STANDING AT ARMAGEDDON

STANDING AT ARMAGEDDON

A Grassroots History
of the Progressive Era

NELL IRVIN PAINTER

W. W. NORTON & COMPANY

Independent Publishers Since 1923

For information about permission to reproduce selections from this book, write to
Permissions, W. W. Norton & Company, Inc., 500 Fifth Avenue, New York, NY 10110.

Manufacturing by Lakeside Book Company

A previous edition of this book was cataloged by the Library of Congress as follows:

Painter, Nell Irvin.
Standing at Armageddon.
Includes bibliographies and index.
1. United States—History—1865–1921. 2. United States—Social
conditions—1865–1919. I. Title.
E661.P33   1987   973.8   86–33111

ISBN 978-1-324-05060-5 pbk

W. W. Norton & Company, Inc.
500 Fifth Avenue, New York, N. Y. 10110
www.wwnorton.com

W. W. Norton & Company Ltd.
15 Carlisle Street, London W1D 3BS

1 2 3 4 5 6 7 8 9 0

FOR FRANK AND MADELINE FREIDEL

CONTENTS

HOW THIS BOOK WORKS

I admit it: *Standing at Armageddon* is an old-fashioned book of political economy. *Political economy?* What's that? Political economy investigates the relationship between politics and money: it's voting and taxes and governmental policy, the nuts and bolts of who gets and who pays. In a democracy like the United States, it's the tension between the power of the people and the power of wealth, a tension recognized at the turn of the twentieth century, before there were income taxes, before concepts of a social safety net, a time when the wealthy were extremely rich and the poor exceedingly impoverished. I know political economy isn't sexy like entertainment or social media and stars in the cultural firmament, the stuff of so much of our lives today—or so it would seem. But political economy remains absolutely fundamental to our lives as individuals and families and within our public life. To be effective citizens, we need to understand political economy. Here's how *Standing at Armageddon* can help with that.

First of all, *Standing at Armageddon* gives you three kinds of information about historical events that you can look for today: (1) what happened, (2) what meanings people took out of what happened, and (3) how people processed the event over time. You will often see the word "symbolize," as in, the Lawrence, Massachusetts, textile strike of 1912 "came to symbolize the state of labor relations in general and the potential for profound unrest" (p. 269). The strike itself was a January interruption in the manufacturing of textiles in one Massachusetts town, but it was led by members of the Industrial Workers of the World. That leadership changed a local event into a portent of disorder on the national scale, so that the strike symbolized something most Americans found scary: "profound unrest" and unbridled radicalism. That one strike at Lawrence rekindled debates about immigration because so many of the workers were foreigners.

Second, *Standing at Armageddon* explains important economic concepts and how they played out in public life. The theme running right throughout this book is taxes—not only what kind, how big, who pays, and how much, but also what it means not to have them at all. I need not tell you how central taxes are, because taxes are still news. But you may not be aware of the disconnect between kind of taxes, the tax revenue they produce, and whether they are intended to raise revenue or not. To give two instances, I discuss how protective tariffs imposed on foreign-made goods (back then, made in Europe, today made in Asia) influence the prices of goods produced within the United States (p. 94). You will consider how people with different levels of income thought about paying for World War I and how its enormous costs encouraged federal income taxation (pp. 321–22).

Banks, too, affect the economy on the national and personal levels. And we still hope that banking policy can influence the economy by avoiding depressions and easing the burden of debt. Throughout the late nineteenth century, money and banking remained crucial issues, even for ordinary people, such as farmers supporting the People's Party—Populists—in the 1890s. (Back then, "populism" meant politics intended to address the concerns of ordinary working people, not, as so often today, nationalist and authoritarian regimes that squelch human rights.) The Federal Reserve System created in 1913 meant so much more than just the creation of a big national bank. It was intended to address demands that could hardly be reconciled (pp. 282–83). Most fundamentally, it was to end economic hard times by managing the money supply. But it was also to break the power of the "money trust"—big banks and bankers like J. P. Morgan—and at the same time to create a central bank under the control of those very same bankers. Such were the Federal Reserve's obvious but unavoidable conflicts.

This book is unusual in making ordinary working people and their concerns its central focus, for in the long decades when organized labor lost ground the struggles of workers and unions rarely figured in the news. In the late twentieth and early twenty-first centuries it was difficult to stay focused on the everyday issues that count for most people, such as hourly wages, the length of the workday, and workplace safety, even though these very matters play so large a part in most people's lives, a much larger part than, say, the steps and missteps of our showy billionaires. Today, at last, working people, often very well-educated working people, are striking and organizing anew.

As I write these words, not only are workers on the railroads, delivery trucks, hotel rooms, and in online commerce's warehouses striking and organizing, they are joined by screenwriters, actors, graduate students, museum workers, and coffee house employees—people with educational backgrounds associated with the middle class. Workplace conditions were easy to see as crucial concerns in the late nineteenth and early twentieth centuries, and they ultimately permeated the American political economy. Workers today need to know their struggles have a history.

The New Deal of the 1930s falls outside the purview of this book, but it's important to recognize the New Deal as a culmination of Progressive Era politics. The 1940s and 1960s brought the Fair Deal and Great Society programs seeking to make government a protector of working people by regulating business and enacting a social safety net. Looking back on the turn of the twentieth century, we see that it took decades for regulation and the social safety net to move from demands of working people and their allies on the fringes of public life—people like Populists and organized labor and social workers—into the mainstream and on to national policy. That long trajectory reminds us that the mainstream and policy continue to change.

Closer to our own times, the philosophy of the federal and some state governments has returned to the laissez-faire—leave alone— policies of the nineteenth century (with today's glaring exception of regulations of sexualities and gender). Since about 1980, the demand for deregulation in the interests of stimulating the economy has been loud enough to undo much of the regulation enacted in and shortly after the New Deal to protect people. Deregulation fostered economic competition, a soaring economy, and lower prices, but also economic instability, dangerous workplaces, the "gig" economy of transient, disempowered workers, a focus on cheap imported consumer goods, and what the Progressive Era called "trustification," the merging of companies into huge, wealthy, and powerful corporations. Today, the call for regulation is rising once again, for instance, in the interest of the environment, a cause that hardly existed at the turn of the twentieth century.

The financing of political campaigns represents another issue of the political economy still very much alive in the present. The presidential election of 1896, when Marcus Alonzo Hanna engineered Republican William McKinley's victory over his Democratic and Populist opponent William Jennings Bryan, marked a crucial turning point (p. 158). Hanna collected millions of dollars from big business, with an interest in keeping government away from regulation, while Bryan represented the people who would use government to regulate the economy in the interests of farmers and workers.

We still debate the role of money in politics: Is campaign financing an exercise of free speech? Or does it buy wealthy individuals and corporations privileged access to the people who make and enforce the laws? With such vast disparities of wealth today, and with far more money than ever before influencing elections after *Citizens United* v. *Federal Elections Commission* (2010), political money is very much on our minds.

My attention to the political economy doesn't narrow my definition of who is American. Throughout this book you will find people of color and White women as historical actors, even when they disagree among themselves. A certain complexity and density result; the fact is that life—even life in the past—is not, was not, simple. Just like people living today, just like you, Americans at the turn of the twentieth century changed their minds as their awareness of conditions around them changed. For one famous example, follow the course of President Theodore Roosevelt as he loses a New York City mayoral election, coming in behind the Single Taxer Henry George, then reappears, and reappears. Roosevelt faces a crucial strike in the coal industry, dealing with people he came to call "malefactors of great wealth," denouncing organized labor, and preaching preparedness for war. Follow the courses of two lesser-known figures, journalists William Allen White and Ida B. Wells. He grows from a conceited young dandy deploring Populists to a clear-eyed observer of the Great Unrest of 1919, and she, an anti-lynching crusader, seeks refuge from her native Mississippi in 1895, becomes a founder of the National Association for the Advancement of Colored People, and has her request for a passport to attend the Versailles conference denied.

In short, more than a century ago, and under many now unfamiliar names, thoughtful Americans of various races, classes, and genders pondered the meanings of wealth generated by a modern economy. They asked how it could be that the people who worked the hardest were the poorest, but the people who seemed not to work at all rolled in dough. How could it be that political power served the people with the most but did so little for the people with the least? What is—what should be—the relationship between the power of money and the power of the people? We still ask those very same questions today, and knowing this history can help us find answers.

STANDING AT
ARMAGEDDON

1

LATE-NINETEENTH-CENTURY AMERICA BY THE NUMBERS

Late-nineteenth-century American speakers and essayists rarely resisted the impulse to list figures with many zeros. Almost any argument—the impossibility of raising wages in the railroad industry in the 1870s, the need to reduce agricultural production in the 1880s, the desirability of remonetizing silver in the 1890s—served as a pretext for demonstrating how American production had soared. These astronomical measures of output functioned practically as a talisman, to be touched and paraded whenever possible: In 1889 the United States produced 1,705,000 tons of rails; in 1900, 2,672,000 tons. In 1889 factories, mines, and railroads used 23,679,000 horsepower; in 1900, 37,729,000, not counting the use of the popular new electric motors. Between 1889 and 1900 the production of raw steel doubled, from 5,865,000 tons to 11,227,000 tons. Total manufacturing capital soared from $5,697,000,000,000 in 1889 to $8,663,000,000,000 in 1900.[1]

Steel production, that symbol of development, summed up the story. By the end of the century the United States had exceeded the combined output of its two rivals, Great Britain and Germany. The president of the American Bankers Association exulted in 1898: "We hold now three of the winning cards in the game for commercial greatness, to wit—iron, steel and coal. . . . We have long been the granary of the world," he said, "we now aspire to be its workshop, then we want to be its clearing house."[2]

Spoken at the end of a devastating depression, these words represented braggadocio as much as confidence in the recent return of prosperity. But the banker knew which way the economic currents were running. In the 1890s foreign investment had been crucial to this country's growth. A generation later the money flow had changed course. By the end of the European War New York had replaced London as the world's financial capital, and Europe was heavily in our debt. In 1919 the United States outproduced the rest of the world in agriculture, manufactured goods, and credit.

Technological innovation made possible dramatic increases in industrial and agricultural productivity. Older inventions such as the steam engine, the generator, and the sewing machine became common in many industries. Tractors and reapers allowed a few men to do the cultivating and harvesting that had demanded the labor of hundreds. New inventions that harnessed electricity revolutionized industrial production and lit up millions of homes.

In the fast-growing cities, subways and street railroads altered urban topography, allowing people to live miles from their work—the middle classes in verdant suburbs; well-paid workers in jerry-built subdivisions. Elevators allowed the erection of the skyscrapers that gave large cities their characteristic twentieth-century skylines, another hallmark of modernity. While telephones, typewriters, cash registers, and adding machines sped and routinized the conduct of business, cameras, phonographs, bicycles, moving pictures, amusement parks, and professional sports defined the mass popular culture that still dominates our times.

In 1919 most Americans could hope to live more healthful and longer lives than their parents, thanks to the discovery of causes and cures for endemic diseases such as malaria, yellow fever, hookworm, typhoid, and diphtheria. In the first decades of the twentieth century the death rate dropped one-third, and life expectancy increased by six years. Improvements in canning and the wide use of refrigerated railroad cars brought a variety of meats and vegetables to markets distant from California, Texas, and Florida and put varied diets within reach of large numbers of Americans. Rising standards of living indicated real improvement in millions of lives.

The popular symbol of progress was the automobile. At the very beginning of the twentieth century only a handful of Americans could afford cars. But in 1909 automaker Henry Ford vowed to democratize the automobile, and he was as good as his word. Adopting the moving assembly line to the manufacture of automobiles in 1914, the Ford company produced nearly a quarter of a million cars per year, which sold at one-fourth of their price a decade earlier.

Automobiles were only one spectacular indicator of the extraordinary productivity of the American industrial economy. The gross national product (GNP), reckoned in current prices, rose from about $11 billion in the mid-1880s to $84 billion in 1919. Population growth provides part of the explanation: in 1880, 50,155,800 and in 1920, 105,710,600. But per capita GNP also increased impressively, from $208 in the mid-1880s to $804 in 1919.[3] This wealth was not distributed evenly, however.

FIGURES ON the distribution of wealth (property) and income (wages, salaries, rents, and dividends) are hard to come by for the late nineteenth and early twentieth centuries, before the income tax made such statistics available. But the most reliable estimate of differences in family wealth in 1890 produced the results in the accompanying table.[4]

The wealthiest 1 percent of families in 1890 owned 51 percent of the real and personal property; the 44 percent of families at the bottom owned only 1.2 percent of all the property. Together, the wealthy and well-to-do (12 percent of families) owned 86 percent of the wealth. The poorer and middle classes, who represented 88 percent of families, owned 14 percent of the wealth.

Family income from wages and salaries was distributed less inequitably than wealth. The poorest one-half of families received one-fifth of wages and salaries. Adding in income from rent, however, produced more marked contrasts. The wealthiest 2 percent of families received

DISTRIBUTION OF WEALTH AND INCOME IN 1890

ESTATES (BY ANNUAL INCOME)	NUMBER OF FAMILIES	AGGREGATE WEALTH	AVERAGE WEALTH PER FAMILY
Wealthy classes ($50,000 and over)	125,000	$33,000,000,000	$264,000
Well-to-do classes ($5,000 to $50,000)	1,375,000	23,000,000,000	16,000
Middle classes ($500 to $5,000)	5,500,000	8,200,000,000	1,500
Poorer classes (under $500)	5,500,000	800,000,000	150
	12,500,000	$65,000,000,000	$5,200

more than half the aggregate income (whereas the wealthiest 1 percent owned more than half the property). This tiny class of rentiers received as large a total income from its property as the poor half of the families received from both property and wages.[5] Living off their investments, wealthy rentiers did not need to work.

Over the long term, wages changed little in the late nineteenth century, when most workers earned less than about $800 a year. After 1901 inflation came into the picture, and wages increased along with the cost of living. According to one recent estimate, the poverty line moved from $506 per year in 1877 to $540 in 1886, $544 in 1893, $553 in 1900, and $660 in 1909.[6] Throughout the period many heads of household— servants, and agricultural and industrial laborers—made less than the $506 to $660 needed to keep a family out of poverty.

Large numbers of working people were needy because of regularly experienced unemployment in the form of layoffs. In the late nineteenth and early twentieth centuries between 23 percent and 30 percent of the work force was out of work for some period every year. Unemployment made working class life uncertain, for the loss of a job might mean leaving home to search for work as well as a lack of income.[7] Men searching for work were called tramps, and they became symbols of the "dangerous classes," as though they were evil men who had chosen not to work.

Differences in income depended on more than occupation. For the same work, northern workers made more than southerners, Whites made more than Blacks, men made more than women. Industrial work paid better than agricultural work, so that unskilled industrial workers made about $360 per year and unskilled agricultural workers about $260 per year in the North at the turn of the century. In the South incomes were about one-fourth lower.

For many farmers, even those who owned their farms, the period was a disaster. A crisis in farm indebtedness meant that more and more farmers lost their farms. In 1880, 25 percent of those who farmed did not own their land. Large numbers of White farmers in the Midwest were tenants and sharecroppers; even greater proportions of southerners farmed land that was not their own. In 1910 half the tenant farmers in the country lived in the cotton South, and more than half the farms in eight southern states were farmed by tenants.[8] Many of these landless farmers were Black.

At the turn of the twentieth century nine out of ten Blacks lived in the South, and three-quarters of Black farmers were tenants or sharecroppers. In the generation since emancipation, Blacks, who constituted about 40 percent of the southern population, had bought one-eighth of the region's farms. Even so, nearly all African Americans, even the landowning minority, were poor. The most oppressed lived as peons, tied to planters by long-term contracts that deprived them of the right to change employers for as much as ten years, or as convicts, whom the states leased to planters and industrialists. In either situation, employers, who cared only about extracting a maximum of work from actual or virtual prisoners, provided wretched living and working conditions. These southern Blacks, who earned bare subsistence and often died before earning their freedom, represented the worst-paid workers in the U.S. More numerous among the Black poor were agricultural workers, who labored on cotton plantations for annual incomes of less than $400.

Other Americans were not so badly off, but their situations varied widely. Within one family and within one lifetime, fortunes could rise and fall. Some actual examples will show how particular families in various economic classes lived.

Miners were at the low end of the income scale. They made as much as $60 per month when they were working, but they seldom worked year-round. Regular layoffs ordinarily reduced their annual pay to less than $500 per year. A thirty-five-year-old native-born American anthracite coal miner in Pennsylvania explained his income and expenditures in 1902:

> ... my wages were $29.47 for the two weeks, or at the rate of $58.94 per month. My rent is $10.50 per month. My coal costs me almost $4 per month. ... Light does not cost so much, we use coal oil altogether.
>
> When it comes down to groceries is where you get hit the hardest. Everybody knows the cost of living has been extremely high all winter. Butter has been 32, 36, and 38 cents a pound; eggs as high as 32 cents a dozen; ham, 12 and 16 cents a pound. ... Flour and sugar did not advance, but they were about the only staples that didn't. Anyhow, my store bill for those two weeks was $11. That makes $22 per month. The butcher gets $5 per month. Add them all, and it costs me, just to live, $42.40.[9]

As in many other families whose principal earner made $500 a year or less, this miner's children worked after about the age of ten. In 1900 nearly one-fifth of the children under fifteen earned wages in nonagricultural work, and uncounted millions of others worked on farms. Spouses also contributed to family income by taking in washing and ironing, keeping boarders, working in the fields, or, less frequently, working for wages.

Jane Addams, founder of the best known of the settlement houses, described the working-class Halsted Street neighborhood in Chicago where Hull House was situated, showing that poor neighborhoods often lacked the minimum public services stipulated by law:

The streets are inexpressibly dirty, the number of schools inadequate, sanitary legislation unenforced, the street lighting bad, the paving miserable and altogether lacking in the alleys and smaller streets, and the stables foul beyond description. Hundreds of houses are unconnected with the street sewer. . . . Rear tenements flourish; many houses have no water supply save the faucet in the back yards, there are no fire escapes, the garbage and ashes are placed in wooden boxes which are fastened to the street pavements.[10]

Industrial workers and their families usually lived in small houses crowded on streets near factories. At the turn of the century such houses might have running water, but they would have lacked indoor plumbing and electricity. Agricultural workers' houses stood alone in the fields, with outhouses, water from hand-operated pumps, and no electricity. In either case, two rooms for a large family, and perhaps unrelated boarders in addition, would have been usual.

In the late nineteenth century industrial workers put in sixty-hour weeks, and farmers might work still longer hours on a weekly basis. Working people did not take vacations and could not afford to retire, although they might have to stop working because of injury or incapacity. Around the turn of the century commercial parks, like Coney Island in New York, began to offer workers a respite from the drab everyday existence.

About $800 per year represented a comfortable working-class income that would permit children to remain in school and wives to work only for their families. At the upper end of the working-class spectrum, highly skilled northern mechanics might take home as much as $1,000 per year, making them the aristocrats of labor and putting them on the borderline that divided the working class from the middle class.

MIDDLE-CLASS FAMILY INCOME varied from about $900 per year to about $3,500. At the lower end were male employees: salesmen, clerks, and government workers, who wore jackets and ties and worked in offices where their hands and feet stayed clean. Teachers, most of whom were women, belonged to the middle class socially, although their incomes—only about $250 per year—were lower than those of most workers. Poorly paid but thoroughly respectable, teachers provide the most obvious example of the ambiguity of class identification in the United States, for while income provided the single clearest indicator of class standing, it did not tell the whole story. Class in the United States has been more and less than a matter of struggle or relations of production, by which social scientists generally define classes. Class, particularly when it comes to the middle class, is a fluid category that includes individual (or family) self-definition, tastes, and attitudes.

Just as ethnic and racial divisions make it misleading (though convenient) to speak of a single American working class, there was no single middle class either. There were working classes and middle classes, not only agricultural and industrial but also of many ethnicities and races. At any moment, say, 1880, several sorts of families might identify themselves as middle-class, whether or not they lived in a middle-class neighborhood and whether or not each member had finished high school.

Classes were not formed once and for all, in the sense that a middle-class family's antecedents might have been in other classes, and its descendants, too, might also belong to the working or upper classes. Middle-class parents did not always succeed in keeping their progeny out of the working class, for downward mobility was common. All ethnic groups, even the poorest, such as Blacks and Italians in the early twentieth century, included some families that were middle-class. In addition, the composition of the middle class in the 1870s differed from its counterpart in the 1910s.

In both 1877 and 1919 native-born White Protestant Americans were presumed to belong to the middle (or upper) classes, even though in the South, West, and Midwest large numbers of such people belonged to the agricultural and industrial working classes. The standing of descendants of immigrants changed over time because the arrival of new groups of immigrants altered assumptions about relative class status. The Irish, who had seemed in 1877 to constitute a permanent class of casual laborers and domestic servants, had by 1919 become skilled workers and foremen, while many Irishwomen had become the teachers of the eastern and southern European immigrants who early in the twentieth century formed a new industrial working class. Similarly, German Jews, many of whom in the mid-nineteenth century had been itinerant peddlers, were largely middle- and upper-class by the time of heavy Russian Jewish immigration after 1905. And the process continued. By 1920 the children of Europeans who had immigrated in the late nineteenth century had become the teachers and foremen of southern Black migrants in the North and Midwest. Each new group moved in at the bottom, nudging its neighbors upward, even though mobility might reach only one step up within the working class.[11]

While most Blacks and immigrants, as well as their children, were wage workers in 1877 and 1919, their neighborhoods, even when solidly working-class, divided between the rough and the respectable. Rough elements—especially men—set little premium on education and ignored the dictates of respectability. Not everyone who saw herself as respectable—and women were more likely than men to value respectability and education—based that identity on income. Rough and respectable neighbors might share economic status and live side by side. Aspirations as much as wealth separated "shanty Irish" from "lace curtain Irish" and their equivalents in other working-class groups.

The respectable were more likely than the rough to attend church and to belong to temperance organizations. And the respectable were more likely than self-proclaimed roughs to be active in labor organizations. The Grand Master Workman of the Knights of Labor (the leader of the national labor federation that flourished in the 1880s) was an Irish American named Terence V. Powderly. Although head of a labor organization, he prided himself on his gentleman's appearance. Like many other Knights, Powderly was active in the temperance movement, a clear signal of respectability among members of the working class.[12]

In addition to the respectable within the working classes, a small but influential group of Blacks and immigrants belonged to the economic middle class. These families achieved their upward mobility through education, the priesthood, entrepreneurship, and leadership in political, fraternal, or labor organizations. Wealthier than workers, they were also better educated, better clothed, and better fed.[13]

Middle-class families earned enough to support themselves without having to count pennies, as the miner quoted above had to do every day. The middle class lived in relatively large, single-family dwellings and employed some sort of household help, if only a laundress. The heads of the more precarious of such households, male teachers, clerks, and telegraph operators, earned about $900 per year and would have attended high school. Ministers made about the same amount but probably would have received further schooling. Church-supplied housing would often compensate for low ministerial salaries, making a middle-class style of life possible on a relatively small income. But in the 1870s a nationally famous preacher like the Reverend Henry Ward Beecher of the Brooklyn, New York, Plymouth Church earned a salary of $20,000 per year plus generous fees from lecturing.

Lawyers and doctors, who averaged about $1,200 per year, would have undergone specialized training, but not necessarily college, law school, or medical school. Although both legal and medical training were being professionalized at the turn of the century, one might still prepare for qualifying examinations in the office of an established practitioner. Professionals enjoyed not only prestige but a comfortable standard of living that would allow the better-paid to save and invest surplus income.

A southern Black woman, the wife of a physician and the mother of three, explained the state of their finances in 1904. Both she and her husband had attended college in the South, and he had also completed medical school. After ten years her husband earned about $1,200 per year from his medical practice. "By most frugal living and strict economy he saved enough to buy a home, a house of four rooms, which has since been increased to eight. Since our marriage we have bought and paid for two other places, which we rent. . . . We have an iron-bound rule that we must save at least fifty dollars a month. Some months we lay by more, but never less. We do not find this very hard to do with the rent from our places, as I do all my [housework] except the washing and ironing."[14]

Another middle-class woman who had been active in the woman suffrage movement remembered the household of her grandfather, a judge in Ithaca, New York, where she grew up:

> The house was very large. That was the day, of course, when you still had sleep-in servants. Down in the rather large, halfway basement was the dining room, a large pantry, a huge kitchen and what was called the maids' sitting room. . . .
>
> The first floor had a big central hall, a music room, a library, front and back parlors, and a very large bed / sitting room and bath for my grandfather and grandmother. . . .
>
> Up on the second floor there were one, two, three bedrooms and a bath in the front of the house, and what was then called the sewing room. Then you went down a flight of steps to a door, and there were one or two rooms for servants, and a big storage room. . . .[15]

The upper class received annual incomes of more than $3,500, little of which would have been earned as wages and salaries, as in the case of the working and middle classes. Upper-class people like Eleanor Roosevelt of New York (niece of President Theodore Roosevelt) traveled to Europe as children, attended colleges or academies after secondary school, owned more than one house, boats, carriages, and automobiles. They employed several servants and took vacations.

Jay Gould, who owned the southwestern railroad system at the time of the great strike of 1886, lived with his family in a brownstone at 579 Fifth Avenue, New York City. In addition, Gould owned Lyndhurst, an estate built to resemble a Gothic castle at Tarrytown, which he had purchased in 1880 for $250,000. The art gallery on the second floor at Lyndhurst boasted paintings by Rousseau, Corot, Daubigny, and other painters of the then fashionable Barbizon school. Gould's pride and joy was a 380-foot-long greenhouse resplendent with $40,000 worth of plants. He often commuted from Tarrytown to his office in lower Manhattan on his 230-foot-long white yacht, the *Atalanta*.

His niece remembered Christmas in the Gould mansion on Fifth Avenue in the early 1880s. Among her presents were a gold Swiss watch, a fine brooch, and a check from her uncle. After opening the multitude of gifts, the family entered the dining room, where the table was ornamented with one huge and several smaller vases full of scarlet anthuriums and poinsettias. The dinner consisted of terrapin (turtle, a late-nineteenth-century delicacy), oysters, turkey with stuffing, cranberry jelly, vegetables, and plum pudding. Silver compotes holding hothouse fruit, candied fruit, and bonbons were scattered across the table. After dinner the family assembled around the tall, ornate Christmas tree in the library, where everyone received a box of candy and another gift.[16]

The very rich included families such as the Vanderbilts (who made their money in railroads) and the Rockefellers (oil refining and, later, banking). The Vanderbilts owned several mansions on Fifth Avenue in New York City as well as houses throughout the country, including young George Vanderbilt's Biltmore House, in Asheville, North Carolina. Modeled after a French château, Biltmore House stands on an estate of more than 8,000 acres, is 1,000 feet long, and has 250 rooms, including 40 master bedrooms, an indoor swimming pool and gymnasium, and a dining room 72 feet long. Undiminished by income or inheritance taxes, the fortunes that paid for such estates piled up faster than they could be spent. When he died of tuberculosis at the age of fifty-two in 1892, Jay Gould's estate was valued at $77,000,000. Henry Clay Frick of the Carnegie Steel Company left $150,000,000 on his death in 1919.

THE WEALTHY REPRESENTED about 1 percent of families, and even the comfortable and middle classes were greatly outnumbered by the millions of working people who lived close to subsistence levels in prosperous times and suffered the wage cuts, layoffs, and unemployment that accompanied the periodic depressions. Whenever hard times came, strikes and violence occurred. And hard times arrived with an awful regularity: 1873–1879, 1882–1885, 1893–1897, 1907–1908, 1913–1915.

Working people were not unique in dreading the distress and conflict that depressions produced. Middle- and upper-class people were frightened by the labor disturbances that revealed a seemingly unbridgeable gulf between classes and threatened to destroy American society. But more than that, labor violence reminded nonworkers of the very existence of the poor, whose presence they otherwise ignored. For many in the middle and upper classes, workers were a different sort of people, unpredictable and unamenable to reason, belonging to what were then called different races. Whereas the middle and upper classes were largely Protestant, native-born, of British descent, the working classes, particularly the industrial working classes, consisted of many peoples who were foreign, Catholic, and, in the South, Black.

When brought face-to-face with the existence of workers, the middle and upper classes envisioned foreigners—people from Ireland and Germany—in terms of stereotypes. Germans, known to many Americans as Deutsch or Dutch, were thought of as sturdy, hardworking, serious people. After the upheavals of these decades, however, Germans acquired another connotation, that of socialists, anarchists, and communists. By belonging to the Republican party, which stood for Protestant respectability, progress, and the Union, many Germans took a giant step toward probity. While Germans were thought to enjoy a glass of beer after a hard day's work, their work was seen as honest and productive. The Irish did not benefit from such generosity. Irishmen were thought of as notorious drunkards who might as well drink as work. Even though Germans were Catholics and Jews as well as Protestants, the stigma of Catholicism—mindless, slavish superstition—did not taint Germans as it did the Irish.

Irish Catholics regularly appear in writing of the 1870s and 1880s as pawns of the pope, the local political boss (a saloonkeeper), or both. While it was often accepted that the problem with the Irish was their religion or their social habits, the fundamental—usually unstated—objection was that they were mostly poor people who lived in cities and who were afflicted with the misfortunes that accompany that condition.

Millions of Irish immigrants to the United States in the middle of the nineteenth century were more likely to see themselves as involuntary exiles from their homeland, whose politics continued to interest them keenly. Irish immigrants left an exploited colony in which living conditions had deteriorated tragically in the mid-1840s, when the main food crop failed during the potato blight. Between 1841 and 1860, 1,700,000 Irish people, more than half of them women, immigrated to the United States, 120,000 during the two worst years of the potato famine, 1845 and 1846. During the century beginning in 1820 4,700,000 Irish people came to the United States, a total exceeded only by the number of German immigrants.[17]

Irishwomen were subject to the stereotypes usually attached to domestic servants: frivolity, laziness, and stupidity. But they did not inspire apprehension in the minds of the well-educated and respectable Protestant native middle and upper classes, as did their male counterparts. To Yankees, Irishmen, like poor people throughout the industrialized world, seemed to be ignorant, dirty, immoral, drunken, and violent—far more likely to be rough than respectable. Too poor to buy land, the Irish became in both subjective and objective reality the first American proletariat, thereby forfeiting any claim on the mythology of upward mobility that persisted after the Civil War.[18]

President Abraham Lincoln, in an eloquent summary of the free-labor ideology, had declared in the late 1850s that "there is no permanent class of hired laborers among us."[19] According to the free-labor myth, a poor man who worked steadily and soberly and who saved his surplus wages could, using his savings as capital, go into business on his own. He would then hire young workers, who would save their wages and start on the road to independence in their turn. By the 1870s this portrait of mobility held good for only a small minority of workers born in the U.S. Most people took it for granted that the more than 2,000,000 Irish would never attain upward mobility, but Irish Americans began to make their way into the middle classes, often using politics as a hoist.

In cities like New York, Boston, San Francisco, and Chicago, Democratic organizers had quickly seized upon the English-speaking Irish immigrants as potential voters, procuring the naturalization papers that at mid-century made voting relatively easy for White men, no matter what their nativity. Nearly all Irishmen became Democrats, and their adherence lent the Democratic party some unsavory connotations: bossism, herd voting, and corruption, even though these were national phenomena not limited to one party. Thanks to their numbers, Irish Americans came to exercise considerable local influence in urban, northern, and western politics by the 1870s and 1880s.

In 1878 Scranton, Pennsylvania, elected the nation's first Irish American mayor, Terence Powderly, who had run on a Greenback-Labor ticket. New York followed in 1880; Lawrence, Massachusetts, in 1881; and Boston, in 1890. By the end of the 1890s the Irish held firm political control of several other cities, including San Francisco, Chicago, and New Haven. The civil service reform movement of the 1870s and 1880s, which sought to reserve political office for educated people instead of party regulars, was in large part a nativist, class-bound reaction against the success of the Irish—foreign, Catholic, working-class people—in urban politics.

The Irish had not created the broad-based political organizations that they soon came to dominate. The first city bosses, such as Boss William Marcy Tweed of New York, were Yankees. But the Irish entered city politics just as the minimal politics of deference gave way to the politics of careers and service to masses of poor constituents. In the new politics, young men without education could make a living, through either holding patronage offices or supplying votes. It mattered little that they disregarded the larger political issues of the day, such as tariffs, currency, or, indeed, civil service reform. As politics became a job, the means for getting along—bribes, jobs, levies on office-holders' salaries, payments for voters—assumed a larger role in political life. And large cities offered patronage jobs in abundance. In New York, in the late 1870s, about one out of twelve heads of household worked for one or another level of government. According to another estimate, one out of eight of the city's voters was employed by government.[20]

ONE REASON the Irish did so well in American politics was their perma-
nence. Unlike many other immigrants, the Irish came to stay.[21] Temporary immigrants—sojourners—came intending to work in the U.S.
just long enough to save a bit of money to buy some land, pay some
debts, or start a business, then return home. As a child in Guangzhou
(Canton), China, Lew Chew was impressed when "a man of our tribe
came back from America and took ground as large as four city blocks
and made a paradise of it. . . . The man had gone away from our village a poor boy. Now he returned with unlimited wealth, which he had
obtained in the country of the American wizards. After many amazing
adventures he had become a merchant in a city called Mott Street, so it
was said. . . . Having made his wealth among the barbarians this man
had faithfully returned to pour it out among his tribesmen, and he is
living in our village now very happy."[22] Following his neighbor's example, Chew immigrated in the early 1880s, opened a laundry business
in California, and saved his profits. He returned to China in 1887 and
then came back to the U.S. to start a laundry business in Buffalo, having earned the right to return by immigrating before the passage of the
Chinese Exclusion Act. Like Chew, hundreds of thousands of sojourners
went home and returned to the United States repeatedly.

The proportion of sojourners varied widely from group to group.
Between 1899 and 1924 nearly all the Chinese, about half the Italians
and Greeks, about 12 percent of the Irish, and 5 percent of the Jews
returned home. Overall about one-quarter as many foreigners left for
home as came to the U.S. every year at the turn of the century.[23]

Many who intended to return home ended up staying and having American children. By 1910 one third of the American population was either foreign-born or had at least one foreign-born parent.
In many cities, including Fall River, Massachusetts, Chicago, Milwaukee, New York, Cleveland, Minneapolis, and San Francisco, the
foreign-born and second-generation residents constituted more than
three-quarters of the population. By that time the immigrant population had changed dramatically.

Between 1880 and 1920 the provenance of the foreign-born population in the United States shifted away from Germany, Ireland, north-western Europe, and China to central, eastern, and southern Europe. In 1880, 29 percent of the foreign-born had come from Germany, 28 percent from Ireland, and 25 percent from elsewhere in northwestern Europe. In addition, 11 percent came from Canada, 4 percent from central, eastern, and southern Europe, and 1.6 percent from China and Japan. In 1920, in contrast, 46 percent of the foreign-born population came from central, eastern, and southern Europe, 20 percent from northwestern Europe (excluding Ireland and Germany), 12 percent from Germany, 7 percent from Ireland, and less than 1 percent from China and Japan.[24]

THESE IMMIGRANT WORKERS came to fill millions of jobs that the rapidly expanding industrial economy created. Working in textile, clothing, and agricultural equipment factories, railroad roundhouses, coal mines, and steel mills, the men and women of the new industrial working classes quickly overshadowed agricultural workers in economic importance. In 1880 about one-half the United States work force was in agriculture. By 1920 only a little more than a quarter remained on the land.[25]

During the 1880s the factory system of production first became widespread, reflecting the unprecedented level of industrial mechanization that occurred during the decade. Factory work underwent striking changes, as capital investment increased one and one-half times during the decade. In addition to technological advances, new managerial techniques made workers into what Henry George called mere feeders of machines.

From the point of view of workers, this increased use of machinery and the huge size of mechanized factories entailed what a member of the Knights of Labor called the degradation of labor: "The men are looked upon as nothing more than parts of the machinery that they work. They are labeled and tagged, as the parts of a machine would be, and are only taken into account as a part of the machinery used for the profit of the manufacturer."[26] These monotonous jobs required relatively little training or skill because increasingly managers, not workers, made decisions about the industrial process.[27] This was only one example of the conflict between how workers and employers perceived the new industrial order and the society it shaped.

Workers often resented mechanized work and laborsaving devices. A cotton spinner in Fall River, Massachusetts, doubted that laborsaving machinery had been of the "slightest aid to the operatives. They are in a worse condition now than they were with the old hand-loom," he explained, because "the tendency has been not only to reduce wages, but also to dismiss help."[28] A brass worker complained that mechanization harmed workers by dividing the industrial process into small, discrete jobs, each done by a different worker, so that a man working on a machine would learn little beyond his particular task. Having been a skilled craft before mechanization, brass working was deskilled in the 1880s, and reduced pay indicated the change. Previously considered a cut above ordinary workers, a brass worker had then "felt he was somebody; he was a skilled mechanic." But now brass workers were part of the semiskilled, homogenized work force whose low wages forced them to live in tenements, "surrounded by the poorest class, the cheapest class; the cheapest element of the laboring people." Once proud craftsmen, brass workers were now no better than anybody else.[29]

For many managers, especially in large factories, workers were merely interchangeable sellers of the commodity of their labor, just another cog in the machine that was the factory. As soon as one worker left hard, dangerous, or dirty work, another quickly stepped in. In these years of virtually unlimited immigration, workers were in abundant supply. Employers considered their pay subject to the rules of supply and demand, no matter what amount sufficed to support a worker decently or a worker and family. A stockholder in a Lawrence, Massachusetts, textile mill explained that "if [a manager] can secure men for $6 [a week] and pays more, he is stealing from the company."[30] Industrial wages were low, but most immigrants could earn more in the United States than they could at home.

An Italian or Hungarian who made 30 cents a day at home could make $1.50 or more in the United States, a fact that established the

American reputation in Europe and Asia as a place in which to prosper. Rocco Corresca, a Neapolitan fisherman, heard in the late nineteenth century that America "was a far off country where everybody was rich and that Italians went there and made plenty of money so that they could return to Italy and live in pleasure ever after. One day I met a young man who pulled out a handful of gold and told me he had made that in America in a few days."[31] Corresca immigrated shortly afterward, only one of millions of immigrants and migrants from American farms attracted to the dynamic American urban economy. Arriving penniless, he had by 1902 saved $1,000, decided against returning to Italy, and was opening a new shoeshine parlor near South Ferry in lower Manhattan. Success stories like Corresca's occurred often enough to nurture in many the hope of dramatically improving their prospects.

The possibility of economic mobility was a fundamental part of what most Americans, old or new, thought made the United States different from the Old World. Not only could virtually all White male workers vote in the late nineteenth century, but American society was widely thought to lack Europe's class structure. Believing that poverty stemmed from individual shortcomings, most Americans prized this supposed classlessness as one of the foundations of the American political system. They commonly interpreted threats to the economic order as threats to democracy itself—that is, as attacks on the political order. Just as a member of the Knights of Labor could warn that "the political structure of this country is resting on a sand heap" because industry was grinding workers down, an official of the United States Steel Corporation could also contend that the great steel strike of 1919 threatened to overthrow the government.[32] Time and again Americans thought about economic issues in political terms, especially in hard times, when the suffering and the violence (or fear of violence) of the desperate set off searches for remedies for depressions and methods of harmonizing the class conflicts that depressions exacerbated.

IN THE late nineteenth century the cures for depressions and class conflict tended to be simple and comprehensive. In the 1870s Henry George argued that if only one tax were levied, on the increase in the value of land as settlement increased, speculation would cease, everyone would be able to buy land, workers would become farmers, and the resulting labor shortage would drive up wages and end unemployment. Poverty and crime would disappear together. In the 1880s Edward Bellamy thought that his brand of state socialism would engender a bloodless revolution that would abolish money, unemployment, strikes, and all other manifestations of social conflict. In the 1890s silver enthusiasts like William ("Coin") Harvey preached that bimetallism would increase the money supply, raise agricultural prices, increase purchasing power, cure depressions, and end unemployment and hunger. Although many admired the purported benefits of each new scheme, the means for reaching utopian goals were never clear.

By the end of the nineteenth century sweeping panaceas had lost much of their attractiveness, as reformers, often members of the first generation of college-trained women, visited work sites and working-class homes and offered specific cures for specific problems. Florence Kelley and Alice Hamilton inspected factories in Illinois and New York and proposed legislation to attack particular occupational hazards. Lillian Wald of the Henry Street Settlement in New York trained pioneer public health nurses. They were just three of hundreds of women and men who lived comfortable middle- and upper-class lives but were perturbed and frightened by the injustices of industrial society.

The reforms of the early twentieth century were many and varied: woman suffrage; prohibition; railroad regulation; maximum hours of work; abolition of child labor; the initiative, referendum, and recall; workmen's compensation; Black civil rights; graduated income taxes; and banking reform. The great reform movements were, however, more ambiguous than a straightforward story of altruism, for the nativism, racism, and sexism that characterized the period appeared among the well-meaning. Such shortcomings were to be found in the ranks of labor reformers purporting to uphold the claims of all working people at the same time that they denigrated the needs of important segments of the American working classes, whether women, Blacks, or foreigners. Similarly, supporters of a reform as necessary and right as votes for women sometimes couched their arguments in phrases that narrowed the definition of "women" and undermined the claims to citizenship of poor men who were Black or foreign.[33]

As a result, reformers who advocated much needed positive change sometimes seemed at once to protect the interests of groups with legitimate grievances even as they defined themselves as a privileged subset within their larger group. Thus the spokesmen of organized labor were the most constant and most positive protectors of working people at the same time that they were the opponents of the poorest-paid workers, called contract labor. Women workers, for instance, could hardly look to employers to further their interests as workers. Yet organized labor itself rarely welcomed women workers or took up their specific grievances. The best representatives of workers not only conducted a campaign to prohibit the immigration of Asian workers to the United States but also neglected and opposed the interests of Black workers.

Despite difficulties and contradictions, changes occurred, some for the better. Between the late nineteenth and early twentieth centuries large numbers of Americans came to realize that economic, social, and demographic changes needed to be taken into account politically or grave injustices would result. By 1913, for instance, nearly everyone agreed that reforms that had seemed extreme in the 1870s were now absolutely necessary, and in that year the graduated income tax—an old Socialist and Populist reform—became law. In 1914 Congress passed a bill that appeared to satisfy labor's decades-old demand for exemption from antitrust prosecution as well. By the second decade of the century most Americans had accepted as commonplace many new policies that promised to make the economic order more equitable. This fundamental shift marked weakening of the assumptions that had dominated discussions of politics and economics in the 1870s. The federal government could now proclaim an intention of acting in the interests of ordinary people that a generation earlier would have been unthinkable in all but labor circles. In the 1870s a willingness to meet the needs of farmers and workers would have stirred a storm of protest. But in the

1910s the same effect would have followed a refusal to acknowledge the demands of common citizens, by regulating railroads or imposing a graduated income tax.

Political thought changed significantly between 1877 and 1919; technological change was even more dramatic. But throughout the period different groups advocated conflicting interpretations of how society works. One group spoke the persuasive idiom of prosperity; the other, the equally positive language of democracy. Advocates of prosperity prized order, which would issue from a hierarchical arrangement of society in which the more able few would make decisions for everyone. Advocates of democracy, on the other hand, reclaimed the right of each man to speak for himself. Both drew on the legacy of antebellum Republicanism, so that in the 1870s the two ideals of prosperity and democracy did not necessarily seem contradictory, and spokesmen for labor and business embraced them both.

Champions of prosperity invoked an identity of interest among all members of society, be they owners or workers. This view grew out of the producer-centered philosophy that had gained acceptance before factories were the main locus of industrial production and millions became permanent wage hands. When employers and employees had worked side by side, both claimed to be producers and deemed merchants, bankers, and speculators, in contrast, to be nonproducers. The Republican party of the 1850s embraced this vision, but like much else in Republicanism, the producer mentality changed after the Civil War. By the late nineteenth century this comfortable but archaic conception misrepresented a reality in which employers were more likely to preside over a factory or railroad than work alongside their employees. Appropriating the producerite rhetoric of mid-century, owners (increasingly assumed to be better educated than workers) claimed the right to decide what was best for all.[34]

According to the hierarchical view, capital and labor were not natural antagonists, but each played its part in a harmonious whole. In the agricultural South a planter could explain this ordering of society: "The planter feels an interest in the welfare of his laborers, and the latter in turn look to him for advice and assistance."[35] In industry Jay Gould, owner of the southwestern railroad system in the 1880s and a very wealthy man, believed that "capital and labor, if let alone, generally come together and mutually regulate their relations to each other." Gould was convinced that strikes and other forms of class conflict were nothing more than the work of demagogues. Unions, he said, created tensions that would not otherwise exist.[36] Some working people accepted the assumptions of identity of interest, but this philosophy was most useful to those who already wielded some power.

Identity of interest served as an argument against change, for buried within it was the assurance that the existing order of things was not only just but also decreed by laws of God or Science. Survival of the fittest—Social Darwinism—purported to prove that the best people had already succeeded and the least fit had already lost out in the struggle. Various groups (classes, races, even sexes) were said to have inherited different capabilities. Because abilities were immutable, the prevailing arrangement could never be adjusted, and struggle was vain.

The social economy would function in an orderly and efficient manner, with each group playing its proper role, provided different classes realized that their interests were identical. Workers who stayed sober and appeared promptly every morning, including Mondays, who worked without slacking or striking or quitting suddenly (despite better-paying jobs elsewhere or family emergencies) would ensure high productivity. High productivity would mean large profits, permitting the payment of high wages, so that profits would benefit workers as well as owners. Well-paid workers would buy their own homes, save money, go into business, and prosper in their turn. With a stake in society they would have more reason to preserve the American polity than to disrupt it. In time of war citizens would follow their leaders without the doubts or divisions that would hinder a war effort undertaken for the good of all. These were the commonplaces of the identity-of-interest view of the world.

Although Christianity and Darwinian evolution conflicted philosophically, church attendance generally complemented attitudes embodied in the interpretation of social relations that was called Social Darwinism. Congregants who gave generously comforted themselves with the thought that they were worthy members in a Christian moral order that dictated a single value system. Every thought and act could be judged according to one standard of virtue because what was right for one group was right for all. Therefore, attending church, obeying the law, and keeping the peace could be seen as acts of absolute rightness rather than as the upholding of an entire economic system that worked in the interests of some but against those of others. A labor newspaper railed against this brand of religion, asking rhetorically, "Why in the world is it that nearly all our preachers are taking the serpent's side in this tragedy of labor? Why is it that the land is filled with their bawling against every effort of the working people for self-elevation?"[37]

Christianity, however, served more than to buttress the status quo. Labor reformers like Terence Powderly argued that true Christianity validated the claims of labor. By this reasoning, many churches were not so much moralists for the society as a whole as they were the servants of the rich. As if to illustrate Powderly's point, a minister working among the poor reported that they believed that the "Christian church has forgotten its Master's gospel, and become the Church of respectability and wealth and 'society'; now it has become the upholder of civilization as it is."[38] At the turn of the century a Princeton professor who wrote a book about working-class life after a year's firsthand experience quoted a Chicago worker's disdain for organized religion: "'I don't take no stock in church, anyway,' he explained. 'Fellows like us ain't expected there, and we ain't wanted.'" Another worker called the Princetonian-turned-worker "a dude" for attending church at all.[39] This sense that churches were mere temples of hypocrisy—not houses of Jesus—grew strong enough to inspire ministers like the Reverend Washington Gladden to try to recapture Christianity for the ideals of social justice through the Social Gospel movement. Seeing drink at the root of many social evils, churchgoing women began to protest against the saloon in the 1870s, leading many into a wide range of public action. The identity-of-interest argument sounded more convincing during prosperous times, when the economy and, by extension, the polity seemed to function smoothly. Hard times limited the persuasiveness of an identity of interest of all segments of society because when battles raged in the streets between workers on strike and troops guarding property, when armies of unemployed men marched on Washington demanding work, and when factories closed and the poor suffered, people were less willing to entertain the notion that they did not fully understand their own interests. In those times a belief in the inevitability of what a New York machinist called "antagonism" seemed more realistic.[40]

The hierarchical view of identity of interest stressed eternal truths and laws that decreed one, absolute concept of right. But people who accepted the possibility of antagonism or conflict thought that more than one interpretation of right existed. They said, in essence, that what was right was related to whose interests were being served. They saw society as consisting of a series of competing interests, some more powerful than others, and they identified the existing state as the servant of a particular class, not of all the people. In the words of a freight handler in the 1880s, "the whole machinery of the law and all its forces are on the side of the corporations and of the money power."[41] Economic privilege was therefore creating an aristocracy that would ultimately undermine democracy.

Comparing the lavish lives of the aristocrats who did not work with the poverty of the working masses, many thoughtful observers questioned the existence of immutable natural laws and worried instead that their society was out of joint. From the 1870s to the 1910s (and beyond) some Americans feared that a society in which the privileged wielded enormous power to further their own interests could not at the same time function as a democracy in which all were created equal. At the turn of the century Americans came increasingly to feel that society needed to be democratized to ensure everyone a decent chance for life, liberty, and the pursuit of happiness.

Democratizers believed that society naturally entailed conflict, and in the conflict of interests they championed those of the disadvantaged, which seemed, on the surface, at least, to be an impeccably American aim. But just as the identity-of-interest argument was marred by the demand of obedience from those at the bottom with or without their consent, so the ideal of equity, of every person's claim to an equal hearing, contained the germs of anarchy (the enemy of prosperity), as each interest group reclaimed its rights. If every group of workers facing a wage cut walked off the job, thousands of strikes would create tremendous disorder, which happened in 1877 and 1919 and in many years in between. The years of upheaval intensified the debate between hierarchy and democracy, between order and equity, evidence that during the intervening generations the contest had not been settled.

Americans did not consciously abdicate their political and economic rights in exchange for prosperity, although at the turn of the century they came very close indeed. Representatives of business (who spoke of an identity of interest of all the American people) succeeded far better than the spokesmen of workers (who defended the interests of workers against the depredations of wealth) in portraying their interests as those of Americans as a whole. In the late nineteenth and early twentieth centuries, organized labor failed to convince its fellow citizens that what was good for workers was good for America. As in other industrial societies, organized labor in the United States seemed to represent a special interest that in times of crisis held the potential for destroying the state. For many Americans, the promise of the identity of interests was prosperity, while the specter of the claims of the working majority was disorder.

The United States remained the country whose most attractive promise was mobility upward and out of the working class. Remarkable national wealth, on the one hand, and ethnic and racial divisions within the working class, on the other, meant that broad working-class solidarity materialized briefly in moments of crisis and endured only until the inevitable red scare scattered the forces of labor. But the search for a cure for depressions and class conflict continued.

2

THE TOCSIN SOUNDS

The end of Reconstruction in 1877, tragic as it was for poor southern Blacks, could only be termed anticlimactic. After so much bloodshed and endless, outraged charges of corruption, debt, and incompetence, most southern states had already reverted to Democratic rule. The states that in the mid-1870s remained Republican—Mississippi, South Carolina, Louisiana, and Florida—seemed embroiled in a ceaseless round of violence that still demanded federal attention a decade after the end of the Civil War.

Former supporters, previously staunch antislavery men, such as the Reverend Henry Ward Beecher and editor Horace Greeley, had already pulled back from the daunting task of implanting democracy in the South several years previously. Egalitarianism now seemed visionary, some said sentimental and unrealistic. In 1872 Greeley had gone so far as to announce to a crowd in Indiana, "I was, in the days of slavery, an enemy of slavery, because I thought slavery inconsistent with the rights, the dignity, the highest well-being of free labor. That might have been a mistake."[1] In addition, several other reforms encompassed within the antislavery spirit—state-sponsored education and woman suffrage, to mention two—also lost support, as governments turned away from policies of social equity and embraced the regulation of morals. The nationalist, reforming temper of the 1860s lapsed into the reaction of the economically depressed 1870s, with demands of government retrenchment and less government spending. Already the myth of the carpetbagger-scalawag-Negro-era-of-misrule, which held sway until well into the twentieth century, was wearing thin from repetition.

Pronouncing the southern record closed, northerners anxious to get on with the business of business expressed satisfaction in April 1877, when Republican President-by-Compromise Rutherford B. Hayes removed the last United States troops from southern state capitols.[2] This withdrawal was of particular consequence in the states of South Carolina and Louisiana, where contested elections had produced rival governors and legislatures and federal troops had buttressed the Republicans' claims. Hayes's action left Democratic "redeemers" in control of their states and ended an era in American politics. Sighs of relief greeted the compromise that made Hayes President and welcomed the end of sectional conflict. No longer would "the South" bedevil national politics.

Calling themselves the "wealth and intelligence of the South," White supremacist Democrats had "redeemed" or recaptured the former Confederate states through rhetorical campaigns against the debts, incompetence, and corruption (all national phenomena in the 1860s and 1870s) that they said typified the Republican regimes of the South. Redeemers had also made extensive use of terrorism, which fell heavily on Blacks and which in Mississippi and Arkansas had erupted into statewide civil wars.

Northern Republicans had come to the aid of southern Republicans protesting the violence of the early 1870s by holding congressional hearings on the Ku Klux Klan and passing legislation against terrorism. But as the decade progressed, northern Republicans reinterpreted anti-Black and anti-Republican violence in the South less as criminal action and more as proof that traditional political elites needed to return to power. One of the most influential periodicals of the time, *The Nation*, spoke of wealthy former Confederates as "the persons who must eventually purify Southern politics, if they can be purified."[3]

Led by new elements in southern politics, the Reconstruction governments had given eleven southern states modern constitutions, public schools for Black and White, modern prisons, social welfare organizations, and universal manhood suffrage (although some states temporarily disfranchised many former Confederates). But not only had this new leadership included elements that the old elites despised (poor Whites and Blacks), but the new constitutions also embodied an active role for government, which ran counter to southern traditions. For these two reasons, as well as the anarchy and bitterness that had followed the Confederate defeat, modernization had come at the cost of unceasing turmoil. By 1877 many northerners were as relieved as southern Democrats to see Reconstruction end and supposedly, if not actually, efficient and honest government return. While the abolition of slavery had irrevocably altered southern society, much of the antebellum relations of power was restored.

The southern Black masses, however, feared the return to power of the very people who had kept virtually all southern Blacks enslaved. In the lower Mississippi Valley tens of thousands of freedpeople responded to renewed Democratic control by migrating to Kansas in 1879, fleeing violence and the threat of actual or practical reenslavement. The Exodus to Kansas was an emphatic Black vote of no confidence in redeemers.[4] But in the North and the South, people whose concerns did not extend to the welfare or apprehensions of poor southern Blacks assumed that racial and sectional tensions would now end and the nation could get on with the work of restoring prosperity. And the very word *prosperity* appeared frequently in American discussions of politics everywhere in the world, underscoring the preoccupation of the age.

The mid-1870s had been hard. Even the celebration of the nation's centennial in Philadelphia took place under the pall of hard times. Inside the park, smiling workers demonstrated the latest inventions— the typewriter and the telephone—and new manufacturing technologies in the tobacco and textile industries. Exotic natives from faraway, exotic lands highlighted the contrast between so-called savages and (White) Americans. A modern Corliss steam engine as tall as a three-story building dazzled visitors and provided electricity for the whole exposition.[5] But beyond the confines of the centennial exposition's ceremonial glorification of American power and progress, the unemployed, the hungry, the tramps searched for their next meal. Because wages and hours had been cut repeatedly since the onset of the crisis, even the families of men and women who were still employed suffered. Increasingly devastating depressions represented the somber side of the dramatic industrialization celebrated in the centennial exposition.

The depression of the 1870s was the worst the United States had yet experienced. A Wall Street panic in 1873 had set off a wave of bankruptcies, and in succeeding years businesses had failed by the thousands, 6,000 in 1874 alone.[6] Worried observers attempted to count the masses of unemployed workers for the first time. In industrialized states like Massachusetts, well above 30 percent of the work force was out of work for four months a year during the worst years.[7] Faced with widespread suffering even in agricultural regions, Americans sought to fathom the crisis. One of the many explanations concerned the South.

While a few nonsoutherners blamed the whole nation's difficulties on upheaval in the South, this view did not prevail in the North. Yet most southerners held Reconstruction responsible for hard times in the South. Most southern Democrats and even some leading Republicans (Black and White) blamed the economic crisis on politics, especially on the failure of the Reconstruction regimes to secure the backing of the "wealth and intelligence of the South." Leadership by migrant northerners ("carpetbaggers"), modest southern Whites ("scalawags"), and Blacks of varying levels of wealth and education was said to have weakened business confidence in the South, thereby undermining economic growth.

By this reasoning, the fundamental problem lay in the split between the upper classes and the mass of Republican voters who supported Reconstruction regimes. The latter were men of moderate means who demanded services from state government (schools, institutions for the poor, infirm, and criminal) that did not subsidize businesses. South Carolina made this case with great clarity, for not only had it provided the vanguard of secession, but its antebellum government had been the most oligarchical in the South. Both the upper and lower houses of the state legislature had been dominated by planters, and the lower house had even designated the governor. As was the case nationally, the State Senate selected United States senators.

Reconstruction had destroyed this order of things. South Carolina's population was more than half Black, and although Blacks never held political office in proportion to their numbers, any Black representation at all was a novelty. Although the Senate was generally dominated by Whites, and only the lower house ever had a Black majority, the Reconstruction experience was still traumatic enough for Whites to inspire the terrifying and long-lived southern call to arms against what may be paraphrased as "Negro domination." The presence of Black legislators may have become the focus of attention in South Carolina and other southern states, but the real issue was that Blacks could vote at all. Overwhelming numbers of Black voters were desperately poor, and they voted their economic concerns. Their poverty and vulnerability to economic coercion and violence meant that any state government dependent on their votes would have priorities different from governments that represented planters and businessmen, who were employers. This combination of race and economics changed the face of southern state politics.

Reconstruction governments did not turn out to be positively proworker or pro-small farmer. Rather, they refrained from passing legislation that would victimize or immobilize farm workers that planters were demanding. But even this modest tilt toward the poor disgruntled the representatives of planters, whose ideas of the proper regulation of labor were to be found in the postwar Black Codes. These were a series of statutes that severely limited the mobility of Blacks, sealing them in the status of a vulnerable, landless agricultural work force. In 1866 the Black Codes' resemblance to antebellum slave codes had impelled Congress to wrest control of the process of Reconstruction from President Andrew Johnson. A decade later Democratic planters and businessmen (looking over their shoulders at Washington) hesitated to demand reenactment of the Black Codes as they campaigned to regain power.

Instead, "conservative citizens" and "taxpayers" met in "taxpayers' conventions" to demand honesty and efficiency. Their leader was the man whose government redeemed South Carolina.

Wade Hampton III, a planter who owned 1,200 acres of plantations in South Carolina and Mississippi and who had owned 900 people before the Civil War, protested the "venal and corrupt" Republican regime in South Carolina. However, what annoyed him most was "not only taxation without representation, but representation without taxation." The 1867 constitutional convention mandated by Congress and the legislature that it designed had used population (Black as well as White) as the sole basis for representation in the state legislature, a change from the antebellum system, which recognized White population and taxes paid—i.e., wealth. (South Carolina was unusual in this explicit recognition of the foundation of the politics of deference.)[8]

To underscore the justice of their complaint about the new method of legislative apportionment, the taxpayers' convention offered a detailed, if flawed, listing of the property holdings of all the delegates elected under the novel rule of universal manhood suffrage to the constitutional convention. The list was intended to demonstrate that the state's new rulers were poor men who paid little or no taxes. Hampton found it unfair that men of his class were "misrepresented in not having our property, the property of the State, represented."[9]

Such complaints had carried little weight in the period immediately following the Civil War, when Radical Republicans in Washington wanted most to reshape the South in the image of the North and before they appreciated the immensity of the task. In 1867 this objective had seemed to entail displacing the planter class, which had taken the South out of the Union. In South Carolina, as throughout the South, planters and plantation districts had provided the impetus for secession and had shown the greatest enthusiasm for the Confederacy. After the war, understandably, national Republicans had wanted to exclude these former Confederates and Democrats from politics. The old elites were to be replaced by pro-Union elements, a new, "loyal" political class that consisted of Blacks (northern and southern), northerners (Black and White), and southern White unionists.

Continual political battles and outright terrorism had marred the effort to reconstitute political life in the South. The enforcement of new federal legislation against the Ku Klux Klan in the early 1870s diminished terrorism for a time, but the mid-1870s saw a renewed wave of violence against Republicans of both races. In Colfax, Louisiana, and Hamburg, South Carolina, bloody-minded mobs of Whites attacked besieged Blacks with cannon. Reconstruction's attempt to displace a traditional ruling class seemed an increasingly impractical idea, even to egalitarian-minded Republicans like Albion W. Tourgée, who recorded his frustrations with North Carolina's intractable social order in the thinly veiled fiction of *A Fool's Errand* (1879).

After the Panic of 1873 and the reorientation of political issues it entailed, northern Republicans were far less ready to support the fragile Republican regimes of the South. In 1875, in the midst of a partisan civil war in Mississippi, President Ulysses S. Grant refused to send federal troops to support the Republican side, on the ground that "the whole public are tired out with these annual autumnal outbreaks in the South, and the great majority are now ready to condemn any interference on the part of the government."[10] Without federal support southern Republicans of both races were subject to more or less violent persuasion either not to vote or to support Democrats. Unrestrained by federal oversight, redeemers, like the forces of William Marcy Tweed of New York, won elections in the counting, not in the casting, of ballots.

The United States Supreme Court reflected the weakening commitment to political revolution in the South. Beginning with the Slaughterhouse Cases of 1873, the Court increasingly used the due process clause of the Fourteenth Amendment to protect corporations from state regulation rather than the civil rights of persons. The *Reese* and *Cruikshank* decisions of 1876, related to antiBlack political violence in Kentucky and Louisiana respectively, further limited the scope of the Fourteenth and Fifteenth Amendments by removing individual infringements of civil rights from the purview of federal law. Holding that Congress could legislate only on the actions of states, the Court made it virtually impossible for federal authorities to punish political violence. The Court's assault on Black civil rights did not end in the 1870s. In 1883 it ruled the Civil Rights Act of 1875 unconstitutional, thereby permitting discrimination in public accommodations. In 1896 it approved racial segregation, according to the fictional "separate but equal" formula, in *Plessy* v. *Ferguson*. And in 1898, in *Williams* v. *Mississippi*, it ruled against a Black man who had sued the state of Mississippi for racist disfranchisement in its 1890 Constitution. The Court decided that the Mississippi provisions, which through a series of subterfuges made it nearly impossible for Black men to vote, did not constitute racial discrimination because they did not mention race by name. Together these decisions undergirded the legal segregation, disfranchisement, and racial degradation that characterized the South during the first half of the twentieth century.

CORRUPTION AND elevated government spending characterized the Reconstruction regimes of the South as they plagued other governments as well. The Crédit Mobilier (railroads), Whiskey Ring (internal revenue), and Star Route (mail) scandals of the early 1870s spoiled reputations in Congress and in the Grant administration. In New York City the Tweed Ring of William Marcy Tweed stole and embezzled millions. As politics became the affair of "machines" whose whole point was holding office and distributing patronage, men of education and wealth began to demand clean, efficient government, through the agency of an educated bureaucracy. At a time when educational level was directly related to wealth, this meant putting government back into the hands of men who were more prosperous than the party faithful so prominent in local government, North and South.

By the 1870s Wade Hampton's argument that government rightly belonged in the hands of the "wealth and intelligence of the South" was gaining acceptance among many southerners, including some of the Black elite. P. B. S. Pinchback of Louisiana and Martin Delany of South

Carolina, both prominent Black men, shared the conviction that men of the better classes could end the violence and bring back prosperity. Like most abolitionists before the war, Delany had held what were then called republican ideals, according to which every man had the inherent right to participate in the political process, no matter what his level of education or his income. But after the war Delany came face-to-face with the realities of government by the impoverished masses in South Carolina and pulled away from the Republican party.

What repelled Delany, Hampton, and others who called for the return of the better classes to political leadership was the use that many poor men—new in politics in the South—made of political office. Whereas Delany, Hampton, and others who had formed their political views before the war idealized office-holding as service to society as a whole, many of the carpetbaggers, scalawags, and Blacks of Reconstruction saw politics as a livelihood and political power as an avenue to personal wealth.

This same sort of organizational politics appeared in the North, where the southern argument for the restoration to political power of the so-called better classes also made sense to elites. Their spokesmen were men of letters such as E. L. Godkin, editor of *The Nation*, former abolitionist essayist James Russell Lowell, Harvard historian and writer Henry Adams, and journalist Charles Nordhoff. Many of these were newly conservative voices that had earlier opposed slavery and supported Black civil rights. Now, considering themselves the best men in the nation, they spoke for the prosperous, educated classes. Identifying with wealthy and articulate White southerners, they applied the southern contrast between taxpayers (property owners) and voters (propertyless workers) to an analysis of local government in the North. Nonsouthern rhetoric assigned to Irishmen the role of southern Blacks.[11]

Just as the specter of "Negro domination" had served to discredit government elected by the southern masses, so Irish bossism was said to have caused the crisis of city government in the North. And just as the service of Blacks in the late conflict no longer served to validate their claims to full citizenship, so the service of the Irish in the Civil War also faded from view with the revival of 1850s-style nativism. The symbol of Irish character for nativists was no longer that of poor people seeking refuge from famine or the sturdy, indispensable builders of the transcontinental railroad, but rather the mobs of the Draft Riots of 1863 and the Orange and Green riots during annual celebrations of the Irish Battle of the Boyne. The pointed political cartoons of Thomas Nast stereotyped Irishmen in English fashion, so that man resembled ape and woman appeared as the perpetual victim of her man.

Ignoring the realities of contemporary public life, nativists blamed the largest group of poor immigrants readily at hand. "It is most curious that the most of these city plunderers work by means of Irishmen," journalist Charles Nordhoff observed in 1871, locating the causes of corruption in two Irish "traits": "The Irish emigrants [sic] to our shores display an extraordinary aptitude for misgovernment of cities," and "the Irish, more readily than any other people amongst us, accept charity." Such "traits" had changed the political process into a matter of helping out the poor, which Nordhoff and his peers saw as a perversion of municipal government.[12]

In fact, the Irish did not represent anywhere near the majority of workers and voters in the North. Actual figures do not support the rhetoric of the "best men," who saw the working class and the Irish as the same thing. In 1870 the vast majority of industrial workers in the U.S., 65 percent (2,255,100), were American born, part of the massive rural-urban migration of the late nineteenth century. Of the remainder, 11 percent (373,000) were born in Germany, 5 percent in England and Wales (159,000), and 12 percent (421,000) in Ireland.[13] Nonetheless, the Irish were undeniably poor, a working class of largely unskilled laborers, who were succeeding in urban politics.

Although the men who ran this new politics in both North and South were often from working-class neighborhoods, they did not consciously serve the interests of workers, or at least not those of organized labor. In the post-Civil War period labor's main issues were the eight-hour day, the establishment of bureaus of labor statistics, development of consumers' and producers' cooperatives, and opposition to convict and contract labor, notably the Chinese who had immigrated to the Pacific coast in large numbers in the 1840s, 1850s, and 1860s. Virtually all the Chinese immigrants were men in the prime of life who came as sojourners. They had built the western section of the transcontinental railroad, provided crucial services in the mining camps, and formed much of the work force in western cities. By 1870 nearly 9 percent of the population and about a quarter of the work force in California were Chinese, who numbered about 160,000 in the United States in 1880. The issue of "coolie labor" became national in 1870, when a shoe manufacturer in North Adams, Massachusetts, imported 75 Chinese men and boys to break a strike by the Knights of St. Crispin. While non-Chinese workers—native Whites and Irish—often stressed that they opposed "contract labor," not the Chinese themselves, the movement to protect jobs was not innocent of racial prejudice. Employers who used Chinese workers as a bulwark against unionism also aggravated racial tensions among workers.[14]

Like the elites who saw the influence of immigrants in politics as a threat to democracy, labor reformers were also skeptical of politics as practiced in the 1870s. Far from representing working people, democracy in the United States was a sham, wrote a union man who thought that the wealthy were able to manipulate the political process through the agency of the poor. The rich, he said, "buy idlers and vagabonds enough to swell the ranks . . . and run up a majority whenever a show of hands is required."[15] But labor's skepticism toward politics did not prevent the new labor federation from pursuing its goals through the political process.

The National Labor Union (NLU), organized in Baltimore in 1866 under the leadership of iron molder William H. Sylvis, became the largest national federation until that time. This yearly convention of labor delegates pursued its immediate goals, notably the eight-hour day, through political action. The keystone of organized labor for decades, the eight-hour workday was designed to spread work around and thereby lessen unemployment and to give workers leisure time for education and cultural pursuits. Deprecating strikes, the NLU took as its long-range goal the abolition of the wage system and the organization of all workers except the Chinese. Initially delegates welcomed workers regardless of race and gender, but this openness narrowed with time. Blacks accordingly founded their own National Colored Labor Union in 1869, which separated from the White National Labor Union in 1870.[16]

Both National Labor Unions shared the same weaknesses, chiefly tensions between delegates and leaders who were actually workers and those who were middle-class reformers, such as former abolitionists like Frederick Douglass and Wendell Phillips, who had been the Labor Reform gubernatorial candidate in Massachusetts in 1870. Whereas the working people tended to focus on immediate, concrete goals like the eight-hour day, middle-class reformers wanted to pursue what they saw as broader aims. In the early 1870s Phillips embraced greenback currency reform and insisted that organized labor follow him. At the same time Douglass, who had acquired a thoroughly conventional respectability, championed the Republican party and attempted to refashion the Black NLU into a partisan organization. Neither man acted frivolously, for each enjoyed significant support within his organization. But majority support was not the same as unanimity, and enough opposition remained to provoke serious controversies. Weakened by internal divisions, both National Labor Unions fell victim to the hard times that followed the Panic of 1873.

Before the depression the White NLU apparently achieved a measure of success in politics. During the late 1860s the legislatures of Connecticut, Wisconsin, Illinois, Missouri, California, Pennsylvania, and New York adopted laws making the legal workday eight instead of ten or twelve hours. This would seem to have marked a stunning victory for labor, which had made the eight-hour day its first priority. But the laws contained no enforcement mechanisms, and all of labor's demonstrations, strikes, and speeches failed to secure any implementation whatever.

For the NLU, lack of enforcement amounted to a betrayal that soured organized labor on the political process. At the same time, however, labor's success in state legislatures frightened many in the middle class. What labor saw as a demonstration of its powerlessness in politics, nonworkers took as a warning of impending labor takeover of American politics. Throughout the balance of the nineteenth century and well into the twentieth, labor would denounce two-party politics as the servant of wealth, while at the same time men of letters complained that the poor and uneducated controlled the political process.

The very passage of eight-hour laws seemed to many to signal a new phase in United States history, in which one class would be pitted against another and workers would dictate the law to employers. A friend of one of the new banker millionaires argued that "this universal suffrage country will never see the end of attempts of demagogues to excite the poor against the rich, labor against capital, and all who haven't money against the banks who have it."[17] Labor's continuing interest in currency reform, its support of greenback currency, and its opposition to national banks during the rest of the nineteenth century further alarmed conservatives.

Labor reformers as well as conservatives realized in the mid-1870s that the conflicts that would henceforth rend American society were of a new sort, pitting class against class, not North against South. This is not to say that the capital-owning classes were suddenly and monolithically arrayed against all workingmen and women. As in Europe, organizations concerned with the interests of workers attracted various non-working-class allies. Some former abolitionists, notably Wendell Phillips, continued to manifest their concern for the poor by joining the ranks of organized labor. Depending on the issue (currency, temperance, cooperatives), labor attracted the support of men and women who did not belong to the working classes: farmers; small businessmen; woman suffragists; socialists; Blacks. But one essential point cleanly divided labor and its allies from conservatives who viewed economic issues from the perspective of employers. That issue was wages and their relation to labor.

FOR WORKERS, wages represented not merely payment for performing work designated by their employers but also the main means of subsistence. One labor spokesman said that the worker was entitled "to wages sufficient to provide him with enough food, shelter, and clothing to sustain and preserve his health and strength. We [in the labor movement] contend that the employer has no right to speculate on starvation when he reduces wages below a living figure, saying, if we refuse that remuneration, there are plenty of starving men out of work that will gladly accept half a loaf instead of no bread."[18]

But for employers, labor was a commodity, subject to what were called the iron laws of nature or of supply and demand. "Labor is a value which a large number of men put into the market for sale," explained the editor of the genteel *Scribner's Monthly*, whose readers saw economic issues from the shareholders' point of view. "If the man who has it to offer cannot get the price he asks for it, he has an undoubted right to withhold it, precisely as if his labor were a bushel of wheat, or any other commodity."[19] By this reasoning, which was exceedingly popular in the 1870s, workers had a perfect right to strike, but not to make strikes effective by preventing strikebreakers—men who would work for prevailing and therefore seemingly natural wages—from taking the vacated jobs. This argument, often but by no means exclusively that of Republicans, deplored the organization of unions as a curse on both employers and employees and saw strikes as mistakes (at best) or crimes (at worst) against employers. To this turn of mind, strikes not only halted production but also distorted what conservatives saw as the natural identity of interests of labor and capital.

THE DEPRESSION of the 1870s undermined belief in the harmony of interests as strikes broke out in many industries—notably in textiles in Massachusetts and anthracite coal mining in northeastern Pennsylvania. The anthracite strike provoked a long, bloody battle, which ended in mid-1877 with the execution of twenty Irish miners, members of the Ancient Order of Hibernians (known as the Molly Maguires). The hangings provided labor with martyrs and conservatives with their proof that the formation of unions naturally entailed bloodshed. However, this most sensational case of labor unrest of the decade up to the summer of 1877 seemed to most other observers to be merely an isolated incident without lessons beyond the wildness of the Irish. For the next few years the Molly Maguires provided a symbol of senseless conflict, but they did not seem to threaten the country's basic stability. The strikes that began in Baltimore, Maryland, and Martinsburg, West Virginia, on the Baltimore & Ohio Railroad in July 1877 were of an entirely different order.

Early in July several railroads simultaneously alerted their employees that wages would be cut by 10 percent for the second time since 1873. Complaining that they would not be earning enough to sustain life, firemen and brakemen walked off the job and refused to let the trains of the Baltimore & Ohio Railroad run. The governor of West Virginia sent militiamen to get the trains moving, but the militia fraternized with the strikers and their supporters. One militia officer explained the reason: "Many of us have reason to know what long hours and low pay mean and any movement that aims at one or the other will have our sympathy and support. We may be militiamen, but we are workmen first."[20] The governor then obtained federal troops from President Hayes.

This was the first time since the presidency of Andrew Jackson that federal forces had been used to break a strike, setting a precedent for future federal intervention. Former President Ulysses S. Grant reflected on the popularity of using United States troops against strikers compared with the criticism that had surrounded the use of troops in the South: "During my two terms of office the whole Democratic press, and the morbidly honest and 'reformatory' portion of the Republican press, thought it horrible to keep U.S. troops stationed in the Southern States, and when they were called upon to protect the lives of negroes—as much citizens under the Constitution as if their skins were White—the country was scarcely large enough to hold the sound of indignation belched forth by them for some years. Now, however, there is no hesitation about exhausting the whole power of the government to suppress a strike on the slightest intimation that danger threatens."[21] In Martinsburg strikers erected barricades against the soldiers, but the troops succeeded in freeing a few trains. By that time violence had erupted in Baltimore.

The streets of Baltimore were packed with workers, few of whom were actually strikers, most of whom were skilled workers, and all of whom seemed threatening in their poverty and anger to observers from the privileged classes. The crowd set fires and waged pitched battles with the Maryland troops, whom they pelted with paving stones and bricks. As a result of Baltimore's outburst, 10 people died, 16 were injured, and 250 arrested.[22] James A. Dacus, a St. Louis journalist who appointed himself historian of the railroad strike of 1877, described events in Baltimore as "a spectacle that made one feel as though it was a tearful witnessing in perspective of the last day, when the secrets of life, more loathsome than those of death, shall be laid bare in their hideous deformity and ghastly shame."[23] This symbolic Armageddon grew more ugly when the ill-disciplined militia fired on a rock-throwing crowd of tormentors, killing 10 and wounding 23.

The most sensational events of the bloody nationwide strike occurred in Pittsburgh, where the Pennsylvania Railroad exercised monopoly power and virtually everyone—shipper, passenger, or worker—hated it. As in Martinsburg, the local militia in Pittsburgh mingled with the crowds that gathered around the strikers in the streets. The authorities then replaced the local forces with soldiers from Philadelphia, who found no friends in the mob. Seeing the Philadelphia forces as the tool of the railroads, the crowd attacked. Outnumbered and besieged, the Philadelphia militia opened fire as it retreated, leaving the crowds in control of the city. On Sunday, July 22, the crowd looted stores and freight cars and burned railroad property in a show of inchoate anger. Only the arrival of federal troops reestablished order, with the aid of two large rapid-fire machine (Gatling) guns. Twenty-five people died during the upheaval in Pittsburgh.[24]

Along all the major railroad lines of the Northeast and Midwest, in Albany and Buffalo, Newark and Trenton, Chicago, Erie, Reading,

Altoona, Harrisburg, Columbus and Cincinnati, Fort Wayne, Terre Haute, Peoria, and Kansas City, the strike paralyzed rail transport and brought crowds of strikers and sympathizers into the streets. In Chicago, as in several eastern cities, the Workingmen's party sponsored demonstrations in support of the railroad strikers. The Chicago demonstration attracted some 20,000 people, who heard speeches by the anarchist Albert Parsons, whose name became famous in the following decade. Street fighting between workers and police in Chicago killed some 40 or 50 people. In border state cities, Black and White workers went out on strike together and together prevented the movement of freight trains. In San Francisco the protest was as much against Chinese workers as against the Southern Pacific Railroad, which controlled the state's economy and politics.

The violent confrontations pitting working-class men and women against the forces of order reminded many of the sensational uprising that had occurred in Paris in 1871. In particular, several observers noted the presence of women as full-fledged participants in the working-class mobs that supported the strikers. Newspapers often described these unshrinking, uninhibited working-class women as "petroleuses." This was the term that anti-Communard journalists had used to define the Frenchwomen like Louise Michel and Josephine Courtois who had upheld the Paris Commune in 1871 by building barricades, preparing rifles, and setting fires. According to the *Baltimore Sun*, "the singular part of the disturbances is the very active part taken by the women, who are the wives and mothers of the firemen. They look famished and wild, and declare for starvation rather than have their people work for the reduced wages. Better to starve outright, they say, than to die by slow starvation."[25]

For one week St. Louis was the scene of a general strike; the city's workers took pride, briefly, in having set up the nation's only *"genuine Commune."*[26] James Dacus reflected what became the prevalent and distinctly negative imagery of the great strike of 1877 when he characterized events in Pittsburgh: "The Commune has risen in its dangerous might, and threatened a deluge of blood."[27]

Again and again, Americans saw the strike as the American equivalent of the Paris Commune, and throughout the balance of the century the Commune, with its scenes of violent confrontation, served as the prevailing image for Americans faced with labor unrest.

THE PARIS COMMUNE had occurred six years earlier, its progress followed closely by Americans. Napoleon III had declared war on Prussia in July 1870, but defeat had forced him to surrender at Sedan in northeastern France three months later. His government had fallen, replaced by the Third French Republic. Two weeks later Prussian armies encircled and besieged Paris. In March 1871 the French government fled Paris for Versailles, and the people of Paris proclaimed the Commune. Communards occupied the Hôtel de Ville (city hall).

The Commune's government began to demonstrate what a workers' regime would be like—separation of church and state; support of free, secular, public education for girls as well as boys; government salaries set at the pay of a skilled worker; vacant lodgings requisitioned for the homeless; trade unions allowed to take over abandoned workshops and set up cooperatives; employers forbidden to deduct penalties from workers' wages—earning the Commune a glorious reputation in labor circles. But shocked and fascinated American elites overlooked the reforms to concentrate on the violence.

On May 16, 1871, Communards pulled down the Vendôme column, which one of the Communards had numbered foremost among the city's "monuments of oppression."[28] Louis Philippe had erected a statue of Napoleon I on the top of the column, which became a symbol of the apotheosis not only of Napoleon but also of empire. Under attack by the Versailles government's "forces of order," the Communards arrested, then, in the middle of the Place Voltaire, shot to death the archbishop of Paris, the curé of the Church of the Madeleine, and more than thirty priests.

During "Bloody Week," May 21–28, the fighting between Communards and the Versailles army went street by street and house by house. Communards burned more memorials of the empire, including the Tuileries, the Palais Royal, the Hôtel de Ville, the prime minister's residence, the Pavillons de Floral and de Marsan, and the buildings containing the archives of the empire, including the Ministry of Finance.

After breaking through the barricades erected by the Communards, government troops had stood survivors against buildings and shot them dead. After the defeat the army stacked up a pile of 1,100 bodies near the Trocadéro, and bodies lay three deep in the yard of the École Polytechnique. Heaps of corpses lay scattered throughout the city.[29]

The massacres of Bloody Week ended the seventy-three-day life of the Commune and created its myths. About 870 of the Versailles forces died, but 20,000 to 25,000 Parisians lost their lives in the fighting and in the fires started by both Communards and troops.[30]

Although government forces were responsible for most of the bloodshed, a reputation for incendiarism and butchery remained with the Communards, who had killed far fewer people but who had murdered priests and demolished icons of French civilization. For a century opponents of socialism used the fires and assassinations associated with the Commune to discredit socialists of all sorts. Paris in flames remained the Commune's enduring image.

AT FIRST Americans saw the bloodshed as a purely French phenomenon, an outgrowth of the supposedly volatile French national character. But soon the larger similarities emerged with more or less urgency, with particular poignancy among former abolitionists who still liked to think of themselves as reformers. Unlike lifelong conservatives, they felt a malaise when faced with the conflicts accompanying industrialization. "America has no Vendôme column to overturn, no palaces to fire, no priesthood to spoil and slay," began one such Massachusetts minister, disturbed by the increasingly effective organization of workers in his shoe-manufacturing town of Lynn. Convinced that the United States, like France and other European nations, was endangered by what he called the spirit of the Commune, he feared the "perilous fascination for intensely democratic instincts in the theory that property has no rights which the majority may not abrogate at will."[31]

Wendell Phillips was one of only a few Americans, including those counting themselves partisans of labor, who did not reject the Commune's every feature. The Chicago *Workingman's Advocate*, while it reprinted the Commune's manifesto and refuted the outrageous condemnation in much of this nation's press, did not endorse the Commune.[32] In *The Nation* E. L. Godkin lamented the weakening of patriotism, which was once thought to be the strongest sentiment in the bosoms of workers but which was now fast ceding place to class feeling and hatred of capitalists.[33] Frederick Douglass summed up the conventional wisdom, citing class conflict as a pervasive fact of modern life. But he concluded that liberty, individualism, tolerance, and republican institutions would spare the United States the violent extremes of civil war in France.[34]

In 1871 the Commune seemed to hold a warning for Americans, but in only the broadest of terms. By 1877 other similarities beyond class conflict and workers' murderous anger at the rich had struck Americans reflecting on the significance of their own massive railroad strike. Strategic questions came to mind.

In Paris the empire, whose monuments the Communards had so eagerly attacked, had simplified the government's reconquest of the city. For Napoleon III, with the aid of Baron Georges Eugène Haussmann, had purposefully transformed the Paris of Louis Philippe from a city of narrow, winding streets, easily barricaded and protected by insurrectionists in 1830 and 1848, into a city of broad boulevards and radiating intersections. The new Paris reflected the strategic concerns of the French government, and now large numbers of mounted troops could move easily down the boulevards and concentrate in the spacious squares. Americans reflecting on the Commune of Paris and their own commune of 1877 reached similar conclusions about military needs.

Incensed by the property damages sustained by the railroads at the hands of striking workers, Pennsylvania Railroad President Thomas A. Scott elevated the companies' losses to the status of a national crisis. Accordingly, Scott recommended, à la Baron Haussmann, the permanent garrisoning of United States troops "at prominent points, large cities and other great business centres . . . [where] their movements can be combined rapidly, and they may be directed against points of danger. . . ."[35] E. L. Godkin clamored for a doubling in size of the United States Army, which by tradition had been extremely small. But the U.S.'s long-standing republican conviction opposed a standing army, preferring an armed citizen militia, particularly because potential enemy nations were oceans away. The only peoples who had regularly challenged United States power militarily were Native Americans. Although Indian wars were fierce, protracted, and deadly during the 1870s, such conflicts did not demand an enormous standing army. But now, it seemed, a great new threat existed in the nation's very bosom, in the form of strikers and what were called the dangerous classes, who had figured so prominently in the crowds of Baltimore and Pittsburgh. Newspapers described these groups as though they constituted a separate racial group, like Blacks or Indians, who were incapable of altering their supposedly inherently uncivilized and uncivilizable nature.[36]

Godkin believed that a regular army with 25,000 more trained men could have prevented the destruction of property and the bloodshed that had accompanied the railroad strike. Augmentation of the regular army did not prove a very popular idea, but the creation of a National Guard, modeled on the French Garde Nationale, had begun gaining support even before the railroad strike. In 1876 Civil War veterans and businessmen had formed a National Guard Association to lobby Congress for the enactment of a new Militia Act to modernize that of 1792. Labor unrest made the idea of a National Guard all the more attractive after 1877, when industrialized northeastern states created National Guard units, whose budgets were supplemented by donations from businessmen. After the 1877 disturbances Chicagoans, for instance, created a National Guard battalion of five cavalry companies out of the cavalry of businessmen hastily convened during the strike. The subsequent battalion was equipped and uniformed by the Citizens' Association of the City of Chicago, which consisted of businessmen who, according to a National Guard colonel, "look after the best interests of our city."[37]

In the late nineteenth century all the states established National

Guards, which accounted for state military expenditures of nearly $3 million by 1896. Everywhere National Guard officers came from the middle and upper classes, and everywhere, too, wealthy city dwellers subscribed funds to build massive armories, as Thomas Scott had recommended.

While businessmen went about the work of building a National Guard and putting up armories, a much broader spectrum of public opinion seeking to understand how such an upheaval could have occurred looked around for outside instigators, called "communists," who might have been behind the railroad strike. As in the case of the Paris Commune, "communists," "socialists," and "reds" seemed, if not the causes of the anarchy and bloodshed, then opportunist agitators goading the "dangerous classes" into acts of violence or anarchist frenzy.

In its most narrow and best-informed version the red bashing that followed the 1877 strike focused on the International Workingmen's Association, the International. James Dacus called the International a "promoting power" in the strike that manipulated the people and organized the riots. A monthly review aimed at the well-educated and well-heeled charged that "the gaunt Communist has placed his foot on American soil. . . ."[38]

In fact, the First International, a small and weak organization, had been founded in London in 1864 with the blessings of Karl Marx. But doubting that a revolution could succeed in France, which lacked a well-organized working-class movement, Marx himself was initially ambivalent about the Paris Commune. Factional conflict within the International distressed him further. After losing control of the organization in 1872, he withdrew from the International completely.[39]

Organizations influenced by the International or affiliated with it supported both the Paris Communards and the railroad strikers of 1877. But in neither case were these organizations or their members numerous or influential enough to determine the course of events. Leading Communards had been inspired by several brands of socialism flourishing in Europe, including Marxism. But Marxists directed neither the Paris Commune nor the railroad strikes. Although ten sections of the International existed in the U.S. (eight in New York, two in Chicago), it could do no more than organize meetings in support of the strikers.

The International's actual weakness bore no relation to the role that the fearful imputed to it or to various other hazy categories of leftists characterized as "communists." More often than not the "communists" were simply union men or other supporters of workingmen's organizations. As early as 1877 large numbers of Americans assumed without reflection that any organization or action undertaken by workers was subversive by definition.

Charges that "communists" were manipulating working people subsided without triggering a full-blown red scare in 1877. But the strike began to change American life and thought. It fixed the image of the Commune—violence, burning, and bloodshed—on the very idea of organized workers and socialists of any sort, images that reappeared in fiction, especially, throughout the balance of the century. And the strike awakened everyone to the existence of an intense, formless anger among poor and working people that was too shocking to be consonant with the older ideal of an American society spared class conflict. A New Orleans journalist pulled together the bloody connotation of the Commune and new sense of fear by envisioning the "millionaire" as alarmed as never before, having "seen the ghost of the Commune [that] will stalk through his dreams every night until he can feel with his prototype of the old world the security of mercenary bayonets enough to garrison every considerable town."[40]

The strike, although spontaneous, showed the advocates of labor the real strength of working people acting together. Samuel Gompers, then a cigar maker in New York City, recalled that he and his fellow workers were "stirred deeply" and were "heartened" by the courage the railroad strikers had shown in protesting against injustice. For Gompers, the great railroad strike was a tocsin that sounded "a ringing message of hope" to American workers.[41] But whether the bell rang out hope or fear, the strike gave notice that American society, long accustomed to seeing itself as exempt from the class struggles that rent Europe, no longer enjoyed this exemption.

DURING THE YEARS following the great railroad strike Americans of varying stations acted on what they took to be the lessons of 1877. In California the strike inspired a journalist originally from Philadelphia to write what became a classic of political economy for the discontented. Henry George revealed his intent in his long title: *Progress and Poverty, An Inquiry into the Cause of Industrial Depressions and of Increase of Want with Increase of Wealth. The Remedy* (1879). Elaborately argued to refute established economic wisdom, *Progress and Poverty*'s message was strikingly simple. The problem of our time, according to George, was that as civilization advanced and laborsaving devices multiplied, industrial progress led to depressions and extremes of wealth and poverty instead of producing ease. "Where the conditions to which material progress everywhere tends are most fully realized," he wrote, "we find the deepest poverty, and sharpest struggle for existence, and the most of enforced idleness."[42] For George, the curse of modern civilization was the "unequal distribution of wealth," which, in turn, rested on the private monopolization of land, particularly land held off the market by speculators hoping to reap future profits. His remedy was a tax on land that would supply all the revenue the government would need, hence the later designation the "single tax."

George did not advocate the confiscation of land or taxes on improvements, but he would levy taxes equal to the amount by which land values increased purely because its location had become more attractive. With such a tax, speculation (holding empty land off the market until settlements grew up around it and its value increased) would become prohibitively expensive. Once the market for land had opened, workers would be able to afford farms, thereby creating a labor shortage and raising wages. This one reform, according to George, would bring America back from the brink of disaster and usher in a golden age, stamping out inequalities of wealth, corruption in politics, conflicts between labor and capital, and all crime and poverty. His remedy would permanently cure the evils of civilization. Should his advice not be heeded, he warned of catastrophe in apocalyptic tones.

Without dimming its appeal, the economics in *Progress and Pov-*

erty mystified many of its millions of readers. The book's world view, not its painstakingly argued refutation of academic economics, touched a sympathetic chord among its devotees. George offered a scientific explanation for the wealth of people who did not work and the poverty of those who labored. He repudiated the usual hereditary explanations for wealth or poverty, stressing the importance of environment rather than blood. Insisting that the conditions in which people lived shaped the outcomes of their lives, George freed the poor from the burden of hereditary sloth and inferiority. Although he was not at that time an especial champion of organized labor and suggested that landowners, not employers, were labor's main oppressors, George's book sympathized with the plight of working people. The spirit more than the remedy of *Progress and Poverty* made George a hero of labor and embedded a tax on unused land in the reform and labor platforms in the next few decades.

Progress and Poverty was only one of several books inspired by the railroad strike of 1877 that indicated the degree to which the strikes had shaken the public.[43] The most widely read novel of the strike, *The Bread-Winners* (1884), was by an antilabor corporation lawyer, formerly Abraham Lincoln's private secretary, later secretary of state, John Hay, who warned of impending ruin unless the upper class organized to turn back the ambitions of unscrupulous labor agitators and their easily duped followers.

Hay's hero, Arthur Farnham, is a well-bred rentier living in the poshest section of a city called Buffland. Farnham's antagonist, Andy Offit, a ne'er-do-well-turned-labor-organizer, rallies support by playing on the jealousies of workers, including a naïve carpenter whose girlfriend, educated beyond her station, seeks to punish Farnham for spurning her. (Here education ruins rather than improves the poor.)

Buffland's good, conscientious workers make no complaint, leaving only the lazy and drunken susceptible to the message of "a few tonguey vagrants and convicts" who are "preaching what they called socialism, but what was merely riot and plunder."[44] When these ruffians, who belong to a secret society of workers called the Bread-Winners, invade

Farnham's neighborhood, he organizes other Civil War veterans into a volunteer cavalry (such as those providing a basis for the new National Guard units) to drive out the invaders.

Hay's novel leaves its readers with four messages, three straightforward, one implicit: first, that only the preaching of unscrupulous outsiders who are not workers causes labor upheaval; second, that unions and strikes mean that the poor will invade the homes of nice people; and third, that to prevent such occurrences, the better classes must recapture local government from the spineless, corrupt foreigners (here German and Irish) who pander to the lower orders. In the political parlance of the day, Hay was preaching civil service reform—government by the educated.

Hay's fourth lesson, the natural superiority of the rich, directly contradicts *Progress and Poverty*. The inherent excellence of his protagonists emanates from loving portraits of handsome, conscientious Farnham—a former officer who is every inch the natural leader of men—and his neighbors, including the beautiful, modest, educated young woman (young enough to be his daughter) to whom he becomes engaged.[45] These people are portrayed as attractive representatives of a class whose education, physical beauty, and good taste justify their making momentous decisions about their entire society. Because he saw public life as too important to be left to corrupt politicians and greasy workers, Hay stressed Farnham's good judgment and cool objectivity. While the labor leaders preach class hatred, confusing personal passions with social issues, Arthur Farnham pursues the common good. Hay probably did not realize it at the time, but the very people whose influence he sought to undermine were reaching similar conclusions about the necessity of political action.

THE RAILROAD STRIKE produced a dramatic increase of support for the Independent (Greenback) party in 1878 and, in the 1880s, the organization of Workingmen's parties. The great attraction of Greenbackism for men who had awakened politically in 1877 was its anticapitalist and antibanking rhetoric (although many entrepreneurs and small-scale manufacturers, who were not anticapitalist, were Greenbackers out of a conviction that the retention of paper currency would lower interest rates and stimulate investment). Both labor Greenbackers and manufacturer Greenbackers saw themselves as "producers" and bankers as parasites. Although Greenback philosophy satisfied many who mastered its analysis of the roles of currency and usury in the economy, not everyone could follow the meaning of "fiat currency" or "interconvertible bonds." Even without understanding all the logic of Greenbackism's economics, however, many voters realized in 1878 that the Independent party offered a way to attack the forces suspected of subverting democracy, "monopolies"—which at that time meant the railroads—and the rich, personified by bankers.[46]

Greenbackism had its roots in the antebellum work of Edward Kellogg, a New York merchant bankrupted in the Panic of 1837. Kellogg recorded his views on money and the need for a flexible supply of "fiat" or paper currency in *Remarks upon Usury and Its Effects: A National Bank a Remedy* (1841) and *Labor and Other Capital* (1849), which together earned him the name "father of Greenbackism." Kellogg believed, first, that the government, not private banks, should issue currency, and second, that the government should print paper money, to serve as a circulating medium, and sell low-interest bonds, to attract investment. The one would be exchangeable for the other, or "interconvertible," producing a flexible money supply. In inflationary times people could exchange their money for bonds, thereby reducing an overabundant supply of currency. In deflationary times they could cash in bonds for money, and the attendant increase in the money supply would drive prices up. As important as were his views on currency and interest, it was Kellogg's concern for working people and his assertion that special interests kept workers poor that explain a great deal of Greenbackism's popularity over the years. Kellogg died in 1858, before government-issued currency seemed feasible. But the Civil War made government-issued paper money, called greenbacks, a reality.

In order to meet the financial demands of the Civil War, the federal government began issuing its own currency in 1862 in addition to selling bonds that could be bought with greenbacks. Reconversion from paper to specie (gold or silver) and payment of the interest and principal of wartime bonds bedeviled postwar politics right down to the end of the century. The "money question" also included national banks, another wartime expedient for raising money. These were private banks chartered by the federal government whose amount of circulating banknotes was limited by law. In Greenbackism—and in later protest movements—the national banks became symbols of the inordinate power of wealthy eastern speculators who did not work but who profited from the manipulation of money evidently at the expense of "producers": farmers, laborers, and small businessmen.

By the mid-1860s Alexander Campbell, a Pennsylvanian who had gone into the ironmaking businesses and land speculation in Illinois and who came to be known as the father of the Greenback party, had translated Kellogg's views into a political movement, stressing the interconvertible bond and the viciousness of "usurers." Campbell's writings brought into the Greenback fold labor reformers, notably William H. Sylvis, leader of the National Labor Union, and Andrew C. Cameron, founder of the *Workingman's Advocate*. Like the work of Henry George and Karl Marx, Campbell's writing offered not only an emotionally satisfying and "scientific" explanation for the poverty of working people and the increasing wealth of financiers but simple, comprehensive remedies as well. The interconvertible bond and government-issued currency promised to break the power of bankers and distribute wealth more equitably. Campbell's indictment of moneylenders satisfied William Sylvis, who explained that before becoming a Greenbacker, he had been trying for twenty years "to discover some remedy for the great wrongs imposed upon labor—to find the reasons why a small portion of the population enjoyed ninety percent of the wealth of the nation, while the many whose labor produced everything lived in poverty and want." Campbell taught Sylvis that interest "produces nothing; all it does is to transfer the products of labor to the pockets of the money lenders, bankers, and bondholders." Drawing on the powerful Jacksonian distrust of bankers and bondholders, Campbellite Greenbackism proffered a means of restoring to labor its rights and bringing justice to the economic system.[47] Campbell's political success included two terms as mayor of La Salle, Illinois, and election to Congress on the Independent (Greenback) ticket in the mid-1870s.

While Greenbackism had attracted a shifting medley of supporters in the 1860s and 1870s, the Greenbacker fold always included labor reformers, like Wendell Phillips. The short-lived National Labor Reform party of the early 1870s embraced Campbell's views, as did the more important Independent (Greenback) party, founded in 1876. The latter party fared badly at the polls in 1876, receiving only 80,000 votes nationwide. Two years later, however, strengthened by the increase in class consciousness produced by the railroad strike and the participation of the Knights of Labor, Independents received 870,000 votes, electing fifteen Greenbackers to Congress and scores of local and state officials.[48]

THE KNIGHTS OF LABOR had begun in Philadelphia in 1869 as a secret society organized by a handful of tailors afraid of being blacklisted or losing their jobs should their union sympathies become known. Uriah S. Stephens, who became the organization's first leader, or Grand Master Workman, had begun study for the Baptist ministry when the Panic of 1837 forced him to go to work. He ended up as a tailor in Philadelphia. During the Civil War he helped organize the Garment Cutters' Association, but Stephens was no radical. He espoused the prevalent antebellum view that workers and capitalists share an identity of interest as producers.

Stephens's vision of increasing the "Brotherhood of Man" under the protection of the "Fatherhood of God" did not include an inevitable class conflict.[49] Placing great emphasis on solidarity—the uniting of workers of all skill levels, races, and ethnicities—Stephens believed in cooperation, which the National Labor Union of the 1860s and early 1870s had also stressed, and in education of the laboring classes. He insisted that Knights discuss economics and politics and learn to pursue their own interests as citizens.[50]

The Knights of Labor remained secret and fairly small with local assemblies (locals) and district assemblies (made up of delegates from local assemblies) clustered in Pennsylvania, New Jersey, and New York until after the great railroad strike of 1877. The strike's disorder convinced the Knights' leadership that only tighter, more centralized organization would prevent new outbursts of radicalism and violence. In 1878 the order abandoned secrecy and organized openly on a national scale, welcoming all male wage earners and former wage earners (women were accepted in 1881, and one of the first female local assemblies was Chicago's 1789, which had been the Working Women's Union, organized in 1878), with the exception of lawyers, bankers, saloonkeepers, gamblers, and speculators, who were seen as representatives of the parasitic classes.

The Knights' 1878 constitution echoed many of labor's older demands, including the establishment of cooperatives, public lands for bona fide settlers only, the eight-hour day, equal pay for women doing the same work as men, as well as a set of demands associated with Greenbackism that echoed throughout the rest of the nineteenth century: government ownership of railroads, elimination of the private banks (to be replaced by a system of government-owned postal savings banks), and paper currency to be issued by the federal government.

The election of 1878 marked Greenbackism's apogee. Despite the Greenbackers' insistence on the repeal of the Specie Resumption Act of 1875, which would return the nation to metal currency and retire greenbacks, the law stood. Specie payments resumed on January 1, 1879. The argument now centered on whether the specie in question should be silver or gold. Greenbackers had favored silver (quietly demonetized by the Coinage Act of 1873), and in the years that followed, the silver cause acquired Greenbackism's tone of antimonopoly protest. Over the veto of President Hayes, Congress passed a compromise measure in 1878 intended to balance the interests of bankers and insurance men and those of western farmer-labor-creditor proponents of the unlimited coinage of silver. The Bland-Allison Act provided for the limited purchase of silver and, with the return of prosperity in 1879, quieted agitation over currency until the 1890s.

WITH THE RETURN of prosperity the crisis of 1877 no longer seemed so fundamental. The great political issue of the early 1880s returned to the theme of the 1870s before the railroad strike: political corruption. Concern over patronage intensified with the assassination of President James A. Garfield in 1881 by a disappointed office seeker. The editors of two prominent, respectable periodicals, George W. Curtis of *Harper's Weekly* and E. L. Godkin of *The Nation,* formed the Civil Service Reform League in 1881. Even with the passage of the Pendleton Civil Service Act in 1883, political corruption continued as an issue in national politics.

The federal government took cognizance of the crisis in industrial relations in two unprecedented ways. First, Congress in 1884 set up a Bureau of Labor Statistics, which organized labor had been demanding since the 1860s. (Massachusetts had set up such a bureau in 1869, headed after 1873 by Carroll D. Wright, who took over the federal bureau once it got started.) The National Labor Union, the Federation of Organized Trades and Labor Unions, and the Knights of Labor all had supported the creation of a federal Bureau of Labor Statistics as the first step in procuring legislation in labor's interest. Samuel Gompers testified in 1883 that a federal Bureau of Labor Statistics "would give our legislators an opportunity to know, not from mere conjecture, but actually, the condition of our industries, our production, and our consumption, and what could be done by law to improve both [*sic*]."[51] Secondly, the Senate undertook an investigation in 1883 and 1884 of the relations between labor and capital in the United States that produced five volumes of testimony, entitled *Senate Committee on the Relations Between Labor and Capital* (1885). However, the presidential campaign of 1884 approached the issue of labor only obliquely. The ostensible leading issue was corruption, although cartoons and campaign rhetoric equated political corruption with municipal corruption, both captured in the stereotyped figure of an Irishman.

Republican candidate James G. Blaine of Maine was tarred with the brush of corruption, and in fact, Blaine's own letters implicated him in railroad scandals. Political cartoonists caricatured Blaine's followers as corrupt Irishmen and tied every bloody act of Irish nationalists to Blaine. But Blaine's links with men of very great wealth did him incalculable harm, particularly after a group of New York financiers gave him in October a banquet at Delmonico's, which the newspapers seized upon as "Belshazzar's Feast." Jay Gould, one of Blaine's wealthy supporters, was not among the organizers of the dinner, but his notoriety was such that newspapers played upon his presence to trumpet stories of GOULD'S BANQUET TO BLAINE. A series of editorials wondered whether "Jay Gould Blaine" would, once elected, serve "Jay Gould or the People?"[52] Democrat Grover Cleveland of New York ran as the candidate of reform in general and civil service reform in particular. Cleveland became the first Democratic President since the Civil War, and his victory represented his party's triumph over the taint of disloyalty in the era of the Civil War.

PARTISAN POLITICS mattered little in the wave of railroad consolidation occurring in the wake of the Panic of 1873. Here the watchwords were the *elimination of competition*. One of the most spectacularly successful of the speculating railroad barons was Jason ("Jay") Gould, who had once boasted that he could "hire one half of the working class to kill the other half" and who was known since the Civil War years as "the most hated man in America."[53] Beginning as a New York mapmaker, Gould had gone into brokerage by the late 1850s. During and after the war he bought several railroads, notably the Erie, known as the very symbol of political corruption and financial rot. With his then partners, Daniel Drew and James ("Jubilee Jim") Fisk, Gould inflated ("watered") the stock of the Erie threefold without adding to the railroad's actual value, earning the Erie, which paid no dividends in those years, a reputation as the "scarlet woman of Wall Street."[54] (Drew, a former cattle dealer, is said to have originated the phrase *watered stock* by feeding cattle salt, then having them drink water before being weighed for sale, to inflate their value.)

Gould and his partner Jim Fisk had produced the Panic of 1869 by attempting to corner the market in gold. During the hard times following the Panic of 1873 Gould and his backer, Russell Sage ("the Money King"), bought up midwestern and southwestern railroads, so that by 1880 they controlled the Union Pacific, the Kansas Pacific, the Denver Pacific, the Texas Pacific, the Rio Grande & Western, the St. Louis & Iron Mountain, the Wabash, and a network of regional feeder lines. Throughout their careers Gould and Sage gutted their railroads by watering stock and siphoning off money rather than plowing back profits into maintenance and improvements.

The 15,000-mile-long "Gould System" covered the entire central and western portions of the country, starting in Ohio and radiating out from St. Louis through the Midwest and Southwest to the Pacific coast. In 1880 Sage and Gould brought the Western Union telegraph system under their control, giving it a virtual monopoly by running its lines along the Gould System tracks.[55] During the early 1880s Gould also bought the *New York World*.

By the mid-1880s the Gould System had begun to face financial trouble. The ill-managed Wabash went bankrupt and into the hands of receivers, followed a year later by the Texas Pacific. At this point a nervous and ill Gould was vulnerable financially, but his style of management characterized American railroads generally. These first great American corporations embodied the arrogance associated with monopoly in the minds of the businessmen and farmers who depended upon them to ship their produce as well as the hundreds of thousands of railroad employees. Embedded in the controversies surrounding the railroads was the problem that, at bottom, the railroads, like all businesses, served two sets of interests. For the owners and managers, businesses existed to make money (and labor was just another cost to be driven as low as possible). But for consumers, the role of business was to deliver reasonably priced, dependable, good-quality goods and services. These two different needs sometimes conflicted, particularly in economic hard times.

THE DEPRESSION of the 1870s starkly demarcated the post-Civil War era of hopes for the extension of democracy into the South from the grim era of class conflict. Whereas the newly enfranchised freedmen and the workers organized in national labor unions captured the spirit of the early years of the decade, the figure of the financier inherited the crisis-ridden times that followed the great railroad strike of 1877. With the defeat of the eight-hour movement and the Greenbackers, the 1870s' great and hopeful movements toward equity, another figure captured the imagination. Jay Gould stood for many things in different circles: a rapacious financier; an adventurous builder of empires; a heartless oppressor of labor; a genius at seizing the opportunities offered by a rapidly expanding economy. At the same time that Gould was making his several reputations, the Knights of Labor were growing into labor's great hope for the future, an immense conspiracy against capital, the workers' answer to great corporations, or a threat to American democracy. Americans were not united in their interpretations of contemporary events. But they would no longer be able to comfort themselves with the assurance that the United States was different from the Old World. By the end of the 1870s the depth of class cleavages was not obvious. But anyone looking at the railroads acknowledged that workers and owners did not agree.

3

THE GREAT UPHEAVAL

After thirteen years of construction the greatest bridge in the world opened on May 24, 1883. A long-span suspension bridge, the Brooklyn Bridge over the East River linked the largest and the third-largest cities in the United States.[1] Even before its completion the Brooklyn Bridge had acquired significance that transcended engineering and transportation. The Statue of Liberty, dedicated three years later, served a symbolic rather than a practical purpose. The Statue of Liberty came to symbolize patriotism while the Brooklyn Bridge became an emblem of progress, the American enterprise of taming nature and bending natural resources to human ends. Fittingly enough, the Brooklyn Bridge was mostly made of steel, another distinctively modern material.

The President of the United States, Chester A. Arthur (a New Yorker), led the dignitaries at the opening ceremonies, whose featured speakers were the Reverend Richard S. Storrs and Congressman Abram S. Hewitt. Storrs called the bridge a great achievement of technology that would open a new era in American history and "make nature subservient to human designs." Storrs recognized in turn the investors and politicians, then the engineers and the workers who actually built the bridge, which represented a "durable monument to Democracy itself."[2]

Congressman Hewitt attempted to clear the taint of political corruption from the reputation of this Eighth Wonder of the World. Conceived in 1865, the bridge had been built by the Brooklyn Bridge Company, in which the cities of Brooklyn and New York owned shares, but it would not have come into being had the bridge company not bribed legislators in Albany. Once construction was under way, dishonest contractors had supplied shoddy materials. Writing in April 1883, Henry George had referred to the use of substandard wire in the great bridge, contrasting scientific progress with the persistence of small-minded iniquity: "We have brought machinery to a pitch of perfection that, fifty years ago could not have been imagined," George said, "but in the presence of political corruption, we seem as helpless as idiots."[3]

Congressman Hewitt differed, claiming that the downfall of the Tweed Ring had taken New York into a new era of clean politics, of which the bridge was a product. While Hewitt spoke of vindication, he also paired the bridge with the age's most potent symbol of progress, the railroad. Connecting Long Island with Manhattan, the Brooklyn Bridge closed the last gap in the coast-to-coast railroad link that provided a physical representation of national unity. American fascination with railroads dated back to the 1830s and 1840s, when they had become the main means of transporting settlers across vast distances in the West. Popular painters like Thomas Cole, Jasper Francis Cropsey, and George Inness recognized the qualities possessed by the railroad that embodied the new industrial order: metal and fire, noise and smoke. The nation's favorite essayist, Ralph Waldo Emerson, called the iron in railroads "a magician's rod" whose power could "evoke the sleeping energies of land and water."[4]

By the 1880s the railroad stood for technology in popular rhetoric, and Americans endowed technology with qualities they imagined to be uniquely American: prosperity, mobility, and democracy. Andrew Carnegie contrasted the United States with Europe in *Triumphant Democracy* (1886): "The old nations of the earth creep on at a snail's pace; the Republic thunders past with the rush of the express."[5] The railroad inspired speeches, articles, and novels in which it not only connected the rural or small-town American to destiny in the great city but also provided adventure and romance.

Going forward meant going West, getting rich, moving up, and the transcontinental railroad inherited the resonance of the prewar slogan Manifest Destiny. The handiest index of progress was the increase in railroad trackage that knitted the nation's farms and industries together, so that each thousand miles of railroad tracks meant efficient transportation, and efficient transportation meant profit.[6] And in this Republic in which all men supposedly enjoyed civil and political liberty, every man could make a profit, if only he had the ability to work hard and save. Liberty meant that each man began life with limitless opportunities, and liberty meant not only that governments would not interfere with the making of money but that they were expected to promote enterprises likely to produce profits. Although few recognized it, this common wisdom, so prevalent in the 1880s, contained a fundamental contradiction. At the same time that the economic system and the political system were seen as one—any attack on economic institutions appeared to endanger the polity—most people believed that the government should not regulate or own any economic institution.

Abram S. Hewitt's Brooklyn Bridge speech also addressed a controversial aspect of progress which railroads, the greatest corporations of the mid-nineteenth century, also embodied: the millionaires who lived magnificently and seemed infinitely powerful—the Harrimans, Stanfords, Vanderbilts, and Goulds. Citing an immutable law of the steady improvement of society, Hewitt tried to explain that the wealth created by technological progress, now seemingly monopolized by a few, would ultimately contribute to the common good and produce "absolute justice between man and man."[7]

Although few Americans could resist the rhetoric of progress in which the railroad played so central a part, here and there a voice warned that progress was not all to the good. *John's Swinton's Paper,* a prominent New York labor newspaper, sounded the alarm against the "new corporacy," in which the railroads were only some of the great corporations that were "sapping the foundations of commercial integrity, destroying respect for honesty and purity, levying tribute upon the food you eat—and often, very often, adulterating it. . . . Awake, O sleeper! thy chains are forged. Thine arms are bound. Thy hands are fettered—thy feet are linked together."[8]

For all their happy connotations of modernity, the railroads were still places where thousands of men daily worked and died. Between July 1888 and June 1889 railroads employed 704,443 men, of whom 20,028 were injured and 1,972 were killed on the job.[9] The railroads— and the telegraph lines that ran alongside them—were also the setting of several important strikes in the economically depressed mid-1880s, the most notable against companies owned by the financially vulnerable Jay Gould. In 1883 the telegraphers organized by the Knights of Labor successfully struck Gould's Western Union Telegraph Company nation-wide. Two years later Knights of Labor working on the Gould railroads struck to protest wage cuts accompanying the economic downturn.

The 1885 strike was brief and successful, the Knights of Labor win-ning the promise of the restoration of lost wages and the reinstatement of strikers without discrimination. Not realizing that the victory also reflected Gould's precarious finances and failing health, the Knights seemed to have achieved the unusual feat of forcing a millionaire to deal with his workers as worthy opponents. This well-publicized vic-tory projected the Knights of Labor as a powerful organization of work-ers which, with the easing of the recession, produced a phenomenal growth of the Knights all across the country. More than 700,000 strong in 1886, the Noble Order of the Knights of Labor figured centrally in the tumultuous, pivotal year of the Great Upheaval.

The year 1886 began with riots and strikes in the bituminous coal-fields of southwestern Pennsylvania. By mid-March 50,000 workers were on strike.[10] Hundreds of workers struck the McCormick reaper works in Chicago, but the streetcar strikes in New York, in which police drove streetcars through barricades and strikers threw rocks, generated bigger headlines.[11] As soon as the streetcar strikes were won, the year's most sensational strike broke out in the West.

The triggering incident of the great southwestern strike, what Ter-ence Powderly called the "last straw," was mundane. C. A. Hall, a leading member of the Knights of Labor in Marshall, Texas, was fired by the very foreman who had earlier given him permission to leave work to attend a meeting of the Knights District Assembly 101, a regional grouping of several local assemblies centered in Sedalia, Missouri, which represented all the Knights of Labor working on the Gould railroads in the Southwest.[12]

Hall's dismissal came in the midst of tense times, for District Assembly 101 had already been considering a strike to protest low wages, arbitrary management (as in the Hall case), and union busting (firing union activists to frighten other workers away from the union). According to the leader of District Assembly 101, a Scots machinist named Martin Irons, the Knights had tried repeatedly to negotiate with the management of the railroad. "Every avenue was closed by a barrier of unapproachableness. . . . One hour's gentlemanly courtesy on the part of the manager would have averted all this disaster [the strike]."[13]

Arrogant management was only one of several grievances that had made the Knights consider striking, even before Hall's dismissal. The Knights of Labor had wanted to raise the wages of unskilled workers— mostly section men, many of whom were Black. This first demand was characteristic of the Knights, who, unlike other established unions of the time, included unskilled as well as skilled workers, Blacks and Whites, men and women. By organizing unskilled as well as skilled workers by industry, the Knights of Labor were acting on the principle of industrial unionism, which did not become widespread and enduring in the United States until the 1930s.

With the exception of the United Mine Workers, most nineteenth-century unions were trade unions, organizing only skilled members or particular trades, who preferred their unionism "pure and simple"— that is, unencumbered by long-term aims, such as the abolition of the wage system, and by seemingly impractical policies, such as the admission of unskilled workers, who, being easily replaced, had virtually no leverage with their employers. The crafts unions looked out for only their own members, restricting their numbers by requiring members to be skilled (and usually also White and male), so they could negotiate improved working conditions, notably shorter hours and better pay. Whereas the philosophy of the Knights of Labor downplayed the strike, the crafts unions used strikes selectively, which, thanks to the difficulty of replacing skilled workers, they were better able to win. The engineers on the Gould railroads belonged to one such organization, the Brotherhood of Locomotive Engineers, who stayed on the job throughout the strike, a course that the Grand Chief of the brotherhood, P. M. Arthur, called heroic and manly but that greatly weakened the strike. Weighing the virtues of showing solidarity with the Knights against keeping to the engineers' agreement with management, Arthur preferred strengthening his own union's reputation for respecting contracts, in the hope that railroad managers would be inspired to fulfill their part of the contractual bargain as well. Like many crafts unionists, Arthur doubted that workers of many occupations and skills levels could combine to serve all their interests equally. He questioned not only the wisdom of the great southwestern strike but also the long-term viability of the Knights of Labor.

The Knights' second demand in the southwestern strike—to secure recognition by the company as the workers' representatives—was intended to protect workers from capricious foremen and unreasonable orders. In the absence of grievance procedures, foremen tyrannized the workplace and were one of the main objects of complaint among workers across the country.

Without recognized unions—and in 1885 Gould had not recognized the Knights, though acceding to their demands—workers on the southwestern railroad system and elsewhere in American industry often felt themselves the victims of their employers, great corporations that workers faced as individuals. There were other discontents as well. Not only were wages low, but workers were assessed a number of petty fines that further reduced their pay. Workers paid for damages to company property that occurred while they worked, whether or not they were at fault; they also paid for imperfect products, even when these were caused by faulty materials or mechanical malfunction. Workers were not compensated for time spent on the job unproductively, which for Gould

System workers meant, for instance, that repairmen sent away from home received no pay for time spent traveling to and from the work site, sometimes twenty-four hours or more. In addition to these chronic grievances, the company had failed to live up to the agreement that had settled the strike of 1885.

THE SOUTHWESTERN STRIKE began on March 1, 1886, at several Texas locations: Marshall, Big Spring Creek, Fort Worth, and Dallas. News of the walkout spread quickly to the 9,000 Knights in District Assembly 101, who struck all along the 4,500-mile Gould System of railroads in Texas, Missouri, Arkansas, and Kansas, tying up freight throughout the Southwest. The first violence associated with the strike occurred on March 2, as a freight train attempted to leave Big Spring Creek and 25 masked men took over the train, forced the fireman and engineer from the cab, and disabled the engine. Such incidents occurred repeatedly, as strikers sabotaged and "killed" engines by throwing bits of iron into their working parts and emptying the engines of water and removing the screws without which the engines could not move. Violence began on March 10, when strikers beat up a strikebreaker at Fort Worth. As the walkout spread, mounting destruction threatened to halt the movement of freight in the entire central section of the country.

H. M. ("Hub") Hoxie, the manager of the Missouri Pacific, steadfastly refused to bargain with Martin Irons, the Master Workman of District 101. Hoxie faced the conflict with what a reporter described as a "grim, unswerving fixedness of purpose," believing that the fundamental question was whether management or the Knights of Labor should run the railroad.[14] With negotiations at a stalemate in Missouri, Terence Powderly, the national leader of the Knights of Labor, began meeting with Jay Gould in New York City. Powderly called off the strike in anticipation of a settlement, then Gould reneged on his side of the bargain, and the agreement fell apart. The conviction that Gould was making a fight to the death against the Knights of Labor fueled the bitterness of the strikers and their supporters. A Kansan sent this anti-Gould poem to a leading labor newspaper:

Ye serfs! who toil wearily year after year,
With no ray of hope your existence to cheer;
Be patient, like asses, and don't fail to bring,
The fruits of your toil to our harsh railroad king,
Don't think by submission you'll ever be free,
From oppression, extortion, or monopoly;
For Emperor, nor Sultan, nor Czar ever ruled,
With sway more relentless than old King Gould.

————

Your armed militia their banners may flaunt,
And haughty oppressors the masses may taunt;
But men of America, to liberty born,
Shall hurl back the insult and menace in scorn.
A giant is rising, who'll burst every chain,
The eagles shall scream in the heavens again;
And cursed be the dog that submits to be ruled,
By a plundering usurper like old King Gould.[15]

The breakdown of negotiations triggered more violence, including riots in several Texas railroad centers. But destruction in East St. Louis, Illinois, beginning on April 7, recalled events of 1877. A crowd of 1,000 marched to every railroad yard in the city, threatening at each place to block the freights. At most of the roundhouses, armed marshals stood guard. Two days later the guards at the Louisville & Nashville railroad yard fired into a crowd of 300 strikers and sympathizers, wounding 6 men and a woman. The mob scattered, then regrouped near City Hall. A Knights of Labor organizer begged the crowd to go home, arguing that rioting threatened to ruin the organization that the Knights had nurtured so painstakingly. The crowd defied him, pushed hundreds of railroad cars off the tracks, and set railroad property on fire in several different yards. Strike-related violence in East St. Louis killed 11 persons and destroyed railroad property worth $75,000. By early May the strike was faltering, however, and the Knights called it off, claiming victory in the face of defeat.

The significance of the great southwestern strike lay less in its failure to secure the demands of the Knights than in the attention it attracted to the phenomenal growth of the labor federation. Suddenly, it seemed, masses of workers not only were willing to throw the economy into chaos to secure their demands but belonged to an organization that appeared eager to demonstrate its power. The southwestern strike seemed to take the events of 1877 one step farther, a possibility that exhilarated some and frightened others. These impressions were only partly valid.

AFTER THE ostensibly successful strikes of 1883 and 1885 workers stung by years of abusive management flocked to join the Knights of Labor. The order had had only 28,100 members in 1880, but membership climbed to 71,300 in 1884, 104,000 in 1885, and 729,000 in 1886. Much of its leadership and its rank and file were Irish American, although Black tobacco workers, some of whom were women, played an important part in southern industrial centers like Richmond, Virginia. By 1886 the Knights had become the first massive organization of workers in American history. Newspapers reported membership totals that ranged into the millions, exaggerating the power of the order and overlooking the disarray resulting from such sudden growth.

Early in 1886 the Executive Council, receiving more applications for membership than it could handle, refused to admit new members for forty days, until applicants could be screened and initiated into the aims and methods of the organization. With good cause, the leadership worried that workers nursing old grievances against their employers would join the order merely to organize strikes, without understanding that it opposed striking until all other remedies had been exhausted. In some cases, in fact, workers were striking first and attempting to join the Knights later, a procedure directly contradictory to the organization's philosophy.

With roots in the older traditions of organized labor and reflecting the nonconfrontational views of its founder, Uriah Stephens, the Knights of Labor emphasized cooperative production rather than the abuses of wage work. The order hoped to replace capitalism's wage system (rather than merely to raise wages) by creating an economy in which all workers would be the owners of cooperative factories, in which all would work and share profits. Cooperative enterprises would abolish the conflict between employees and owners because workers would be their own employers.

In view of the Knights' objective of refashioning the economic order by abolishing wage labor, strikes represented diversions from more important, long-range goals; strikes were exercises in impatience more likely to be lost than won. During the southwestern and several concurrent strikes, Grand Master Workman Powderly expressed his doubts about striking without "an extreme necessity" and counseled workers to exercise patience rather than walk off the job. Powderly's conception of the American economy drew on antebellum models of mobility, in which every worker could aspire to ownership of an enterprise and large corporations had no permanent place. Imbued with this philosophy, Powderly and the older leadership of the Knights found it difficult to comprehend the demands of workers who saw themselves as permanent wage hands and their employers as perpetual adversaries. He understood neither the anger nor the impatience of the strikers of 1886, who in many instances showed a positive hatred of their employers. This conflict between the leadership and the rank and file—the one temperate, the other angry—fatally weakened the Knights of Labor in the long run. Although it was not evident in the spring of 1886, another labor federation that recognized the permanent nature of the wage economy would inherit the mantle of labor leadership from the Knights of Labor. The organization soon to be known as the American Federation of Labor also staged a protest over working conditions in 1886.

MANY CRAFTS UNIONS were affiliated with the Federation of Organized Trades and Labor Unions under the leadership of Samuel Gompers. An English immigrant of Jewish background, Gompers had come to the United States at the age of thirteen, in the early 1860s. President of the national cigar makers' union before he was thirty, Gompers was one of the founders of the Federation of Organized Trades and Labor Unions, which in the fall of 1886 became the American Federation of Labor (AFL). The AFL accepted the existence of two conflicting classes, workers and employers, and saw the strike as the workers' most telling weapon in the battle.

Although the philosophies of the two great labor federations differed on means and ends, both strove on the day-to-day level to protect workers from exploitation by employers. The division between the AFL and the Knights of Labor was not always clear, for not only had new recruits to the Knights—anxious to strike—acted on assumptions more appropriate to the philosophy of the crafts unions, but many workers also belonged to both federations at once, as did Gompers. However, the crises of 1886 put an end to coexistence.

On the leadership level, at least, the Knights of Labor and the AFL disagreed on the 1886 general strike for an eight-hour workday. The AFL supported the eight-hour movement, but the leadership of the Knights of Labor saw the campaign as "a waste of energy." The eight-hour movement dated back to mid-century and had been revived in 1884 by the Federation of Organized Trades and Labor Unions, which had begun planning for a nationwide general strike on May 1, 1886, after which eight hours would constitute a day's work.[16] Although Terence Powderly opposed the drive for shorter workdays because it would distract workers from the struggle for more fundamental reforms, thousands of Knights joined local strikes, along with members of the skilled trade unions, socialists of many sorts, and anarchists (revolutionaries who believed that government was by its nature the servant of the rich and must be replaced by militant trade unionism, which would become the nucleus of a decentralized, egalitarian social order).

Nearly 200,000 workers struck on May 1, 1886, with the greatest numbers going out in New York, Chicago, Cincinnati, and Milwaukee. Strikers attended open-air meetings that called for an eight-hour workday, which would reduce unemployment and give workers the leisure time needed to improve their minds. In most cities the eight-hour strikes simply died out without incident after a day or two. But in Milwaukee and Chicago the May Day demonstrations ended in bloodshed.

In Milwaukee Polish workers marched from plant to plant, calling workers out of the farm machinery factories and rolling mills. On May 5 militia guarding one of the mills fired into a crowd of marchers, killing five and injuring a dozen more. In the wake of the shootings, wild rumors of bomb plots circulated. The police rounded up local socialists and anarchists and refused to let them meet.

In Chicago events went farther. The eight-hour general strike and parade of 40,000 merged into the McCormick reaper strike that had been dragging on for several weeks. On May 3 participants in both strikes congregated in front of the McCormick plant, where Chicago police, already known for brutality against workers, beat up strikers and fired into the crowd. One striker died immediately; three others, later on.[17] The International Working People's Association (IWPA), a small, mostly German anarchist group, called a mass meeting to protest police brutality, to take place in Haymarket Square the following day. The IWPA circulated flyers in German and English that challenged workers to "Arm Yourselves and Appear in Full Force!" A national organization of workers, the 5,000-member IWPA had locals in New York, Philadelphia, St. Louis, and other industrial cities throughout the country, including the Far West and New Orleans. Its strongest organization was in Chicago, where every year its 100 members commemorated the Paris Commune as the greatest achievement in the workers' struggle.[18]

The Haymarket meeting of 2,000 to 3,000 took place on a drizzly evening and proved to be entirely peaceful. Toward the end only about 300 remained in the crowd, but as they began to disperse, a bomb exploded among the policemen who had just arrived in Haymarket Square. Fifty policemen fell, and the remainder fired into the crowd for two or three minutes. The bomb killed 1 officer immediately, and 7 others died later of injuries, while 60 were injured by their fellow officers' fire. The number of casualties sustained in the crowd was never ascertained, but the "wild carnage" probably killed 7 or 8 and wounded 30 to 40. Blood flowed in the streets; but no one knew where the bomb had come from, and few noted that police had done all the killing except that of the policemen killed by the bomb.[19]

Even before the Haymarket bombing Chicagoans had been anxious and excited. The eight-hour crusade had attracted a broad spectrum of supporters, and a labor newspaper had reported "eight-hour agitation everywhere." A socialist had predicted that "the next time the commune is established it must be all over the world at once—and there must be no more failures or partial failures."[20] On the other side, police and state militia stood prepared to put down any popular uprising. Chicago police, Pinkertons—private police with a long history of antilabor brutality—and respectable citizens who had been made sheriff's deputies for the day patrolled the rooftops along the route of the eighthour May Day parade. The state militia, armed with Gatling guns, had waited behind the scenes. The violence at the McCormick reaper works and then the Haymarket bombing and shootings had occurred during a time of expectation of impending confrontation. After the Haymarket bombing panic seized the city. A witness remembered "one of the strangest frenzies of fear that ever distracted a whole community."[21]

Chicago experienced the first full-blown red scare, months of antiradical (antisocialist, antianarchist, antiforeign, anti-anything-too-critical-of-things-in-general) hysteria, from which even laborites were not immune. As in 1871, organized labor distanced itself from the revolutionaries. With conservatives, liberals, and even Knights of Labor calling anarchists "wild beasts," the Chicago police initiated eight weeks of what Richard T. Ely, a professor at Johns Hopkins University, termed "police terrorism."[22] Three hundred prominent citizens, led by department store magnate Marshall Field, meat-packing millionaire Philip D. Armour, and George M. Pullman, owner of a company that manufactured railroad sleeping cars, pledged $100,000 to eradicate anarchy and sedition. The police raided more than fifty meeting places of anarchists, socialists, and other sorts of radicals, taking hundreds into detention, where many were badly beaten. Rumors of conspiracies and bombings circulated among a populace whose hysteria police encouraged.

The trial of the anarchists lasted from late June to late August. The judge in the case intimidated jurors (none of whom was a worker), frustrated the defense's attempt to disprove the charge of conspiracy, and instructed the jury that advocating violence was the same as committing murder. Although testimony showed that six of the eight defendants were not in Haymarket Square when the bomb was thrown, and the other two were in full view on the speakers' wagon, the state's attorney tried to prove that they had formed a conspiracy to bomb and that while "perhaps none of these men personally threw the bomb, they each and all abetted, encouraged and advised the throwing of it and are therefore as guilty as the individual who in fact threw it."[23] Without any indication of who threw the bomb, this allegation could not be proved. Moreover, all the purported incitement to violence had occurred in public, which hardly fitted with the charge of conspiracy.

Nonetheless, the jury found all eight anarchists guilty of murder and sentenced seven to death. Before he and three others were hanged, one of the convicted anarchists, Albert Parsons, an Alabamian from an old American family, wrote to a friend:

> There is no evidence that I or any of us killed or had anything to do with the killing of, policemen at the Haymarket. None at all. But it was proven clearly that we were, all of us, anarchists, socialists, communists, Knights of Labor, unionists. It was proven that three of us were editors of labor papers; that five of us were labor organizers and speakers at workingmen's mass meetings. They, this class court, jury, law and verdict, have decided that we must be put to death because, as they say, we were "leaders" of men who denounce and battle against the oppression, slaveries, robbery and influences of the monopolists. Of these crimes against the capitalist class they found us guilty beyond any reasonable doubt.

Another of the convicted men concluded that "he who speaks for the workingman today must hang."[24]

In the summer of 1886 the verdict was exceedingly popular. But as passions cooled with the passage of time, a few liberals—notably the nation's leading man of letters and editor of *The Atlantic* William Dean Howells, the Chicago writer and publisher Henry Demarest Lloyd, and Henry George—began to have second thoughts. By the end of the year hundreds were reexamining their views. Labor organizations and newspapers began demanding a reconsideration of the verdict, although Terence Powderly of the Knights of Labor opposed the anarchists' cause steadfastly. Local assemblies of the Knights of Labor defied Powderly and participated in a movement for clemency, as did the American Federation of Labor. Despite a wave of support for reduced sentences, four of the seven convicted to die were hanged in November 1887, although the governor of Illinois commuted the sentences of two to life imprisonment. (One anarchist hanged himself in prison.)

Exacting retribution for the incendiary, anticapitalist rhetoric of the Chicago anarchists, the executions polarized American opinion. For some, Haymarket jumbled several scary entities: organized labor (Jay Gould had called the striking Knights of Labor "conspirators"), revolutionaries (with all the images of the Paris Commune attached), and unAmerican immigrants. Before 1886 the word *immigrant* carried the connotation of Irishman, with overtones of Catholicism and municipal corruption rather than labor radicalism. After Haymarket the stereotype of the foreign (especially Germanic), bearded, swarthy, bomb-throwing anarchist gained currency. But in liberal and labor circles *Haymarket* stood for something very different: the persecution of the advocates of labor and the willingness of authorities to trample American traditions of free speech.

While the Haymarket tragedy facilitated the identification of organized labor with incendiary radicalism in the popular mind and saddled labor with the burden of proving that it was not out to destroy American institutions, it did not halt labor's momentum in 1886. Labor union membership stood at nearly 1 million people, three-quarters of whom were in the Knights of Labor. The press was full of discussions of what was called the labor problem, which meant strikes and riots as well as poverty and unemployment.

In a year of 1,400 strikes involving nearly half a million workers and of significant local success of Workingmen's or Knights of Labor political parties, the great question was how labor would use its newfound strength. Many labor supporters assumed that the labor problem was part of a larger, political problem that would endure until workingmen used their ballots in their own interests. After all, a worker's vote counted as much as a millionaire's. A man prominent in organizations of both workers and farmers agreed with many of his fellows that "a great deal of the crime that is in society is brought about by a system of class legislation in the U.S. tending to make the rich richer and the poor poorer. . . . I do not consider there can be any settlement of a permanent character in the country except by a system of legislation."[25] By entering politics, the Knights of Labor saw themselves as "recapturing government for the people."[26] This argument—that government should protect citizen consumers from being oppressed by monopolies—stood in sharp contrast with the more conventional assumptions about liberty from governmental regulation of the economy. The idea that government could protect the poor was not new in the 1880s—the National Labor Unions of the 1860s and 1870s had demanded eight-hour legislation and the creation of bureaus of labor in state government—but the call for governmental protection of people, as opposed to business interests, now struck most people as a novelty.

To its proponents, this logic seemed all the more persuasive considering that police in cities like Kansas City, Kansas, had been used on the behalf of employers against the southwestern railroad strikers and that the laws of many states prohibited (as "criminal syndicalism") or severely curtailed workers' rights to picket or boycott employers they considered unfair. Even successful strikes could not remove laws of this sort from the books, and strikes in the second half of 1886 were succeeding less and less. Political action appeared increasingly appealing, and even though Terence Powderly called labor politics the "most arrant nonsense," his censure did not stop local assemblies of the Knights of Labor in more than 200 cities and towns from joining with trade unionists and socialists to organize their own slates of candidates.[27]

In Wisconsin the labor party called itself the People's party. In Chicago it was the Union Labor party. In Baltimore it was the Industrial party, and in Boston it was the Central Labor Union. Usually the labor slates were simply called Knights of Labor or Workingmen's parties, and they ran on similar platforms in the fall of 1886. The Knights of Labor and Workingmen's parties embraced issues that were purely local—such as police brutality or the punishment of individuals unfriendly to labor—as well as a series of national reforms associated with the Greenback-Independent parties of the mid-1870s, notably the substitution of paper currency for national bank notes. The Workingmen's parties of 1886 also brought to the fore some of the Greenbackers' minor demands, such as the graduated income tax and government ownership of railroads and telegraphs. (These two demands, originating in mid-century European socialism, fitted in well with the Greenbackers' and Workingmen's parties' dislike of the railroads, which seemed to exercise the powers of monopolies.) The workingmen's parties also called for the abolition of low-paid labor (child, convict, and contract labor) that brought down wages generally.

In 189 towns and cities throughout the country—including Lynn, Massachusetts; Milwaukee, Wisconsin; Rutland, Vermont; Key West, Florida; Richmond, Virginia; Leadville, Colorado; and Newark, New Jersey—the Workingmen's parties fielded slates of candidates.[28] But no matter how complete their failures or how sweeping their victories, none attracted as much attention as the Henry George campaign in New York City.

BY THE MID-1880s George had become a pivotal figure in the closely related movements of labor politics, Irish nationalism, and economic reform. His 1879 best-seller, *Progress and Poverty*, had quickly attracted large numbers of Irish American readers, and George had subsequently published articles in New York's *Irish World*, a prolabor newspaper whose masthead read "Land for the people." The motto referred primarily to Ireland, where millions of landless Catholic tenants had been forced off land monopolized by a handful of aristocratic, Protestant families. Although formulated in California, Henry George's ideas about land applied to both Ireland and the United States, particularly when they appeared in the columns of an Irish American labor newspaper.

In the early 1880s, after George had moved to New York from California, the *Irish World* had sent him to Ireland to report on the land question. On his return, Terence Powderly, who was also a national vice-president of the Irish-American Land League, invited George to join the Knights of Labor. After each of George's visits to the British Isles, New York workingmen and reformers had welcomed him with public dinners. After being taken up by the *Irish World*, many of whose readers were also Knights of Labor, George became increasingly identified with the labor movement.[29]

In the summer of 1886, when George returned to New York for the third time, delegates from the Central Labor Union (representing 50,000 workers in 207 unions) asked him to run for mayor on a labor ticket. After a good deal of persuasion George accepted the nomination on the condition that the Central Labor Union present him a petition with at least 30,000 signatures, which would ensure him broad support. By the end of August the petition bore 39,000 names, and George was ready to enter the electoral contest to propagate his ideas on land reform.

Two separate groups nominated George for mayor. First a nominating convention of the trade and labor conference presented its platform, which combined George's land reform with issues favored by the labor organizations. It upheld the "sacred right of private property" and blamed political corruption and workers' poverty on a system of landownership that permitted the monopolizers of land to charge prices beyond workers' pocketbooks. Then the platform listed labor's own demands: government ownership of railroads, highways, telegraphs; employment on public works; abolition of property qualifications for jurors; and the simplification of court procedures to make the poor equal to the rich before the bar.

The following day middle-class reformers held another meeting to nominate George. Their views, stressing land reform and Christian val-

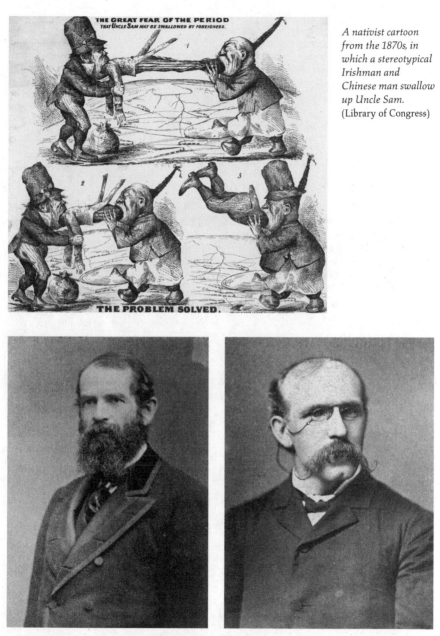

A nativist cartoon from the 1870s, in which a stereotypical Irishman and Chinese man swallow up Uncle Sam. (Library of Congress)

(LEFT) *Jay Gould, owner of the southwestern railroad system.* (Library of Congress / George Grantham Bain Collection) (RIGHT) *Terence V. Powderly, Grand Master Workman of the Knights of Labor.* (Courtesy of the Ohio History Connection)

(RIGHT, TOP) *Surveying the damage at Pittsburgh after the great railroad strike of 1877.* (Carnegie Library of Pittsburgh)

(RIGHT, CENTER) *Women delegates to the 1886 convention of the Knights of Labor.* (Library of Congress)

(BELOW) *Haymarket Square, May 4, 1886, according to an artist in* Harper's Weekly. (Library of Congress)

ues, paralleled those of George more closely than had the unions'. But the unions refused to accept the middle-class party name, Land and Labor, and George's vehicle was known as the United Labor party.[30] The George campaign embraced a wide spectrum of reformers, including Father Edward McGlynn, a prominent spokesman for the Irish-American Land League, and Professor Daniel De Leon of Columbia University, who later joined and led the Socialist Workers party, Samuel Gompers, and other intellectuals and labor supporters. The Central Labor Union, the Greenback party, the Anti-Monopoly party, and the American Federation of Labor cooperated in the campaign alongside individual land reform followers of Henry George.[31]

George's main opponent was Abram S. Hewitt, the son-in-law of Peter Cooper, who had run for president on the Independent-Greenback ticket in 1876. Known as a friend of labor and a man of honor, Congressman Hewitt represented the Democratic machine's answer to the challenge of Henry George.[32]

George spoke several times a day to working-class audiences, mostly on his own remedy for economic inequality, the single tax on land values. He endorsed neither socialism nor anarchy, but his Democratic opponent denounced him for stirring up class hatred. "An attempt is being made to organize one class of our citizens against all other classes," Hewitt charged, "and to place the government of the city in the hands of men willing to represent the special interests of this class, to the exclusion of the just rights of the other classes." Hewitt accused George of trying to "substitute the ideas of anarchists, nihilists, communists, socialists, and mere theorists for the democratic principle of individual liberty" and warned that if George were elected, the atrocities of the Paris Commune would occur in the streets of New York.[33]

Most newspaper editors were profoundly ignorant of George's bourgeois dislike of extremes and sided with Hewitt, reading irresponsible and incendiary meaning into George's speeches and warning that his election would unleash the lawless forces that had burned East St. Louis, thrown bombs in Chicago, and barricaded the streets of New York. Although George's own views might be moderate, the editors warned, his ideas would let loose the "thousands of desperate men who infest large cities [and who] cannot be fed on abstract socialism." Instead of conscientious, moderate, organized workingmen, George's followers were called "men who plot and theorize and agitate, and who live the lives of vagabonds."[34]

Hewitt won the election with 90,550 votes; George came in second with 68,110; and the well-bred young Republican candidate, Theodore Roosevelt, got 60,440 votes. There was evidence of a good deal of fraud. George suspected that fraudulent counting had denied him victory and vowed to lead a massive reform movement that would refashion American politics. By organizing Land and Labor clubs nationally, starting a newspaper, and pulling together a United Labor party on what it hoped would be a permanent basis, the George movement had already mobilized enough political support to frighten the New York legislature, which in 1887 passed several labor laws, including the regulation of the employment of women and children, the limitation of hours of employment on the street and elevated railroads, the marking of convict-made goods, and the creation of a Board of Mediation and Arbitration.

Georgeites became permanent members of the ranks of reform, and single taxers like Father McGlynn remained influential in reform politics long after the George coalition of labor, middle-class reformers, and socialists had splintered. In 1887 socialists tried to incline the United Labor party toward socialist positions, prompting George to expel them from his coalition. Committed to the free market, George had never believed in any form of socialism, insisting that government ownership of the means of production was wrong-headed and that "there is no conflict between labor and capital. . . ." He assumed that his single tax would cure all economic and social problems once and for all.[35] Such views contradicted every brand of socialist thought, making further collaboration between George and socialists impossible.

Having alienated one side of his coalition, George forfeited non-socialist labor support when he reversed his views on the Haymarket martyrs. Although he had earlier spoken for clemency, he later decided that the anarchists were guilty of conspiring to cause the throwing of the bomb and were therefore guilty as charged. Such views set George outside the labor pale entirely. Divorced from many of his supporters, George slid out of labor politics until 1897, when he once again ran for mayor of New York. The campaign of 1897 killed an already sick man.

The Henry George campaign of 1886 was only the most spectacular example of labor's entry into local politics in the year of the Great Upheaval. Across the country urban workers were fielding slates of candidates who stood (more or less) for their own interests, and in the countryside the Farmers' Alliances were also turning to political action.

FARMERS HAD BEGUN to come together in the 1860s and early 1870s, when local Granges had organized farm families across the country. The Granges initially functioned as social groups, but by 1874 the national convention had called for the formation of consumer and marketing cooperatives. Such undertakings lasted only briefly, weakened by cash shortages and competition from large corporations. But the Grange initiative was not merely social and economic. During the early 1870s Grangers had succeeded in electing legislators sympathetic to farmers, and a series of midwestern states passed Granger laws regulating railroads and grain elevators, which the United States Supreme Court invalidated (setting the stage for federal regulation of interstate commerce). Although the Grangers did not survive the depression as much more than a social organization, by the late 1870s other farm organizations had appeared in Texas and the Midwest.

The Farmers' Alliance in the South began in 1877, in Lampasas County, Texas, but it did not grow until 1884, when an organizer— "traveling lecturer"—began visiting other farming communities to speak of the need to protest falling crop prices, high interest rates, and farm foreclosures. The traveling lecturer's efforts paid off quickly, and with the addition of others, the Alliance became a movement with more than 300 suballiances in north and west Texas by 1885. In the Midwest the Farmers' Alliance started in Chicago in 1880, without growing much until wheat prices began to fall during the recession of the mid-1880s. By the time the midwestern Alliances met in 1886, membership had grown to somewhere between 50,000 and 100,000. Meanwhile, a Colored Alliance for Blacks was growing up parallel to the southern Alliance, which was a Whites-only organization. The three Alliances met together in St. Louis in 1889 and claimed to have more than 4 million members, a majority of whom belonged to the southern Alliance.

According to the largest and most influential Alliance, monopolistic railroads, greedy bankers, and a punitive credit system represented the evils that kept southern farmers poor. In an economy chronically short of cash, southern farmers had to purchase the seed, tools, food, and clothing needed during the crop year on credit; that meant paying elevated "credit" prices as well as interest. After the cotton crop had been picked and sold, farmers repaid shopkeepers' or planters' heavily inflated bills. The credit system kept thousands of southern farmers in debt year after year.

The Alliance was convinced that if farmers could "bulk" their cotton—combine the produce of hundreds of individuals and sell directly to fair-minded buyers—they might circumvent and eventually abolish the pernicious credit system, with its continual cycle of debt. In its emphasis on cooperative enterprise, the southern Alliance echoed the favored remedy of the Grangers and the Knights of Labor, without much more success.

Many Alliancemen were anxious to join with the Knights of Labor, whom they saw as natural allies and fellow producers. Even before the great southwestern railroad strike of 1886 the Farmers' Alliances had passed resolutions calling for "unity of action" with the Knights. In September 1885 the Knights of Labor and the Farmers' Alliance had held a joint meeting in north Texas and cheered advocates of unity. A sympathetic newspaper noted that "it is only by such combinations as the Knights of Labor and the Farmers Alliance that the laborers or producers can expect to cope with the organized power of capital, and the measure of their worth will be determined by the thoroughness of their organization."[36]

The joint organization of what were called the producing classes seemed even more logical when the southwestern strike drew farmers and workers together in actions that had started in Texas. Although many Alliancemen balked at close association with organized workers, who sometimes seemed as threatening as organized capital, generally the cooperation-minded Alliance saw the interests of the Knights of Labor as kindred to its own. Like members of the Knights of Labor, Alliancemen worried about the accumulation of vast fortunes in a few hands, a concentration of wealth that appeared powerful enough to distort the rule of law and to plunder the laboring and farming classes. Both workers and farmers seemed to be victims of the corporations that set the level of wages paid to labor and the prices paid to farmers. Alliance members refused to buy goods boycotted by the Knights, and they offered aid to strikers. This support was all the more natural because many people, including Martin Irons, Master Workman of District Assembly 101, belonged to both groups.

THE KNIGHTS OF LABOR and the Farmers' Alliances spoke for millions who had directly experienced the evils of which they complained. But the Great Upheaval also perturbed middle-class women and men who had not suffered directly. Alarmed by their growing conviction that the conflicts of the 1870s and 1880s portended greater crises, reform-minded people tried to alert the middle and upper classes of the need to close the gap between workers and owners, lest society be destroyed by class war. Many individuals, like Frances Willard, president of the Woman's Christian Temperance Union, and the prominent liberal Chicago journalist Henry Demarest Lloyd viewed labor issues differently after 1886. Using different means, each shaped public opinion in ways that were obvious only to his or her particular audience in the late nineteenth century but that would influence public life in the twentieth.

From 1879 to 1898 Frances Willard was president of the Woman's Christian Temperance Union (WCTU), the nation's largest organization of women during the 1880s.[37] The temperance movement was as old as the century, and abolitionism had had a strong temperance cast. Growing out of a women's antisaloon crusade in Ohio following the Panic of 1873, the WCTU had been founded as a national organization of women in 1874 and attracted thousands of churchgoing Protestant, mostly White, women. Willard had been one of the founders, but her background was academic rather than in temperance. Before working full-time for the WCTU, she had been dean of women and professor at Northwestern University, then president of the Evanston College for Ladies after its absorption by Northwestern.

Although deeply committed to temperance and women's rights, Willard began to think about labor questions more broadly in 1886. The WCTU organized a Department for the Prevention of Pauperism, which concentrated on workers, and Willard herself went further. She endorsed the eight-hour workday and expressed her support for organized labor, notably the Knights of Labor, which organized female as well as male workers and whose Grand Master Workman Powderly was a temperance man of long standing. The WCTU sent greetings to an Ohio meeting of the Knights in 1886, and Willard sent a letter of solidarity to several labor organizations across the country. In 1887 Willard actually joined the Knights of Labor, but her rapprochement with labor did not receive unanimous WCTU support. Nonetheless, Willard's views were influential in shaping the organization's approach to workers.

During the Great Upheaval the WCTU revised its explanation of the relationship between drunkenness and poverty. Having argued previously that drunkenness caused poverty among working people because laborers squandered their pay in saloons instead of supporting their families, the WCTU began to see drunkenness as a result of poverty. Before 1886 Willard herself had believed that the burning issue for labor was not so much higher wages as "how to turn present wages to better account"—i.e., how not to waste them on liquor. After the Great Upheaval, however, the WCTU newspaper, the *Union Signal*, ran a series of articles on child labor and the use of alcohol as a consequence of overwork and deprivation. By the 1890s the *Union Signal* was writing that "men and women, overworked, with a state of low vitality and innumerable difficulties to meet, naturally turn toward anything that will afford temporary relief. . . . In the midst of misery, drinking is almost inevitable."[38] This reversal meant that after 1886 women organized for temperance were less likely than before to blame workers for drinking. In the last decade of the century the WCTU took increasing interest in working people, particularly young women.

HENRY DEMAREST LLOYD reached large numbers through writing rather than organizing. He had grown up in New York, attended Columbia College in the 1860s, and was admitted to the New York bar in 1869. In the early 1870s he had organized the Young Man's Municipal Reform Association, in a vain attempt to bring the "best people" into politics and defeat Tammany Hall. Leaving the law, Lloyd turned to journalism and the *Chicago Tribune*, the daughter of whose publisher he married.

Like Henry George, Lloyd had been shaken by the railroad strike of 1877, observing that "either the attention of the people must be arrested & turned into resolution & resolution into action or else the country will drift into a convulsion as much greater than the convulsion that wrecked the Roman Empire as the Americans are more numerous than the Romans."[39] Lloyd began studying the great corporations and, beginning with "The Story of a Great Monopoly" (1881), a critical history of the Standard Oil Company, published several indictments of big business, including studies of Jay Gould and the Chicago Board of Trade. A denunciation of financial conspiracy and corruption, "The Story of a Great Monopoly" served as a first draft of his 1894 book on the same subject, *Wealth Against Commonwealth*, and provided an influential model of the investigative journalism that in the early twentieth century would become known as muckraking.

Wealth Against Commonwealth sounded one of the first alarms against big business to emanate from elite circles. It was one thing for Greenbackers, *John Swinton's Paper*, Knights of Labor, and Farmers' Alliancemen to denounce the monopolies but quite another for a college-educated journalist to present a well-researched explanation of how the large corporations—now increasingly referred to as trusts—victimized a wide range of ordinary people. While Lloyd never became as popular as Edward Bellamy, his remedy—socialism peaceably achieved—was the same as Bellamy's in the most famous of several utopian novels that appeared after 1886.

THE UTOPIAN WRITING that came out of the Great Upheaval drew on a centuries-old European and American tradition that flourished in the late nineteenth century. Assuming the people were perfectible, utopian writers, notably Edward Bellamy and Ignatius Donnelly, set their novels a century in the future, far enough away from the present to make radical change credible, for better or worse. Scores of turn-of-the-century utopian authors imagined means of democratizing society, even though the writers themselves were not workers or farmers.

Some utopians garnished their portraits with amazing, futuristic inventions that betrayed the authors' faith in both technological progress and the human capacity for improvement. Others showed the horrendous class struggles in which society would inevitably end unless something were done. Bellamy described the promise of a nonviolent, revolutionary future; Donnelly showed the violent class conflict that he feared would occur if contemporary social trends were to continue. In books that reached millions of readers, Bellamy and Donnelly set their middle-class peers thinking about the possibilities for change.

Edward Bellamy, a Massachusetts journalist who, like Lloyd, had trained originally to practice law, began writing his best-seller *Looking Backward* during the Henry George campaign. The book sold 60,000 copies in 1888, its first year; 100,000 in the next. *Looking Backward* spoke to the concerns of millions in the United States and throughout the industrialized world. An observer with a distaste for actual workers, Bellamy produced a book that is mostly dialogue between a respectable nineteenth-century Bostonian, who falls asleep in 1887 and awakens in the year 2000, and his twentieth-century host.

In 2000 Boston is a parklike city without lawyers, politics, or extremes of poverty or wealth. In the novel's peaceful solution to the labor problem, the entire population belongs to an industrial army, all of whose members are paid equally through credit allowances instead of money. Bellamy's twentieth century answered the fantasies of many middle-class Americans in the 1880s by eschewing class war and pushing industry out of sight. In the oddly preindustrial future of *Looking Backward* the working class has disappeared completely.

The main characters experience life as a pleasant round of consuming goods and entertainment. But Boston in 2000 is not in the least democratic, having exchanged democracy, which Bellamy and many others saw as little more than a wellspring of political corruption, for permanent hierarchical industrial peace. Order was Bellamy's main concern, and to underscore his point, he spoke to readers directly in a nonfictional postscript warning that workers were on the verge of insurrection and that unless their lives improved drastically, society would collapse. Before his death in 1898 Bellamy moved thousands of educated men and women by offering a vision of what seemed to them a more appealing world. But *Looking Backward* offers no description of any procedure that would lead from the crisis-ridden present to utopia, for as the book begins, monopoly has already evolved into state capitalism.

Another well-known utopian, Ignatius Donnelly, belonged to the Independent-Greenback party and others that in the 1880s and 1890s followed in its tradition of protest. Unlike Bellamy, Donnelly actually played a leading role in the new politics.[40] In *Caesar's Column* (1891) the corruption that Donnelly railed against as a political activist endures for another century, producing a society that is rigidly divided between a brutalized proletariat, encompassing seven-eighths of the population, and a tiny, depraved oligarchy. In scenes recalling the bloodshed of the Paris Commune, the proletariat rises up in a desperate, sanguinary revolution that devastates civilization but allows the middle-class protagonists and their wives (all beautiful blondes) to escape to Uganda in airships.

To forestall a repetition of the conditions that had precipitated the revolution, Donnelly's colonists, transplanted Swiss and a handful of Americans, institute all the reforms demanded by Greenbackers, Knights of Labor, and the Farmers' Alliances. Donnelly included Swiss because he thought their canton-based system of government presented the most successful example of democracy in practice. The colony, although situated in Uganda, includes no Africans, presumably because Donnelly was concerned solely with the preservation of Western civilization.

Although Donnelly professes to show the way to a better future through state-owned railroads, paper money, and limits on personal wealth, he is no more able than Bellamy to articulate how the class conflict of his time is to be resolved on a step-by-step basis. Like Bellamy, he believed that the best in American culture could be separated from the unfairness, then preserved by itself, if only economic justice prevailed.

The utopian novels ignored the thorny truth that no economic order could reconcile all conflicts or make everyone happy. Recognizing that the interests of different classes were antagonistic in the world in which they lived, Bellamy and Donnelly envisioned utopias in which everyone's interests would be served fairly. Only by stepping into distant worlds could they resolve the conflicting ideals of order and equity. Meanwhile, immediate problems demanded immediate solutions.

STARTING IN BOSTON, *Looking Backward* inspired the organization of Nationalist Clubs named after the system of "Nationalism," as Bellamy called his version of non-Marxist socialism. The Nationalist movement advocated moderate reform and took great pride in representing only the best people. A self-conscious movement of the well-off and well-bred, afraid of radical change or contact with actual workers, Nationalism embodied Bellamy's sense of the need for change along with his fear of confrontation.

Nationalist Clubs sprang up in Kansas, Ohio, Rhode Island, Michigan, Massachusetts, and California, and they talked a good deal about visionary change. In the 1890s they entered the political arena, campaigning primarily for municipal ownership of utilities but occasionally pursuing more fundamental reforms. Although Nationalists supported third-party politics in the 1890s, in the long run this elitist movement did not contribute significant ideas or leaders to the new political movement. Socially distant and disdainful of actual farmers or workers and deprived of leadership after Bellamy's death, Nationalism as a movement faded without making a lasting mark on the politics of the 1890s. In the short run, however, Nationalism brought a handful of well-educated people face-to-face with the pressing social and economic problems of their times. Ignatius Donnelly, an actual participant in the new politics that followed 1886, verbalized the thoughts and frustrations of people who had previously seen themselves as victims rather than actors.

THE GREAT UPHEAVAL brought new constituencies and their issues into the American political arena. In the mid-1880s the clearest manifestations of the new forces in public life were the Workingmen's parties associated with the Knights of Labor and the Farmers' Alliances. Toward the end of the decade these organizations attempted to join forces nationally. In 1889 the Knights of Labor and the three Farmers' Alliances (northern, Black, and southern) met jointly with the Farmers' Mutual Benefit Association in St. Louis. The meeting failed to achieve unity, but delegates accepted a joint platform codifying several demands that had been circulating since the mid-1880s, including the free and unlimited coinage of silver and the subtreasury plan.

The central demand of the southern Alliance in the 1880s was the subtreasury plan of Charles Macune of Texas (a former Greenbacker), which called for the establishment of federal subtreasury offices alongside warehouses or elevators, in which farmers could store their nonperishable produce, notably grains, corn, and cotton. Subtreasuries would issue farmers negotiable government notes worth up to 80 percent of the value of the stored commodities, and farmers would have to pay modest storage fees and interest on the notes. Farmers would therefore be able to market their produce at any time of the year, not merely at harvest, when prices inevitably went down. The scheme offered farmers relief from the credit system they saw as the root cause of their poverty.

During the 1880s, when the federal purchase and coinage of silver were severely limited in order not to inflate the value of currency, free and unlimited silver coinage also promised to put more money in the hands of farmers and workers. "Free silver," as the free and unlimited coinage of silver at a ratio of 16 units of silver to 1 of gold came to be known, had been a supplementary demand of the Independent-Greenback party in the 1870s. With specie resumption in 1879, the demand of inflationists shifted from paper currency to silver. Of enormous political importance was the transfer of much of the rhetoric and imagery of protest from greenbacks to silver. "Free silver" was not merely a cry for a larger money supply; it was a slap at the symbols of wealth and power: the railroads ("monopolies"), eastern bankers ("national banks"), and large corporations ("trusts").[41] As in the 1870s, a keen sense of oppression and a resentment of great wealth lay at the core of new money demands.

IN 1890 THE Alliances and the Knights of Labor met again, in Ocala, Florida, and added to their demands the direct election of United States senators and government loans secured by land. Direct election of U.S. senators was intended to reduce the influence of railroads and other large corporations in electing their men and purchasing votes in state legislatures. The corrupting role of railroads in politics had been publicized as early as the 1860s. But by the late 1880s the role of corporations in politics had begun to rival the issue of supposed corruption of working-class politicians as a source of concern in educated circles. Henry Demarest Lloyd had written that the Standard Oil Company had "done everything with the Pennsylvania legislature except refine it" and showed how the company had purchased a seat in the United States Senate for its man, Henry B. Payne of Ohio.[42] Legislatures were especially susceptible to bribery, and they elected men to the United States Senate, who in turn killed any legislation that the Knights and Alliancemen favored. A poor man's vote might count equally with a rich man's in a congressional election, but this was not the case when state legislatures elected U.S. senators. The demand for direct election of U.S. senators expressed a profound distrust of the way politics worked.

The demand for government loans to farmers took its place alongside free silver and the subtreasury plan as a way of providing farmers with access to sufficient credit. Outside the East, credit was tight and banks were scarce. Were the government to make loans, presumably each citizen with land would be eligible for credit. The fulfillment of this demand would not offer relief to landless tenants and sharecroppers, the poorest of farmers, whose numbers were growing rapidly in the South. But it would have increased tremendously farmers' access to credit.

DESPITE THE BRIBERY and corruption that they thought typical of existing politics (*John Swinton's Paper* spoke of the "legal hacks, party hacks, alcoholists and money sharps who now rule us"[43]), entering the political arena had come to seem inevitable to many of the delegates at Ocala, for electoral politics, in a democracy, seemed to offer the best means of influencing the economic order. Beyond the ballot box, farmers and workers lacked the prestige or wealth to shape the economy directly, other than through strikes, boycotts, and cooperative enterprises, all of which worked only in the short term and were subject to legal controls. Knights and Alliancemen began to conclude that they would have to take a hand in shaping the laws that governed them. If they did not own the railroads that they claimed overcharged them for shipping, they would try to pass legislation that would make overcharging illegal. If state laws declared the striking and boycotting of unfair employers to be unlawful, they would have to draft new laws to prohibit unfair labor practices. Now the men and women of the Farmers' Alliances and the Knights of Labor increasingly saw independent politics as a means of wresting power from Republicans and Democrats, whom they thought served only the interests of the better-off. The new constituencies sought to reclaim politics from the politicians and reorient it toward their own needs.

The Alliances and the Knights spoke openly of class conflict, denying the policies which served one privileged group—such as the owners of railroads or steel mills—could serve the interests of farmers or workers equally well, although in the late 1880s they smudged the conflicting interests of workers and farmers. In the wake of the Great Upheaval of 1886—as after the great railroad strike of 1877—the rhetoric of class conflict sharpened, as organized farmers and workers noted what they saw as a growing gap between the people whom they called the producing classes (themselves) and the rich.

The issues were primarily economic because in the eyes of the new constituencies the fundamental evil was the inequitable distribution of the great wealth the American economy yielded. Knights and Alliancemen did not object to the abundance brought by new technologies. But they wanted the new economic power of corporate capitalism to be exercised in the interests of the great masses of Americans, not merely the few, and they wanted the state and federal governments to seize the power to regulate on their behalf. In an economic way and, by extension, in a political way the great question for the newly politicized in the late 1880s was whether or not the United States would continue to be a democracy, by which the Knights and Alliancemen and their middle-class allies meant democracy in Jeffersonian terms, by equalizing standards of living. They wanted to reorient the nation's economy so that its incredible productivity would benefit, not impoverish, the millions who worked as well as the thousands who owned.

4

REMEDIES

"The eighties dripped with blood," the famous muckraking journalist Ida M. Tarbell remembered of a decade filled with conflict.[1] After the events of the Great Upheaval—the thousands of strikes, especially the great southwestern railroad strike, and the riots and bombings, especially the Haymarket bomb and the hysteria that followed it—few denied the existence of a serious labor problem in the United States. The question was what to do about it. Remedies proliferated, many of them political.

The demands presented in the St. Louis and Ocala platforms struck most Democrats and nearly all Republicans as extreme. But as the weight of the new constituencies began to be felt politically, Democratic and Republican officeholders realized that they would have at least to appear to take the welfare of workers and farmers more seriously.

President Grover Cleveland, a Democrat, attempted to do that in his annual address to Congress in December 1886. Echoing the Grangers', Farmers' Alliances', and Knights of Labor's concern over the power of huge corporations, Cleveland conceded that governmental policy had permitted the owners of certain industries to gain abnormal profits that had contributed to the accumulation of enormous fortunes in the hands of a few, whose wealth rivaled the aristocracies of undemocratic countries. Such riches contradicted "the natural growth of a steady, plain, and industrious republic." While American farmers competed at a disadvantage in international markets, Cleveland said, they paid unreasonably inflated prices for necessities and luxuries at home.[2]

The industries Cleveland singled out for criticism were "protected"—that is, their products were sheltered from overseas competition by a series of "protective tariffs" that raised the prices of imported goods. In his condemnation of protective tariffs, Cleveland agreed with the St. Louis and Ocala platforms, although the tariff had not been high on their list of demands. Cleveland opposed any more than a minimum of governmental activity and thus rejected the St. Louis and Ocala remedies that would have extended the reach of the government or limited the workings of the free market. The protective tariff, which had attracted Democratic attack since well before the Civil War, became Grover Cleveland's own crusade for economic and political reform.[3]

The British writer Rudyard Kipling noticed on a visit to the United States in 1889 that Americans felt strongly about the tariff, particularly if they were Democrats and particularly if they were drunk. Without understanding the workings of the tariff, Kipling said, Americans were convinced that it either protected the nation from ruin or ensured its destruction.[4]

The question of imposing tariffs on imported goods had flared up periodically during the nineteenth century, especially in 1828, with the "tariff of abominations," and again during the Civil War, when high tariffs (and several other taxes) had raised much needed revenue. After surrender, wartime taxes had been either discontinued or reduced, so that the tariff had not been an important issue in the 1870s. In 1883 Congress had passed a tariff that had raised some duties and lowered others, but most notably it had raised duties on goods whose American producers had spokesmen in Congress or influential lobbyists. During the late 1880s and 1890s this systematic favoritism strengthened the suspicion that government was coming to represent business interests rather than people's interests.

Protective tariffs divided Democrats and Republicans more cleanly than most other issues. To put it simply, Republicans supported them, Democrats opposed them. The two major parties overlapped ideologically, but their divergent constituencies shaped their differing approaches to the issues. Democrats traditionally represented working people in industrial cities like New York and Chicago and White southerners, most of whom were farmers. They saw themselves as consumers wanting to pay lower prices for goods they had to buy. The Republican party represented farmers in the Midwest, workers in a few cities like Philadelphia and Cincinnati, and southern Blacks.[5] But most of all, the Republican party was the party of business. As the party of manufacturers it supported high tariffs that would protect industrialists from stiff foreign competition that would drive down prices and profits. Although many businessmen were Democrats, their party presented itself rhetorically as the protector of the plain people. While both parties prized prosperity and feared radical change, they approached political issues differently. Democrats emphasized economic equity, while Republicans spoke of identity of interest as they argued over tariffs, currency, and banking, which were the national political issues of the late 1880s and 1890s.

Congress dragged its feet after President Cleveland's call for tariff revision in 1886, but he refused to let the issue drop. With most of his fellow citizens, the President believed that the health of the American democracy depended on a fluid class structure, and his own preferred means of discouraging the accumulation of large fortunes was the reduction of protective tariffs. Dedicating his entire annual message of 1887 to the tariff, Cleveland predicted "financial convulsion and widespread disaster" if high protective tariffs continued. He called protective tariffs "vicious, inequitable, and illogical" and accused them of nurturing the huge corporations that did business nationally and seemed to threaten open competition. Without charging conspiracy outright, Cleveland labeled manufacturers who prospered under tariff protection and who constantly lobbied Congress to keep tariffs high "an organized combination all along the line."[6]

Congressional Democrats, fortified by growing popular opposition to protection, introduced several tariff-cutting measures, the most important of which bore the name of Texas Democrat Roger Q. Mills.

During the spring of 1888 Democrats framed a series of arguments against high protective tariffs, stressing the conflict of interest between laborers and farmers, on the one hand, and manufacturers, on the other. They often branded large manufacturers "trusts" and "monopolies," referring to business combinations on the order of the earliest trust, Standard Oil Company, which John D. Rockefeller and Henry M. Flagler had forged out of several independent refineries in 1879. Trusts were large industrial combinations integrated horizontally and vertically. Horizontal integration brought competing companies together in the same corporation. In vertical integration the corporation gained control of the entire manufacturing and distributing process, owning or controlling sources of raw materials, factories, and means of transportation. Although it owned its pipelines, Standard Oil did not own the railroads it used, but through a series of rebates and special rates it shipped more cheaply than its competitors. In fact, many businesses organized regionally or nationally did wield tremendous economic power, which in turn intruded increasingly into politics.

When the word *trust* appeared in political rhetoric, its meaning was a good deal broader than merely vertical integration of production and distribution. Trusts were thought to be powerful enough to set their own prices for raw materials, labor, and the sale of their own products. Most people assumed (correctly) that they made astronomical profits which allowed them to drive local competition to the wall. In Democratic rhetoric, the trusts and monopolies were depicted as enemies of the people and thereby enemies of the people's protector, the Democratic party.

The Democratic argument assumed that the tariff filled the pockets of the privileged class of protected manufacturers by overcharging working people and farmers, who spent their entire incomes for subsistence, for the necessities of everyday life. One congressman drew up a list of items that farmers used regularly and showed the percent increase in prices caused by protective tariffs, including the iron that went into cooking stoves (raised by 45 percent), sugar (raised by 48 percent), woolen hosiery and undershirts (raised by 75 percent), woolen dresses (raised by 70 percent), castor oil (raised by 102 percent), and white lead paint (raised by 54 percent).[7]

The bagging used for grain furnished a handy example of how tariffs victimized farmers. This bagging was subject to a tariff of 54 percent, which meant that for every $100 worth of bagging that was imported, the farmer paid $154. But this was not the crucial point. Far more damaging was the effect on prices of domestically produced bagging. Even if this amount of bagging could be manufactured in the United States and sold profitably for $100 or $125, the manufacturer could charge any price under $154, undersell imports, and pocket the additional profit, thanks to the protective tariff. "This is called protection to the American bagging manufacturer," said the congressman, but "it can be plainly seen that what is prosperity and advantage to the American bagging industry is an injury and disadvantage to the farming classes."[8]

To aggravate matters further, higher costs for implements, clothing, and bagging put the American farmer at a disadvantage in the free-trade market of Liverpool, England. By keeping the costs of agricultural production artificially high in the United States, protective tariffs stifled American foreign trade, 75 to 80 percent of which was agricultural, notably cotton, grains, meat, and dairy products. As producers and consumers, farmers were the double victims of protective tariffs.

"The tariff is not for the benefit of the workingman," argued Democratic Representative Mills, in the face of the Republican contention that tariffs kept American wages high. Reading from a Bureau of Statistics report, he showed that manufacturers pocketed much of the price increases that protection made possible: the tariff on a yard of flannel costing 18 cents was 8 cents, yet the worker who made it earned only 3 cents. Similarly, a pound of sewing silk costing $5.66 bore a tariff of $1.69, while labor received 85 cents. Foundry pig iron cost $11 per ton, with the tariff representing $6.72 of that price, and the labor, $1.64. Obviously workers' wages did not increase at anywhere near the rate that tariffs increased prices. Manufacturers, he said, went "into the highways and hedges" to hire labor at the lowest possible price; consequently, "the 'great American system' that is intended to secure high wages for our laborers is so perverted that all its beneficence intended for the poor workman stops in the pocket of his employer, and the laborer only gets what he can command in the open market."[9]

Democrats conceded that American workers were better paid than Europeans and that immigrants flocked to the U.S. for that reason. But seeking the explanation for relatively high wages, Democrats pointed to technologically advanced machinery, mechanized production methods, skilled workers, and abundant raw materials and power sources, which meant high worker productivity. They used productivity, not protective tariffs, to explain high wages. Not only did the tariff not increase wages, Democrats argued, but it reduced workers' net income by inflating the prices of necessities. Democrats predicted the disappearance of the middle class and the undermining of the foundations of democracy, as the population divided into a large, impoverished class of the poor and powerless and a tiny class of the rich and powerful.[10]

By Democratic logic, the protective tariff enriched manufacturers at the expense of farmers and workers, priced American producers out of world markets, and encouraged the consolidation of wealth into trusts and monopolies that kept prices unnecessarily high. The tariff fostered political corruption by making the government the source of private profit, and it created a surplus of governmental revenues of about $100,000,000 that should have remained in the pockets of the people.

The revenue surplus underscored the particular nature of protective tariffs. At first glance tariffs seemed a necessary source of federal revenue. But a second look would show that they provided far more revenue than the federal government was spending. Democrats demanded what they termed "a tariff for revenue only," which would mean lower tariffs that would bring only as much money as the government needed to continue functioning. They said tariffs should be lower because they were, in fact, a regressive tax that fell most heavily on the poor, thereby accentuating class differences. For President Cleveland and many congressional Democrats, the root cause of the inequitable distribution of wealth was protective tariffs. Lowering tariffs was their remedy for the maldistribution of wealth.

Republicans initially responded to President Cleveland's indictment by thinking up schemes for spending the troublesome surplus. All outstanding government bonds could be retired before reaching maturity. However, this would provide a windfall to bondholders, who were generally assumed to be identical with the bloated rich, whose further enrichment was not politically attractive at this time. Pensions for Union veterans and their families might be broadened, a suggestion that ultimately prevailed. Or one of the most resented of the tariffs, the duty on sugar, might be reduced.

The sugar tariff provided Republicans an exceptionally fine rhetorical target. Regressive in the extreme, the sugar tariff raised the cost of an item used by every American, from the poorest to the richest. The sugar trust was one of the most arrogant and therefore most hated of the trusts. Nine-tenths of the sugar consumed by Americans was imported (from Cuba and the Sandwich [Hawaiian] Islands), and the duties on various sorts of sugars contributed $55,000,000, about half the offending surplus. Sugar, too, was the main protected item produced in a Democratic state—Louisiana. If you really want to help the little people, said the Republicans to the Democrats, reduce the tariff on sugar.

Many Republicans, including Blacks and the Woman's Christian Temperance Union (most of whom were Republicans), suggested that the answer to the surplus was passage of a bill introduced by Henry W. Blair of New Hampshire that would have distributed millions of dollars to aid education in states with large proportions of illiterate voters— that is, in the South. The need for funds for education in the South was so great that half the southern senators (Democrats all) overcame their states' rights prejudices and voted for the bill. But the Blair bill never enjoyed enthusiastic southern Democratic endorsement because it would do something for Blacks and at the same time legitimize protective tariffs. Lacking persistent Republican support and opposed by many Democrats, the Blair bill died in 1888.

Republicans argued persuasively and with some labor backing that American workers were better off than workers anywhere else in the world. A congressman from the manufacturing state of Massachusetts painted a rosy picture of industry and industrial workers under the system of protective tariffs:

> I wish I could take this body of men to the heights opposite the city of Lowell, Mass., where, with one glance of the eye sweeping up and down the stream, would be literally seen miles of cotton-mills, perhaps the finest in the world . . . and filled from basement to roof with a thinking, throbbing army of intelligent and skillful men and women. . . . [S]tanding upon this spot in the early evening as the sun goes down, you would see first from one and then another of the thousands of windows the lights flashing out. . . . Listen, and the bells ring out their peal, the gates fly open, and from them issue thousands of working men and women, well clothed, well fed, well housed, pleasant to look upon, happy and contented, moving quietly to their homes . . . the ideal laboring wage-earners of a New England manufacturing city.[11]

The immigration of hundreds of thousands of foreign workers to the United States every year proved the attractiveness of what Republicans called the American system of protection. American industry need not compete in world markets, said Republicans in 1888; there were markets enough here. If American products alone supplied American markets, American workers would never want for work. Protection was therefore the American way of self-help and development, providing ample jobs for American workers. "I would not permit a single ton of steel to come into the United States if our own labor could make it," said Congressman William McKinley of Ohio to an appreciative audience in the House galleries. "Let American labor . . . manufacture American products. (Applause.) . . . This Government is made for Americans, native-born and naturalized; and every pound, every bushel, every ton, every yard of foreign product that comes into this country to compete with ours deprives American labor of what justly belongs to it."[12]

For McKinley, protection was in the best interests of all Americans, especially poor men seeking to better themselves by starting out in business. Rejecting the main Democratic argument that protection hurt the many and enriched the few, McKinley said that the interests of American producers and consumers were one and that the President should have been ashamed to pit one class against the other. Protectionism's most eloquent defender explained that protection stimulated American industry, which enriched all Americans. Every factory spread prosperity throughout its neighborhood because workers found employment, farmers sold their produce to workers, and tradesmen sold to workers and farmers. Abolition of protective tariffs would cause unemployment and poverty.

This Republican argument enjoyed a measure of support from labor. An ironworker and union man agreed that protection would benefit a great many workers by providing more jobs in the ore and coal mines that supplied the foundries and in the foundries themselves. A textile worker preferred to see prices high "because cheap goods result from too close competition, and that ends in bringing down wages."[13] For these workers as well as for Republican spokesmen, protection meant prosperity for the American people in general.

Prosperity was William McKinley's favorite theme, and he countered the Democrats' image of the suffering poor and class conflict with one that was far sunnier. Embracing protectionism, he promised that Americans producing for an American market would realize a utopia of production and exchange. Unemployment would disappear. Dissatisfied workingmen would find fulfillment. Farmers would get fat prices for their crops. And legislators, no longer subject to temptation from corporate boodlers, would act only in the interest of the general commonweal. The tariff was McKinley's answer to Henry George.

THE TARIFF WAS the great issue of the 1888 presidential campaign, which pitted Democrat Grover Cleveland, calling for tariff revision downward in the name of farmers and workers, against Republican Benjamin Harrison, calling for protective tariffs in the name of prosperity and the general good. The persuasiveness of the latter argument received a substantial assist from abundant campaign funds raised by John Wanamaker, the Philadelphia department store founder. Wanamaker addressed audiences of industrialists across the country, impressing upon them their stake in protection and, by extension, in the Republican party. "How much would you pay for insurance upon your business?" Wanamaker asked. "If you were confronted by from one to three years of general depression by a change in our revenue and protective measures affecting our manufacturers, wages, and good times, what would you pay to be insured for a better year?"[14]

This appeal proved effective in 1888 and in later campaigns as well, in which financing from business interests played a significant role. The redistribution of the burden of campaign financing had begun in the early 1880s, when civil service rules began to prohibit political parties' assessments on the salaries of officeholders. Issues of clear financial import for business had always been important in government, but now political campaigns needed even more to draw money from the groups who stood to profit from governmental policies.

Because the Republican party enunciated positions that were more valuable to the wealthier segments of the population, it benefited more than the Democrats from large corporate contributions. Whatever their party, most U.S. senators were suspected of representing corporate interests, and this link between money interests and congressional representation distressed the new constituencies, whose issues Congress defeated or diluted.

The election of 1888 was close, but Republicans kept a slight majority in the Senate, gained a narrow majority in the House of Representatives for the first time in more than a decade, and captured the presidency (although Cleveland had polled 100,000 more popular votes than Harrison). Republicans interpreted the victory as a mandate for protectionism and set about revising the Mills tariff bill. It emerged in the fall of 1890 as the McKinley tariff and epitomized Republican tariff orthodoxy.

A high tariff bill, the McKinley tariff contained only one noteworthy reduction: on sugar. By admitting raw sugar free, retaining a tariff on refined sugar, and paying a bounty to domestic sugar producers, the McKinley tariff managed to cut the duty collected on sugar, protect the sugar trust, protect Louisiana growers (and sow disturbance in the Sandwich Islands that finally led sugar planters to revolt against the Hawaiian monarchy and ultimately make the islands an American protectorate), revise one schedule downward, and spend a good part of the surplus on bounties. Democrats had argued for the lowering of tariffs on the ground that the surplus revenue proved that the tariff collected too much money. The bounty paid to Louisianian growers came out of the embarrassing revenue surplus and, by reducing the surplus, weakened one Democratic argument against protectionism. The McKinley bill further lessened the surplus by lowering internal taxes on tobacco and increasing pension expenditures for Union Civil War veterans.[15] Within a few years the revenue surplus had entirely disappeared. The man whose name adorned this cunning piece of legislation grew increasingly attractive as a presidential candidate.

No sooner had Republicans enacted what they saw as the perfect tariff bill than they suffered a resounding defeat in the 1890 congressional elections, after prices had soared in the wake of passage of the Republican tariff and after Farmers' Alliances and their allies had elected their own representatives. In the presidential election of 1892 the antiprotectionist Democrat, Grover Cleveland, faced the Republican incumbent, Benjamin Harrison, and defeated him. This time the Democrats read a mandate into the election returns, and they set about revising the tariff downward, or so they said. By then, however, the economy was faltering, and the currency question—reintroduced into politics in the Ocala platform of 1890—had begun to overshadow the tariff in public debate. The increasing salience of the silver issue, as the protective tariff faded from view, indicated the strength of the new constituencies, notably the Farmers' Alliances. Building on Greenback tradition, the Alliances cared more for increasing the money supply than raising or lowering tariffs.

Believing that silver currency would reverse the long-term deflationary trend of the late nineteenth century that had generally reduced prices, including crop prices, the Farmers' Alliances had added the free and unlimited coinage of silver ("free silver") to the Ocala demands of 1890. The currency demand was related to the Alliances' opposition to national banks, for both free silver and the abolition of national banks promised to make life easier for the "producing classes" and redress the maldistribution of income by ending what seemed like governmental favoritism toward banks, which also symbolized the rich. Thus the history of currency and banking reform mixed up Civil War economic policies, the need to satisfy bankers of the safety and profitability of laws regarding money and banking, and the meandering history of legislation regarding currency.

THE FREE SILVER and antinational bank demands of the 1890s had their roots in the Greenback movement of the 1860s and 1870s, although different coalitions had supported the retention of paper currency, then the coinage of silver, over the decades. National banks and paper currency both grew out of Civil War monetary policies. During the war the federal government had issued paper currency—greenbacks—to meet the vastly increased need for money. To this end the government chartered national banks, which were privately owned and issued bank notes that also circulated as currency. The government had also sold millions of dollars' worth of bonds to finance the war. The bonds did not circulate as currency, but they, like greenbacks and national bank notes, all were to have been redeemed—paid off—in metallic currency (specie—i.e., gold and silver). Greenbackers wanted to continue the circulation of paper money, which they called fiat money. Like today's paper money, fiat money lacked any but symbolic value, and its worth depended on the health of the economy and the strength of the government. Precious metals, in contrast, were considered intrinsically valuable no matter what the state of the economy. Whatever the intentions of Civil War legislators, the issue of whether or not and when to redeem these several types of paper in specie, and whether the specie should be gold or silver, bedeviled national politics on and off throughout the balance of the nineteenth century. The underlying problem was a long-term deflationary trend, which meant that wages and prices, especially for agricultural produce, declined.

Between the 1860s and 1897 prices declined on a long-term basis for a combination of reasons, even though commercial banking developed several mechanisms other than currency that increased the money supply. But currency in circulation did not keep pace with economic growth, resulting in the contraction of money and credit that resulted in lower prices, which is termed deflation.[16] In the 1860s and 1870s Greenbackers had opposed specie resumption because whether gold or silver were used, money would immediately become dearer and cause more deflation. Greenbackers preferred a flexible paper money supply that could be increased to cause inflation during hard times. While inflation would encourage higher farm prices, more abundant money would be worth less. On balance, Greenbackers concluded that inflation would do more good by increasing prices than damage by making money cheaper. They believed correctly that the inflation resulting from more paper money would help the masses of farmers, by raising crop prices and enabling farmers to pay their debts with inflated, cheaper dollars. Tight currency favored only the rich, by making debts contracted in cheaper money harder to pay. When a farm mortgage had been contracted in dollars that equaled one bushel of wheat or nine pounds of raw cotton but had to be paid off in dollars that equaled one and one-half or two bushels of wheat or fourteen pounds of raw cotton, such debts became extremely difficult to repay and ensnared southern farmers in debt and led to foreclosure on mortgaged farms in the West. Inflationists maintained that tight money impoverished honest toilers, who were debtors, and benefited only the rich and the bankers, who were lenders of money.

Deflationists, on the other hand, supported national banks (which

they saw as bulwarks against uncontrolled growth of the money supply), opposed the circulation of fiat money (which had lost value during the Civil War), and favored gold (or paper certificates redeemable
in gold) as the only proper form of money. Many business leaders also
assumed that free silver would produce rampant inflation, which, in
addition to cheapening currency, would cause irresponsible speculation and, inevitably in its wake, economic crises. In the 1870s Congress had heeded these fears, disregarded the demands of Greenbackers
and other inflationists, and passed two pieces of controversial legislation. The Specie Resumption Act of 1875 began the substitution of
specie for greenbacks on January 1, 1879. But because the Coinage Act
of 1873 had abolished the traditional silver standard, redemption in
specie meant redemption in gold. Although Greenbackers persisted
well into the 1880s, the Resumption Act defeated them in the long run.
By the late 1880s and early 1890s "free silver" had become the ral-
lying cry of inflationists, who claimed to have discovered what they
called the "Crime of '73," which had taken the United States off the
silver standard.

During most of the nineteenth century the United States had been
on a bimetallic standard: both silver and gold circulated, at least in theory, and both were fully legal for any payments. Before the Civil War,
however, silver was actually worth more than its Treasury Department
equivalent in gold (one unit of gold was worth sixteen of silver). Silver,
worth more in the United States as jewelry or cutlery and widely used
in Latin America as a slightly lighter substitute for Spanish dollars,
tended not to circulate as currency.[17]

Before the 1860s several European countries used either silver or
silver and gold as currency. Some of the German principalities used
gold; others, silver. But in the 1860s several European nations left the
silver standard and began selling off silver for gold. As Germany united
into a single nation in 1871, it adopted the gold standard, and the Scandinavian countries followed suit. At the same time silver production
in the United States began to increase. With supplies of silver up and
demand down, silver dollars fell in value in relation to gold.

This increase in silver supplies led conservative Republicans and Democrats to term silver dollars "depreciated" and to attempt to ensure that United States bonds would be repaid only in gold. By the late 1860s and 1870s a second controversy on money was raging between the advocates of bimetallism and gold monometallism. This debate was not the same as the battle between paper currency and specie, but the two issues were related. Bimetallists preferred a larger currency supply—inflation—and gold monometallists wanted a more limited supply—deflation.

During the late 1860s and early 1870s, a time of relative prosperity, money was less in the public eye than Reconstruction. What debate there was centered more on greenbacks than silver. In the United States Senate, however, John Sherman, a conservative Republican from Ohio, took particular interest in money, to the point of attending an international monetary conference in 1867. Noting the increasing popularity of gold monometallism in Europe, Sherman sponsored legislation that would demonetize silver and put the United States in the gold van.

For Sherman and other monetary conservatives, silver carried several unfortunate connotations that were reinforced internationally. The European nations that they thought stood for advanced civilization used gold, whereas the Asian and Latin American nations that they thought backward used silver. England, which they admired as the embodiment of progress, had been on the gold standard for nearly the entire nineteenth century. The virile new nation of Germany had soundly defeated the effete French in 1871, and the Germans were going onto the gold standard, while the vanquished French used silver and gold. Gold seemed to be the natural currency of modernity and superiority, as decreed by "laws" of economics that were considered as inflexible as the laws of mathematics. Such were the pro-gold arguments.

Against this international backdrop, Sherman succeeded in 1873, after trying for several years, to get the Coinage Act passed. Sherman and his allies intended to preserve American creditworthiness by preventing the redemption of greenbacks and government bonds in depreciated silver dollars. They claimed afterward that no silver dollars were being presented to the U.S. mints, but quite the opposite was true. The silver boom in the American West was presenting too much silver: in 1869, $902,000; in 1870, $1,300,000; in 1871, $3,650,000; and more than $7,000,000 in 1872.[18] Silver was too plentiful, and Sherman feared that without demonetization, the United States would become the international dumping ground for silver.

Hard times hit Western Europe and the United States just as the Coinage Act became law, and during the depression of the 1870s silver advocates grew in number, exerting tremendous popular pressure on Congress in 1877 and 1878 to restore the unlimited coinage of silver. The House passed the Bland free silver bill in 1878, but the conservative forces controlling the Senate watered it down, changing it from a free to a limited silver coinage act. President Hayes vetoed the act to save the nation from "a stain on its honor." But Congress passed the Bland-Allison Act over the veto.[19] Improvement in the economy at the end of the 1870s and early 1880s calmed passions, but the depression of the mid-1880s and very low crop prices in 1889 reignited the silver issue.

As the Farmers' Alliances and their labor allies pressed for unlimited coinage of silver at the traditional ratio of 16 to 1, the increased pressure made itself felt in Congress, where several free silver bills circulated.[20] As in the late 1870s, the force of the new bills was muted by senators who feared cheapening the dollar, notably the influential John Sherman. Considering the burgeoning popular pressure for free silver, he saw the Sherman Silver Purchase Act as the best compromise possible between his own sense of economic soundness and the sort of inflationary disaster he associated with free silver. "Being compelled to choose between the measure proposed and the free coinage of silver," Sherman had supported the bill that bore his name because "it was better to stop the compulsory coinage of the bullion into dollars," he wrote in his autobiography.[21]

The Sherman Silver Purchase Act of 1890 that emerged from the Senate provided for the buying—but not necessarily the coining and circulating—of 4,500,000 ounces of silver per month. Although this represented approximately twice the amount of silver purchased under the Bland-Allison Act of 1878, it was by no means free silver and did not provide for the purchase and coining of all silver presented to the Treasury and, above all, did not restore silver to equality with gold as a legal standard of money. As a political issue and a remedy for farmers' poverty, silver did not die in 1890, nor did the related protest against the national banks, which focused on the Coinage Act of 1873.

Silverites denounced Sherman's Coinage Act as the "Crime of '73" for depriving the producing classes of adequate currency in order to protect a tiny group of plutocrats. In the words of Ignatius Donnelly in 1892:

National power to create money is appropriated to enrich bondholders. Silver, which has been accepted as coin since the dawn of history, has been demonetized to add to the purchasing power of gold by decreasing the value of all forms of property as well as human labor, and the supply of currency is purposely abridged to fatten usurers, bankrupt enterprise, and enslave industry. A vast conspiracy against mankind has been organized on two continents, and it is rapidly taking possession of the world. If not met and overthrown at once it forebodes terrible social convulsions, the destruction of civilization, or the establishment of an absolute despotism.[22]

One great difference between the inflationary and deflationary forces was the breadth of their outlook. For the inflationists, domestic questions were paramount. Uninterested in attracting foreign investment (more likely, in fact, to oppose foreign investment in land) and convinced that inadequate supplies of gold had caused hard times, they were not interested in what other countries did with their money or how foreigners reacted to American monetary policies. For this reason, first the Greenbackers and later the free silver advocates placed little importance on the international ramifications of American monetary policy. It mattered not to Greenbackers and silver supporters that Britain used gold and that international bond purchasers would not buy bonds redeemable only in a domestic paper currency.

Fearing that a devalued U.S. currency would dry up foreign investment in the United States, hard money advocates paid careful attention to the ebb and flow of money at a time when the United States depended heavily on investment from abroad. Gold standard advocates and protectionists (who were often but not always the same people) held positions that were in apparent contradiction. They advocated an international outlook on the currency question and at the same time looked no farther than an American market for American products in tariff debates. But American manufacturers supplying American markets still needed investment from overseas—especially from Great Britain—which made dependable, profitable investments in the United States in order to attract investors.

SINCE THE END OF the Civil War Greenbackers, Workingmen's and Knights of Labor parties, and the Farmers' Alliances in turn had targeted the national banks as the chief villains among the handful of powerful men who monopolized the nation's money supply and kept the "producing classes" poor. As with hard money and gold currency, the national banks functioned as a potent symbol of economic unfairness. Again, the underlying issue was a limited money supply, for by law the national banks operated along extremely conservative lines that tended to keep money tight.

Like other monetary practices of the late nineteenth century, national banking grew out of the government's financial needs during the Civil War, when the federal government had chartered national banks by selling each bank a large block of U.S. bonds for gold. In exchange for having paid gold for the bonds, the national banks were allowed to issue their own paper currencies, which circulated like government-issued greenbacks, up to a national dollar limit. This meant that the amount of currency in circulation related to the state of the bond market rather than directly to the currency needs of the economy, and the resultant rigid limitation on currency was believed to deepen difficulties in times of inflation (as during the Civil War) or crisis (as in the panics of 1873 and 1893). Because the government placed a 10 percent tax on the notes of other, state-chartered banks, the state banks were placed at a great disadvantage and were virtually taxed out of issuing their own notes. This, in turn, further cramped the total supply of bank notes. The combination of the dollar limit on national bank note issues, the requirement that national bank notes be secured with specie, and the expansion of the economy together produced deflation and its unpopular manifestation, lower prices. And lower prices meant lower wages.

The national bank controversy also had a sectional dimension. Westerners and southerners complained about the unfair geographical distribution that cut them off from access to the richest banks. And in fact, the national banks were clustered disproportionally in the Northeast. The scarcity of national banks outside the Northeast, combined with the discouragement of state bank issues, created a chronic shortage of cash in the South and West, which in turn made money dearer. The new demand for the abolition of national banks aimed at breaking the predominance of the national bankers, encouraging inflation, and supplying the South and West with an adequate supply of currency.

THE ST. LOUIS AND OCALA platforms contained further economic demands, notably for government ownership (St. Louis platform) or government control (Ocala platform) of the means of communication and transportation, including the telegraph but pointing particularly to the railroads. Government ownership was a standard feature of late nineteenth-century reform that grew out of antimonopolism, which opposed the concentration of ownership of the railroads—the symbol of monopoly—on the grounds that concentrated ownership stifled competition, raised shipping charges, and encouraged the railroad's high-handed treatment of shippers. In pursuit of railroad rate regulation, if not government ownership, small businessmen who shipped goods by rail joined the Knights and Alliancemen. Big businesses responded to this crisis by supporting two pieces of federal legislation that attempted to quiet the public outcry against the arbitrary power of the railroads.

The 1887 Act to Regulate Commerce, also known as the Interstate Commerce Act, created the first, prototypical federal regulatory body, the Interstate Commerce Commission (ICC) and sought to prohibit discriminatory and unjust rates charged by railroads, especially higher rates for short hauls relative to long hauls. In the *Wabash, St. Louis & Pacific Railroad Company* v. *Illinois* decision of 1886 the United States Supreme Court had decided that states could not regulate interstate commerce, making federal legislation necessary for any regulation of the major railroads. In light of the various regulations being passed by the states, the growing popularity of regulation, and the indication that federal regulation would prove less restrictive than regulation by the states, the owners of railroads offered no serious opposition to the less than stringent ICC. Jay Gould, owner of the southwestern railroad system, said of the bill, "[L]et it go, or we will get a worse dose next season."[23] Gould's instincts were right, for the ICC never seriously inhibited the railroads' shipping practices. Not surprisingly, its passage did not end the clamor for control of huge corporations like the railroads and Standard Oil.

In the years immediately following the creation of the ICC, congressional representatives introduced nearly twenty bills calling for control of other trusts and monopolies. All but one of the bills died in committee in the Senate, the lone exception being the Sherman Antitrust Act. As in the case of free silver, Congress, the Senate in particular, tried to quiet public outcry with as little change as possible. After a good deal of stalling, Congress passed a watered-down bill in the guise of reform. In the course of debate over the Sherman antitrust bill, Senator Orville Platt, himself a conservative, accused the Senate of demagoguery. All the Senate wanted, he said, was a weak measure that could be paraded as "A Bill to Punish Trusts."[24]

The Sherman Antitrust Act proved to be a dead letter in the nineteenth century, at least against the trusts. This was due partly to the law's vague wording and partly to the difficulty of discriminating between lawful and unlawful business combinations. Sherman himself had made the distinction, but federal judges, who were not anxious to dismember large corporations, refused to rule that any given combination actually broke the law.

Another difficulty in enforcing the Antitrust Act was the disjunction between Sherman's position in debate and the law's actual wording. Sherman had spoken for a bill that would make illegal "trusts and combinations in restraint of trade and production"—that is, in manufacturing as well as exchange. But the law, as enacted, prohibited "every contract, combination in the form of trust or otherwise, or conspiracy, in restraint of trade or commerce among the several states, or with foreign nations"—i.e., only in exchange, not in manufacture.[25]

This omission proved to be critical in 1895, in the decision of *U.S. v. E. C. Knight, Co.*, the first case to come before the United States Supreme Court under the Sherman Antitrust Act. The producer of 98 percent of the refined sugar in the United States, the E. C. Knight Company was unmistakably a monopoly. But the Court declared it beyond the reach of the Sherman Act because sugar refining was manufacturing, not trade or commerce. It mattered little that production ultimately affected commerce because the justices insisted that a monopoly have a "direct" effect on commerce before it becomes subject to federal regulation. (Justice John Harlan dissented from a decision that he thought left the public at the mercy of combinations that bought, sold, and transported necessities.) Through this sort of decision the Court narrowed the scope of antitrust legislation and effectively thwarted any attack on large corporations in the late nineteenth century.

IN MUTING THE demand for public control of companies seen as monopolies and trusts, Congress and the courts accepted the conventional wisdom that great aggregations of capital did not represent sinister combinations formed expressly to overcharge farmers, fleece consumers, or grind down workers. Large corporations often seemed to be the natural products of the results of impressive technological advances or of economies of scale, according to which the more a company produced, the less each unit cost. By this logic, the larger a business, the greater its efficiency, and the more cheaply it could produce and distribute its goods.[26] "Sentimentality," which meant concern for the human costs of economic judgments, was said to have no place in the business arena, where survival of the fittest—according to Herbert Spencer's Social Darwinism—was assumed to be the rule, the most efficient producers survived and the less efficient "went to the wall" (perished). The late nineteenth century was said to represent a new day of technological progress, in which old-fashioned producers, who refused to adopt the advances of mass production, were mere relics, whom the more fit would inexorably shoulder aside.

Many Americans saw business conducted on a national scale—the bigger, the better—as proof of the country's continued progress. Undeniably the big new businesses, like James B. Duke's American Tobacco Company and John D. Rockefeller's Standard Oil Company, reaped unheard-of profits. Operating on a scale hitherto unimaginable, they could afford to employ the latest laborsaving devices, the automated production techniques that Henry George had marveled at in *Progress and Poverty*. The possibility of economies of scale of big business was obvious to all, and at least theoretically mass production would ultimately raise the standard and reduce the cost of living for everyone.

Andrew Carnegie, the nation's foremost steel manufacturer and a conspicuous apologist for the new order, spoke and wrote widely of its benefits. A singular millionaire, Carnegie had immigrated to New York with his family from Dunfermline, Scotland, in 1848 at the age of thirteen and had begun his working life in a textile factory. His mother was a washerwoman, and his father worked himself to death in a cotton mill within five years of the family's arrival in the United States. Andrew Carnegie took bookkeeping classes at night, and when an uncle found him a job as a telegraph messenger boy, he began his climb out of the working classes. Rising from telegraph operator to clerk, to secretary, and then to superintendent, Carnegie by the age of twenty had bought stock in a delivery company. Continuing to speculate and reinvest, he earned nearly $50,000 per year in the 1860s. At thirty he entered the iron industry, organizing it vertically so that his own companies supplied one another. In the 1880s he gradually acquired several steel factories around Pittsburgh.

With many of his contemporaries, Carnegie welcomed enormity in business. The trend to bigness, he said, followed an irresistible law that made the accumulation of vast aggregations of capital in a few hands an "overpowerful tendency." For Carnegie, as for other proponents of big business, holding out against the inevitable was both useless and wrongheaded. The bigger the scale of operations, the better for what Carnegie called the "race" (presumably, but not assuredly, the human race), for in the measure that the few accumulated fortunes, the lives of the toiling masses improved. To an ever-greater degree, the poor would find in their own homes luxuries previously within reach of only the rich. Small-scale businesses had produced men of small minds, he said, but "this bigger system grows bigger men, and it is by the big men that the standard of the race is raised."[27]

A conspicuous philanthropist, Carnegie was his own best example, having given 2,500 libraries to various towns in the United States and Great Britain.[28] Fascinated by education, he was both a booster of the African American educator Booker T. Washington's Tuskegee Institute and an indefatigable propagandist, preaching his gospel of wealth in essays, articles, and an autobiography. Carnegie preferred great inequities of wealth to what he took to be the only alternative: universal squalor. He thought that in the long run extreme disparities of wealth were also good for the "race," for the very rich added to the store of civilization. The very gulf between the mansions of millionaires and the huts of workers measured the advance of civilization: "It is well, nay, essential, for the progress of the race that the houses of some should be homes for all that is highest and best in literature and the arts, and for all the refinements of civilization."[29]

In the late 1880s and early 1890s conservatives like Andrew Carnegie and William McKinley eloquently integrated the identity-of-interest argument with the political issues of the time, including protective tariffs, hard currency, and big corporations, to show that all Americans benefited from high prices, full employment, sound money, and mass production and distribution. Their arguments persuaded many, but not the organized thousands who perceived themselves to be victims rather than beneficiaries, ground down rather than uplifted by what they disparagingly called trusts and monopolies.

At the same time, the rhetoric of class conflict grew sharper, as the Knights of Labor, Farmers' Alliances, trade unionists, and their middle-class allies like Nationalists and Henry George and his followers, followed the meandering courses of their favorite political remedies (as expressed in the St. Louis and Ocala platforms) through the labyrinths of state legislatures and Congress. Politics was turning out not to be a straightforward undertaking.

THE YEAR 1890 marked a turning point for the Farmers' Alliances, as they entered national politics wholeheartedly and successfully, the subtreasury plan for agricultural credit prominently displayed. By then the Alliances were the more vital part of the farmer-worker coalition that had come out of the great upheaval. The Workingmen's parties had suffered serious reverses in the late 1880s, as the Knights of Labor had declined in membership. Employers' associations had effectively disrupted the order by blacklisting leading Knights, so that no employers would give them jobs. And employees had to sign "yellow dog contracts" or take "ironclad oaths," according to which they promised not to join any union on pain of losing their jobs. Private police (notably the much hated Pinkertons) spied on workers inside factories and off the job. Several states enacted laws that limited the unions' freedom of action. A split in the labor movement between the Knights of Labor and the AFL also hurt the Knights in the long run, as workers were forced to choose between the two competing federations. Finally, Terence Powderly's cautious leadership wasted rank-and-file mobilization by countermanding strikes and forbidding political action. The masses of workers who had flocked to the Knights of Labor during the mid-1880s fell away as strikes failed. Membership in the order declined to

548,000 in 1887; 220,600 in 1889; and 100,000 in 1890. The Farmers' Alliances, in contrast, seemed to be going from strength to strength.

ALLIANCE NEWSPAPERS praised the virtues of the subtreasury plan in their columns as they explained over and over how it worked. In February 1890 the Alliances persuaded Democratic Senator Zebulon B. Vance of North Carolina and Republican Representative John A. Pickier of South Dakota (representatives of two of the strongest Alliance states) to introduce subtreasury legislation in Congress and sent petitions bearing a million signatures in support of the bill.

Yet the subtreasury bill died in committee because Republicans who were no friends of the Alliances controlled Congress and because even many congressmen friendly to the Alliances—a great number of southern Democrats—dismissed the subtreasury plan, with its then unheard-of dependence on direct federal aid to farmers, as a crackpot scheme. The speedy failure of their central issue convinced even those Alliancemen least interested in pulling away from the two major parties of the need for more reliable representation in Congress, which became the goal of the campaign of 1890.

The Alliances would support only candidates who measured up to the "Alliance yardstick," the St. Louis platform of 1889. In an impressive debut the Alliances took control of eight southern and two western state legislatures and forged important blocks of strength even where they failed to muster majorities. Ten representatives and two U.S. senators, William A. Peffer of Kansas and James H. Kyle of South Dakota, ran successfully on Alliance platforms. In Lincoln, Nebraska, a young Democrat friendly to Alliance doctrine and later the most famous Democrat in the country, William Jennings Bryan, went to Congress for the first time. The farmers' movement seemed on the verge of achieving considerable political influence.

Despite their numbers in western and southern state assemblies, representatives elected in 1890 who had measured up to the Alliance yardstick enacted little Alliance legislation. Only in Texas and North Carolina did Alliancemen succeed in translating their platforms into law to any significant extent. In three southern states legislators who had gained Alliance backing in their campaigns repudiated the St. Louis platform and, once in office, opposed railroad regulation. Such failures stemmed from inexperience, lack of discipline, ideological rigidity, well-organized opposition, and the temptations of lobbyists.

Hamlin Garland, a novelist sympathetic to the Alliances, illustrated how well-meaning but inexperienced legislators could find themselves subject to other than popular pressures in his 1892 novel *A Spoil of Office*. The novel's hero, Bradley Talcott, newly elected to the Iowa House of Representatives, is initiated into the subversive ways of big corporations, especially the railroads, by a denizen of the capital who has seen many a state legislator corrupted:

I wonder if you know how these infernal corporations capture a State! . . . I want to warn you. I've known many a fine, honest fellow to get involved. Now I'll tell you how it's done. Before you have been here a week, some of these railroads will send for you, and tell you they've heard of you as a prominent young lawyer in the State. Oh, they've heard of you, we've all heard of your canvass; and as they are in need of an attorney in your county, they'd like very much to have you take charge, etc., of any legislation that may arise there, and so on. There may not be a week's work during the year, and there may be a great deal, etc. but they will be glad to pay you six hundred dollars or eight hundred dollars, if you will take the position.

Well, we'll suppose you take it. You go back to Rock [Talcott's home district], there is very little business for the railroad, but your salary comes in regularly. You say to yourself that, in case any work comes in which is dishonorable, you'll refuse to take hold of it. But that money comes in nicely. You marry on the expectations of its continuance. You don't find anything which they demand of you really dishonest, and you keep on; but really cases of the railroad against the people do come up, and your sense of justice isn't so acute as it used to be. You manage to argue yourself into doing it. If you don't do it, somebody else will, etc., and so you keep on. Suddenly the war of the corporation against the people is on us, and you find you are the paid tool of the corporation. . . .[30]

Although Garland's example implicated a state legislator, the same methods worked equally well on the federal level, particularly in the Senate, but the legislators were far less naïve than Bradley Talcott. (Each great corporation had its senator, who was known as its man. The most famous was Republican Senate leader Nelson Aldrich of Rhode Island, who was the man of the Standard Oil Company.) Seduction by businesses presented great temptations to representatives who had been elected with Alliance support, but a good deal more made it difficult for them to vote in accordance with the St. Louis platform.

The problems were twofold. First, the Alliances themselves were heterogeneous associations that brought together impoverished farmers, prosperous planters, and rural merchants who did not always agree, especially on the radical subtreasury plan. In addition, representatives supported by the Alliances also represented other constituencies. Townspeople who did not face the farmers' frustrations were likely to dismiss Alliancemen as cranks, as did the young William Allen White, the editor of a small-town newspaper in rural Butler County, Kansas, an Alliance stronghold. White denigrated the Alliance as a "fly-up-the-creek, rag, tag, and bobtail" movement, and his criticism reflected the cultural and political distance that separated townspeople from farmers. Democrats and Republicans, who were usually lawyers who lived in town, when trying to represent both the William Allen Whites and the Alliancemen in their districts often came down on the side of the town.

By 1891 it had become clear that members of the established parties, even when the votes of Alliancemen elected them, were also subject to social pressure and increasingly, to party leaders' "iron discipline."[31] When their parties pressed them, they abandoned Alliance reforms on money, banking, and transportation. Even before the hard lessons of 1890 and 1891, however, the option of an independent, third party had seemed attractive to many members of the Farmers' Alliances. By 1891 it looked like a natural solution. Delegates of the Alliances, the Knights of Labor, the American Federation of Labor, and other reform groups, including Nationalists, met in St. Louis to discuss the formation of a new party, which required another meeting to realize.

In 1892, 1,300 delegates from the Alliances, Knights of Labor, Nationalist and Land and Labor parties, and a series of smaller groups met in Omaha, Nebraska, and formed an independent party, which they called the People's party, whose adherents became known as Populists. The Omaha platform presented a broad range of economic reforms that had been circulating in protest circles for years: government ownership of railroads and telegraphs; limitation of government land grants to bona fide settlers instead of to railroads; a flexible currency based on free silver; the graduated income tax (which would redistribute wealth by taxing the incomes of the wealthy more heavily than the incomes of the poor); postal savings banks (which would provide the poor with a safe savings repository run by the government); the direct election of U.S. senators; and the eight-hour day. Mary Elizabeth Lease, one of many women active in the Farmers' Alliances, seconded the nomination of General James B. Weaver for President.

Lease was an Irish American Kansan who had grown up in Pennsylvania. After she and her husband had failed at farming in the mid-1880s, she began her career as a public speaker, first on Irish nationalism, then on the farm crisis, speaking for the Union Labor party, which had absorbed supporters of the Greenback and Anti-Monopoly parties. By the late 1880s she belonged to the Farmers' Alliance and served as master workman of one of the largest local assemblies of the Knights of Labor in Kansas.[32] General James B. Weaver had been an abolitionist before rising to the rank of general in the Union army. During the 1870s he left the Iowa Republican party to join the Greenbackers and was elected to Congress as a Greenbacker in 1878. In 1880 he was the Independent-Greenback party's presidential nominee.

"We are nearing a serious crisis," Weaver had written. "If the present strained relations between wealth owners and wealth producers continue much longer they will ripen into a frightful disaster. . . . A bold and aggressive plutocracy has usurped the Government and is using it as a policeman to enforce its insolent decrees. . . . The corporation has been placed above the individual and an armed body of cruel mercenaries permitted, in times of public peril, to discharge police duties which clearly belong to the State." Echoing Henry George's paradox of poverty in the midst of progress, Weaver noted that "our supply of raw material is abundant, and our facilities for manufacturing without a parallel. We have every variety of climate with fruits and cereals ample to supply the wants of the world. . . . [I]nstead . . . we find that discontent, debt and destitution exist throughout every state and territory in the Union. . . . We find millions of people homeless and out of employment. . . ."[33]

The first imperative facing the leaders of the new People's party was the creation of national unity. Populist leaders from the West, notably Jeremiah ("Sockless Jerry") Simpson and Mary Elizabeth Lease, visited the South. Simpson, a former sailor and farmer, had moved to Kansas from New York in the late 1870s. Initially a Republican, he had become a Greenbacker before joining the Farmers' Alliance. He was a Populist congressman from 1891 to 1895, but both Republicans and Democrats nominated him for his last term, 1897 to 1899. Simpson had embraced the title of "Sockless Jerry" (which a hostile journalist had coined) during his first congressional campaign in 1890, when he said that his opponent, whose nickname was Prince, must wear silk stockings, whereas Simpson—a man of the people—wore no socks at all.

At the same time southerners like Tom Watson of Georgia and Leonidas L. Polk of North Carolina addressed large, enthusiastic audiences in the West. Polk was a farmer and a Democrat whose interest in the welfare of farmers dated to the 1870s, when he had designed the North Carolina Department of Agriculture and served as its first commissioner. He had founded the Alliance newspaper in Raleigh, North Carolina, the *Progressive Farmer*, in 1886 and had led the campaign for an agricultural college, which became North Carolina State University. Tom Watson was a lawyer descended from slaveholders who had by the 1880s regained the family's planter status without losing his concern for poor farmers. After a victorious campaign for Congress in 1890 that was as "hot as Nebuchadnezzar's furnace," Watson had joined Jeremiah Simpson in the losing battle for the subtreasury plan.[34]

In countless speeches Simpson, Lease, Polk, Watson, and scores of other Populist speakers denounced sectionalism as a false creation of money-grubbing politicians who had advanced themselves by keeping the people divided. Blaming the two established parties for having caused the Civil War, Leonidas Polk exhorted farmers to throw off the fetters of sectionalism and unite to address their common needs. But unity was not to be so readily achieved.[35]

Northern speakers on the sectional theme imposed conditions, trading the abolition of sectionalism for the elimination of racial discrimination. Terence Powderly had bluntly told southern White Alliancemen: "[W]hen you recognize the nigger as a man, we of the north will join you heart and hand for reform." Ignatius Donnelly of Minnesota envisioned a new Populist order that would let producers keep what they produced, remove the hand of the "robber class" from the throats of industry, obliterate the Mason and Dixon Line, and "wipe the color line all off our politics."[36] Not all of this pleased White southerners deciding whether to join the People's party.

The racial egalitarianism of the nascent third-party movement antagonized many southern White Alliancemen, but there were important exceptions. Leonidas Polk—whose death at the age of fifty-five in June 1892 prevented his nomination for President on the third-party ticket—and Tom Watson of Georgia supported the independent party and soft-pedaled White supremacy in the 1890s. Watson believed that southern farmers would continue to be exploited as long as they let race prevent them from protesting together. He told Black and White farmers in Georgia they were "kept apart that you may be separately fleeced of your earnings."[37] But Polk and Watson were exceptions. After the meeting of February 1892, when Donnelly delivered the speech quoted above, another White southerner doubted whether White farmers in Georgia would accept interracial organization. "They believe this is a white man's government, and we should rule this country. [Black participation] may please alliancemen living north of Mason and Dixon's line, but it will not be endorsed in Georgia."[38]

The southern Alliances were segregated racially, and although instances of individual Whites' cooperating with individual Blacks occurred, the Colored Alliance could not count on support from its White counterparts because the White and Black southern Alliances stood on opposite sides of several fundamental questions concerning race, party, and economic interest.[39]

Southern Whites were nearly always Democrats, and they usually supported the White supremacist and antiBlack legislation that southern Democrats initiated. In 1889 White Alliancemen in Tennessee supported disfranchising legislation, and in Georgia and Louisiana they backed the continuing assault on Black civil rights. In South Carolina the celebrated Negrophobe, "Pitchfork" Benjamin Tillman, enjoyed enthusiastic White Alliance support first as governor, then as U.S. senator. Throughout the 1890s southern Alliancemen and independents rarely dissented when the segregation and disfranchisement of Blacks occurred.

When several members of the Mississippi Colored Alliance boycotted unfair merchants in 1889—a tactic White Alliancemen used commonly—they were murdered for having challenged the economic and racial status quo. Such violence was not unheard of in the Deep South in the late nineteenth century, and the fact that the victims were Alliancemen did not disturb local White Alliancemen, who made no protest.

Black and White southern Alliances also found themselves at loggerheads over the Lodge federal election bill of 1890, which, had it passed, would have protected Black suffrage in federal elections. In the cotton regions of the South, Black and White Alliances opposed one another again in 1891, when the Colored Alliance organized a strike of cotton pickers that White Alliancemen, who employed the cotton pickers, helped break.

White Southerners were reluctant to leave the Democratic party, the bulwark of White supremacy, which assured them certain powers and privileges on the basis of race. The *Atlanta Constitution* had been sympathetic to the Alliance movement, but it balked at the creation of an independent party. Rejecting the idea of leaving the Democratic party, the *Constitution* warned that a third party would destroy unity among Whites, which was essential to the safety of their property and the southern way of life. A third party would be "farcical in its conception and tragical in its results."[40] The *Constitution* voiced the fears of many White southerners, but it did not speak for all the Whites in the Alliance. Many went into the third party with Tom Watson.

Nonetheless, the overwhelming southern strength in the Alliances did not translate directly into preponderant southern influence in the People's party. The most prominent Populist, Leonidas Polk of North Carolina, had, like many southerners, seen free silver as a step in the right direction, but he had added in 1891 that "we do not believe that free and unlimited coinage would give us all that is needed." For Polk and many others, particularly southerners, the whole financial system needed questioning. Free silver was a palliative; only fundamental reform would provide adequate currency supplies, keep up the prices paid for agricultural products, and distribute money more fairly. As long as money was controlled by a few men, Polk said, farmers would not be treated equitably.[41]

Despite the economic radicalism born of their precarious economic circumstances, racial concerns kept many southern farmers, Black and White, out of the new party. Lacking massive southern participation in support of the subtreasury plan—a southern idea—the People's party veered away from the southern economic remedy to the favored midwestern solution. Free silver became the foremost demand of the third party, one that was easier for large numbers of people to grasp.

The creation of an independent People's party had taken place in relatively prosperous times, yet the party's platform bristled with the language of class conflict. A political event that attracted wide newspaper coverage, this challenge to the hegemony of the wealthy and the corporations attracted enormous attention. But politics, particularly the politics of class struggle, did not represent the entire range of remedies for the social crisis. Beyond politics and political parties, many Americans who identified themselves more or less overtly as Christians stressed morality and the interdependency of all groups in this increasingly complex, industrial society.

THE MOST purely Christian response to the upheavals of the 1880s were those of ministers of the Gospel, such as the Reverend Washington Gladden, pastor of the First Congregational Church of Columbus, Ohio. At the turn of the century Gladden became known as the leader of the Social Gospel movement, which pursued social reform along lines of justice and equality through personal regeneration. Social Gospelers did not believe in the inevitability of class conflict, and as they tried to mediate between managers and labor unions, they emphasized the brotherhood of man.

During the 1870s Wendell Phillips's speeches had intrigued Gladden, then a minister in Springfield, Massachusetts. Gladden's approach to labor was paternalistic and critical of unions in the 1870s, but by 1884 he was living in Ohio and saw at first hand the bloody, expensive strike of the Hocking Valley miners. Two vice-presidents of the company against which the miners were striking belonged to his church's board of trustees, and the company treasurer was a church member. Having employed all his powers of persuasion to defend the miners' right to organize, Gladden failed to persuade his congregants that recognizing the union was the Christian thing to do. One of the vice-presidents told Gladden that he would break the union even at the cost of half a million dollars.[42]

During the class conflict of the mid-1880s Gladden, like many other ministers, investigated the economic background of local churchgoers. As in other American cities, only about a third of the workers attended any church at all, and most who did were Catholic. Gladden also discovered that a quarter of the population of Columbus but only one-tenth of his First Church congregation belonged to the working classes.[43] One way to reach the poor was to open branch churches in working-class districts, as the First Church did between 1886 and 1891.

Another solution, to which Gladden and other Social Gospelers turned repeatedly, was lecturing and writing. In 1887 Gladden gave a series of lectures at Yale Seminary, which he published in 1893 as *Working People, Tools and the Man: Property and Industry Under the Christian Law.* Criticizing the existing economic order, Gladden denied that property owners' rights were absolute and maintained instead that each individual had a right to subsistence. In an imprecise manner he advocated government regulation of private property, which would finally result in communal property ownership. During the early years of the twentieth century Gladden's analysis of industrial society persuaded him that some form of socialism would benefit the masses; at the same time, however, God remained central to his vision of the good society, which must be fundamentally Christian.

THE WORD CHRISTIAN figured in the name of the Woman's Christian Temperance Union. The WCTU newspaper, the *Union Signal,* published in Chicago, had a circulation of 100,000, making it the largest women's newspaper in the world.[44] During the late 1880s and 1890s the *Union Signal* reflected the organization's motto, Do Everything, by running articles on many social issues, including the problems of workers, particularly women and children. The WCTU's concern for working people extended into practice in the late 1880s and early 1890s, as locals across the country found their own remedies for society's problems and opened centers that met various workers' needs.

WCTU locals in the Connecticut River valley of Massachusetts established schools and homes for alcoholic women and prostitutes, while the Chicago WCTU, the nation's most active, ran (among other undertakings) day nurseries, an industrial school, a free pharmacy, a restaurant, lodging houses for workingmen and women, and a shelter for homeless women. A local in Tennessee tried to get the hours of factory workers reduced to half a day on Saturday. During these years the WCTU extended its definition of temperance and began to provide social services that might prevent alcoholism.[45] Not all advocates of temperance construed their mandate as broadly as the WCTU under Frances Willard, however. The Anti-Saloon League, founded in 1893 and modeled on centralized business enterprises, saw drink as a cause of poverty, as the WCTU had before the Great Upheaval. The Anti-Saloon League received cooperation from the WCTU and also from employers who saw in temperance a means of increasing workers' efficiency. Support for temperance grew steadily, and by 1900 one-fourth of Americans were living in communities with restrictions on the consumption of alcohol.

Other middle-class women sought remedies for the evils of the new urban and industrial society by initiating what they called municipal housekeeping. Simultaneously reaffirming the importance of women's place in the home and engaging in public action, women concentrated on the quality of life in poor neighborhoods: street cleaning, slaughterhouses and butchering, sanitation in public schools, pure milk and water, and the suppression of vice. The women in the municipal housekeeping and temperance movements believed that the home and the community were inextricably enmeshed in modern society at the same time that they suspected that governments at all levels were more interested in economic growth than in human welfare.[46]

INITIALLY the settlement movement combined Christian philanthropy and a generalized concern for the working class that shared much with the WCTU, the Social Gospelers, and the municipal housekeeping movement. But within a very few years its best-known example, Hull House in Chicago, had begun to mount a systematic attack on dangerous and ill-paid working conditions. Hull House was not the first settlement house in the United States; Stanton Coit, a graduate of Amherst College with a Ph.D. from the University of Berlin, founded the Neighborhood Guild settlement on New York's Lower East Side in 1886. Yet the settlement at 335 Halsted Street in Chicago is generally thought of as the oldest.[47]

Two 1882 graduates of the Rockford (Illinois) Female Academy, Jane Addams and Ellen Gates Starr, founded Hull House in 1889, inventing a useful vocation for themselves. As members of the first generation of college-educated American women, Addams and Starr had few careers to choose from, one of which was medicine, Addams's choice until a year's study at the Woman's Medical College of Pennsylvania revealed her lack of aptitude in that field. Addams drifted for several years, claiming later that she had come to understand the need to live among workers after seeing poverty in England and after visiting Toynbee Hall, the original urban settlement, in London's East End.

For Ellen Starr, however, conditions in the United States supplied sufficient imperative. In 1889 she wrote a friend that "people are coming to the conclusion that if anything is to be done towards tearing down these walls . . . between classes, that are making anarchists and strikers the order of the day it must be done by actual contact and done voluntarily from the top."[48] For Addams, living among the poor would give meaning to the lives of young, college-educated people who needed firsthand contact with the realities of their time. Initially offering useful employment to people of the middle class, Hull House quickly began to fill some of the infinite needs of its immigrant neighborhood by organizing clubs, English courses, a playground, and a working girls' boardinghouse. The cooperative boardinghouse was the creation of Mary Kenney, a bookbinder who later served as an organizer for the American Federation of Labor and as a factory inspector for the state of Illinois.

Kenney's job as one of the nation's first female factory inspectors had grown out of a collaborative effort by several women's organizations in Chicago, one of which, the Illinois Woman's Alliance, had begun a campaign in 1889 against sweatshops, for limited working hours for women and children, and for the appointment of female factory inspectors.[49] By 1891 Florence Kelley, a well-educated resident of Hull House, had taken over leadership of the movement. An 1882 graduate of Cornell University who had done graduate work at the University of Zurich, translated Friedrich Engels, become a socialist, and married in

Europe, Kelley had already helped organize the successful campaign for women factory inspectors of the New York Working Women's Society.

When the reform administration of Governor John Peter Altgeld came into office, Illinois passed a stronger factory inspection law in 1893, and Kelley became chief inspector, a post she held until Altgeld lost the election of 1896. Kelley lived at Hull House, and her assistants were Abraham Bisno, a talented garment industry organizer with close ties to Hull House, and Mary Kenney, who had organized the Hull House workingwomen's boardinghouse. Factory inspection was only one of Hull House's efforts toward improving work conditions in Chicago. In 1895 the settlement published *Hull House Maps and Papers*, a detailed description of working-class housing, sweatshops, and child labor.

As a well-educated individual of strong convictions Florence Kelley was a pioneer of occupational safety legislation, to which her fellow Hull House resident Alice Hamilton added occupational medicine. Kelley was an extraordinary person. Of her a prominent lawyer said later that she had "probably the largest single share in shaping the social history of the United States during the first thirty years of this century . . . [by playing] a powerful if not decisive role in securing legislation for the removal of the most glaring abuses of our hectic industrialization. . . ."[50] With the help of other similarly inclined residents, Kelley turned the work of Hull House toward obtaining legislation to regulate hours and working conditions for women and children.

For all the considerable achievements of Kelley and of Hull House, the settlement movement was more than the record of one woman or one group. Many of the settlement house residents were men—for example, Graham Taylor of the Chicago Commons and Robert Woods of South End House in Boston—and Black women, such as Victoria Earle Matthews, who founded the White Rose Industrial Association in 1897 in New York for Black women migrating from the South. This was preeminently a women's movement, more exactly a movement of White, northeastern and midwestern, college-educated women from prosperous backgrounds. Educated enough to see beyond the household but prohibited from taking a direct part in politics by voting or holding office, these elite women found much to be done in working-class neighborhoods.

The women sustained the work of the settlements, which in turn provided invaluable resources to many of the first generation of college women, who often remained unmarried: a family setting, the moral support and expertise with which to deal with employers and bureaucrats, and a network of sympathetic, influential, nonresident men, like Henry Demarest Lloyd, who could help further their goals.[51] The creation of a third political party provided the spectacular remedies to the crises exposed in the years of the Great Upheaval, but not everyone who was disturbed by the unrest could follow that course. A few educated women pursued alternative reforms, and some men who did not accept analyses that stressed conflict found Christian remedies of their own.

Both the People's party and the settlement movement were new in the early 1890s; only six settlements existed in the United States in 1891, and the People's party had come into being only in 1892. Each presented remedies to the economic problems that had become so frightening in the 1880s. But very shortly, another depression, harsher than any in living memory, would lend credence to the Populist critique of American society, multiply the numbers of middle-class people living among the poor, and redouble the search for remedies.

5

THE DEPRESSION OF THE 1890s

The showpiece of American progress, the American steel industry in the valleys of the Monongahela, Mahoning, and Ohio rivers of western Pennsylvania, northeastern Ohio, and northern West Virginia, was technologically sophisticated and efficient. Millions of tons of steel and steel products—rails, armor for railroad cars and locomotives, machines and the machines that made machines (the crucial capital goods sector of the economy)—poured out of the steel region in quantities that rivaled Europe's total output. For Americans who prized progress, this industry offered a splendid symbol of modernity.

The plants of Andrew Carnegie turned out a quarter of the nation's steel production in the mid-1890s, but the industry was still competitive, divided among three or four large companies and several small ones. But labor conditions in the steel industry were exceedingly harsh. For less than subsistence wages, workers put in twelve-hour days and seven-day weeks. In 1892 wage cuts, the early manifestation of hard times, struck the heart of the steel region. A sensational strike at Homestead, Pennsylvania, in 1892 pitted the nation's largest steel producer against the nation's strongest trade union. The bloody struggle ended in military occupation.

Writer Hamlin Garland found the steel town of Homestead "squalid and unlovely," a place whose people seemed "discouraged and sullen." The hot, onerous, dangerous work of attending the gigantic furnaces of the Carnegie mills struck him as downright inhuman. Once every two weeks steelworkers switched shifts and worked a long shift of twenty-four hours, then had twenty-four hours off. Considering the hours and the extremes of heat and cold, Garland wondered after a tour of the open-hearth works how steelworkers survived.[1]

A factory town on the Monongahela River a few miles upstream from Pittsburgh, Homestead was the site of the most modern steelworks in the country. Andrew Carnegie—the "star-spangled Scotchman"—had bought the mill from Henry Clay Frick in 1882. Carnegie also owned twelve neighboring plants, at Beaver Falls, Duquesne, Braddock, Pittsburgh, and other nearby locations. The Carnegie Steel Company owned every facet of the business, from ore mining to steel distribution, a vertically integrated trust. Thanks to efficient management and the scope of operations, Carnegie's industrial empire made more than $40,000,000 in profits per year in the early 1890s.

During the 1870s and 1880s Carnegie had written about labor sympathetically, insisting that manufacturers should "meet the men *more than half way*" and that "the right of the workingmen to combine and form trades-unions is not less sacred than the right of the manufacturer to enter into association and conferences with his fellows." He said experience had taught him that in general at least, unions were beneficial to both capital and labor, which were natural allies. An apostle of identity of interest, Carnegie preached that cooperative effort served the interests of capital and labor simultaneously.[2] During strikes in the 1880s he had advised Henry Clay Frick, now his plant manager, to bargain with strikers. But in the 1890s Carnegie strengthened his position in the industry and took a harder line.

Carnegie and Frick's adversary at Homestead was the Amalgamated Association of Iron, Steel, and Tin Workers, formed in 1876. At its largest—in 1891—the Amalgamated Association had more than 24,000 members. The best organized and strongest union in the American Federation of Labor, the Amalgamated Association had won a strike at Homestead in 1889. But in 1892 Frick decided to break the union. According to the Homestead managers, the union undermined efficiency by objecting to workers' being fired when laborsaving equipment was installed and by demanding that workers receive higher wages when productivity increased. The union "placed a tax on improvement," a Carnegie partner concluded, "therefore the Amalgamated had to go."[3]

When the contract between the Amalgamated Association and the Homestead mill expired in June 1892, Carnegie was at his castle in Scotland, and he gave Frick a free hand. Carnegie remained in Europe, while Frick broke the strike and the union, using wage cuts as an entering wedge. Instead of bargaining when the union rejected his terms, Frick locked workers out and erected a fence that was eight feet high and three miles long, surrounding the whole property of the Carnegie mill from the railroad to the river. Topped with barbed wire, the fence had a series of holes in it that appeared to have been designed for sharpshooters. At the ends of the mill buildings, twelve-foot-high platforms supported electric searchlights. As much as the wage cut, Frick's fortifications angered the workers, who interpreted his refusal to bargain as arrogance. They saw his barricading the plant, which they called Fort Frick, as warlike provocation, which it was.

The lockout began on June 28. The workers immediately established an advisory committee and began patrolling the town and the riverfront. On July 2 the company discharged all workers, with the intention of bringing in 300 Pinkerton agents, a private police force, to protect the new, nonunion workers from attack as they came into the plant.

The Pinkerton National Detective Agency had served in similar circumstances since the railroad strike of 1877. For working people, Pinkertons had come to symbolize the tyranny of corporate power and strikebreaking. A mercenary army independent of local police and beyond the reach of local politics, Pinkertons protected strikebreakers (scabs) from strikers, a role in which workers found the agents careless and trigger-happy. In 1890 Pinkertons had killed five people in a railroad strike.

When the Pinkertons appeared the morning of July 6 on two covered barges, the discharged workers understood the plan and stormed down to the river to prevent the Pinkertons from landing at the mill.

As the agents attempted to land, the workers tore down Frick's fence and rushed onto the pier. From a barge, one of the Pinkertons looked out at the riverbank to see "what appeared to be a lot of young men and boys on the bank, swearing and cursing and having large sticks. I did not see a gun or anything. They were swearing at our men. I did not see any more, but came back and resumed my position at the door. I had not been back more than two minutes when I heard a sharp pistol shot, and then there were 30, 40, or 100 of them, and our men came running and stampeding back as fast as they could and they got in the shelter of the door, and then they turned around and blazed away."[4]

Throughout the day Pinkertons traded gunfire with workers, who had hastily erected barricades of pig and scrap iron. Workers fired upon the barges with rifles and a cannon and attempted twice to set the barges afire with a burning barge and a flaming oil-doused handcart. They threw stones, metal, bricks, and lighted dynamite at the barges, injuring several Pinkertons, some fatally. The Pinkertons continued to return the fire. As it became clear that the workers could neither burn up nor kill off the Pinkertons and that the Pinkertons could neither return to Pittsburgh nor land, a committee of union men arranged an armistice. The Pinkertons were allowed to land, but they had to run a 600-yard-long gauntlet of workers, beating and kicking them.

When hostilities ceased, nearly 150 of the 300 Pinkertons were injured; 9 steelworkers and 7 Pinkertons were dead. Most Americans, shocked at the bloodshed and the passion displayed by the workers, blamed the Carnegie management for provocation through wage cuts and the fortification of the mill. But this was not the end of the chaos at Homestead.

Governor William Stone of Pennsylvania sent 8,000 militiamen to the town in the middle of July to maintain order. Thanks to a tightening of discipline after the 1877 railroad strike, the Pennsylvania militia was the best drilled in the country at a time when state militia routinely served to protect strikebreakers and company property in labor disturbances. Once the militia occupied Homestead, new workers began to come to the mill, which resumed operations, department by department, on July 15.

The regular work force, convinced that Frick would not be able to find enough skilled workers to run a nonunion plant, continued to strike. They gained support when workers at the Carnegie plants at Beaver Falls and Pittsburgh struck in sympathy. But the Homestead mill's schedule grew more normal every day. Even an assassination attempt failed to remedy the deterioration of the strikers' position. On July 23 Alexander Berkman, an anarchist (who was the friend of the nation's most articulate and attractive anarchist Emma Goldman), shot Henry Clay Frick, thereby creating the first sympathy for Frick in the whole affair. Berkman was quickly sentenced to twenty-two years' imprisonment, and Frick recovered speedily.

In September affairs in Homestead took a new turn. Scores of striking workers were indicted on 167 counts of murder, rioting, and conspiracy. Some charges were dropped, and workers were acquitted of others; but as soon as the first round of trials ended, thirty-five of the leading union men were charged with treason under a hitherto unused 1860 Pennsylvania law that transformed what had been assaults against an employer into crimes against the state.[5]

Unable to make their bail, the union men languished in jail until the middle of October, when the jury found them all not guilty. By then the Amalgamated leaders had been immobilized and isolated from their men for three weeks while their legal costs mounted. Meanwhile, the leaderless steelworkers of Homestead watched with resentment as new workers, many Black, took their jobs. The Amalgamated Association barred Blacks, and strikebreaking was one of the few avenues through which Black workers could secure what were, for them, well-paid jobs in industry.

The last of the soldiers left Homestead in the middle of October, leaving a legacy of intense bitterness and a demoralized work force. The Homestead tragedy, where sixteen men lost their lives and thousands lost their jobs, was the first of the tremendous labor upheavels of the 1890s, and it showed that a strong employer could break a union that was strong if the company could hire a mercenary police force and could count on the cooperation of the courts. A company wealthy enough to shut down operations for a time could eventually starve its employees back to work on its terms.

IN THE FALL of the presidential election year of 1892 Democratic marchers in working-class neighborhoods in western Pennsylvania ignored the two candidates, Democrat Grover Cleveland and Republican President Benjamin Harrison, and shouted this jingle:

> Show us a man in a Pittsburgh mill
> Who had his wages raised by the McKinley bill!

Although this was a Democratic slogan aimed at a Republican policy, it reflected the cynicism of the people in the steel towns toward the central partisan issues of the time. Wedded to older issues like the tariff and needing to take positions in their regard, the major parties found themselves in a quandary. The Democratic platform tried to combine old and new issues by denouncing the McKinley tariff but advocating strong antitrust laws and legislation to protect labor. Republicans ventured no further than a reaffirmation of their support for protectionism. The hottest political issue of the year, silver, split both parties into opposing gold and silver factions and made it impossible for platform committees to find phrases acceptable to strong majorities of either party. Lacking consensus and fearful of offending their wealthy backers, Democrats and Republicans straddled the issue of free silver.

In Omaha, Nebraska, the People's party attacked Democrats and Republicans in the same breath. Ignatius Donnelly ridiculed the two major parties' subservience to the rich by imagining a wedding between Democrats and Republicans: "They will be married at the altar of plutocracy, and Grover Cleveland and Ben Harrison will act as bridesmaids. (Great laughter.) The devil will give away the bride—(Great laughter and applause, renewed laughter and cheering)—and Jay Gould will pronounce the benediction. (Applause.)"[6] The People's party platform on which General James B. Weaver ran for President demanded free silver, postal savings banks, the initiative and referendum (to let the people bypass corrupt legislatures and effect laws directly), the direct election of U.S. senators, and the graduated income tax.

Populists did well at the polls, electing three governors, five U.S. senators, and ten representatives. In all, nearly 1,500 Populist candidates won election in 1892. General Weaver received 1,041,000 votes, 8.5 percent of the total vote, and carried six western states. Fraud, especially in the South, probably reduced the recorded number of Populist votes. Former President Grover Cleveland defeated President Harrison 5,557,000 to 5,176,000 votes. Careless with patronage, the President had never been a popular man. He reminded some Republicans of "a pig blinking in a cold wind."[7] Just as Cleveland was inaugurated in March 1893, the economy collapsed.

Even before the crash the American economy had been vulnerable. The failure of the London banking house of Baring Brothers in 1890 had sent shocks through financial circles in the United States and precipitated a gradual withdrawal of European capital that reduced the money supply. The wage cuts that had provoked strikes at Homestead, Coeur d'Alene, Idaho (in the mining industry), and New Orleans (a multiracial general strike) reflected industrial weakness.

IN MAY 1893 the National Cordage Company, one of the largest corporations in the country—also known as the twine trust—failed, triggering the collapse of the stock market. Banks canceled their outstanding loans, and several railroads went bankrupt. In six months in 1893, 8,000 businesses and 360 banks (including 141 national banks) failed, and farm prices, depressed since the late 1880s, fell further. Employers who did not discharge workers outright cut wages drastically. Unemployment reached catastrophic proportions, estimated at 2,000,000 by Richard T. Ely, an economist at the University of Wisconsin, and at 3,000,000 by Samuel Gompers of the American Federation of Labor. At least one-fifth of the industrial work force was idle in the winter of 1893–1894.

In San Francisco 7,000 were unemployed; 50,000 in California all told. In Atlanta 3,000 were out of work; in Chicago, 100,000; in New York, between 100,000 and 200,000. A relief camp in Denver attracted so many destitute homeless that it was forced to close. Schoolteachers in Iowa found homeless men sleeping in their classrooms. Families broke up as men took to the roads, searching for work.[8] No one could recall times as hard as these.

During that terrible winter Ray Stannard Baker, a young reporter in Chicago, watched the phenomenal Columbian Exposition—with its specially built White City of 400 buildings lit with 10,000 incandescent lights, full of the latest mechanical inventions on 700 acres—give way to wretchedness, cold, and hunger:

> The bright banners, the music, and the tinsel of the World's Fair, gorgeous as they were, soon faded. They were followed with dizzying haste by another pageant, sombre and threatening, that of the depression and panic of 1893–1894, nowhere else so severe as in Chicago. It was marked by unprecedented extremes of poverty, unemployment, and unrest. Every day during that bitter winter the crowds seemed to increase. . . . I was fascinated by what I was seeing and hearing. What a spectacle! What a human downfall after the magnificence and prodigality of the World Fair which had so recently closed its doors![9]

The glamour of the Columbian Exposition and the suffering of the depression made an especially poignant contrast in Chicago, but evidence of hard times scarred every part of the nation. In the fall of 1893, as the depression made jobs scarce, groups of unemployed workers in the Far West who had taken to the road looking for work had organized themselves along military lines, calling themselves industrial armies or industrials. Numbering from 50 to 300 each, these tramp armies overpowered railroad guards and rode about on trains for free. They personified the problem of joblessness as well as their hope that a political democracy would provide economic democracy, which they saw as the chance to get paid for a day's work.

Jacob S. Coxey led the best known of the industrial armies. Coxey's Army, also known as the "Commonweal of Christ," set out from Coxey's hometown of Massillon, Ohio (20 miles south of Akron), on Easter Sunday, March 25, 1894, intending to reach Washington on May Day. Forty years old and by no means unemployed, Coxey was a self-made businessman worth $200,000 who wore costly, hand-tailored suits and bred horses. Despite his prosperous appearance, he had been a currency reformer for years, having left the Democratic party for the Independent-Greenback party and the Greenbackers for the People's party.

Coxey's remedy for unemployment was a pair of bills that he had introduced in Congress in 1892 and 1894 and that had won AFL backing in 1893. The non-interest-bearing bond bill, recalling the Greenbackers' interconvertible bond of the 1860s and 1870s, never gained congressional support because bonds that paid no interest were a contradiction in terms. Coxey's good roads bill, intended to put the unemployed to work, attracted wider support, particularly from labor, Populists, and the unemployed. According to Coxey's proposal, Congress would issue $500,000,000 in paper currency (greenbacks) at the rate of $20,000,000 per month, which would pay the unemployed $1.50 per day for eight-hour days, building good roads throughout the country, and would provide work for all who applied. To lobby Congress on the good roads bill, Coxey led his Commonweal of Christ to Washington, calling his army "a petition in boots."

An army of the unemployed was not Jacob Coxey's idea, but Coxey's name is remembered, thanks to abundant newspaper coverage and the press agent's skills of his flamboyant partner, Carl Browne, a Californian who had converted Coxey to the western idea of industrial armies. According to one of the many journalists who accompanied Coxey's Army, Browne was "a great, big strong fellow with a hearty bass voice, part fakir, part religionist, part Wild West cowboy, and withal a natural leader of men."[10] Browne always wore a fanciful western outfit: boots that reached over his knees, a buckskin jacket with Mexican silver half-dollars for buttons, a sombrero, and a fur cape. Instead of a tie, he wore a string of amber beads as a memento of his dead wife. Among the various religious and political banners that Coxey's Army carried on its march, Brown had painted one that read "Peace on Earth Good Will to Men. He Hath Risen, But Death to Interest on Bonds."

The Commonweal of Christ, about 100 strong and led by a young Black man carrying an American flag, set out in snow flurries on Easter Sunday. Browne rode behind the color bearer on one of Coxey's Kentucky horses, followed by 16 mounted men, including Jesse Coxey, Jacob Coxey's sixteen-year-old son, dressed in a blue and gray uniform symbolizing sectional unity. Behind a trumpeter Jacob Coxey, his wife, and baby son—named Legal Tender Coxey—rode in their coach. From time to time the army sang songs such as "Coxey's Army Song," written by Commonweal member George Nixon, to the air of the Union army song "Marching Through Georgia":

> Come, we'll tell a story, boys, we'll sing another song,
> As we go trudging with sore feet,
> The road to Washington!
> We never shall forget this tramp,
> Which sounds the nation's gong.
> As we go marching to Congress.
>
> CHORUS
> Hurrah, hurrah, we'll sound the jubilee;
> Hurrah, hurrah for the flag that makes you free;
> So we'll sing the chorus now,
> Wherever we may be,
> While we go marching to Congress. . . .[11]

All along the way the army received generous contributions of food and shelter from working-class settlements hard hit by the depression, a fact that impressed even skeptical observers. In labor and populist strongholds the welcome was especially enthusiastic, and the marchers received assistance from the WCTU at several points. Greeting committees, bands, and hundreds of volunteers met the Commonweal at Homestead and Beaver Falls, Pennsylvania, where workers had confronted the Carnegie Steel Company in 1892. At Homestead the Commonweal reached its greatest strength of 600 men.

When Coxey's Army reached Washington at the end of April, it was only one of several industrial armies converging on the capital from every part of the country except the South. A small but extremely radical army had left Boston on April 22, and several armies had left midwestern cities like St. Louis and Chicago (which contributed a Polish army). The biggest and most troublesome armies for the authorities and the railroads came from the West. Several armies left the San Francisco Bay Area, one of them included the eighteen-year-old Oaklander Jack London, who later became a popular writer, and another that was led by Anna Ferry Smith, a Farmers' Alliance, Bellamyite, Populist lecturer.[12] Industrial armies left from Los Angeles, Tacoma, Seattle, Spokane, and Portland. But all the western armies faced difficulties securing provisions and crossing the great distances between the West Coast and Washington, D.C. Industrial armies from Montana, Colorado, and Utah commandeered trains and waged pitched battles with sheriffs' deputies, winning the fights but losing volunteers for lack of food. By the time the remnants of these western armies reached Washington, Coxey had long since attempted to present his views.

Coxey's Army had marched through the city, 500 strong, accompanied by Annie L. Diggs, a Populist organizer and lecturer from Kansas. On a splendid white horse Jacob Coxey's seventeen-year-old daughter represented the goddess of peace. Carl Browne rode a gray horse, and Coxey, his wife, and baby Legal Tender rode in their carriage. The parade had stopped at the Capitol, where Coxey had mounted the steps and removed his hat to speak. Before he could begin his address, two policemen had grabbed him and other police had dragged Carl Browne off his horse. Mayhem broke loose, and police began clubbing spectators. As their supporters had expected, Coxey and his lieutenants were charged with walking on the grass.[13]

Various industrial armies continued to arrive at the Coxey campground during the late spring and summer, swelling the numbers to 800 in mid-May and to more than 1,000 in July. The demonstration ended on August 10, after authorities had broken up all the camps and scattered 1,200 men.

Jacob Coxey died in 1951 at the age of ninety-seven, still believing in his good roads scheme and feeling vindicated by the federal government's adoption of much of his program in the Civilian Conservation Corps and the Works Progress Administration in the 1930s.[14] By then few remembered Coxey, but in the 1890s his movement had alerted many who belonged to the middle and upper classes to the magnitude of unemployment and the desperation of the jobless. The industrial armies made a permanent impression on many educated contemporaries who were not then reformers, such as Ray Stannard Baker.

Baker had marched with the army as a reporter for the *Chicago Record*. Like most members of the middle class, he had initially dismissed the Commonwealers as fanatics, but Baker came to take the industrial army phenomenon seriously: "I soon made up my mind that there could have been no such demonstration in a civilized country unless there was profound and deep-seated distress, disorganization, unrest, unhappiness behind it—and that the public would not be cheering the army and feeding it voluntarily without a recognition, however vague, that the conditions in the country warranted some such explosion."[15]

As catastrophic incidents succeeded one another without pause, the spring of 1894 permitted little leisurely reflection on the larger meaning of recent events for the evolution of industrial society in the United States. No sooner had the Commonweal of Christ marched into Washington than labor unrest flared up in Chicago, throttling rail traffic throughout the central section of the country. The Pullman strike precipitated such chaos that it was called the Debs rebellion, after the Indianan Eugene Debs, who led a union of railroad employees.

THE PULLMAN STRIKE in Chicago shared four characteristics with other labor disturbances of the 1890s: A cut in wages during a depression precipitated a strike sharpened by long-standing conflicts; George Pullman and the Pullman company management dealt with workers arrogantly; government entered the struggle on the employers' side; and the strikers and the unemployed attacked railroad property with an angry ferocity. But in this hostile exchange the government in question was not the state of Illinois. The Democratic administration in Washington initiated governmental support of the Pullman company and other railroads in Chicago against the American Railway Union (ARU), led by Eugene V. Debs, who had served his apprenticeship with the Brotherhood of Locomotive Engineers. What began as a strike against one company ended as a war between workers and the combined forces of the U.S. Army and the General [Railroad] Managers' Association.

In the wake of the railroad strike of 1877—which in Chicago had pitted strikers and supporters against police in a four-day battle that killed 13 and injured hundreds—George Pullman had conceived his own remedy for unrest and built a model town for his workers near his Pullman Palace Car Company. Carefully planned, Pullman village was clean, orderly, rationally arranged, carefully maintained, expensive, and dry (no liquor allowed). Pullman's purpose was to inculcate what he called "habits of respectability," and he predicted that housing workers in uplifting surroundings would initiate "a new era for labor" free from strikes and unrest.[16] The town of Pullman epitomized the hierarchical ideal.

But workers rarely remained in Pullman for more than a few years. They preferred living beyond the village limits, where rents were lower and they could do as they pleased, including taking a drink at a favorite saloon, unobserved by informers. Workers complained that foremen pressured them to live in Pullman and that when workers were rehired after layoffs, the residents of Pullman came back first. Resisting such pressures, Pullman workers stayed as briefly as possible in a town in which they constantly felt spied upon.

At the outset of the Panic of 1893 the Pullman company had cut wages an average of 28 percent, without cutting rents in Pullman village. As rents were ordinarily deducted from pay, workers sometimes received pay envelopes containing $1 or $2 for two weeks' work, even less than $1 on occasion. In May 1894 a delegation of Pullman employees had petitioned for the restoration of wages to their 1892 level, but as at Homestead, the company refused to bargain; within a week three members of the committee had been laid off. The Pullman workers called a strike and asked the American Railway Union to represent them. Led by Eugene Debs and organized by industry instead of by craft, the ARU failed to persuade the Pullman workers not to go out during hard times. When the Pullman workers steadfastly refused to call off their strike, the 150,000 ARU members supported them and stopped handling Pullman sleeping cars.[17] The strike began on May 12, 1894. By the end of June rail traffic through Chicago had stopped, shipping was tied up from California to Ohio, and the shortages that resulted sent food prices soaring in Chicago.

The General Managers' Association, formed in 1886 by managers of twenty-four railroads centered or terminating in Chicago, backed the Pullman company fully. However, the association's most powerful ally, Richard Olney, the attorney general of the United States, formerly a railroad officer and lawyer, was not in Chicago. After he had authorized the deputizing of U.S. marshals, railroad companies deputized their own personnel, making company men into law enforcement officers of the United States government. On July 2 Olney obtained a blanket injunction ordering strikers back to work for having blocked the U.S. mails. Strikers denied that they were interfering with the passage of mail and continued the strike.

Seeing Debs as a demagogic leader of the ignorant and lawless and the strike as a prelude to class war, President Cleveland ordered U.S. troops into Chicago on July 3 to disperse the crowds that he contended

were obstructing the mails. (They had scrupulously avoided obstructing the passage of mail.) Troops arrived on the Fourth of July, over the
strenuous objections of the governor of Illinois, John P. Altgeld. At that
point violence began in earnest. Crowds stoned, burned, and wrecked
trains and fought in the streets with police, state militia, and the U.S.
Army numbering 14,000.

The combined military forces brought the strike to an end on July 8,
after it had spread to several states and cost 34 lives. Debs was convicted
for contempt of court (ignoring the blanket injunction), and he served
six months in a federal penitentiary.

WHAT CAME TO BE called the labor injunction made striking, an activity
that had not previously been defined as illegal, a crime—contempt of
court. The use of labor injunctions triggered a torrent of criticism, not
only from Populists and organized labor but also from liberals in the
legal field. The injunction served on Debs and the ARU leadership was
the best publicized early such response, but it was not the first. During
earlier strikes in 1893 judges had enjoined "all persons generally" from
striking, notably in Milwaukee in December, on the ground that strikes
that threatened to hinder the operations of the corporation in question
(a railroad) might damage company property and intimidate strikebreakers.[18] In the Pullman strike the injunction effectively rendered all
strike activity illegal. After Pullman, courts used the labor injunction
widely to declare strikes conspiracies to interfere with commerce and
thereby within the purview of the Sherman Antitrust Act of 1890.

Like the labor injunction, President Cleveland's dispatch of federal
troops to Chicago over the governor's protests also proved controversial. On the one hand, college men joined militia companies, sharing
the belief of one Harvard alumnus "that it was a necessary police force.
Like almost everyone else I was totally in the dark as to the merits of
the Pullman strike of 1894 which led me to enlist. I approved President
Cleveland's intervention in that strike and for many years considered
Governor Altgeld a very dangerous person."[19]

On the other hand, others criticized the President if only for his flagrant overriding of states' rights. Henry George, who had voted for Cleveland in 1888 and had attended the Democratic National Convention in 1892, now sided with Governor Altgeld. Accusing the General Managers' Association of conspiring to block the mails expressly to bring the federal government into the struggle, George blamed capitalists for seeking to increase the standing army for use against the masses "because the millionaire monopolists are becoming afraid of the armies of poverty-stricken people which their oppressive trusts and combinations are creating."[20]

Eugene Debs saw federal intervention as decisive. The American Railway Union had challenged corporate power as never before, and the union would have won but for the managers' enlistment of federal courts and armies, he said in a speech following his release from the penitentiary. Debs termed this an "exhibition of the debauching power of money," which Americans were seeing more often than ever before.[21]

Quickly realizing that the Pullman strike had effectively destroyed the 150,000-member American Railway Union, Debs concluded, as Terence Powderly had eight years earlier, that strikes were self-defeating. Strikers were economically vulnerable, particularly in the hard times that caused so many strikes, and unions could not control the crowds (many of whom were not union members but people angry at the rich) that furnished a rationale for military intervention. Before organizing a new political party, the Social Democracy of America, out of the remnants of the ARU in 1897, Debs worked with the People's party.

SUCH HARD TIMES hurt farmers as well as workers, as interest rates soared to more than 10 percent—in an era when 4 to 5 percent was the norm—and plunging crop prices combined to cause farmers ever-greater difficulty in securing fresh credit to repay outstanding debts and mortgages. A Kansan noted sadly that the dollar's worth of mortgage that could be repaid with one bushel of wheat in good times now consumed four bushels of wheat.[22] More than ever, Populists claimed, the depression proved the accuracy of their analysis of American conditions.

To illustrate their point that the few impoverished the many, they wrote articles, songs, even poems, like "The Plutocrat's Jubilee":

> We own all the money—we will own the land.
> The Courts and the Congress are at our command.
> Our fortunes have gone up like beautiful rockets'
> We've the Dems and the Republicans both in our pockets;
> And to please the fool people, we make our salam,
> And let them choose either—we don't give a damn!

> We own all the railroads, the coal and the oil,—
> All wealth is secure in our octopus coil;
> The State legislatures, from East to the West,
> Bought up by our bribes, will for us do their best,
> Whatever we ask, be it better or worse,
> They'll do it with promptness, and not care a curse!

> We've serfs on the railroad, and serfs in the mine,
> In the shop, on the farm—all the places, in fine;
> And millions in idleness, willing to work
> For the pittance we give them, from morning till murk.
> When we call, round the polls all these fellows will jam,
> And vote as we'll tell them and not care a damn![23]

Concluding that too few people had too much money, Populists favored a graduated income tax that would redistribute wealth, rather than protective tariffs that they said taxed the farmers and workers for the benefit of manufacturers.

Meanwhile, a Democratic Congress was trying to pass a Democratic tariff bill that would presumably lower tariff rates in accordance with campaign rhetoric. As it left the House of Representatives, the tariff bearing the name of William L. Wilson—a former Confederate gold Democrat—reduced rates and also included a federal income tax.[24] In the Senate, Maryland Democrat and protectionist Arthur Pue Gorman refashioned the bill, and various senators added 634 amendments, nearly all of which revised tariffs upward. The Wilson-Gorman Tariff Act of 1894 emerged as a protective measure worthy of Republicans, although the income tax provision survived. (President Cleveland refused to sign the bill, which became law without his signature.)

FOR ALL THIS CONTROVERSY, the Wilson-Gorman federal income tax of 1894 was not the first in the nation's history. A graduated income tax had helped finance the Civil War, and during the war the constitutionality of direct taxation on incomes had been settled, and the income tax extended until 1872. After its repeal the idea of a graduated federal income tax remained attractive to those preferring a more equitable form of taxation than the regressive excise taxes and tariffs. Between 1874 and 1894 sixteen bills proposing a new graduated income tax were introduced in Congress. The income tax of 1894, which was more a flat tax on unusually high incomes than a graduated tax, called for a levy of 2 percent on annual individual incomes, net corporate profits, inheritances, and gifts of more than $4,000. In March 1895 the U.S. Supreme Court considered a challenge to the income tax in *Pollock* v. *Farmers' Loan and Trust Co.*

Arguments on the *Pollock* case revolved around what was called class legislation—laws that unfairly victimized or favored one group of citizens over another—and the constitutionality of the income tax. For advocates of the income tax, the protective tariff represented class legislation. The income tax was fair, they contended, because it taxed those best able to pay.[25]

Joseph H. Choate, the leading corporation lawyer of the era, counsel for Standard Oil, and later U.S. ambassador to Great Britain, served as chief counsel against the income tax. Building his argument around what he called the communistic, socialistic, populistic nature of the income tax, Choate reasoned that the income tax penalized the thrifty and industrious by taking from them to reward the poor. Choate won over the Court by skillfully linking income from rents to taxes on real property ("direct taxes"), which were prohibited by the Constitution.

The Supreme Court's decision of April 1895 was badly fragmented, striking down the tax on rents by six to two, but dividing on other provisions, four to four (one justice had been absent from the bench). Justice Stephen J. Field, who had been a corporation lawyer in New York and who represented a judiciary increasingly recruited from the ranks of corporate lawyers, filed a widely quoted separate opinion warning of impending class conflict should the income tax stand: "The present assault upon capital is but the beginning. It will be but the stepping stone to others, larger and more sweeping, till our political contests will become a war of the poor against the rich; a war constantly growing in intensity and bitterness."[26]

After a new hearing before a full Court in May, the justices, still divided, declared the entire income tax unconstitutional, five to four. All parts of the income tax were construed as direct taxes prohibited by the Constitution. The dissenters condemned the decision as a disaster. Justice John Harlan was disturbed that the income tax had been struck down while the protective tariff endured because the special advantages accorded the wealthy threatened the nation's stability. As though to illustrate Harlan's point, the Supreme Court, in the same session that struck down the income tax, reached other decisions that relieved large corporations and hobbled labor.

IN MAY 1894 the Court upheld the labor injunction that had allowed Debs's conviction for contempt of court in the Pullman strike. Deciding that it violated freedom of contract and protection of private property, the Court also invalidated the 1893 Illinois statute limiting women and children in the garment industry to eight-hour workdays, the law that women's groups under the leadership of Florence Kelley of Hull House had demanded. A month later, in June 1894, the Court decided the *E. C. Knight* case under the Sherman Antitrust Act.

Taken together, these cases showed how completely the U.S.

Supreme Court had come to embrace the logic of corporations. These decisions outlawed virtually any attempt by states to limit maximum hours of work, of unions to strike, and of the federal government to curb or regulate monopolies or to curb the accumulation of vast fortunes. Shaping the federal jurisprudence of conflicts between workers and employers and between consumers and manufacturers, these decisions gave a green light to wealthy individuals and corporations that shone for almost forty years.

The decisions of 1895 enormously strengthened conservative responses to pressures for economic equity, whether in the form of strikes, taxes, or regulation. But the Court's actions also dismayed many in the privileged classes. The depression spectacle of unemployment, hardship, disorder, and conservative reaction shook many moderate people out of complacency; some of them even became susceptible to the Populist claim that the government was the servant of privilege. A few middle- and upper-class people were prompted to take action, following the lead of the best-known member of the middle class to espouse Populist positions, William Jennings Bryan, Democratic congressman from Nebraska.

Elected to Congress for the first time in 1890, when his issues had been tariff reform and the income tax, Bryan had been returned to the House in 1892, after Populist leaders like Mary Elizabeth Lease and James B. Weaver had begun to emphasize free silver. In 1893 he had been touted for the presidency on the strength of his prosilver speeches.

DURING THE MID-1890S, the currency issue completely eclipsed taxes and tariffs, not only as a means of making the distribution of wealth more equitable but also as a remedy for the depression. A compromise measure, the Sherman Silver Purchase Act of 1890—to purchase, not to coin silver—had not increased the money supply or halted the collapse of prices. As economic conditions worsened, the silver forces once again pressed for the unlimited coinage of silver (free silver), and a little book on the subject, William ("Coin") Harvey's *Coin's Financial School* (1894), became a wild best-seller.

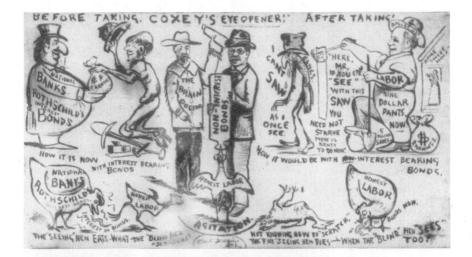

(ABOVE) *A banner drawn by Carl Browne and carried by Coxey's Army in 1894. Browne and Coxey are the figures on the top row in the center. On the left, the national banks are fat and prosperous but honest labor—man and chicken—are poor and scrawny. In the middle honest labor stands on agitation and takes Coxey's non-interest-bearing-bonds remedy. On the right the banks are poor, but honest labor is fat.* (Library of Congress)

(LEFT) *Workers on a Bessemer converter in a Pittsburgh steel mill in the 1880s.* (Library of Congress)

(LEFT) *Ray Stannard Baker, a journalist who covered Coxey's Army and served as Woodrow Wilson's press attaché in Paris in 1919.* (Library of Congress / George Grantham Bain Collection)

(BELOW) *Pinkertons running the gauntlet at Homestead, as seen by an artist in* Harper's Weekly, *1892.* (Library of Congress)

United States troops escort a train past strikers in Chicago, the Pullman strike, 1894, by an artist in Harper's Weekly. (Library of Congress)

Eugene V. Debs, head of the American Railway Union and later presidential candidate of the Socialist party, in 1904. (Library of Congress)

Former President Grover Cleveland at home in Princeton, New Jersey, in 1905. (Library of Congress)

William H. Harvey was an Illinois Populist whose influential pamphlet explained free silver to millions of ill-educated silverites. The protagonist, a fictional young Chicago financier named Coin, conducts a school for the city's leading men, who learn that American and British bankers lie at the root of the nation's economic troubles. Coin teaches that hardship in the 1890s was caused by the Coinage Act of 1873, "commonly known as the *crime of 1873*. A crime because it has confiscated millions of dollars worth of property. A crime, because it had made thousands of paupers. A crime, because it has made tens of thousands of tramps. A crime, because it had made thousands of suicides. A crime, because it has brought tears to strong men's eyes, and hunger and pinching want to widows and orphans. A crime, because it is destroying the honest yeomanry of the nation. A crime, because it has brought this one great republic to the verge of ruin, where it is now in imminent danger of tottering to its fall."[27] The problem was not a shortage of food to eat or work to be done; it was a shortage of means of exchange—of money. Recalling Henry George, Harvey observed that "in the midst of plenty, we are in want." Only the remonetization of silver and its coinage at the official ratio of 16 to 1 would restore prosperity.

Opponents of free silver, like President Grover Cleveland, insisted that only the repeal of the Sherman Silver Purchase Act of 1890 would cure the depression. Before the crash of 1893 Cleveland had termed free silver the nation's "greatest peril" and predicted disaster.[28] Indeed, the economy had weakened after the passage of the Sherman Silver Purchase Act, and for Cleveland, the connection was casual. He called Congress into special session in August 1893 to repeal the law.

Speaking on behalf of free silver, William Jennings Bryan echoed Harvey's argument that there was insufficient gold to meet the needs of all the countries that used it as currency and that the monometallic gold standard had severely and artificially contracted the money supply. This deflation—which he called a purposeful policy designed to enrich creditors (mainly bankers)—created a dishonest dollar that increased the value of debts above their original amount.

At the very time that the effects of the crash were being felt across the land, Bryan predicted that the contraction of the currency would cause unemployment in industry and foreclosures of the mortgages secured by family farms. Like his fellow Democrat the President, Bryan blamed the depression directly on currency. But he challenged his party to commit the country to bimetallism and to the needs of the plain people. Bryan did not persuade enough members of Congress to disregard the President, and the Sherman Silver Purchase Act was repealed.

Unfortunately repeal did not create greater confidence among bankers, nor did it halt the fall of farm prices or slow the spread of unemployment. It did not safeguard gold, either, for under pressure of demand from bonds reaching maturity and overseas investors redeeming bank notes, the nation's gold reserves fell precipitously in June 1894, February 1895, and January 1896. (The McKinley tariff of 1890 had eliminated the revenue surplus.)

To raise the gold reserves, the Treasury Department issued interest-bearing bonds in large denominations (which only the very rich could afford) and made a spectacular sale to bankers J. P. Morgan and August Belmont in 1895. Morgan's name was already synonymous with fantastic riches, and Belmont was the American representative of the great European banking house of Rothschild. Together they epitomized enormous wealth and power and, for Populists, bloated, conspiratorial plutocracy. On the $65,000,000 bond sale, Morgan and Belmont made a perfectly legal profit somewhere between $1,500,000 and $16,000,000; no one outside the banks knew exactly how much. Bryan saw this as profit fleeced from taxpayers, remarking that the American people owed the President the sort of gratitude that "a passenger feels toward a trainman who had opened a switch and precipitated a wreck."[29]

All sides blamed President Cleveland for bungling the gold crisis and for failing to bring the nation out of the depression. Personally satisfied that he had restored the proper currency, he nonetheless left office a terribly unpopular man. In 1896 the grip of the depression was as firm as ever, and money still seemed to hold the key to prosperity. Silver versus gold was the pivotal issue of the 1896 presidential campaign.

SILVER HAD BECOME the favorite cause of Populists, silver Democrats, silver Republicans, and the owners and miners in the silver-producing areas of the West which stood to gain from the massive purchases of silver that would follow unlimited coinage. By and large—but with significant exceptions—free silver was the cause of westerners and southerners. The darling of silver Democrats since 1893, William Jennings Bryan put the party in his pocket at the nominating convention of 1896 by warning goldbugs in his party that they must respond to the needs of the producing classes. He defied Democratic supporters of gold in phrases he had tested on the stump:

> You tell us that the great cities are in favor of the gold standard; we reply that the great cities rest upon our broad and fertile prairies. Burn down your cities and leave our farms, and your cities will spring up again as if by magic; but destroy our farms and the grass will grow in the streets of every city in the country. . . . Having behind us the producing masses of this nation . . . we will answer [the] demands for a gold standard by saying to them: "You shall not press down upon the brow of labor this crown of thorns, you shall not crucify mankind on a cross of gold."[30]

The convention burst into a wild half hour demonstration. For the young writer Edgar Lee Masters, Bryan's speech marked a watershed, "the beginning of a changed America."[31]

KANSAS NEWSPAPERMAN William Allen White found the Republican National Convention listless. "There is no life in it. The applause is hollow; the enthusiasm dreary and the delegates sit like hogs in a car and know nothing about anything."[32] In order to nominate his man, William McKinley, Marcus Alonzo Hanna managed the convention from beginning to end. Hanna, a Cleveland oil refiner who had entered the oil business on the ground floor with John D. Rockefeller, had prospered along with Rockefeller and made a fortune in oil, coal, and refineries. His principal concern was protective tariffs (on currency, however, McKinley and Hanna were more moderate than Grover Cleveland), and he had begun his campaign to nominate McKinley in the early 1890s.

Hanna represented a philosophy of government that was coming into its own at the end of the nineteenth and beginning of the twentieth centuries. Hanna and his peers had entered politics with the single aim of helping themselves and their business associates. They controlled whole states, so that government served the interests of powerful businesses, such as streetcar companies and utilities. Corporations handpicked their representatives, often lawyers who had been in their employ, who would pass or kill bills according to the needs of the corporations. Men like Hanna assumed that the state and federal governments existed primarily for their own benefit.

To ensure the election of his nominee, Mark Hanna raised an astonishing campaign fund of at least $3,500,000 from the managers of railroads, banks, and large industries. With all this money he could afford to print literature tailored to the interests of several constituencies, pay what was necessary to get (or purchase) the vote, and bring trainloads of voters to McKinley, who campaigned from his front porch in Canton, Ohio (which was only a few miles from Jacob Coxey's Massillon). The candidate delivered bland speeches about the return of prosperity without addressing the pressing economic questions that the depression had raised. McKinley needed only to appear reassuring, because after the Democrats had nominated Bryan, the burning issue for many conservatives—Republicans and Democrats—was whether Bryan would utterly ruin the country by bringing Populists, socialists, and anarchists into the government.

One effective piece of campaign literature that Hanna distributed widely was a sarcastic editorial from a small-town newspaperman, William Allen White, that characterized Populist rhetoric about helping the little man as nothing more than sour-grapes complaints of ne'er-do-wells. "We don't need population, we don't need wealth, we don't need well-dressed men on the streets," White grumbled. By his own account, the well-fed twenty-eight-year-old White was known for sartorial elegance spiced by his penchant for gaudy neckties. Just before he had written his piece, a crowd of shabbily dressed older men—Populists— had jeered him on the street, complaining about the hostile editorials in his Republican newspaper. Pretending to speak for the Populists, White pitched into them: "What we are after is the money power. Because we have become poorer and ornerier and meaner than a spavined, dis- tempered mule, we, the people of Kansas, propose to kick; we don't care to build up, we wish to tear down." White reminded his readers that Bryan had suggested that instead of letting prosperity trickle down to the masses from above, the masses should be made prosperous and let prosperity trickle up. "That's the stuff!" White protested. "Give the prosperous man the dickens! Legislate the thriftless man into ease, whack the stuffing out of the creditors and tell the debtors . . . that the contraction of currency gives him a right to repudiate. . . . What we need is not the respect of our fellow men, but the chance to get something for nothing." The "something for nothing" line proved especially popular.[33]

In later life White came to respect Bryan and to recognize that the Democrat was the first man of his generation to lead a major party as an unashamed champion of the poor. Clearly Bryan's nomination in 1896 marked a change in the Democratic party. In shifting leader- ship from conservative, New York-based goldbugs to Populist-leaning western and southern silverites, the Democratic party now reinforced its claim as the party of the "producing classes." The People's party had changed the Democratic party, but the process worked both ways.

THE POPULISTS' very success in persuading large numbers of voters that the gold standard caused misery and that free silver would restore eco- nomic justice threatened the integrity of the People's party as an inde- pendent force. Watching Democrats and Republicans by the thousands climb onto the silver bandwagon, the leaders of the People's party came face-to-face with a strategic dilemma, as the allure of fusion with the Democratic party, now led by Bryan, split Populists into fusionists and middle-of-the-road purists. Willing to downplay everything but the silver issue in the interest of converting millions of Americans, fusionists wanted to join the Democrats to tap their numbers and, in the South, their respectability. The chairman of the People's party, U.S. Senator Marion Butler of North Carolina, belonged to this group. The most prominent middle-of-the-roader was Congressman Thomas Watson of Georgia, the vice presidential nominee of the People's party in 1896, who insisted that all the Populist demands—including the subtreasury— should be stressed equally.

In 1896 the People's party nominated Bryan for President and Watson for Vice President. But because Bryan never properly acknowledged the Populist nomination, the People's party campaign began on a note of uncertainty. To make matters worse, Butler's uncritical admiration of Bryan (more becoming to a Democrat than a Populist), his open feuding with Watson (Butler delayed several weeks in notifying Watson of his nomination), and his flaccid leadership of the People's party left Populists confused and ultimately weakened the party irremediably at a time when its philosophy made increasing sense to moderates. The Democratic party, divided between a prosilver majority and a progold minority, was in no condition to shore up the Populists.

With only limited access to the moneyed interests, Bryan and the silver Democrats raised a meager $300,000, in contrast with something between $3,500,000 and $7,000,000 for McKinley, which even at its minimum represented an astronomical figure. McKinley stayed at home and Hanna brought voters to him, while Bryan stumped the country—often carrying his own bags—speaking scores of times a day. The ill-financed, ill-organized campaign was no match for the sleek McKinley machine. Hanna swamped voters with specialized appeals that reinforced employers' warnings that if Bryan won, business would be ruined, and ruined businesses provided no jobs.

McKinley won the election by one-half million votes by uniting middle-class people against the threat to their way of life that Bryan seemed to represent and by convincing many workers that a Bryan victory would cost them their jobs, even though the Bryan campaign had excited farmers and workers as no other presidential contest had done in the past or would for years to come.

After the campaign, Anna ("Nettie") Cabot Davis Lodge, the much admired wife of conservative Massachusetts Republican Senator Henry Cabot Lodge, acknowledged that Republicans had won through superior organization, the support of the press, the aura of respectability, and "with both hands full of money." The Democrats had begun as only a disorganized mob, out of which "burst into sight, hearing, and force—one man, but such a man! Alone, penniless, without backing, without money, with scarce a [news] paper, without speakers, that man fought such a fight that even those in the East can call him a crusader, an inspired fanatic—a prophet! ... He alone spoke for his party, but speeches which spoke to the intelligence and hearts of the people, and with a capital P. It is over now, but the vote is 7 millions to 6 millions and a half."[34]

THE 1890s had been a period of hard, hard times, political instability, and popular explosions that seemed to be harbingers of revolution. But as serious as the crises of the nineties had been, power relationships did not change radically. In part this was due to the removal of some of the unemployed who were so volatile a part of the masses. Europeans and Canadians who lacked work—their motive for migrating in the first place—simply went home.[35] And in cases of labor unrest, like the Pullman strike of 1894, the federal government stepped in to undermine the bargaining power of organized labor and thereby curb serious challenges to the economic status quo. The army and courts of the United States attempted with considerable success to control strikes and related disorders through the use of labor injunctions and National Guards.

The new political party that had seemed so promising in 1892 failed to build on its successes. Nonetheless, the Populist influence on political debate made the election of 1896 the most passionate of the period. Voters faced an unusually clear-cut ideological choice, between McKinley's identity of interest promises of prosperity and Bryan's commitment to fairness to those at the bottom, by representing them directly rather than through the people at the top.

Although voters could not know it at the time, the election of 1896 marked a turning point in American politics. As the party of prosperity and respectability, Republicans became the majority party on the federal level and in all but southern states. But even though prosperity and remarkable political unanimity returned, the country was left with a bad case of the jitters. Seared by hard times, Americans were weary of unemployment, strikes, and conflict. An easy foreign war offered a welcome opportunity to wave the flag in unison, almost.

THE WHITE MAN'S BURDEN

After years of suffering—caused by a civil war in Cuba between the Spanish government and nationalist forces—frustrating diplomacy, and suspense, the United States entered the war against Spain. Bands played, flags flew, children on fences yelled, threw firecrackers, and shot toy pistols; women wept, crowds filled train stations to press flowers on the volunteers departing for what John Hay, author of *The Bread-Winners* and United States ambassador to Great Britain, called "a splendid little war; begun with the highest motives, carried on with magnificent intelligence and spirit, favored by that fortune which loves the brave."[1]

The war itself was amazingly brief—declared in April, over in August—a few campaigns in Cuba and Puerto Rico and a stunning naval victory in Manila. Cuba gained nominal independence (but lost it to a de facto American protectorate under the Platt Amendment) in this "little war" that gave the triumphant United States an island empire that included Puerto Rico and the Philippines and stretched halfway across the earth.[2] Prosperity, industrial might, and colonial possessions symbolized the greatness of the United States, its coming of age, its sudden awakening to an expanding world in which it had a major role to play.

According to a leading Republican, the old America had been a closed, isolated, provincial country, "a hibernating nation, living off its own fat—a hermit nation."³ Plain and self-contained, the sleepy American Republic lacked the dash of a military establishment and the magnificence of an aristocracy, hallmarks of the great European powers. But now America was waking up and seizing opportunities, no longer shirking its duties on the international stage. More and more Americans were going to Europe, acquiring European educations, European tastes, European sophistication, European titled husbands, and European ambitions. On a certain level Americans were becoming cosmopolitan, and they showed off with celebrations of transatlantic friendships and the new fashion of English-style spelling. Proclaiming the brotherhood of the English-speaking peoples, a highly articulate minority embraced Englishness, particularly in regards to empire. The very word *England* connoted imperial mastery, which American expansionists found attractive.

Captain Alfred Thayer Mahan, lecturer in the Naval War College and exponent of sea power, discerned the predominance of the splendid English strain in his own personality, despite his mongrel American ancestry. He was one-quarter English, one-quarter Franco-American, and one-half Irish, but he said he was not in the least gregarious.⁴ In a stream of books and articles he urged the United States to put aside the "outlived plea" of isolation and (like the English) recognize its duties and seize its fate in the world at large. Mahan preached the English virtues—empire, military preparedness, and a big navy. For expansionists, a fine new America, a superb people were emerging from the chrysalis of isolation.

THE EXPANSIONIST RHETORIC of the late 1890s was exceedingly clamorous. With much less noise, however, secretaries of state had more or less discreetly extended the reach of American power in the preceding decades. Despite opposition, William Seward had acquired Alaska in 1867; James G. Blaine had consolidated American hegemony in Latin America in the 1880s; and the Harrison administration came close to annexing the Sandwich Islands (Hawaii), which had been considered a possibility since Seward's time.

Democrats were more likely to oppose expansion in the 1890s. Yet Grover Cleveland's secretary of state, Richard Olney (who had been U.S. attorney general, 1893–1895), nearly propelled the United States into military confrontation with Great Britain over a boundary between Venezuela and the British colony of Guiana that crossed territory thought to bear gold. To open the age of the jingo, Olney in 1895 resurrected the Monroe Doctrine's strictures against new European colonization and interference in the affairs of the Americas. His bellicose diplomacy coincided with renewed difficulties for Britain with the Boers (Dutch settlers) in South Africa that precluded an all-out fight. With Venezuela a mute bystander throughout, the British submitted the Venezuelan boundary dispute to arbitration. Henceforth Britain and the United States celebrated their identity of interests in a world divided into discrete national spheres of interest. The Caribbean belonged to the United States.[5]

THE WESTERN HEMISPHERE offered the United States a favored field, notably in the Spanish colony of Cuba, which had tempted American expansionists throughout the nineteenth century. By the mid-1890s American investment in Cuba amounted to some $50,000,000 ($10,000,000 more than Andrew Carnegie's annual profit from steel manufacture), with an annual trade of about $100,000,000. But a renewed war for independence had broken out in 1895, one of several serious anticolonial insurrections within living memory. Between 1868 and 1878 Cubans had challenged Spanish control, waging a guerrilla war and emancipating slaves. As a result of the Ten Years' War, slavery was abolished permanently and American investors bought many sugar plantations from planters bankrupted by the war. In the 1890s, therefore, the rebellion entailed losses for Americans as well as Cubans and Spaniards.

American property losses and the war's appalling human cost were widely reported in the United States. Both sides inflicted heavy casualties on noncombatants, but the concentration camp policy of the Spanish general Valeriano Weyler Y Nicolau proved especially deadly. In order to isolate the rebels and create free-fire zones, Weyler herded

Cuban farm families into crowded and unsanitary camps, where thousands died of disease and malnutrition. The suffering was equally pitiable in the cities; in Santiago, starvation and sickness were common, and the dead piled up, unburied.

The commander of the USS *Montgomery* reported in February 1895 that in the province of Matanzas 59,000 people had already died of starvation. In the city of Matanzas, with a population of less than 60,000, more than 1,700 people had died in the month of December alone, with an additional 14,000 "emaciated, sick, and almost beyond relief . . . lying about the streets absolutely without food, clothing, or shelter."[6] By 1896 many Americans, especially Populists sympathizing with a people trying to gain independence from a colonial overlord, were petitioning Congress to recognize Cuban belligerency and take active steps to free Cuba from Spanish rule.[7] As the Cuban war dragged on, an ever-widening spectrum of public opinion advocated American entry into the inconclusive struggle to stop the bloodshed and protect American investments. In Congress and in newspapers called the yellow press, enormous pressure for American intervention built up after 1896.

In the autumn of 1897 President McKinley came close to delivering an ultimatum to the Spanish government that would have led to war. The McKinley administration was concerned about American interests in Cuba that were not, in the words of the American minister to Spain, "merely theoretical or sentimental."[8]

The Spanish government promised to institute reforms that would grant Cuba autonomy and, presumably, bring peace. But after a series of riots in Cuba in January 1898 McKinley concluded that the United States would have to intervene. On January 24 the President sent the armored cruiser *Maine* on what he termed "a friendly visit" to Cuba. Newspapers reported "a strong popular suspicion that the administration is preparing for intervention."[9]

Early in February a letter written to a friend in Cuba by the Spanish minister to the United States, Enrique Dupuy de Lôme, became public. The letter not only insulted McKinley but also indicated the Spanish government's lack of good faith in instituting reforms in Cuba. A week later the *Maine* blew up in Havana Harbor, killing 266 of its crew.[10] The President moved toward war painfully but deliberately, sending the Spanish an ultimatum demanding that they cease hostilities and grant Cuba independence immediately. Before the complicated and straggling Spanish response was accounted for and after a great deal of personal agony, the President asked Congress for a declaration of war. He got it just as he wanted it, without assurances to Cuba that the United States would respect its independence, for McKinley realized even before hostilities broke out that unconditional Cuban independence was not necessarily in the best long-term interests of the United States.

The first battle took place in another Spanish colony on the far western edge of the Pacific Ocean early in May, when the American fleet under Commodore George Dewey destroyed the Spanish fleet in Manila Bay in the Philippine Islands.

AN ASIAN VICTORY in the war that had been undertaken supposedly to secure Cuban independence confused many and confronted Americans with unexpected choices. In the immediate aftermath of Dewey's triumph, it was conceivable that the United States would merely use the Philippines as negotiating chips in a settlement centered on Spain's Caribbean possessions. The United States might simply recognize the claims of a two-year-old Philippine independence movement and keep only one harbor as a coaling station, probably Manila. Or the United States might keep the whole island of Luzon, on which Manila is situated.

In humorist Peter Finley Dunne's fictional barroom in Chicago's Archey Road, Mr. Hennessey settled the question: "I know what I'd do if I was Mack. I'd hist a flag over th' Ph'lippeens, and I'd take in th' whole lot iv them." "An' yet," answered Mr. Dooley, the sardonic saloonkeeper, "tis not more thin two months since ye larned whether they were islands or canned goods."[11]

Large numbers of Americans agreed with Mr. Hennessey because they discerned in the Philippines a cure for hard times. Repealing the Sherman Silver Purchase Act had done no good in 1893. The election of 1896 had removed free silver as a cure. Regeneration from within through economic justice, as envisioned by the People's party, had failed at the polls. Yet when McKinley took office in March 1897, times were still grim. In the search for other explanations and new remedies, foreign markets came to the fore.

THE FOREIGN MARKETS explanation sought the cause of depressions not in currency, distribution of wealth, or monopoly. The culprit, it seemed, was agricultural and industrial overproduction. Americans produced too much, it was said; it seemed to matter little that during the recent hard times thousands had run out of the very foodstuffs and manufactured goods reputedly overproduced. What was needed were new markets, especially in Asia, especially in the most populous country in the world, China. It helped the argument that the Chinese already imported enough American cotton textiles, kerosene, flour, iron, and steel to make these American industries partially dependent on Asian sales. Nonetheless, the chimera of markets in China had always outweighed actual trade. During the 1890s American exports to China accounted for only 1.1 percent of all American exports, and during the decade Japan, rather than China, had been the main Asian trading partner of the United States.[12] While foreign markets had beckoned American businessmen for decades, this more urgent quest included the novel expectation that the government of the United States should play an active part in fostering exports.

The Philippine Islands—like Hawaii—represented the perfect stepping-stones to China, stops along the way where coal-burning ships bound for Asia could refuel. Expansionists saw the islands as the opportunity of the century. Manila might become an American version of Hong Kong, the British market city that tapped the markets and produce of South China. Henry Cabot Lodge, who was, with Mahan and Theodore Roosevelt, an ardent, prolific expansionist, spun dazzling promises of "a vast future trade and wealth and power" in American possession of the Philippines, visions that centered on profits for businessmen rather than markets for farmers or jobs for workers.[13]

And Protestant clergymen, one of the most expansionist-minded segments of the American population, imagined the millions of Chinese as potential converts.[14] For many Americans, expansion was the inevitable result of the machine age that had already filled up the continental United States and now seemed to demand the raw materials and foreign markets that overseas colonies promised. The vision of factories running nonstop and workers employed without interruption made this economic argument for annexation straightforward and persuasive. Additional motives existed, as the President discovered.

WILLIAM McKINLEY, as sensitive as anyone to the attractiveness of foreign markets, wrestled with the question of keeping all or part of the Philippines in 1898. To a delegation of Episcopal clergymen this "Christian statesman" gave this explanation of how he had reached his decision. When the islands came "as a gift from the gods," his indecision about their future had kept him from sleeping. Kneeling in prayer for guidance for several nights, McKinley had received an answer:

(1) That we could not give them back to Spain—that would be cowardly and dishonorable; (2) that we could not turn them over to France or Germany—our commercial rivals in the Orient—that would be bad business and discreditable; (3) that we could not leave them to themselves—they were unfit for self-government—and they would soon have anarchy and misrule over there worse than Spain's was; and (4) that there was nothing left for us to do but to take them all, and to educate the Filipinos, and uplift and civilize and Christianize them, and by God's grace do the very best we could by them, as our fellow-men for whom Christ also died. And then I went to bed, and went to sleep, and slept soundly.[15]

Foreign competition in the Pacific actually existed, for the years preceding the Spanish-American War were a time of worldwide European and Japanese expansion. Between 1870 and 1900 Europeans had taken over one-fifth of the land and one-tenth of the population of the globe, trumpeting their conquests as proof of the greatness of each nation.[16] Britain and France led in the late-nineteenth-century scramble for empire that began, symbolically at least, in 1885 at the Berlin Conference, called by King Leopold of Belgium. Leopold successfully claimed as his personal possession the vast central-west African kingdom of Kongo and its dependencies, now known as the Democratic Republic of the Congo. Britain and France simultaneously staked out most of the remainder of Africa in Berlin. The United States, which had never looked much beyond the Caribbean, Canada, and Mexico, took no part in the partition of Africa. In the decade and a half that followed the Berlin Conference, however, many Americans lost their immunity to imperial fever.

Entering the race late, the three up-and-coming colonial powers— Japan, Germany, and the United States—could collect only leftover bits and pieces of territory in the 1890s. German colonial ambitions, more than any other, nettled American expansionists. Recently unified and developing impressively, Germany possessed a big, new navy and omnivorous territorial ambitions. It seemed to have designs on Asia and Africa as well as on the Caribbean and Latin America, which the United States had thought of as its own sphere since the Monroe Doctrine of the 1820s. Unlike the British, who took political control of parts of China and South Africa but left them open to American commerce, the Germans closed their possessions in China, Africa, and the Pacific to foreign trade.

To a considerable extent, therefore, German acquisitiveness influenced American strategy. The United States annexed the harbor of the Pacific island of Pago Pago in 1889, took part in the partition of the rest of Samoa in 1898, and annexed Hawaii and the Philippines largely to prevent Germany's barring American access to markets and coaling stations on the way to China. The creation of a new American battleship navy between 1890 and 1896 was designed to counter the buildup of German naval strength.

Japanese expansion in China and the Pacific worried Americans, but not as much as the Germans'. Japan was a smaller nation, and the territories it occupied in Korea and northeastern China did not threaten

American commerce, as did the German occupation of the eastern Chinese province of Shandong (Shantung), through which American products entered China. Race probably counted for as much as relative strength in American estimates of power because few Americans entertained the possibility that a great power could be nonWhite.

A few denigrated American imperialism as senseless aping of Europeans, but for the most part an overseas empire seemed to admit the United States to an elite club of powerful, advanced, and civilized nations. Preening Americans proclaimed themselves an imperial power and fondly traced the extent of their far-flung—if not massive—new empire. They also located their new-found genius for imperial exploits in their Anglo-Saxon racial ancestry.

As THE BRITISH ACQUIRED the largest and richest shares of imperial bounty in Africa and Asia through wars of conquest and pacification that they called "our little wars," many White Americans—with the glaring exception of Irish Americans—renounced their traditional anglophobia (a legacy of the American Revolution and, especially, the War of 1812) to proclaim the kindredness of the English-speaking people and the natural superiority of Anglo-Saxons. The American nation became the expression of a single "race," the Anglo-Saxon, in a view that swept under the rug the Native American Indians, Irish, Blacks, and Jews who had been Americans since colonial times and the Asians, Slavs, and Italians just now disembarking in increasing numbers.

Anglo-Saxon chauvinism was no novelty in the 1890s. Versions had flared up from time to time during the nineteenth century, and it was once again on the increase; the American Protective Association, a nativist, anti-Catholic organization, had been founded in Iowa in 1887. More recently Josiah Strong, a Congregational minister, had written an influential report on missions in 1885, *Our Country*, extolling the special gifts of Anglo-Saxons: they possessed a sense of fair play, the ability to gain wealth honestly, the enjoyment of broad civil liberties in democracies in which every man had an equal vote, the genius for self-government and for governing others fairly, and the evolution of the highest civilization the world had ever known and could ever know because the sun of empire moved from east to west, starting in China and ending, once and for all, in the United States. Strong did not entertain the possibility that the sun of empire might keep on moving, allowing Japan and China their turns in the twentieth or twenty-first centuries.

These American–Anglo-Saxon attributes, he said, were "peculiarly aggressive traits calculated to impress [their] institutions upon mankind."[17] For Josiah Strong, Anglo-Saxon superiority obligated Congregationalists to convert the remainder of the world to American Protestantism. The seizure of territory was not one of his main concerns. But his rhetoric stressed aggression, thereby sounding other chords of Anglo-Saxonism that prevailed in the writing of Theodore Roosevelt. As early as 1895 Roosevelt had remarked that "this country needs a war," not to conquer territory but to restore manliness and military virtues. Pretending that the true Anglo-Saxon (or Nordic) spirit was that of the warrior, Roosevelt and novelists working in the enormously popular medieval genre, such as Charles Major (*When Knighthood Was in Flower* [2d ed., 1898]) and F. Marion Crawford (*Via Crucis: A Romance of the Second Crusade* [1898]), extolled the grandeur of combat. Crawford's knight characterizes Anglo-Saxons as "men who had the strength to take the world and to be its masters and make it obey whatsoever laws they saw fit to impose."[18] Values like these proved exceedingly convenient during the era of seizing other people's lands.

In justifications of empire, Anglo-Saxonism combined variously with arguments for Anglo-American identity of interest, the White man's burden, manifest and ordinary destiny, and duty. In imperialist reasoning, opposition to expansion was utterly futile. For Alfred Thayer Mahan, expansion was "natural, necessary, irrepressible," and for Henry Cabot Lodge, there existed an "irresistible pressure of events."[19] President McKinley spoke of the peculiarly American destiny that decreed Hawaiian annexation in 1898: "We need Hawaii just as much and a great deal more than we did California. It is manifest destiny." William Allen White recalled that "we were the chosen people . . . imperialism was in the stars."[20] Without their realizing it, jingoists echoed explanations of the inevitability of the trusts.

As often as not appeals to destiny meant race destiny, usually Anglo-Saxon, but for Mahan, Teutonic. The forensically gifted expansionist from Indiana, Senator Albert J. Beveridge, created an unmatched medley of empire, race, destiny, duty, divinity, and necessity: "The American Republic is part of the movement of a race,—the most masterful race in history,—the race movements are not to be stayed by the hand of man. They are mighty answers to Divine commands. Their leaders are not only statesmen of peoples—they are prophets of God. The inherent tendencies of a race are its highest law. They precede and survive all statutes, all constitutions. . . . The sovereign tendencies of all our race are organization and government."[21]

For Beveridge's constituency, the moment was critical, and the mission of the American people central to the enlightenment of all mankind. Expansion rose above politics and laws because within the unity that was human history, Americans were playing a preordained role. Imperialism was elemental, racial, predestined, for God had prepared the English-speaking people, master organizers, for governing what Beveridge called "savage and senile people." Americans must accept colonies and begin the regeneration of the world or see the world relapse into barbarism.[22]

The arguments of the Anglo-Saxonists rested on a specially tailored version of English and American history. In this telling Americans were the descendants of the revolutionaries of 1776, who at Lexington and Concord threw off colonial rule and established the first successful republic in the history of mankind. Earlier attempts at republicanism all had failed for lack of intelligence, morality, self-restraint, and the genius for self-government that ran in the English "blood" of the American people.

Anglo-Saxonists admitted that Anglo-Saxons (or Teutons) had not always possessed this self-governing trait. It had developed slowly over the centuries, they said, since either the Roman occupation of England in the first century A.D. or the signing of the Magna Carta in 1215. Various theories existed on the import of this slow evolution for what were called less developed races. For Benjamin Tillman, Democratic senator from South Carolina, no others could make that journey, because "the Anglo-Saxon is superior to the African or to any other colored people and is alone capable of self-government."[23]

According to Albert Beveridge, the Filipinos had made a false start, not only because they were "not a self-governing race" but also because they had already wasted centuries, while they were "instructed by Spaniards in the latter's worst estate."[24] The fact that even Anglo-Saxons had required a long apprenticeship meant that other peoples (Filipinos, Hawaiians, Africans, Native Americans) would need countless additional generations in which to develop. In the meanwhile, they were unfit for self-government.

Theodore Roosevelt thought a race could spend generations preparing for democracy but still not succeed. Fitness for self-government, for Roosevelt, came "to a race only through the slow growth of centuries, and then only to those races which possess an immense reserve fund of strength, common sense, and morality."[25] The outcome depended on the quality of the racial stock in question, and the adjectives applied to the conquered people, especially to the Filipinos, left little doubt of their supposed quality. They were termed illiterate, pagan, alien, inferior, barbarous, degenerate, debased, ignorant, and, at best, semicivilized. Often the objection was summed up in a single, devastating word: mongrel. The central point was that human history was defined not by individuals or nations but by "races" with lists of "traits" that every individual within a "race" exhibited.

This chain of logic reached an unavoidable conclusion: the United States must rule the Philippines out of duty. This was not mere imperialism; it was mission. Combined with the attraction of foreign markets, the argument of Filipino unfitness for self-government persuaded Americans that keeping the islands was the decent thing to do.

This new mission ignored the original aim of the war—independence for Cuba—and shunted aside the Philippine rebel army that had been fighting for independence since 1896 and that had made it possible for Americans to defeat the Spanish on land and occupy Luzon. When annexation triggered a struggle against American control in 1899, the war (which Americans called an insurrection) became further rhetorical evidence that the Filipinos were unfit for self-government: they had failed to recognize what was good for them. Assuming that American conquest of the islands was an imperative duty, the Philippine-American war amounted to the American version of the White man's burden.

"The White Man's Burden" was the title of a popular seven-stanza poem by the British poet of empire Rudyard Kipling. It first appeared in the United States in the February 1899 issue of *McClure's Magazine*, "circled the earth in a day and by repetition became hackneyed within a week."[26] It began with these verses:

> Take up the White Man's burden—
>   Send forth the best ye breed—
> Go, bind your sons to exile
>   To serve your captives' need;
> To wait, in heavy harness,
>   On fluttered folk and wild—
> Your new-caught sullen peoples,
>   Half devil and half child.

> Take up the White Man's burden—
>   In patience to abide,
> To veil the threat of terror
>   And check the show of pride;
> By open speech and simple,
>   An hundred times made plain,
> To seek another's profit
>   And work another's gain.

Despite the cynicism of Kipling's poem, many Americans took a certain pride in shouldering the White man's burden, particularly when it meant the exploitation of the new colony of Puerto Rico and of the American-controlled republic of Cuba and particularly before the difficulties of empire presented themselves in the Philippine Islands.

THE REALITIES OF CONQUEST quickly turned out to be less glorious than the rhetoric. Even as the Treaty of Paris of 1899 awarded the United States the Philippine Islands in exchange for a payment to Spain of $20,000,000, anti-imperialist Thomas B. Reed, the speaker of the House of Representatives, raised doubts. "We have bought ten million Malays at $2.00 a head unpicked," he warned, "and nobody knows what it will cost to pick them."[27] The Filipinos' refusal to trade one set of colonial masters for another meant the cost would rise.

The seven-year-long Philippine-American war began in January 1899, when rebel leader Emilio Aguinaldo declared the independence of the Philippine Republic. Hundreds of thousands of Filipinos died in battle, of disease, or of other war-related causes. At peak strength, in 1900, American forces numbered 70,000. All told, some 126,000 Americans, Black and White, served in the Philippine war. The ultimate cost to the United States was 4,200 dead, 2,800 wounded, and $400,000,000 expended. In comparison, the Spanish-American war proper had cost 460 American lives.

The long guerrilla war exasperated the American forces, causing General Jacob H. Smith to order his troops to "kill and burn and the more you kill and burn, the better you will please me," as they made the island of Samar "a howling wilderness."[28] The brief and glorious Spanish-American War to free Cuba was one thing. But this long, squalid battle to conquer the ungrateful Filipinos was another that called the high-flown rhetoric of empire into question.

William Jennings Bryan remarked shortly after the outbreak of the Philippine-American war that "'Destiny' is not as manifest as it was a few weeks ago, and the argument of 'duty' is being analyzed."[29] The tawdriness of the war of conquest inspired one of countless parodies of Kipling:

Take up the White Man's burden.
   Send forth your sturdy sons,
And load them down with whisky
   And Testaments and guns.
Throw in a few diseases
   To spread in tropic climes
For there the healthy niggers
   Are quite behind the times.

––––––

Take up the White Man's burden,
   And if you write in verse,
Flatter your Nation's vices
   And strive to make them worse.
Then learn that if with pious words
   You ornament each phrase,
In a world of canting hypocrites,
   This kind of business pays.[30]

For a sizable, vocal minority, it was not simply the Philippine war that discredited overseas expansion. Some Republicans, Democrats, and socialists had criticized imperialism from beginning to end. They condemned, with lawyer and financier Charles Francis Adams, the everlasting "Expansion, World-Power, Inferior Races, Calvination, Duty-and-Destiny" as "twaddle and humbug."[31] Dozens of well-known figures—reformers like Jane Addams and Henry Demarest Lloyd; American Federation of Labor head Samuel Gompers and industrialist Andrew Carnegie; former abolitionist Thomas Wentworth Higginson; prominent Democrats such as William Jennings Bryan and South Carolina Senator Benjamin Tillman; former Republican President Benjamin Harrison; former Democratic President Grover Cleveland; academics such as Stanford University President David Starr Jordan, Harvard University President Charles W. Eliot, and Yale Social Darwinist William Graham Sumner; and writers like Mark Twain, William Dean Howells, Hamlin Garland, and George Washington Cable—all opposed imperialism.

Anti-imperialists found the outright annexation of the Philippines burdensome, unnecessary, immoral, unconstitutional, or strategically unwise. Some would have preferred the arrangements with Cuba that came out of the war. Cuba maintained a nominal independence, but the United States government conducted its foreign policy and ran its political affairs, while American businessmen took over its economy. Andrew Carnegie, Speaker of the House Thomas B. Reed, and E. L. Godkin (former editor of *The Nation*, now editor of the *New York Evening Post*), objected to the forcible annexation of the Philippines as unAmerican because the Constitution contained no provision for island colonies—as opposed to continental North American territories preparing for statehood—or for ruling other peoples against their will and without representation in Congress. Carnegie offered personally to buy the Philippines for $20,000,000, then give them their independence.

William Dean Howells and Mark Twain looked past the flying flags, civilizing missions, and patriotic fervor to the realities of death in war and the tyranny, hypocrisy, and profit in colonialism. Twain's "To the Person Sitting in Darkness" appeared in the *North American Review* in February 1901. "Extending the Blessings of Civilization to our Brother who Sits in Darkness has been a good trade and has paid well," Twain began. "The Blessings of Civilization are all right, and a good commercial property" because they made an attractive lure to the Person in Darkness. But the "Blessings of Civilization" ("JUSTICE, CHRISTIANITY, EDUCATION . . . and so on") are just an outside cover, and they are only for the export trade. The real contents (the "Actual Thing") of Western civilization are the poverty of New York slums and the slaughter in South Africa and the Philippines, where "Civilization" was being resisted. Naked warfare is the "Actual Thing *with the outside cover left off.*" Watching Americans—now playing by European rules—occupy the Philippines, the Person Sitting in Darkness concludes that the United States is "yet *another* Civilized Power, with its banner of the Prince of Peace in one hand and its loot-basket and its butcher-knife in the other. Is there no salvation for us but to adopt Civilization and lift ourselves down to its level?"[32]

William Dean Howells's title character in "Editha" is an ordinary young woman caught up in the jingoism of war. Against his better judgment, Editha persuades her fiancé, George Gerson, to enlist in the glorious cause. George's family has been antiwar since his father lost an arm in the Civil War, but he goes off to the Spanish-American War for Editha.

To Editha's astonishment, George is killed in the war. In a visit to George's mother, Editha is stunned when Mrs. Gerson not only blames her for his death but also scolds Editha for her thoughtlessness: "You just expected him to kill some one else, some of those foreigners. . . . You thought it would be all right for my George, *your* George, to kill the sons of those miserable mothers and the husbands of those girls you would never see the faces of."[33]

Writers like Twain and Howells opposed imperialism and war in any guise. But devotees of war, like Theodore Roosevelt and journalist Richard Harding Davis, deplored the way particular conflicts were conducted. One of the most famous volunteers in the war (William Jennings Bryan was another), Roosevelt complained of army mismanagement: "We are half starved; and our men are sickening daily. The lack of transportation, food and artillery has brought us to the verge of disaster; but above all the lack of any leadership, of any system or any executive capacity."[34]

Richard Harding Davis was one of the era's most famous war correspondents, and he was never, ever antiwar. Nonetheless, the incompetence and lack of rudimentary training and support of the American military in Florida on the eve of the Cuban expedition and the resultant loss of life from disease gave him pause. In the volunteer camps he found tent cities that lacked rain trenches and gutters; latrines and garbage dumps situated windward of the camp; inexperienced regiments, cheap uniforms, and shoddy supplies. "It is sickening to see men being sacrificed as these men will be," he wrote to his brother from Florida.[35] In fact, 5,200 American volunteers died of disease—yellow fever, malaria, typhoid, and dysentery—as opposed to 460 battle deaths. The mounting charges of incompetence and corruption forced the secretary of war to resign after the Caribbean campaign.

RICHARD HARDING DAVIS also covered the South African War, which interested Americans nearly as much as their own. Davis went to South Africa, sympathizing with the British, who were trying to pacify the Dutch-descended Boer republics and bring them under British rule. Davis originally agreed with John Hay that "the fight of England is the fight of civilization and progress and *all of our interests are bound up in her success.*"[36] The Boer farmers of South Africa were intent on keeping political control of the enormous gold field in the Witwatersrand, whose center was Johannesburg and where more than 1,500 Americans worked and resented Boer backwardness and stubbornness as much as the British did. The *New York Times* argued that the Boers were blocking economic development and political freedom in South Africa, for "there is no room in the world for 'peculiar people' who insist on nonconformity, and upon taking up more room than belongs [to] them or that they can use to the utmost advantage. . . . They must conform . . . or be extinguished. . . ."[37]

After having watched the armies in the field and met some Boers, however, Davis began to lose sympathy with the British, whose primary concerns he came to see as maintaining class distinctions and the etiquette of rank. The Boers, whose intelligence and stamina impressed the journalist, reminded Davis of prosperous New Jersey farmers. Writing only enough to justify the trip, Davis left South Africa as quickly as possible.

In the United States opinion on the Boer War divided pretty much along party lines. Republicans favored the British; Democrats and Populists backed the Boers. Irish Americans, the great majority of whom were Democrats, supported the Boers in their fight against England. An Irish brigade from Chicago traveled to South Africa to fight alongside the Boer commandos. The Democratic platform of 1900 included a plank expressing support for the Boers' struggle to maintain their independence. In American politics as well, Democrats tended to be anti-imperialist, with William Jennings Bryan at the forefront.

DEMOCRATIC PRESIDENTIAL CANDIDATE in 1896 and 1900, the leader of his party, Bryan had volunteered the same day Congress declared war on Spain, but he had never reached Cuba. Bryan spent the summer of the war in Camp Cuba Libre, near Jacksonville, Florida, where he contracted typhoid fever. After hostilities had ended in Cuba, Bryan resigned from the service, campaigned against Philippine annexation, and became an eloquent opponent of imperialism. His arguments reflected the concerns of his constituents: workers, farmers, and White southerners.

Recalling the excitement the war had created from the moment the *Maine* exploded, Bryan feared that overseas adventures would permanently distract Americans from the legitimate problems of working-men and that domestic injustices would fade from view in a jingoistic climate of public opinion. A Bryan ally, Populist Senator William V. Allen of Nebraska, predicted that empire would bring American workers into competition with "an endless horde of nondescript populations" who would work for starvation wages and lower the American standard of living. Employers, tempted by large, docile, and cheap pools of labor in the overseas possession, would simply move factories from the United States to Manila or the Hawaiian Islands.[38]

For Bryan and other politicians close to the People's party, imperialism was, at bottom, a class matter. Empire served the interests of only one class, the wealthy, or what People's Party Chairman Marion Butler called the "Syndicates and the Monopolists and Franchise-Grabbers."[39] Then there was the question of armed forces. Colonies would require a large standing army for their control, and farmers and workers would supply the cannon fodder.

An increased military would also cost a great deal, and again, the producers would have to pay the price. Bryan explained that federal taxes were of two sorts, import duties—tariffs, which raised the prices of imported goods and domestic goods that competed with imports—and excise taxes on liquor and tobacco—internal revenue. These were regressive forms of taxation that consumed greater proportions of the incomes of the poor than of the incomes of the rich. Bryan called them "not only an income tax, but a graded income tax, and heaviest in proportion upon the smallest incomes."[40]

What did imperialism offer the ordinary American? Bryan asked. "Heavier taxes, Asiatic emigration and an opportunity to furnish more sons for the army," he answered. Instead of calling imperialism the "white man's burden," Bryan suggested that it be termed the "poor man's load."[41] Dr. Howard S. Taylor, another anti-imperialist, parodied the Kipling poem with his "Poor Man's Burden":

Pile up the poor man's burden—
    The weight of foreign wars;
God shrewdly yoke together
    Great Mercury and Mars.
And march with them to conquest,
    As once did ancient Rome,
With vigor on her borders
    And slow decay at home.

Pile up the poor man's burden,
    Accept Great Britain's plan
She does all things for commerce—
    Scarce anything for man.
Far off among the pagans
    She seeks an open door
While Pity cries in London,
    "God help the British poor!"

———

Pile up the poor man's burden;
    Keep in the old, old track!
Let glory ride, as ever,
    Upon the toiler's back.

Lay tax and tax upon him,
Devised with subtle skill—
Call forth his sons to slaughter
And let him pay the bill![42]

White southerners like Benjamin Tillman contributed other themes to the Democratic opposition to colonialism. Tillman echoed some of Bryan's more Populist anti-imperialist arguments, but mostly, as a White southerner, he fought the inclusion of more colored peoples within the purview of the United States. He likened the African Americans in the South to Polynesians in Hawaii and Malays in the Philippines on what he called racial grounds: African Americans, Polynesians, and Malays all had darker skins than White Americans, and "God Almighty made them inferior and lacking in moral fiber."[43] Regardless of culture or language, humanity thus divided into two parts, Anglo-Saxon and non-Anglo-Saxon, which meant for Tillman White and nonWhite. For most White southern Democrats, annexation of 10,000,000 or so more nonWhites made no sense when White Americans already had their hands full with 8,000,000 Blacks in the South. A prominent conservative Black educator in Alabama, Booker T. Washington, also raised the same question from a different angle: "Until our nation has settled the Indian and Negro problems, I do not think we have a right to assume more social problems."[44]

For anyone concerned with the American race issue, the parallel between White supremacy at home and imperialism abroad was obvious. Southern Democrats took great satisfaction from hearing northern Republicans preach empire and advocate nonvoting status for subject peoples, because southern White Democrats believed that Republicans had forced Black suffrage upon them during the early days of Reconstruction (while most northern states had excluded Blacks from the electorate). The sudden change of heart of Massachusetts Senator Henry Cabot Lodge earned him constant teasing from Tillman and his fellow senator from South Carolina, John L. McLaurin. (Lodge was the author of the federal elections bill of 1890 that would have protected Black voters in the South.) "It is passing strange that Senators who favored universal suffrage and the full enfranchisement of the [N]egro should now advocate imperialism," McLaurin intoned. "If they are sincere in their views as to the Philippines, they should propose an amendment to the Constitution which will put the inferior races in this country and the inhabitants of the Philippines upon an equality as to their civil and political rights."[45] To southern Democrats, Republican espousal of imperialism implied, first, that nonWhite suffrage was wrong and, second, that the White supremacist order in the South, which denied Blacks the vote, was correct in its entirety. Tillman thought that Philippines or U.S. South, it was all the same, and southern Democrats had the answers. "We of the South," he explained, "have borne this white man's burden of a colored race in our midst."[46]

TILLMAN'S USE OF southern examples was not typical of discussion of empire, which generally ignored the existence of people of color in the United States, as though all Americans were cheerfully taking up the White man's burden and carrying out the Anglo-Saxon's civilizing mission. But nonWhites, who suffered disabilities that ranged from dispossession to lynching, were far from unanimous in their support of the imperialist venture. They already understood what it meant to be treated as inferior races.

In the 1840s, 1850s, and 1860s, thousands of Chinese had immigrated from the Pearl River delta near Guangzhou (Canton), in southern China, an area of great social and economic distress in the nineteenth century that also sent immigrants throughout Southeast Asia, to Latin America, and into other parts of China. In 1882, after organized labor had taken up the anti-Chinese demand, Congress passed the Chinese Exclusion Act, making it unlawful for Chinese laborers to enter the U.S. and declaring that they could not vote or become citizens. Disfranchised and relegated to the margins of western life, the Chinese were also targets of White mobs that in Los Angeles in 1871 had lynched 18 Chinese at once and in Rock Springs,

Wyoming, in 1885 murdered 28 Chinese and drove the other 300 out of town.[47] As workers and immigrants, however, their position differed from that of American Indians.

AFTER THE CIVIL WAR non-Indian settlers in the West encroached on Indian lands and slaughtered the buffalo herds upon which Indians depended for food, clothing, and shelter.[48] Settlers demanded military conquest of the Native Americans, a policy that led to bloody clashes throughout the 1870s and 1880s, the most famous of which was the victory of the Sioux, led by Chiefs Rain-in-the-Face, Sitting Bull, and Crazy Horse, over Colonel George A. Custer, near the Little Bighorn River in southern Montana. Settler pressure on Indian lands and Indian resistance convinced Congress to "civilize" Native Americans through the Dawes Severalty Act of 1887, which attempted to break up communally owned reservation land. Reasoning that citizenship and civilization required individually held property—a notion foreign to tribal cultures—the Dawes Act allotted 160 acres to each Indian family head, also including provisions for purchase of "surplus" reservation lands by non-Indian settlers. Congress further reserved the power to allocate rights-of-way to telegraph and railroad companies through Indian lands. In 1887 Native Americans held 138,000,000 acres of land; but by 1900 they held only 78,000,000 acres, and they lost another 12,000,000 before the act was reversed in 1934. In 1889 more than 3,000,000 acres in the Indian Territory, now Oklahoma, were opened to non-Indian homesteaders, so that a territory that had held virtually no non-Indians in 1880 had 730,000 in 1900.

The last burst of Indian resistance, the Ghost Dance, occurred in the winter of 1889–1890. The prophet Wovoka, a Nevada Paiute, had preached that if only all Indians would unite across tribal lines, have faith in the Ghost Dance, and carefully perform its rituals, the ancestors would return, and together they could drive away the non-Indian invaders. The strength of this movement among the Dakota Sioux alarmed government agents, who brought the U.S. Army to the reservation at Wounded Knee, South Dakota. In January 1890, when warriors refused to surrender their guns, the army slaughtered 146 Indian men, women, and children. At the turn of the century the Native American population, encircled and besieged, was shrinking. In 1910 it was at its smallest ever, 220,000—about one-third its number at the end of the eighteenth century.

NUMBERING ABOUT 8,000,000, African Americans were by far the largest nonWhite population in the United States. They were usually seen as synonymous with the "Negro problem" that was invariably identified with the South. For southern Whites, solving the "Negro problem" meant prohibiting Blacks from voting and barring them from the public sphere, which Whites considered exclusively their own.

In 1883 the Supreme Court had struck down the Civil Rights Act of 1875, which had outlawed racial discrimination in public accommodations. In 1890 Mississippi ratified a new constitution that disfranchised Blacks, which the Supreme Court accepted as constitutional in 1898, three years after South Carolina had disfranchised its Black population. The Supreme Court in 1896 accepted segregation on public carriers in *Plessy* v. *Ferguson*, and the separate but equal formula, a fiction from the very beginning, gained legitimacy among Whites. Meanwhile, neither federal nor state governments acted to curb extra-legal violence against Blacks, the worst expression of which was lynching. Between 1885 and 1900, 2,500 lynchings, mostly of Blacks, occurred in the United States, mainly in Mississippi, Alabama, Georgia, and Louisiana. During the Spanish-American War violent incidents of a racist nature continued without pause.

One week after the sinking of the *Maine* (in which twenty-two Black sailors lost their lives), the Black postmaster of Lake City, South Carolina, Frazier B. Baker, was attacked by a White mob that set fire to the post office at the side of his house, shot Baker to death as he fled the flames, killed his infant son, and seriously injured his wife and older children. With most of the country taken up with the excitement of the *Maine*, African Americans mourned Baker almost alone.

After the declaration of war Blacks agonized over whether to fight for a government that ignored incidents like the Lake City tragedy. Despite misgivings, more than 10,000 Black men served in the war during the summer, as members of the regular army (Ninth and Tenth Cavalries, Twenty-fourth and Twenty-fifth Infantries), volunteers, and militia; Black women volunteered as nurses. The question shifted from whether to serve to how to secure Black officers for the segregated Black troops. First Lieutenant Charles Young, a West Pointer, was the only Black officer in the regular army who could lead troops in combat, but he never saw Cuba. A few companies obtained Black officers, but most Black soldiers were led by White officers.

Frustrations increased as Black troops were segregated on trains, in depots, and in rest stops on their way to camps in Florida or Cuba. Southern White soldiers and civilians spat out abuse. Colonel James Tillman, nephew of Benjamin Tillman and commander of a regiment from South Carolina, warned: "We are South Carolinans and white men and no earthly power can force our boys to lift their hats to one of the [N]egro officers. If I hear [of] one of the South Carolina boys saluting a [N]egro I will kick him out of the company. We have enlisted to fight for our country and not to practice social equality with an inferior race whom our fathers held in bondage."[49]

During the summer of the war violence against Blacks at home recurred. In July 1898 a Black newspaper in Richmond, Virginia, listed a dozen lynchings of Blacks since the declaration of war three months earlier. In November White supremacist Democrats overthrew the interracial coalition of Republicans and Populists of Wilmington, North Carolina, in a riot that cost dozens of Blacks their lives. Once again, the shedding of Black blood distressed only Blacks. While Southern Whites excused the Wilmington violence as necessary for the protection of southern civilization, Blacks wondered why the United States could go to war to save Cubans but not Americans in the South. In a play on the name of the Cuban city where Americans had fought the Spanish, Santiago de Cuba, an otherwise unknown Black man in Little Rock, Arkansas, wrote a long poem, "Santiago de Wilmington," which began:

On Santiago's bloody field
    Where Spanish hosts were made to yield
The Negro like a phalanx great
    Fought hard to save the ship of state
And Wilmington with her disgrace
    Stares Santiago in the face
And shows her heartless feelings clear
    For those who fought without a fear.[50]

AntiBlack violence continued in 1899, when a mob of Whites in Palmetto, Georgia, slaughtered half a dozen unarmed Blacks in March. In April the lynching of Sam Hose, also in Georgia, provided a spectacle for 2,000 Whites. Hose had been accused of several crimes, including the rape of a White woman, but the barbarity of his murder shocked White southerners who usually justified the lynching of suspected rapists. Not only did the killing take place in a carnival atmosphere, but spectators mutilated the body for souvenirs. For good measure they also hanged the Reverend Elijah Strickland, who had tried to protect Hose.

In the midst of the Philippine-American war, Blacks protested the Hose lynching and the rising tide of antiBlack terrorism. In Boston a Black member of the Cambridge City Council brought the two together. "What a spectacle America is exhibiting today," said William Lewis. "Columbus stands offering liberty to the Cubans with one hand, cramming liberty down the throats of the Filipinos with the other, but with both feet planted upon the neck of the [N]egro."[51] J. H. Magee of Chicago formed a Black Man's Burden Association to counter antiBlack violence in the United States and promote Philippine independence. Henry T. Johnson, editor of the African Methodist Episcopal Church's newspaper, the *Christian Recorder*, penned one of a score of poems entitled "The Black Man's Burden":

Pile on the Black Man's Burden.
    'Tis nearest at your door;

Why heed long bleeding Cuba,
   or dark Hawaii's shore?
Hail ye your fearless armies,
   which menace feeble folks
Who fight with clubs and arrows
   and brook your rifle's smoke.

Pile on the Black Man's Burden
   His wail with laughter drown
You've sealed the Red Man's problem,
   And will take up the Brown,
In vain ye seek to end it,
   With bullets, blood or death
Better by far defend it
   With honor's holy breath.[52]

As the Philippine war continued in 1900, antiBlack riots erupted in New Orleans, New York, and Akron, Ohio. One hundred Blacks were lynched in 1901.

Amid this slaughter, African Americans derided the rhetoric of Anglo-Saxon superiority, most of all the Anglo-Saxon's reputed genius for democracy and the enlightened governing of others. Citing the Anglo-Saxons of the South, Blacks called Anglo-Saxon civilization a failure and scoffed at the vaunted Anglo-Saxon respect for law. "Their own hot-headed and ignorant will is law," said a Black Missourian, "and this is anarchy."[53]

In response to such charges, White supremacists appealed to an authority higher than law that was akin to McKinley's hand of God and voice of destiny. "Race instinct," White supremacists insisted, transcended mere legislation and justified "the South's" disfranchising and lynching Black men and obeying "a higher law" than that in the statute books or the Constitution. "Race instincts" more powerful than law decreed the protection of Anglo-Saxon civilization by any means necessary, White supremacists argued, and the same imperatives of race made Blacks unfit to vote. "The evil is in the blood of races," John Temple Graves of Georgia concluded, and "the disease is in the bones and the marrow and the skin of antagonistic peoples."[54]

The White supremacist solution to the "Negro problem" was the repeal of the Fifteenth Amendment to the U.S. Constitution, which gave Blacks the vote after the Civil War. White supremacists had wanted to reverse the amendment for years, but northern Republicans had objected. By 1900 the notion no longer seemed so farfetched to the northerners. The realities of empire enlightened northern Republicans who had previously championed universal manhood suffrage for the South. "The mind of the country North and South, especially since the acquisition of Hawaii, Puerto Rico and the Philippines," noted the new mayor of Wilmington, North Carolina, "is in a more favorable condition to consider such a proposition than ever before."[55] The Fifteenth Amendment stood, but in name only. Before the twentieth century had advanced very far, all the sizable nonWhite populations under American control enjoyed only limited civil rights, whether as noncitizen Native Americans or Chinese, subjects in the islands, or disfranchised Black citizens in the South.

ONE RESULT of the rhetoric of empire and the White man's burden was a vastly increased emphasis on race nationally. Of course, race had been a potent political factor before 1898, especially in the South, but the proclamations and debates on war and annexation invariably stressed race by translating a wide variety of political questions into racial terms. American expansion was not interpreted simply as the spread of the American polity, with its ethnically diverse population. It was emphatically and explicitly the expansion of the Anglo-Saxon. Non-Anglo-Saxon Whites were forgotten, and nonWhites everywhere were lumped together as "inferior races."

On the other side, racial exclusion encouraged a tendency among African Americans to identify with the colonized, rather than with the colonizers. In the twentieth century Black Americans would invariably side with Africans and Asians on international political issues that were phrased in terms of race. The African American sociologist W. E. B. Du Bois encapsulated the change in a widely quoted phrase: "The problem of the twentieth century is the problem of the color-line,—the relation of the darker to the lighter races of men in Asia and Africa, in America and the islands of the sea."[56]

Empire also hastened the identification of White Americans with the European colonial powers, with Britain most of all. International ties anchored in the politics of race and empire continued to reduce Americans' sense of the uniqueness of their Republic and its separateness from the class-bound, autocratic, and oppressive regimes of the Old World, building on the realization that in the 1870s, 1880s, and 1890s the U.S. had not escaped class conflicts worthy of Europe.

Most Americans emerged from the conflicts of the 1890s into the prosperous, imperial twentieth century with a great sense of relief. Although the minority of anti-imperialists, particularly Blacks, often cited the trampling of human rights that accompanied colonialism and White supremacy, empire, with its colonialist rule, exclusionary rhetoric, and ranking of races, reinforced the hierarchical side of American values and downplayed fairness. In discussions of politics and economics, too, the new century brought an identity-of-interest emphasis on prosperity that minimized questions of equity.

A wave of prosperity arrived in mid-1898. The war got the federal government spending, and discoveries of gold in South Africa, Alaska, and Colorado increased money supplies.[57] The country enjoyed what Ray Stannard Baker called unparalleled prosperity. Seemingly overnight, factories started up and the unemployed masses found work. Buoyed by empire, the country went from conflict-ridden poverty to balmy prosperity in a matter of months.[58]

7

PROSPERITY

Newly reelected President William McKinley and Vice President Theodore Roosevelt, the Spanish-American War hero and former governor of New York, made a tremendously popular team until the idyll ended abruptly in September 1901, when an anarchist assassinated the President at the Buffalo Pan-American Exposition. Everyone, even his staunchest opponents, mourned McKinley; then attention turned toward the energetic new President. Although Mark Hanna reputedly exclaimed that McKinley's assassination had put "that damned cowboy in the White House," the new President, with the most fascinating personality since Abraham Lincoln, personified the glorious new century.

At forty-two, the youngest man ever to become President, one of the best-educated and most articulate men in public life, Roosevelt descended from privileged New York and Georgia families. Known from his days in Albany as somewhat of a political maverick, he knew nonetheless how to get along with regular republicans. He preserved McKinley's cabinet of corporation lawyers, continued McKinley's pro-business policies, and enjoyed cordial relations with Hanna and other conservative, business-oriented Republicans in the Senate.

In addition to his conservative cohorts, however, the new President associated with men of a relatively broad range of political persuasions and invited a wider circle of acquaintances to the White House than anyone could remember, including liberal journalists like the muckraker Lincoln Steffens and the distinguished Black educator Booker T. Washington, this latter much to the chagrin of White supremacist southerners. Not even a barrage of criticism from the South over the Washington visit diminished Roosevelt's popularity.[1] His was a tremendously attractive personality, well served by the coincidence of his presidency with what he called "noteworthy prosperity."

ROOSEVELT BECAME PRESIDENT as the country was shucking off the debts and troubles of the depressed 1890s and embracing prosperity. McKinley and Roosevelt's campaign slogans of 1900 had been "The Full Dinner Pail" and "Let Well Enough Alone," which translated into standing pat or standpattism. Both slogans seemed well suited to what was now the era of Roosevelt, in which American factories were running full tilt, outproducing Germany, Great Britain, and sometimes the two combined.

The gross national product increased dramatically between the depression year of 1896 and 1901, from $13 billion to $21 billion, which averaged out to $188 per capita in 1896 and $467 in 1901. This extraordinary wealth brought the fruits of technological development into thousands of urban homes, most obviously in the form of electricity and telephones. The airplane and the gasoline-powered automobile, both invented in 1903, fired imaginations. The automobile, at least, quickly inaugurated a new round in the transportation revolution that railroads had begun.

New forms of popular amusements diverted many from dwelling on economic oppression, which, in any case, prosperity had somewhat obscured. More people lived in towns and cities, more work was to be had, wages were rising, workers had more money in their hands, and the new ways of having what was coming to be called "fun" cost only pennies. Two of the older forms of leisure, organized sports and drinking in saloons, had existed long before the twentieth century.

People who lived in large houses continued to drink at home or in clubs, but patterns of liquor consumption changed somewhat for the poor. Although until the 1880s and 1890s working-class people had often taken their drinks in private houses that sold beer or liquor—shebeens—

saloons had all but replaced these informal drinking places, which had usually been run by women. Like saloons, which catered primarily to men, organized sports were male-dominated. Football attracted a college-educated audience, but baseball, with its working-class players, was not so elite a sport. The National League of Professional Baseball Clubs had been founded in 1876, but the first World Series—in which the Boston Red Sox defeated the Pittsburgh Pirates—did not occur until 1903, two years after the founding of the American League.

Middle- and working-class audiences attended circuses, musical comedies, and popular plays, such as the great southern favorite *The Clansman*, by the Reverend Thomas Dixon. Vaudeville and minstrel shows, in which several short pieces of musical entertainment alternated with comedy—usually ethnic or racial humor—attracted a mass working-class, urban audience, but the preeminent twentieth-century amusement was the moving picture.

In the 1870s, 1880s, and 1890s the French scientist Étienne Jules Marey, the American photographer Eadweard Muybridge, and the prolific inventor Thomas Alva Edison all were developing the technology of moving pictures. Marey and Muybridge sought new ways of understanding movement, but Edison, who was his own best press agent, was an entrepreneur attuned to the economic promise of moving pictures. Edison produced the kinetoscope peep show in 1893 and large-screen motion projection in 1896. After 1900, five-cent storefront movie houses—nickelodeons—attracted an enormous working-class audience. By 1908 there were more than 600 nickelodeons in the New York area alone, grossing more than $6,000,000 a year.[2] Nickelodeons created a widely popular form of entertainment not restricted to men, as saloons were. The movies were available to women of all ages and to children—who constituted one-quarter to one-half the audiences.

Amusement parks, another new form of popular entertainment, also appeared at the turn of the century with the increase of the urban population and the extension of trolley lines outside center cities. Places like Coney Island in New York; Paragon Park and Revere Beach in Boston; Atlantic City on the Jersey shore, a train ride from Philadelphia;

and Lincoln Park on Lake Quinsigamond in Worcester, Massachusetts, offered mechanical rides and exotic sideshows. There young people of many ethnic groups and both sexes rode roller coasters, played games, "petted," drank, fought, and forged a new mass culture that repudiated middle-class standards of decorum.[3]

The changing nature of working-class Fourth of July celebrations in Worcester reflected the evolution of popular leisure between the 1870s and the early twentieth century. In the late nineteenth century Worcester's workers celebrated the day off from work with other members of their families, churches, or ethnic societies; women had stayed up all night to prepare food, and children and young men played all the games. But this was not the pattern of entertainment in the new amusement parks, where a few wage-workers operated the rides and games for the men, women, and children who paid to enter and have a good time. The Fourth of July became a "festival of consumption," in which fun was something individuals bought and sold.[4]

ALTHOUGH it would be too strong to call news of Theodore Roosevelt a form of public amusement, the President attracted attention no matter what he did. Many of Roosevelt's activities between 1903 and 1905 concerned foreign affairs, which had interested him over the years. During the Spanish-American War the battleship *Oregon* had taken sixty-eight days to reach Cuba from the West Coast via the southern tip of South America, a fact that had reanimated discussion of an American-controlled canal through the Isthmus of Panama, which belonged to Colombia. The idea of an isthmian canal was 400 years old, but between 1878 and 1889 Ferdinand de Lesseps, builder of the Suez Canal, had failed (at the cost of 20,000 lives) to excavate a sea-level canal across the mountainous isthmus. After de Lesseps abandoned the effort, the United States stepped in. In 1903 it signed a treaty with the newly independent republic of Panama that allowed the United States to build and fortify the canal, to exercise rights, powers, and authority in the ten-mile-wide Canal Zone "as if [the United States] were the sovereign of the territory" as well as to establish a protectorate over all of Panama.

Such one-sided agreements were common in the heyday of colonialism, and Europeans had often set up similar arrangements in territory acquired from China.[5]

Roosevelt claimed later to have taken Panama away from Colombia by himself, but Panamanian nationalism had flared up from time to time since 1830, most recently in 1902, when Roosevelt had recognized that in Panama "you don't have to foment revolution. All you have to do is take your foot off and one will occur."[6] The United States took its foot off by sending the USS *Nashville* there to oversee the revolution and by recognizing Panama's independence within three days of the revolt.

Democrats, in particular, protested against Roosevelt's use of the imperatives of "civilization" to explain the protectorate that he had forced on Panama. A Democratic newspaper in Chicago termed Roosevelt's rationale "a tyrant's plea of necessity."[7] Although criticism of Roosevelt continued for years, the acquisition of the Canal Zone and the building of the canal generally seemed like a good idea, strategically and economically. When completed, the canal promised to give American products easier access to Asian markets. In the meanwhile, the canal's enormous machines, sophisticated engineering, and eradication of tropical diseases (especially malaria and yellow fever) provided an entertaining triumph of science and technology.

In response to a foreign debt crisis and revolutionary instability in the Dominican Republic in 1904, the President promulgated the Roosevelt Corollary, which asserted the American right to police the Western Hemisphere. Because the Monroe Doctrine prohibited Europeans from interfering in Latin America, the United States became (by its own fiat) the sole "civilized nation"—in Roosevelt's terms—allowed to invade countries in the Americas. Between 1900 and 1917 the United States exercised this right repeatedly, not only in the Dominican Republic and Panama but also in Cuba, Nicaragua, Haiti, and Mexico.

For all his jingoism and imperialism, however, Theodore Roosevelt won the Nobel Peace Prize in 1905 for mediating a settlement of the 1904–1905 war between Japan and Russia. Colonial rivalry in Manchuria and Korea had flared into a conflict that the Japanese won, much to the surprise of many who had assumed that nonWhites could not defeat Whites militarily. The loss destroyed the Russian Asian fleet and established Japan as a major regional power, alarming Americans with expansionist dreams. Favoring Japanese claims in Manchuria, Theodore Roosevelt saw the Portsmouth settlement as a means of turning Japanese ambitions away from the Pacific, where they would conflict with those of the United States. The 1907 sail around the world of the United States Great White Fleet was intended to remind the Japanese of American strength in the Pacific. The era of noteworthy prosperity was also one of imperialist competition in which many Americans reveled in playing the role of world power.

EVERYONE COULD SEE that the suffering and unemployment so obvious during the depression had faded from view, but many housewives noticed that since the end of the depression the cost of providing for their families had increased faster than wages, and statistics supported their impression. *Dun's Review,* a business journal, reported that between 1897 and 1900 prices rose by one-third. Joseph Pulitzer's popular daily, the *New York World,* cited figures that showed that during the same period, while capital invested in manufacturing increased by 51 percent, the value of products increased by 39 percent, the cost of management increased by 63 percent, but the total wages (not wages per earner) increased by only 23 percent. A Commonwealth of Massachusetts report showed that the expenses of ordinary workingmen making about $800 per year had increased between 1897 and 1902: 11.2 percent for food, 16.7 percent for dry goods, 52.4 percent for rent, and 9.7 percent for fuel.[8]

Unaware of the inflationary pressure that a growing money supply created, Bryan Democrats and other opponents of business-oriented politics laid the whole blame for rising prices at the door of the trusts. In a critique that exaggerated the extent and the consequences of business consolidations, opponents of the trusts accused them of abusing their power by setting prices too high for workers to buy very much, so that consumption would fall; this would in turn entail reductions in production and thus lead to layoffs. The wages of workers who remained employed would stagnate or fall, critics like Bryan charged, because big business preferred to pay enormous salaries to managers and low wages to laborers. Managers were in short supply, even though the new business schools like the Massachusetts Institute of Technology and the Wharton School of the University of Pennsylvania were producing increasing numbers, but the supply of unskilled workers was virtually unlimited.

A few voices also questioned whether the nation as a whole was enjoying noteworthy prosperity. The census of 1900 showed that 2,000,000 women and 1,700,000 children worked in factories and mills. Since 1890 the percent of children employed in nonagricultural work had grown slightly, from 18.1 to 18.2 percent, and the proportion of women working for wages over the same period increased from 17.4 percent in 1890 to 18.8 percent in 1900.[9] In virtually all cases, women and children worked solely because their families needed the money to survive. Most female workers were young women between school and marriage, but large numbers of Black women, whose husbands received very low wages, worked outside the home. By 1900 several states (including Pennsylvania) had already prohibited child labor; but the laws were not enforced, and needy parents routinely lied about the ages of children who needed to work. Statistics were still scarce and approximate, but they belied assumptions of universal prosperity. The newly created United States Industrial Commission published in 1900 figures which showed that between 60 and 88 percent of Americans were poor or very poor.[10]

Although millions remained poor and businesses seemed to be getting bigger and more powerful every day, the temptation to leave well enough alone was great. In the midst of the welcome prosperity, tampering with the motors of success seemed little short of folly. Moderates like President Roosevelt carefully distinguished between good trusts that helped the economy and bad trusts that hurt. In December 1901 he warned that the nation's economic health was so fragile that

"extreme care must be taken not to interfere with it in a spirit of rash-
ness or ignorance."[11] In the first few years of the century, however, the
economy was robust and undergoing rapid change.

A MERGER MOVEMENT began in 1897 and peaked in 1904, at which point
more than 300 trusts existed in the United States with an aggregate
capitalization of $7,249,343,500. This $7 billion represented a stagger-
ing figure at the time, when even skilled, well-paid workers in trade
unions earned about $1,000 per year. Consolidation had actually begun
just before the Panic of 1893, but only the rare company was capitalized
at $10,000,000 or more in the early 1890s. By 1902 almost 200 cor-
porations were worth that much. The growth of very large companies
was ever more striking. In 1905 less than 1 percent of all manufacturers made $1,000,000 worth of products per year, but those corporations
held more than one-third of the nation's capital and employed more
than one-fourth of all workers in manufacturing. In 1909 just under 5
percent of manufacturing firms employed 62 percent of all workers in
manufacturing, and the 100 largest corporations controlled one-fourth
of the total assets of all the nation's industries. During the first great
merger wave of 1897–1904 one-third of all companies disappeared
through mergers.[12]

Large-scale production and distribution promised to reduce the
costs of production, increase wages, and lower prices. American industry was amazingly productive, thanks in part to the "principles of scientific management," the title of a book by the industrial engineer
Frederick W. Taylor published in 1911 that was popular among managers of large factories. His time-and-motion studies reduced the manufacturing process to a series of discrete steps, which workers performed
repeatedly and quickly to the rhythms of machines. One objective of
Taylorism was to reduce labor costs by making workers produce more
quickly for piecework pay, but these changes in the name of efficiency
also concentrated decisions about the production process in the hands
of managers rather than workers. For both reasons workers universally
resented Taylorism.

AS SHIPPERS OF immense quantities of goods, the trusts were often able to dictate their terms to railroads and smaller competitors. Although rebates and discrimination in railroad shipping rates had been outlawed repeatedly on the state level, these practices were fundamental to the growth of giant corporations like Standard Oil. Smaller businesses complained about rebates and kickbacks that the railroads gave the trusts. Attempts to regulate railroad rates (in the Elkins Act of 1903, to prohibit rebates, and the Hepburn Act of 1906, the first effective federal regulation of railroad rates, for instance) were seen as one way to reduce the power of the trusts, whose control was interconnected. Railroad companies in the United States ostensibly numbered in the hundreds, but seven groups of capitalists controlled 85 percent of the 228,000 miles of railroad in 1906. These seven were organized into four groups, the two most powerful of which were the Morgan-Hill-Vanderbilt-Pennsylvania and the Harriman-Gould-Rock Island.

Businesses operating on a very large scale produced enormous profits, which were used to acquire competitors or to enter other fields of enterprise but not to raise wages. Standard Oil used its profits to found the National City Bank of New York, the richest bank in the country in the early years of the century, which in turn controlled several other big banks. The powerful new banks not only provided capital for industrial production but also invested enormous sums in the stock market. The financial crisis of May 9, 1901, was the result of speculation in the stocks of the Northern Pacific Railroad, mostly on the part of National City Bank.

John Moody, a close observer of the financial world, saw that early in the century what were termed the trusts or the interests consisted of an intricate network of large and small capitalists, all of them sharing interlocking directorates and depending ultimately on one of the two giants who controlled the national economy. John D. Rockefeller ran Standard Oil and the National City Bank; banker J. P. Morgan controlled the House of Morgan, which included the bank of J. P. Morgan and Company, with close ties to European finance. The Morgan company also controlled several other banks: the First National Bank, the National Bank of Commerce, the First National Bank of Chicago, the Liberty National Bank, the Chase National Bank, the Hanover National Bank, and the Astor National Bank. In addition, Morgan controlled important interests in insurance, another industry with large amounts of capital invested in other ventures, including the three largest insurance companies in the country: New York Life, Mutual of New York, and the Equitable Life Assurance Society.

Morgan was the most obvious beneficiary of the early-twentieth-century shift of economic power from industrialists (the manufacturers of goods, or industrial capitalism) to bankers (the suppliers of money and financial services, or finance capitalism) during the process of mergers in which bankers realized huge profits by organizing combinations of manufacturers. The age of mergers produced a new symbol of power, J. P. Morgan, who replaced the steel manufacturer Andrew Carnegie. Like other big bankers, Morgan retained financial control of the trusts he assembled through mergers, the biggest and best known of which was the United States Steel Corporation, which absorbed the Carnegie plants.

ORGANIZED IN 1901, the U.S. Steel Corporation was a vast holding company with 11 huge constituent companies that in turn controlled nearly 800 plants and more than 60 percent of all steel production in the United States. The handiwork of Morgan and Judge Elbert H. Gary (after whom the steel-producing city of Gary, Indiana, is named), the new company issued stock worth $1,402,846,000. The underlying value of the company, however, was $682,000,000. Fully half the value of the stock was "water"—that is, it had no equivalent value in factories or other physical possessions. Some of the water in U.S. Steel stock represented future profits to be won through the strength of the combination in the marketplace; some of it represented fees for promotion of the new stock. Morgan made more than $7,000,000 for putting together U.S. Steel, and the constituent firms paid $63,000,000 in commissions. Having entered the steel business in 1873 with $700,000 capital, Carnegie left with $400,000,000 in cash and U.S. Steel Corporation bonds.[13] The advantages of operating on a large scale seemed worth the expense.

In railroads and manufacturing, combinations were attractive to managers because they permitted more freedom of action, not only in setting prices but in controlling costs, including labor. For managers it was very easy to draw a causal connection between the wave of business consolidation that had begun in 1897 and the prosperity of the 1900s. John W. Gates, a New York financier, called every new trust "a step upward for the social advancement of the laborer."[14] The anthracite coal strike of 1902, the most serious labor disturbance of the decade, illustrated the relationship among big business, labor, and the public good.

ANTHRACITE (HARD) COAL, one of the United States's most valuable industrial resources, exceeded the value of all products except pig iron and bituminous (soft) coal, which was used to produce the coke that ran blast furnaces. Because many cities, including New York, banned the burning of high-sulfur bituminous coal for health reasons, anthracite coal provided the nation's basic source of heat.

This widely used energy source came from nine counties in the Wyoming Valley of northeastern Pennsylvania, around the town of Wilkes-Barre. Early in this century coal miners were a heterogeneous lot; almost half were Slavs or Italians, though the older Irish, British, German, and native-born White mine population held the better jobs and led the union. In 1890 two competing unions, one of which had been a district assembly of the Knights of Labor, had organized the United Mine Workers (UMW). Unusually democratic, the UMW was from the beginning an industrial union that organized skilled and unskilled workers throughout the mining industry and admitted miners regardless of their religion, race, or national origin. In 1897 the UMW had launched an organizing campaign in the anthracite collieries of Pennsylvania that had sparked a confrontation between miners and deputies in Luzerne County, in which deputies had killed 24 unarmed miners.

Three years later the union demanded a wage increase and a broad set of reforms. The owners' refusal to meet the UMW's demands had triggered a strike that ended quickly, thanks to the intervention of Senator Mark Hanna and the Industrial Arbitration Department of the National Civic Federation. Beginning in Chicago in 1893 as a study group to promote better relations between labor and management, the Civic Federation had become a national organization in 1900. It brought together thoroughly respectable businessmen and political leaders like Hanna and Secretary of the Treasury Lyman J. Gage with members of the conservative wing of the labor movement, such as AFL president Samuel Gompers and UMW head John Mitchell. Born in Illinois of Scots-Irish background, Mitchell had belonged to the Knights of Labor before taking over leadership of the UMW in 1899. Both men came in for a good deal of criticism from more class-conscious unionists and socialists for joining the representatives of capital.[15]

In 1900 Mitchell's ties to the National Civic Federation eased relations with Hanna, who in turn approached J. P. Morgan, who headed the Morgan-Hill-Vanderbilt–Pennsylvania group of railroads that controlled the mining of anthracite coal. Hanna convinced Morgan that a coal strike would threaten Republican candidates running in the coming election, Morgan agreed to allow the miners a 10 percent raise, and the strike ended.

The agreement of 1900 expired in March 1901, and again Hanna helped extend it to April 1902. This time the UMW demanded a 20 percent increase in wages, an eight-hour day on account of the dangerous nature of mine work, fair weighing, and recognition of the union. The mineowners, led by George F. Baer—president of the Philadelphia and Reading Coal and Iron Company, the Lehigh and Wilkes-Barre Coal and Iron Company, and the Temple Iron Company—refused to bargain with the miners.

From the beginning the union agreed to submit its demands to arbitration, so sure were its members of the justice of their cause. Miners explained that they could not maintain a decent standard of living because rising prices had more than consumed their previous raise.

On the other side, Baer insisted that a wage increase would raise coal prices, cut consumption, lead to another depression, and was therefore impossible. Besides, he added, "anthracite mining is a business, and not a religious, sentimental or academic proposition." Baer was convinced that the miners "don't suffer . . . why they can't even speak English."[16] In May 150,000 miners struck the anthracite coal mines. Soon 25,000 miners had left the coalfields permanently to seek work elsewhere in the United States or to return to Europe.

The strike continued through the summer, as mineowners refused even to acknowledge the need to bargain and miners would not give up. Coal that ordinarily cost $5 to $6 per ton rose to $14. In the pages of his New York daily, publisher William Randolph Hearst demanded that the federal government prosecute the mineowning, coal-carrying railroads under the Sherman Antitrust Act. In late July and early August disturbances occurred in Wilkes-Barre, causing the loss of life and raising the specter of more violence to come. In July Baer still refused to negotiate with the miners. Defending his right to set wages and conditions of work, he wrote a letter full of hubris, which reached the press and inspired Hearst to call him "Divine Right Baer": "The rights and interests of the laboring man will be protected and cared for—not by the labor agitators, but by the Christian men to whom God has given control of the property rights of the country, and upon the successful management of which so much depends. . . . Pray earnestly that right may triumph, always remembering that the Lord God Ominipotent still reigns, and that His reign is one of law and order and not of violence and crime."[17] With no end to the strike in sight, the coal shortage worsened, and by September coal was at $20 per ton in New York.

A sense of impending crisis spread in the coalfields, where minor altercations continued to occur between strikers and strikebreakers, prompting the governor of Pennsylvania to send state troops into the area to protect strikebreakers entering the mines. As winter approached, mayors and governors in the Northeast urged the President to settle the strike.

Roosevelt realized that a coal famine would cause serious suffering, perhaps violence that in the end would cost him politically. Many Republicans worried that their party, which the popular mind associated with big business, would be hurt by what Senator Henry Cabot Lodge called the "insensate folly" of the mineowners.[18] The President approached Mark Hanna, and the two of them persuaded the coal company heads to meet union officials at the White House on October 3. With his plea for fair play, John Mitchell of the UMW impressed Roosevelt deeply, but the mineowners remained intransigent, professing shock that the President would ask them to deal with "a set of outlaws." Baer reiterated his view that "the duty of the hour is not to waste time negotiating with the fomenters of this anarchy and insolent defiance of law, but to do as was done in [the Civil War], restore the majesty of law."[19] Roosevelt accused the mineowners of courting anarchy and told Hanna that left to themselves, the owners would have long ago provoked "socialistic action."[20]

As fuel shortages forced school and factory closings in the fall and negotiations remained at a standstill, the President faced increased pressure to end the strike. A conference of mayors and governors meeting in Detroit passed resolutions favoring government operation of the mines, and newspapers across the country urged Roosevelt to break up the railroads' control of the coal mines, nationalize the mines, or institute a permanent and compulsory arbitration mechanism, all of which represented the very "socialistic action" the President sought to avoid.

On the strength of what he called a general outburst of wrath, Roosevelt prepared to send federal troops into the coalfields to operate the mines, but not before playing one last card. He had his secretary of war, Elihu Root, who kept close ties with Wall Street, send a letter to J. P. Morgan outlining the plan to send in troops should the owners refuse to negotiate. On October 11 Root and Morgan met on the financier's yacht on the Hudson River, and Morgan agreed to speak to the owners. Morgan's word worked wonders. The owners agreed to arbitration, and the miners returned to work late in October. Roosevelt appointed a private coal commission that investigated conditions in the collieries. The coal companies had contended that paying higher wages was impossible because any additional operating costs would bankrupt them. But counsel for the United Mine Workers—two liberal lawyers known as defenders of unpopular causes, Clarence Darrow and Henry Demarest Lloyd—presented a different story to the coal commission. A handful of railroads, they said, owned the coal mines, and one man, J. P. Morgan, controlled those railroads, making the anthracite coal mining industry a monopoly. The coal companies could cry poverty because on paper their expenses, especially for shipping, appeared crippling. While the railroads billed the coal companies for enormous freight charges (which far outran shipping costs in the bituminous coalfields), the joint ownership of mines and railroads meant that the railroads made generous profits on coal mining that did not appear on the books of the coal-mining companies. Yet the profits ultimately accrued to the mine-railroad owners despite the seeming precariousness of the mining business.

The UMW pressed the coal commission to question evidence that the coal companies had presented pertaining to wages. Mineowners claimed that anthracite miners earned $400 to $450 per year, purportedly enough for a thrifty miner to support his family, buy his own house, and put a little money away for his old age. But the union claimed, with justice, that because at least $600 was necessary to keep a family out of poverty, miners—even accepting the company figures—could not support their families alone. Children would have to leave school to work, and wives needed to take in boarders. The union further disputed the company figures for miners' annual earnings, claiming that when layoffs were taken into account, yearly wages amounted to more like $370, out of which miners had to provide their own mining supplies, such as explosives, which they had to buy at high-priced company stores. Mine companies often paid wages in scrip, forcing miners to purchase everything at company stores.

The commission visited the mining region and saw the miners' living and working conditions firsthand. Speaking of the hut where a Slav miner's family lived, one commissioner remarked that "this is almost as bad as going down a gangway in the mines."[21] Commissioners discovered also that the companies decided not only how much to pay miners for a ton of coal, but also how much a "ton" of coal weighed; what was called a ton of coal varied from mine to mine, from 2,200 to more than 3,000 (instead of the accurate 2,000) pounds. In mines where workers were paid by the carful, the cars were mammoth.

The commissioners learned that the 10 percent raise of 1900 often had not been paid as a straight increase in wages. The owners had reduced by 7½ percent the cost of gunpowder—which the miners supplied at their own expense—as wages were raised 2½ percent. Miners were among the worst paid of American workers, yet mining was one of the most dangerous of occupations. The 148,000 employees in the nine counties of the anthracite field had suffered 513 fatal accidents in 1901.[22] In an industry where deaths and injuries were commonplace, workmen's compensation did not exist. Two Hungarian widows testified that their sons, who were breaker boys, had not received their pay until the company had recovered the house rent their husbands had owed when mining accidents killed them.

Most of the boys in the mine towns and camps worked in what were called the breakers. After leaving the mine, the coal was hoisted up to a cupola, where it was ground into small pieces. It then dropped down a series of chutes, the breakers, beside which sat boys on ladders, picking out the slate and other waste matter as coal dust poured over them—and into their lungs—constantly.

Mother Mary Harris Jones, an outspoken, Irish-born, seventy-two-year-old union organizer familiar with mining families, remembered helping miners' wives bury their children. "The mothers could scarce conceal their relief at the little ones' deaths," she wrote. The mother was invariably pregnant with another child, "destined, if a boy, for the breakers; if a girl, for the silk mills." Indeed, in the silk, underwear, and hosiery mills of Reading, Scranton, Allentown, and Wilkes-Barre, well over half of the employees were under twenty-one.

In the silk mills, workers under sixteen—mostly girls—averaged less than $130 per year; in the hosiery mills, a little over $140. The children of the breakers and the mills were stooped and skinny, often missing thumbs and fingers and always giving the impression of being older than they were. Only when they had been maimed so seriously that they could no longer work did such children attend school. "And you scarcely blamed the children for preferring mills and mines," said Mother Jones. "The schools were wretched, poorly taught, the lessons dull."[23]

Clarence Darrow asked the commission, was "any man so blind that he does not know why that anthracite region is dotted with silk mills? They went there because the miners were there. Every mill in that region is a testimony to the fact that the wages that [the mineowners] pay are so low that you sell your boys to be slaves of the breaker and your girls to be slaves in the mills."[24]

Late in March 1903 the coal commission made its award, to remain in effect until 1906. Some miners gained a 10 percent wage increase; others got reduced working hours. Owners were not to discriminate against union men in rehiring, but the United Mine Workers did not win recognition as the miners' representative. Despite lack of recognition— which was not achieved until the European War—the union counted the award a victory and accepted it. Without the active intervention of the President in the coal strike, even these limited gains would have eluded the miners. For the first time in United States history, a President had entered a labor dispute on other than the employers' side.

Theodore Roosevelt and Mark Hanna collaborated fruitfully on the anthracite strike, convinced that repressing unions merely sowed the seeds of revolution. Both men saw themselves as bulwarks against the upheavals that reactionaries like George Baer would provoke through industrial tyranny. But beyond the platitudes of labor relations and the needs of business, Roosevelt and Hanna parted ways.

HANNA REPRESENTED the prevailing philosophy of government in the very early 1900s in which representatives in state and federal legislatures protected the interests of businesses rather than individuals. (Local politics sometimes reflected the concerns of working-class voters, however.) Hanna represented the Rockefeller interests in the United

States Senate until his death in 1904. His successor as the symbol of the power of great corporations in the Senate was Nelson Aldrich of Rhode Island.[25]

The Senate functioned as an extension of the business relationships that controlled state politics because state legislatures elected U.S. senators, and senators thereby owed their political power to various moneyed interests. William Allen White, who even in his most liberal phase was never an enemy of capital, listed the "interests": "In Kansas, it was the railroads. In western Massachusetts, it was textiles. In eastern Massachusetts it was the banks. In New York, it was amalgamated industry. In Montana, it was copper. But the power which developed and controlled any state went to New York for its borrowed capital, and New York controlled the United States Senate. . . . Only a minority of the people of the United States had any control over the United States Senate. And that minority was interested in its own predatory designs."[26]

Not surprisingly, some observers of the political system concluded that it had been consciously designed to frustrate the will of the people. Frederic C. Howe, a liberal reformer from Cleveland and a protégé of reform Mayor Tom Johnson, saw that politics required management by people who could give it their full time. Howe concluded that when the U.S. Constitution was being drafted, Alexander Hamilton and his rich conservative allies had intentionally divided power and inserted checks and balances so that only professionals could master the intricacies of the machinery. Ordinary citizens, busy making a living, lacked both the time and the expertise to make politics work on their behalf. Great corporations, however, had the money to buy the time of professional politicians. The rare man who was independently wealthy and who chose to enter politics could, in effect, buy himself. Like his friend Henry Cabot Lodge (and his nemesis William Randolph Hearst), Theodore Roosevelt could afford to be his own man.

Roosevelt believed that the success of the Republican party depended upon its playing an intermediate role between ultraconservatives and radicals, which included most organized labor, socialists, William Jennings Bryan, and even Republican Governor and Senator from Wisconsin Robert M. La Follette. Over time Roosevelt's views shifted somewhat, although he remained convinced that he was saving the country from extremists of both sides. Just as Roosevelt would not ignore pressure to settle the coal strike, so he also acted on clamor from the Northwest against the formation of a railroad trust that would monopolize rail traffic from Chicago to Washington state. The Northern Securities case was the first of several antitrust actions that earned Roosevelt the reputation of a trustbuster.

COGNIZANT OF public concern over the power of trusts, but opposed to rash meddling with big business out of hatred or fear, Roosevelt perceived a need for measured antitrust action. Until 1902 the Sherman Antitrust Act had served most spectacularly to convict Eugene V. Debs and to intimidate organized labor. It took labor more than two decades (from 1892 to 1914) of painstaking effort to gain exemption from antitrust action, while the business trusts were virtually immune to such prosecution. Roosevelt, however, was able to reach the most flagrant of the trusts through executive action.

In February 1902 Roosevelt ordered the United States attorney general to prosecute the Northern Securities Company, a recently formed giant holding company of railroads dominated by J. P. Morgan, the Rockefeller interests, James J. Hill, and Edward Harriman. These were the behemoths of the financial world, and the rumor of the merger had already triggered a severe stock market crisis in May 1901. The stock of the Northern Securities Company was heavily watered, meaning that in order to realize a profit, it would need to impose high shipping fees, which as a monopoly it could set with impunity. The governors of several western states that would pay those fees had met to support Minnesota's complaint before the United States Supreme Court, which the United States Department of Justice supported. In 1904 the Court ordered the dissolution of the Northern Securities Company.

Despite warm public response to Roosevelt's prosecution of the Northern Securities Company, the President proceeded cautiously. He instituted one other suit in 1902—against the beef trust—and none during 1903 or 1904, then, after his reelection, several in 1906 and 1907, including suits against the most visible trusts in the land: Du Pont, Standard Oil, and the American Tobacco Company. Court rulings forced the giants to break into smaller companies that still qualified as big business.

Roosevelt's deliberate pace reflected a split in public opinion. While people who did not benefit directly from mergers and huge corporations were frightened by the economic and political power they represented, few dared find fault while memories of hard times were still fresh. Prosperity presented a welcome change, and for those who could afford to pay higher prices, relatively peaceful labor relations more than offset the rise in the cost of living. Families who could not easily absorb higher prices sent children to work a little earlier.

Political protest in these years was muted. With the virtual self-destruction of the People's party and the deaths of Edward Bellamy and Henry George in the late 1890s, the critical parties and movements of the 1880s and 1890s faded. There were still Populists—Tom Watson ran for President on the Populist ticket in 1904—but for the most part, women and men who had been Populists supported the two major parties, dropped out of politics, or became Socialists. Although they no longer constituted a united third party, a few scattered voices spoke up for political reform.

In addition to political reformers, two groups outside government attempted to influence political thought and action, the popular press (including muckraking magazines) and organized labor. Together with those who had begun offering remedies in the nineteenth century, they nudged Americans away from complacency. But the first few years of the century were time in the wilderness for seekers after social justice.

AMONG THE DISSENTERS from regular party politics was Tom Johnson, mayor of Cleveland, whose political education derived from Henry George. In the 1870s, before he was thirty, Johnson had made a fortune in streetcar companies. Then he read *Progress and Poverty* in 1883 and converted to George's egalitarian philosophy. In the mid-1880s Johnson sold his streetcar lines and went into local politics as a reformer. He ran successfully for mayor of Cleveland in 1901, calling for a three-cent streetcar fare, public improvements, and equal taxation of individuals, businesses, and utilities. During his nine years in office Cleveland had clean, well-lit streets, public baths and comfort stations, market inspections, free parks, pure water—and endless controversy.

The equalization of taxes was Johnson's fundamental reform. When he took office, small taxpayers were being charged 100 percent of the taxes they owed according to law, while utilities were paying only 10 to 20 percent. More than half the property and franchises in the city paid no taxes whatever. Johnson established a "Tax School" run by Newton D. Baker—who later served as Woodrow Wilson's secretary of war—to demonstrate how big businesses profited by corrupting public officials in order illegally to lower their taxes.

Although he was not a Socialist, Johnson's attack on what he called the system of public service grants and unfair taxation earned him a reputation as a Socialist, demagogue, or eccentric out to ruin the city of Cleveland. Throughout his controversial nine years as mayor Johnson was the target of more than fifty injunctions. By the time he was voted out in 1909, however, several other cities, notably Toledo, Ohio, had elected reform mayors who, following in Johnson's footsteps, tried to make public service franchises work for the public good. Reform mayors were part of a halting movement away from standing-pat and letting-well-enough-alone politics. One state with sufficient centers of local reform to elect an independent governor was Wisconsin.

AFTER HAVING SERVED one term in the U.S. House of Representatives in the mid-1880s, Robert M. La Follette, a maverick Republican, won the Wisconsin gubernatorial election of 1900. He called for direct primaries, instead of easily manipulated party caucuses, and for taxation of railroads based on property, instead of earnings susceptible to misrepresentation. His insistence that railroads pay their fair share of state taxes paralleled Tom Johnson's concerns on the municipal level. "Fighting Bob," as La Follette was called affectionately, was reelected governor in

1902 and 1904. In 1906 he returned as a senator to Washington, where
he became one of the most respected reform politicians of his time, running for President in 1912 and 1924. La Follette's motto was "The will
of the people shall be the law of the land," and throughout his career
he served the interests of consumers, taxpayers, workers, and farmers,
whether in Wisconsin or Washington.

La Follette was the first of the insurgent politicians (Republicans
who rejected the standpattism of big business Republicanism) to reach
the Senate, and he stood out among the urbane representatives of
wealth. "I think if I had been a wild boar, led about by Mrs. La Follette
with a rope fastened to my hind leg, as a pair, we would not have been
more observed," he remarked to his friends.[27] In the Senate, dominated
by business-oriented conservatives like his Wisconsin colleague John
Coit Spooner, La Follette favored a graduated income tax and stringent regulation of railroads. In 1908 he gained other insurgent col-
leagues: Joseph L. Bristow of Kansas, Coe I. Crawford of South Dakota,
and Albert Cummins of Iowa, and by 1909 and 1910 this minority had
grown strong enough to upset politics-as-usual by dividing Republicans during debate on the Payne-Aldrich tariff.

AT THE SAME TIME that insurgent Republicans were confronting standpat
Republicanism, power relationships were also shifting in the Democratic
party. In 1896 William Jennings Bryan had seized party leadership from
conservatives, represented by New York goldbugs like Grover Cleveland
(who retired to Princeton, New Jersey, after leaving the presidency).
Bryan, the representative of the new constituencies that emerged from
the Great Upheaval, had committed Democrats to free silver and anti-
imperialism but had lost the elections of 1896 and 1900. After the second defeat Bryan had returned to his home in Lincoln, Nebraska, where
he began publishing a weekly newspaper, *The Commoner*, in which
he supported many of the labor and reform ideas that he had championed in the 1890s: opposition to trusts, direct election of U.S. senators,
a graduated income tax, prohibition of the use of injunctions in strikes,
woman suffrage, and anti-imperialism. He gained a fairly broad follow-

ing, but within his party his prestige suffered as the Democratic leadership accommodated to an era of staying the course.

Facing the presidential election of 1904 and seeking a winning strategy, the conservative managers of the Democratic party copied standpat Republicans by nominating a conservative goldbug unsullied by Populism, the chief justice of the New York Court of Appeals, Alton B. Parker. Roosevelt dealt Parker a stinging defeat. By virtue of Parker's failure, Bryan regained control of his party, claiming that voters had repudiated Democratic standpattism. Once again at the head of the Democrats, Bryan continued to press for what he called radical remedies, and he was Roosevelt's most telling critic on foreign as well as domestic matters.

Bryan had been an anti-imperialist since the Spanish-American War, and his convictions deepened after he and his wife, Mary, had made a trip around the world in 1905 and 1906. In Asia the Bryans saw European colonialism in practice and learned that it first and foremost served the interests of the colonizing power, not the conquered peoples. Before the Peace Congress of the Interparliamentary Union in London, Bryan deplored "intolerable expenditures on armaments" and supported the nonviolent arbitration of international disputes.[28]

Returning to New York in August 1906, Bryan placed himself squarely in opposition to war, colonialism, and Rooseveltian militarism as expressed in the big navy policy. In a list of what he called nonpartisan questions—which were very partisan indeed—Bryan called for the popular election of U.S. senators, a graduated income tax, the eight-hour workday, and the arbitration of labor disputes. He provoked a furor by advocating federal government ownership of interstate railroads and municipal ownership of utilities, including streetcar systems. Few Democrats—not to mention Republicans—were willing to go that far, and Bryan subsequently backed down from these advanced positions, calling them long-term, not immediate, goals.

Governmental ownership of railroads and utilities was a staple demand of the Socialist party of America, organized by Eugene V. Debs, Morris Hillquit, Algie M. Simons, and Victor Berger in 1901. The older

Socialist Labor party, founded in 1877 out of one faction of the Marxist Workingmen's party, was headed by Daniel De Leon in the early
twentieth century and remained small, sectarian, and insistent on class
conflict and revolution. While the Socialist Labor party held to the
fundamentals of Marxism—the inevitability of class struggle, the need
for revolution, and the ultimate dictatorship of the proletariat—Debs's
Socialist party welcomed all sorts of people who called themselves
Socialists, most of whom were by no means Marxists. The Socialist
party immediately began winning adherents and a few local elections,
especially in Massachusetts and Oklahoma, growing from 10,000 to
23,000 dues-paying members within its first five years. The Socialist
movement became increasingly well served by periodicals, the most
popular of which was the Girard, Kansas, *Appeal to Reason,* whose circulation grew from about 30,000 in 1900 to nearly 300,000 in 1906, and
whose publisher, Julius Wayland, stressed the compatibility of socialism and American values (like individualism) and saw the membership of Protestant clergymen in the Socialist party as a positive sign.
The *Appeal to Reason* offered a critique of the injustices of American
capitalism, all of which socialism would cure. These years also saw the
creation of a new syndicalist national union, the Industrial Workers of
the World, whose rhetoric in the 1910s attracted attention nationally
and also split the Socialist party.

During the era of "noteworthy prosperity," political critics like Tom
Johnson, Robert M. La Follette, William Jennings Bryan, and Eugene
V. Debs questioned the fairness of the status quo and lectured indefati-
gably. But they were unable to reach great masses of people on a daily
basis. The popular daily press, also known as the yellow press, reached
millions every day and did not hesitate to criticize the political and
economic order.

THE POPULAR PRESS was an innovation of the late nineteenth century,
during which newspapers evolved from speaking for political parties,
with the financial support of parties, to making nonpartisan profits
through advertising and wide circulation. The new-style daily journal-

ism employed Linotypes and modern presses to reduce costs and used photographs, color, and cartoons to make penny newspapers attractive. These inexpensive, exciting, and outspoken daily papers defended the urban masses and were more concerned with pursuing the interests of their audience than with pretensions of respectability. The name "yellow press" came from a popular comic strip called "The Yellow Kid," which appeared originally in the *New York World*.

A Hungarian immigrant, Civil War veteran, lawyer, and St. Louis newspaper publisher, Joseph Pulitzer, bought the *New York Evening World* in 1887, transforming it into a large-circulation daily and adding a Sunday supplement featuring comic strips printed in color. With banner headlines shouting the news of murders and outrages, the unabashedly sensational *World* was newswriting as popular entertainment.

Because the *World*'s huge, working-class readership did not benefit from standing pat, the *World* talked reform. Like Bryan and his followers, the *World* was anti-imperialist, an attitude that Theodore Roosevelt, an archexpansionist, found irritating. The *World* reflected the strength of public antiwar sentiment and severely curbed (without curing) the President's overseas ambitions. After Roosevelt had baldly exploited nationalist sentiment in the Panamanian isthmus and forced a protectorate on the new republic of Panama in 1903, the *World* accused him of having engineered the revolution expressly to seize the Canal Zone.

One of the *World*'s most famous crusades exposed the managers of the Equitable Life Assurance Society, whom the *World* discovered in 1905 to be speculating with policy funds for their own private gain. The insurance industry, full of prestige and dignity, had long appeared above the sharp financial practices that increasingly typified the new age. But according to the *World*, Equitable managers were "gambling with the people's money," and the newspaper launched a full-scale investigation that spread to the Mutual Life and the New York Life Insurance companies. Editor Frank I. Cobb wrote a series of stinging editorials that led to an official state investigation (the Armstrong Commission), headed by a patrician Republican corporation lawyer, Charles Evans Hughes, who was not associated with the Republican machine.

The Hughes investigation substantiated the *World*'s charges and showed, further, that the insurance companies had for decades maintained large political slush funds, which they used to block legislation they considered inexpedient and to encourage passage of laws favorable to the industry. Public outrage elected Hughes governor of New York and prompted the New York legislature to regulate the insurance industry closely.[29]

The other popular New York newspaper belonged to William Randolph Hearst, son of a California mining millionaire. Hearst had copied Pulitzer's methods in his father's *San Francisco Examiner* with great financial success. In attacks on the Southern Pacific Railroad—California's main economic power and dictator of the state's Republican politics—Hearst perfected the techniques he took to New York: sensationalism, professed concern for the underdog, and opposition to entrenched money power. He also took to New York three of his prize *Examiner* journalists: Edward Markham, Ambrose Bierce, and Winifred Black.

In 1895 Hearst had bought the *New York Morning Journal* and raided Pulitzer's staff. He even hired away the cartoonist who drew "The Yellow Kid." Pulitzer started a rival "Yellow Kid" strip, and for a time both papers featured the comic character. The acquisitive Hearst meanwhile bought other newspapers in Chicago, Los Angeles, and Boston.

In the campaign of 1896 the *Journal* was William Jennings Bryan's leading supporter in New York City; the staid *New York Times* and Pulitzer's *World* opposed free silver. Dollar for dollar, Hearst matched the $40,000 his readers contributed to Bryan. The *Journal* moved into municipal politics, blocking the city's award of a gas franchise that would have raised the cost of household gas and ice. The gas franchise stymied, the *Journal* pretended that it alone had protested against the collusion of machine politics and business, claiming all the credit for the reform in a banner headline: WHILE OTHERS TALK THE JOURNAL ACTS. (In fact, the gas franchise had provoked a good deal of public outrage, leading to the creation of a commission to regulate gas companies whose counsel was Charles Evans Hughes, in his first public role.) During the summer the *World*'s "Fresh Air Fund" took poor children on excursions to the country, and the *Journal* took them to the beach. Seeing another need for public service, the *Journal* even ran day care centers for the poor.

The *New York World* and *Journal* were the best-known crusading newspapers, but other newspapers also took the side of the "people" against the "interests." In the 1890s the *New York Commercial Advertiser* had featured the work of Lincoln Steffens, who became a premier muckraker early in the twentieth century; of Hutchins Hapgood and Norman Hapgood, who pioneered in the use of lower-class figures in literature; and of Abraham Cahan, later well known as the editor of New York's *Jewish Daily Forward* and author of the novel *The Rise of David Levinsky* (1917). The *Boston Globe, Philadelphia Record, Baltimore Sun* and *Evening News*, and the papers of the Scripps-McRae chain brought popular journalism to other parts of the country. A self-proclaimed "damned old crank" in rebellion against society, Edward W. Scripps saw himself as the champion of the great masses who were neither rich nor well educated. He retired to a ranch near San Diego at thirty-six, setting editorial policy in California, where he wore ranch clothes and cowboy boots, played poker, smoked countless cigars, and drank, he said, a gallon of whiskey a day. He died in 1926 at the age of seventy-one, worth $50,000,000.

Unlike his fellow publishers, William Randolph Hearst added electoral politics to journalism, financing his political ventures out of his own pocket, thanks to the millions he had inherited from his parents. Early in 1899 he had published a platform that set out his goals: public ownership of public franchises; direct election of U.S. senators; the initiative, referendum, and recall; and the improvement of public schools. He soon added the nationalization of coal mines, railroads, and telegraphs to the list. Throughout the period before the European War,

Hearst gave strong support to organized labor and the poor, and he urged the AFL to go into politics independent of the two major parties. Although Bryan thought labor belonged in the Democratic party, he agreed with much in Hearst's platform. Bryan recommended the *Journal* to his followers and spoke highly of the publisher. The Socialist *Appeal to Reason* also praised the publisher often, because Hearst's platform agreed with that of the Socialist party in several regards. Populist Tom Watson saw eye to eye with Hearst on many issues as well and dedicated his *Life and Times of Thomas Jefferson* (1903) to the publisher.

In 1902 Hearst was elected to the first of two terms in Congress. Although rarely present, he introduced bills to enact several reforms: an eight-hour day for government employees, federal aid to highways, parcel post delivery, direct election of U.S. senators, increased powers for the Interstate Commerce Commission, and the criminalizing of railroad rebates. Hearst remained in Congress until 1907, his eye all the while trained on the presidency.

His nomination seconded by reform lawyer Clarence Darrow, Hearst failed to win the backing of the conservative leaders of the Democratic party in 1904 because he was too much like Bryan, for which reason Bryan himself offered Hearst only lukewarm support. That fall Hearst founded the Municipal Ownership League, whose nomination for mayor of New York he accepted in October 1905. With broad labor and reform backing, Hearst's campaign recalled the Henry George campaign of 1886 and demanded an end to the machine domination of Tammany Hall and its corrupt allocation of public works contracts. George's campaign manager came out enthusiastically for Hearst, who also had the support of several women's groups, including a Women's League for Hearst, headed by Harriot Stanton Blatch, daughter of suffragist Elizabeth Cady Stanton. Hearst lost narrowly, but his astonishing show of strength as an independent indicated that workingmen were not irrevocably wedded to the Democratic party.

As the candidate of the Democratic party and the Independence

League, the reincarnation of the Municipal Ownership League, Hearst ran for governor in 1906 against the popular lawyer Charles Evans Hughes, who was also known as a reformer, albeit of a less prolabor cast. Desperately supporting Hughes, whom he saw as the representative of "decent citizenship," Theodore Roosevelt worried a great deal about Hearst's influence among workers, whom Roosevelt considered impressionable and easily misled. Roosevelt interpreted Hearst's popularity as indicating the growth of socialism and radicalism among New York City workers, and in part to offset Hearst's popularity on the Lower East Side, Roosevelt appointed Oscar Straus secretary of commerce and labor, the first Jew to serve in a presidential cabinet. Other thoughtful New Yorkers detested the idea of Hearst as governor of New York as much as Roosevelt, but they recognized that Hearst was drawing upon a legitimate sense of outrage against the way money and politics had worked together to fleece taxpayers.

Hughes won, but the election signaled the end of an era in New York politics. Hughes was an independent figure whom the old-line Republican bosses could not control, and his victory symbolized the triumph of the forces combating the corrupt alliance of businessmen and politicians revealed in the insurance scandals. Although Hearst did not win, his strength showed that maverick candidates could attract a substantial number of votes.

Hearst's *Cosmopolitan* magazine, an important contributor to the movement of investigative journalism known as muckraking, extended his influence beyond readers and voters in New York State. In 1892 S. S. McClure had started a well-known muckraking journal, *McClure's,* which emerged as the premier muckrake magazine when the single issue of January 1903 contained investigations of municipal corruption in Minneapolis by Lincoln Steffens, of the coal strike by Ray Stannard Baker, and one of a series on the Standard Oil Company by Ida Tarbell. McClure called this the beginning of investigative journalism, but the honor belonged to Henry Demarest Lloyd's *Wealth Against Commonwealth,* published in 1894, and to the yellow press.

Corrupt government and the evil doings of capital and labor equally outraged the writers of *McClure's*, who found acquiescence and blame everywhere. The editorial of the January 1903 number of *McClure's* admonished Americans as a whole for the universal trait of lawlessness but offered no remedies. Unlike Hearst, *McClure's* drew up no list of what was to be done. Hearst's *Cosmopolitan* was sharper and more persistent. David Graham Phillips's "Treason of the Senate" series, the most famous and hard-hitting of the muckraking articles, appeared in *Cosmopolitan* in 1906 and impelled an exasperated Theodore Roosevelt to fasten on the movement the "muckraker" label, which he had borrowed from John Bunyan's 1684 allegory *The Pilgrim's Progress.*

A newspaperman who had begun publishing novels in 1901, Phillips was a favorite of reformers. His novels exposed corruption in the high places of business and politics. *The Cost* (1904) and *The Plum Tree* (1905), two of his early books, were near best-sellers that won the endorsement of reform politicians like Tom Watson, Robert M. La Follette, and Mayor Tom Johnson of Cleveland. But the articles on the Senate made Phillips famous.

"The Treason of the Senate" showed in detail that in 1906, as Congress debated the Hepburn bill, the U.S. Senate was not merely an innocuously deliberative body of national government. Each of Phillips's articles began with a quotation from the Constitution that declared supporting enemies of the United States treason. Phillips began the first essay by calling the Senate "the eager, resourceful, indefatigable agent of interests as hostile to the American people as any invading army could be, and vastly more dangerous; interests that manipulate the prosperity produced by all, so that it heaps up riches for the few; interests whose growth and power can only mean the degradation of the people, of the educated into sycophants, of the masses toward serfdom."[30] This message was far from new, but the series presented it to a wide, new, middle-class audience of magazine readers.[31]

Roosevelt's condemnation of investigative journalism, which he criticized for lacking constructive purposes and serving merely to expose the sordid side of public life—raking up muck—had a chilling effect on the genre. Fewer muckraking pieces appeared, as editors began to fear tiring the public and as publishers who persisted in muckraking lost advertising and bank loans. Only Hearst continued the muckraking tradition wholeheartedly.

In 1908 Hearst's Independent party ran Thomas Hisgen of Massachusetts for President and John Temple Graves of Georgia for Vice President, on Hearst's usual platform. Had the Democratic party not written a prolabor platform, the Independent party might well have attracted more labor support. But the AFL preferred the Democrats, whose nominee was once again William Jennings Bryan.

Defeat in 1908 did not halt Hearst's pursuit of office. He ran for mayor of New York again in 1909 as an independent candidate, provoking Wallace Irwin to write "William Also-Randolph Hearst":

> Willie runs a supplement which always beats the news;
> Willie runs for President, with nothing much to lose—
> Willie's always running, whether by request or not,
> Whenever there's a vacancy, it's Willie-on-the-Spot. . . .[32]

As a publisher and a politician, Hearst played an important part in the growing movement of opposition to inequities in the era of noteworthy prosperity.[33] With other yellow newspapers and muckraking magazines, Hearst's *New York Journal* and *Cosmopolitan* magazine exposed ways in which powerful financial groups manipulated politics to their own ends.

The yellow press, the Socialist press, Bryan Democrats, and a growing number of settlement house residents, social workers, and Social Gospelers, who were well educated and articulate, made their ideas about reform accessible to prosperous Americans during the years of prosperity and complacency. But respectability did not mean that political change would necessarily benefit workers. Labor's central concerns—notably prosecution under the Sherman Antitrust Act—were not pressing issues for nonworkers. Labor itself had to act to protect its rights to organize and strike. In so doing, it made Americans of all classes more sensitive to the needs of working people.

"The Bosses of the Senate," an 1889 cartoon by Joseph Keppler. (Library of Congress)

(LEFT) *Samuel Gompers, head of the American Federation of Labor, in about 1902.* (Library of Congress) (RIGHT) *Henry George, author of* Progress and Poverty. (Library of Congress)

(LEFT) *Andrew Carnegie, head of the Carnegie Steel Company.* (National Portrait Gallery, Smithsonian Institution) (RIGHT) *Frances Willard, head of the Woman's Christian Temperance Union.* (Library of Congress / George Grantham Bain Collection)

Thomas E. Watson as the Populist vice presidential candidate in 1896. (Library of Congress)

Jeremiah ("Sockless Jerry") Simpson on the campaign trail, 1892. (Kansas State Historical Society)

William Jennings Bryan as Populist and Democratic presidential candidate in 1896. (Library of Congress)

Florence Kelley (third from left), pioneer of occupational safety. (Library of Congress)

Jane Addams, founder of Hull House settlement in Chicago. (Library of Congress)

Theodore Roosevelt and his men in the Spanish-American War, 1898. (Library of Congress)

The battleship Maine *the morning after the explosion in Havana Harbor, 1898.*
(Library of Congress)

DURING THE EARLY YEARS of the century working men, women, and children had no effective statutory protection to limit working hours, set minimum wages, provide compensation for accidents on the job, old-age pensions, unemployment compensation, or occupational safety. At the same time the incidence of industrial accidents in the United States was the highest in the world. About half a million workers were injured and 30,000 killed at work every year.

The lack of legislative protection reflected not so much a lack of public support for such measures as the collusion of businesses and their representatives in state legislatures and the U.S. Senate to block laws that would bring the state into the workplace or mandate expensive safety measures. Mobilizing support for labor legislation was also difficult as long as AFL President Samuel Gompers feared that the courts would continue to find ways of turning seemingly innocuous laws against labor and he therefore opposed all labor laws except those prohibiting child labor. Preferring "pure and simple" unionism that kept politics and legislation out of the quest for shorter hours and higher wages, Gompers said that he would like to "tell the politicians to keep their hands off and thus to preserve voluntary institutions . . . [for] the most important human justice comes through agencies other than the political."[34] During the 1890s Gompers and the AFL had eschewed political solutions to what they saw as economic problems and barred partisan politics from AFL conventions, even in the heat of the presidential campaign of 1896, which had stirred workingmen like no other.

Without legal protection, workers' only means of influencing working conditions was through agreement with employers, who preferred to make contracts—usually oral—with individual workers. Two generations earlier, before the spread of factories and the rise of corporations, such agreements would have bound two individuals, an employer and a worker. But by the early twentieth century the majority of workers were employed by corporations, which resisted recognizing unions as the representatives of workers as a group, insisting on "freedom of contract" and "individual rights" as fundamental American values, even when the power relationships between one worker and a corporation were manifestly unequal. Managers' associations, such as the National Association of Manufacturers (NAM), revered the concept of individual rights and the workers' freedom to sign whatever contract might be presented them in terms that made the collective power that unions represented seem downright unAmerican. This kind of opposition to union recognition left workers only two means of pressuring employers: the strike and the boycott. But the increasing use of the labor injunction against these courses of action severely narrowed labor's room for maneuver. By the time of the anthracite coal strike in 1902 the unions' right to strike and boycott unfair employers was under concerted attack.

In the 1890s federal judges had used the labor injunction effectively to prosecute strike leaders like Eugene V. Debs for contempt of court under the Sherman Antitrust Act. Strikers were said to have conspired to interfere with interstate commerce by depriving employers of the free use of their property and the income derived from it. At the end of the nineteenth century the injunction became the blanket injunction, which enjoined anyone from committing certain broadly defined acts, such as picketing and trying to keep strikebreakers from going into plants.

Increasingly judges issued injunctions to prevent strikers from parading, demonstrating, or persuading others to stay off the job. In 1902, while addressing strikers in West Virginia, Mother Jones and other UMW organizers were enjoined from marching and assembling near company property. The trial judge sentenced the men to two months in prison for contempt of court because, he said, "the Constitution don't guarantee rights to the citizens to go into the domain of another state and incite the people to violence." The judge made Mother Jones leave West Virginia, advising her to quit agitating and return to the women's work that "the Allwise Being intended her sex should pursue."[35] (Mother Jones had become a labor organizer in 1867, after the death of her husband.) Such injunctions curbed freedom of speech and rendered illegal acts that were not against the law. Opponents came to call this government by injunction because the courts were in effect creating law. Labor injunctions and blanket injunctions weakened the right of workers to strike and boycott when they could do little other than strike and boycott.

The Danbury Hatters' (*Loewe* v. *Lawlor*) and the Buck's Stove and Range cases, both decided by the U.S. Supreme Court, showed how ready courts were to cripple workers' organizations. In 1901 the hatters' union, attempting to organize the Dietrich E. Loewe hat company of Danbury, Connecticut, had called a strike and boycott of Loewe's products. A manufacturers' association financed Loewe's fight against the union, which culminated in a 1908 decision against the union. The Court decided that secondary boycotts (actions by supporters of the hatters) were conspiracies outlawed by the Sherman Antitrust Act and that individual union members must pay court costs and multiple damages amounting to more than $250,000. Although members' savings accounts were attached and foreclosure proceedings were begun on their homes, contributions to the hatters' union and the AFL ultimately paid off the debt. Nonetheless, the prospect of conspiracy trials and personal financial liability threatened to immobilize unions.[36]

In 1906, while the Danbury Hatters' Case was in the courts, the metal polishers' union struck the Buck's Stove and Range Company of St. Louis, whose president, James W. Van Cleave, was also the president of the National Association of Manufacturers. Van Cleave obtained an injunction against the boycott and also against the discussion of the strike in speech and writing. Seeing this sweeping court order as a patently unconstitutional limitation of free speech, the AFL did not respect it, and Samuel Gompers was sentenced to a year in prison for speaking about the boycott. The judge handing down the sentence called Gompers's conduct "utter, rampant, insolent defiance ... unrefined insult, coarse affront, vulgar indignity," and the AFL leaders "rabble," "public enemies," who would substitute "anarchy and riot" for law and order.[37] The sentence and the judge's words shocked Gompers (a conciliatory labor moderate who had long participated in the National Civic Federation, where he hobnobbed with capitalists and their politicians), who felt he had been treated like an anonymous revolutionary. In the

Buck's Stove suit the small business-oriented NAM set out to destroy organized labor and attempted to establish legal principles that would accomplish that goal. The decision, handed down in 1908, upheld the use of the broadest of labor injunctions and promised to accomplish the NAM's purposes.

In these two crucial defeats for labor, the aggressive, court-supported, antiunion campaign of the managers' associations portended the annihilation of workers' organizations and persuaded Gompers and the AFL finally to abandon the tactics they had relied upon since the decline of the Knights of Labor.

EVEN BEFORE the *Buck's Stove* decision, the need for labor to enter politics had surfaced repeatedly. These were a few of labor's reverses: in 1900 Charles E. Littlefield, a Republican congressman from Maine whom the AFL called "an implacable and conspicuous foe of labor legislation," refused to incorporate a labor exemption into his amendment to the Sherman Antitrust Act; the NAM and other management organizations had systematically entered electoral contests against labor, defeating two of the AFL's rare friends in Congress in 1904; and in 1905 the U.S. Supreme Court had struck down a New York law limiting working hours in bakeries to sixty per week.[38]

Bryan Democrats and Socialists inside and outside the AFL harangued the federation for refusing to act politically. Bryan denounced unionists for supporting the antilabor Republican party, while Socialists saw both major parties as handmaidens of capital and enemies of labor. As long as the Sherman Antitrust Act did not contain an exemption for labor, and as long as federal judges—whom Presidents designated and the Senate confirmed—used injunctions to cripple unions, critics of the AFL insisted that the federation's aloofness from politics would continue to prove costly.

On the national level the AFL in 1906 presented Labor's Bill of Grievances to President Roosevelt and the leaders of both houses of Congress, all of whom ignored it completely. Labor's Bill of Grievances listed organized labor's demands: exemption from prosecution under the Sherman Antitrust Act, relief from the wholesale use of injunctions, immigration restriction, the prohibition of competition from convict labor, and an effective eight-hour law.

After the first rebuff the AFL Executive Council took a lesson from the NAM and decided to try to defeat its enemies. For the first time the council issued concrete plans for the election of union delegates to local and state conventions of the two major parties and entered a congressional election in Maine to defeat Littlefield. Several union organizers and Gompers himself made speeches in Maine and distributed leaflets against "Charles E. Littlefield, the enemy of the common people—he is owned and pledged to defend the trusts." Labor's energetic campaigning alarmed Republicans, including the President, who dispatched to Maine Secretary of War William Howard Taft, Speaker of the U.S. House of Representatives Joseph Cannon (the only man in the House whom labor considered a bigger enemy than Littlefield), and U.S. Senators Albert Beveridge and Henry Cabot Lodge. The President wrote an open letter warning that Littlefield's defeat would represent "a positive calamity to his district and to the country at large."[39] With the support of the National Association of Manufacturers and other business organizations, Littlefield won, but by a narrower margin than ever before.

In 1906 the AFL realized only modest political success, but it helped to elect to the Senate its friend, Robert M. La Follette of Wisconsin, over a NAM ally, the chairman of the Senate Judiciary Committee, who had bottled up all bills against labor injunctions in committee. And four members of trade unions went to Congress.

The AFL entered national politics wholeheartedly in 1908, when Gompers and other members of the executive council presented Labor's Bill of Grievances to the resolutions committees of the Democratic and Republican conventions. The Republicans drew up a platform that supported antilabor court actions, but Democrats incorporated AFL demands into the platform on which Bryan ran. Without specifically endorsing Bryan, the AFL vigorously attacked Republican presidential candidate William Howard Taft's record as an antiunion judge in Ohio, calling him the "father of injunctions."

Organized labor's political demarche succeeded in electing fifteen union members to Congress in 1910. For the first time representatives who were not hostile to labor sat on the House Committee on Labor, alleviating one of labor's frustrations. William B. Wilson, former secretary-treasurer of the United Mine Workers, became chair of the committee. In 1912 the AFL approached both major parties again, and again the Republicans proved unsympathetic, the Democrats cordial. The federation supported Woodrow Wilson's campaign and regarded his election as a great victory. When the Wilson administration included a specific exemption for labor in the 1914 Clayton Antitrust Act, Gompers called it labor's Magna Carta.

As the European War approached, it seemed as though organized labor had begun to gain a voice in influencing public policy affecting workers and as if the iron grip of business were loosening. Increased AFL membership explained part of the change. In 1897 the federation had 250,000 members; in 1900, 868,500; and in 1904, 2,000,000. Membership had declined in 1905 and by 1910 was only 1,562,000. But by 1917 AFL unions had enrolled more than 3,000,000 members.[40] Beyond that, the investigations of muckrakers and the work of governmental commissions of inquiry and bureaus had uncovered a great deal of corruption and collusion between business and politicians at the expense of taxpayers. When the word of one man—J. P. Morgan—dictated the cost of everyone's supply of heat and coal company presidents could claim that God gave them "control of the property rights of the country," it was no longer possible to conclude blithely that what was good for business was necessarily good for everyone else. Business practices now came under closer scrutiny than in the early days of renewed prosperity around 1900.

Theodore Roosevelt sensed this shift in public opinion, and even before the Panic of 1907 he had begun to move away from standing pat, sounding ever less like McKinley and more like Bryan. A reporter asked Bryan if it was true that the President had caught him in swimming and stolen all his clothes. "He didn't get all my clothes," Bryan replied. "I doubt what he did get fit him very well. It is hard, uphill work

for Mr. Roosevelt to make his [Republican] administration respond to
the country's evident demand for reforms."[41] The Panic of 1907 opened
Roosevelt's eyes wider, and he went back to the swimming hole to steal
the rest of Bryan's clothes.

EVEN BEFORE the stock market broke in mid-March 1907, John D. Rockefeller had predicted that Roosevelt's trustbusting and verbal assaults
on business would cause a depression. When a wave of bank and business failures in October swept in a financial panic that threatened to
ruin Wall Street, Roosevelt and the secretary of the treasury cooperated
with the Morgan banks and other large financial institutions to prevent massive bank failures by switching millions of dollars of Treasury
funds from one teetering financial institution to another. The administration bailed out banks by issuing $150,000,000 in Treasury certificates
and bonds.

Despite Roosevelt's efforts to limit the damage, conservatives
blamed him for the panic and spoke of him in the sort of terms that he
would have used to dismiss outspoken critics like William Randolph
Hearst. Supreme Court Justice David J. Brewer called Roosevelt impul-
sive and despotic, and financiers showered the President with abuse for
having undermined business confidence by prosecuting the trusts.

Speculation and mismanagement in the great New York banks and
trust companies had overextended credit and precipitated the panic that
spread hardship all across the land. Kansas journalist William Allen
White described a nation reeling under the impact of the panic: "Factories that had been booming turned glassy-eyed windows to us. Inland
towns in the Ohio Valley and Pennsylvania showed us crowds of idle
workers on the streets.... Cloth signs on store buildings in the little
cities and villages advertised bankrupt sales. The banks were closed.
Commerce and industry stopped dead-still. It was a terrible time."[42]

The President's views shifted dramatically between late 1906 and
early 1908, as he absorbed the calumny of the rich. In 1906, fearing that
a sweeping assault against big business would snuff out prosperity, he
had deplored demands for vigorous prosecution of the trusts. As busi-

nesses began to fail in the early fall of 1907, he saw the panic as something natural, the sort of thing that happened from time to time. He had thought that the acts of the irresponsible capitalists, the Rockefellers and the Harrimans, had caused the panic, but close cooperation with financiers during the worst of the panic transformed his criticism of a few bad apples into anger at the wealthy as a class. By November Roosevelt was echoing middle-class reformer Frederic C. Howe and writing that he neither respected nor admired New York financiers, "the huge monied men to whom money is the be-all and end-all of existence; to whom the acquisition of untold millions is the supreme goal of life, and who are too often utterly indifferent as to how these millions are obtained."[43] By the end of the month he had not only lumped the bad capitalists with the good but also borrowed the vocabulary of the Populists. "The business community of New York," Roosevelt wrote testily, "(by which I mean the New York plutocracy and those who are in the pay of or are led by the plutocracy) ... will themselves tell you how much they suffer from the scoundrelism [of the Harrimans and the Rockefellers] ... but the minute that any action is taken to get rid of the rascality, they fall into a perfect panic and say that business conditions must not be jeopardized. ..."[44]

Inundated by information about how big business actually operated from the Interstate Commerce Commission, the new Bureau of Corporations, the investigation of the beef trust, and muckraking journalists, Roosevelt became convinced that all businesses, not just the villains, would operate counter to the interests of most people unless the government regulated them vigorously and constantly. He began fully to share the growing suspicion that the panic had not been a necessary or natural occurrence. By January 1908 Roosevelt sounded like Hearst or even Debs, denouncing the "malefactors of great wealth." The multimillionaires were positively unAmerican, he said, and no great corporate fortune escaped his wrath. He blasted "predatory wealth," "wrongdoing in many forms," "oppressing wage workers," and "every unscrupulous wrongdoer."[45] Roosevelt's conversion stamped reform as acceptable and brought a flood of respectable people, like William

Allen White—the erstwhile anti-Populist—into opposition to the business-dominated order.

The Panic of 1907, though mild and short-lived in comparison with the depression of the 1890s, broke the "noteworthy prosperity" of the first years of the century, challenging standpatters' claim that things should be let alone and that the wealthy had by their wealth earned the right to direct society. "Fortunes that had been admired as evidence of the glorious opportunity in our happy land," a liberal journalist observed, "turned into exceedingly shaky exploits in thimble-rigging. . . . The Crusade swept into politics and headed for a wholesale redemption."[46] The Panic of 1907 brought labor and local reformers valuable middle-class allies, but the roots of the movement for economic democracy that became respectable in 1908 reached back to the lonely reformers of the early 1900s, Socialists, the strikers and marchers of 1894, the heterogeneous masses of the People's party, Knights of Labor, anarchists, Nationalists, single taxers, Farmers' Alliancemen, and Greenbackers. Although middle-class people supplied their own measure of apprehension, the fundamental themes of the new reform movement had been supplied by labor.

8

RACE AND DISFRANCHISEMENT

The panic of 1907 marked a transition from the uneasy complacency of the prosperous years to a widespread, though far from universal, acceptance of the idea of the need for reform. All sorts of definitions of reform circulated, some moderate, some radical, and they focused on social and economic equity, efficiency in business and politics, and distrust of big business that drew on the old antimonopoly tradition. Americans who called themselves progressives—educated, prosperous, and epitomized by Theodore Roosevelt—embraced many of the remedies that had seemed extreme in the nineteenth century but that now seemed barely sufficient to forestall social breakdown. The crises that most progressives feared concerned class conflict and corporate tyranny, but they remained content to leave race relations in the hands of the "wealth and intelligence of the South" and to ignore the actual racial conflicts and real terrorism that had long been constants of southern history.

With the Democratic recapture of southern state governments in the 1870s, White supremacy had become in effect the official political credo of the South, but not without variation according to region, demography, and chronology. White supremacy posited a racial hierarchy that served economic as well as social ends, providing both an excuse for discriminating against the small numbers of educated Blacks and a way of immobilizing a poor, powerless, largely rural workforce in which most Blacks were to be found. As long as White supremacy seemed a uniquely southern phenomenon, only Blacks and a few White allies protested against it. But in the twentieth century racism seemed to gain vigor outside the South as well, its most noticeable form being mob attacks on Blacks by Whites. One of the most sensational occurred in the New South city of Atlanta, Georgia.

IN AUGUST 1906 Booker T. Washington's National Negro Business League met in racially tense Atlanta to praise the progress of the Negro race through self-reliant enterprise. For Washington and the many who shared his philosophy of racial uplift, property ownership, savings, and dutiful service promised the surest means of advance.[1]

Washington had first risen to prominence in 1895 at the Cotton States Exposition in Atlanta. The best-remembered phrases of the speech that brought him national attention seemed to accept racial seg-regation ("Jim Crow")—"In all things that are purely social we can be as separate as the fingers, yet one as the hand in all things essential to mutual progress"—and disfranchisement—"The wisest among my race understand that the agitation of questions of social equality is the extremest folly, and that progress in the enjoyment of all the privileges that will come to us must be the result of severe and constant struggle rather than of artificial forcing."[2] His autobiography, *Up from Slavery*, which appeared originally in *The Outlook* in 1901, had furthered his reputation nationally as a self-made man. Washington told of having been born a slave in Virginia, having created, by dint of hard work, Tuskegee Institute in Tuskegee, Alabama, one of the finest centers of Black higher education in the United States.

Washington was a thoroughgoing conservative, and his vision of southern society was a harmonious whole without educated Blacks or poor Whites, in which Blacks (labor) and Whites (capital) shared an identity of interest that obviated any need for unions, which he opposed. He flattered what he called the best White men of the South, upon whom he thought the destiny of Blacks depended, and optimisti-cally stressed the improvements in race relations since the late nineteenth century, ignoring segregation, disfranchisement, and lynching. By the early twentieth century he had attracted powerful White backers, controlled several Black newspapers, and influenced the dispensation of federal patronage in the South. For Washington, the future of Blacks lay in the South, and he had told a reporter: "On the whole, I think our meeting not only accomplished good for the race as a whole but especially changed conditions there in Atlanta."[3] But a month after Washington had left Atlanta convinced that he had eased racial tensions, a race riot broke out. A one-sided attack by Whites on unarmed Blacks, this was one of the worst instances of racial violence in the first years of the century. It was not the only one.

ACCORDING TO early reports, the riot was an outraged White population's retaliation for a dozen rapes by Black men against White women, four of which were reported the night of September 22. The *Atlanta News* issued extra after extra, proclaiming in banner headlines eight columns across, TWO ASSAULTS and THIRD ASSAULT. By the time another extra announced a fourth assault, the cry of "Kill the Negroes!" went up. At about 10:00 P.M. a White man mounted a soapbox and brandished the last newspaper. "'Four Assaults by [N]egros on white women. Are we Southern white men going to stand for this?'

"'No!' came a yell from those who heard him.

"'Kill the [N]egros,' was taken up by others, and soon the cry was running along the crowded streets, and those who had been gathering for trouble acted on it."[4] By midnight the mob numbered 10,000 to 15,000 and roved through several areas of the city.

The man who had first mounted the soapbox led a mob to Marietta Street, where a trolley coming down the street held two Black men seated behind two White women. The mob blocked the trolley, dragged the two Black men from their seats, and threw them into the street. A knife-wielding White man killed one Black man, and the mob beat the other to death.

Near the post office a mob armed with clubs, revolvers, rifles, and stones rushed a Black barbershop and tore two barbers from their work.

One barber raised his hands; the mob smashed him in the face with a brick and then beat both barbers to death. An eyewitness driving down Peachtree Street saw a lame Black bootblack trying to outrun a mob. "We saw clubs and fists descending to the accompaniment of savage shouting and cursing. Suddenly a voice cried, 'There goes another nigger!' Its work done, the mob went after new prey. The body with the withered foot lay dead in a pool of blood on the street."[5]

The 3,000 state militiamen ordered to Atlanta by the governor ignored the White mob and went instead to "Brownsville," the home of several Black colleges and respectable Blacks, purportedly to disarm the Blacks. Bent more on humiliating educated Blacks than on protecting them, the militia rounded up professors and students and, with loaded rifles at the ready, marched them through Atlanta's streets to the prison. By the time the riot ended, one White and twenty-five Blacks had died. At least four Black men had been beaten to death.

Following the riot, New York journalist and muckraker Ray Stannard Baker went to Atlanta to investigate. He found an ill-policed city with an unusually high crime rate, even in comparison with cities with larger total populations and larger Black populations. He also discovered that the Reverend Thomas Dixon's play *The Clansman* had been performed in Atlanta just before the outbreak of the riot. Based on the 1905 novel of the same name, the play *The Clansman* was as wildly popular as the book had been.

Dixon was an effective, though lurid, spokesman for White supremacy, the fundamental cause of the Atlanta riot. A well-educated man originally from North Carolina, Dixon had shared a graduate seminar with Woodrow Wilson at the Johns Hopkins University. He had occupied pulpits in Boston and New York City, but his fame rested on his novels, especially the second, *The Clansman*. (D. W. Griffith's pathbreaking, Negrophobic film *Birth of a Nation* was also based on *The Clansman*.) Set in South Carolina immediately after the Civil War, the novel and the play praised the Ku Klux Klan as the only means of assuring the continuation of civilization and White supremacy, which for Dixon were the same thing. He believed that destiny was racial and that

Blacks inherited an incapacity for self-government. Thus race mixing—not violence against women—was the catastrophe in Black/White rape.

Ray Stannard Baker's investigation of the dozen alleged rapes that had triggered the riot revealed two actual and three attempted rapes of White women by Black men. He also discovered three cases of rape of White women by White men, none of which had attracted much attention in the newspapers. He did not investigate assaults against Black women in this extraordinarily violent city.

BAKER MENTIONED the gubernatorial campaign only in a footnote, but Black opinion saw it as the riot's immediate cause. Black Atlanta journalist J. Max Barber, editor of the *Voice of the Negro*, called the riot the "direct fruits of reckless anti-Negro agitation" by Hoke Smith, a gubernatorial candidate, and Tom Watson, his main supporter.[6]

Tom Watson's racial views had shifted since 1896, when he was the Populist vice presidential candidate and had advocated the politics of class solidarity, believing that farmers of both races should stand together against the corporations, the railroads, and the Democratic party. Faced with his enemies' long run of success, Watson had become shrilly antiBlack. He concluded that only if Blacks no longer voted could Whites divide on economic issues. Seeking a gubernatorial candidate who would advocate Black disfranchisement in the 1906 race, he settled on Hoke Smith, a native North Carolinian who had been secretary of the interior in Grover Cleveland's second cabinet. As a Cleveland appointee Smith had been Georgia's leading gold Democrat and Tom Watson's great enemy, but Smith now stood on a platform that embraced much of what the Populists had demanded in the 1890s.

Smith had become known as a supporter of progressive legislation that would prohibit child labor, institute primary elections, elect U.S. senators directly, and outlaw corrupt practices in government, lobbying, and the distribution of free railroad passes. Except for the one plank in his platform calling for Black disfranchisement, Smith ran as a model progressive, the peer of Robert La Follette of Wisconsin and Joseph Folk of Missouri.

Tom Watson brought Populist support to Smith by reassuring poor, illiterate Whites that they would not be affected by measures meant to disfranchise Blacks. Disfranchisers in other states such as Alabama and Virginia had alarmed Georgia's poor Whites by including the "low white man" with Blacks as undesirable voters. And Smith's opponent, Clark Howell, maintained that any disfranchising law that would be constitutional must also disfranchise large numbers of Whites. In fact, voter turnouts in the southern states fell precipitously after disfranchisement. In Georgia the turnout for congressional elections fell by 80 percent after the imposition of a poll tax.[7] Howell, owner of the *Atlanta Constitution*, was not against the disfranchisement of Blacks, but he was skeptical about possible means.

Smith had begun his campaign stressing railroad corruption and charging that Howell was a creature of the railroad-dominated regular Democrats. Howell countercharged that Smith, as secretary of the interior, had appointed Blacks to office. Failing to explain away the transgression, Smith began spending less time attacking the "railroad ring crowd" and more on the necessity of Black disfranchisement.

Smith's own newspaper, the *Atlanta Journal*, claimed that the Democratic "ring" backing Howell preached political equality, which was so near social equality that Blacks had difficulty keeping them apart. Political equality supposedly led to social equality, which led to assaults on the "fair young girlhood of the South." It was time to prevent Blacks from participating in politics, according to the *Journal*, because political power encouraged "the Negro" "in his foul dreams of a mixture of races."[8] By this analysis, Black voting automatically entailed racial amalgamation of the most brutal sort, which was the only kind of Black male / White female miscegenation that White supremacists could imagine.

Not surprisingly, the Smith-Howell campaign was one of Georgia's most violent. Newspapers battled with banner headlines and sanguinary rhetoric, running frequent but unverified reports of outrages and assaults on White women by Black men. In Atlanta in 1906, as in Wilmington, North Carolina, in 1898, a virulent and successful White supremacist campaign produced antiBlack violence.

THE NEWS OF the Atlanta riot deeply distressed Blacks, particularly educated Blacks, because the city's Black population was something of a showpiece of what the race could do with money and education. Booker T. Washington's National Negro Business League had met in Atlanta precisely to highlight Black progress, especially in business. In addition to thriving Black enterprises, the city boasted several Black colleges whose graduates were as respectable and refined as the best the White South could offer.

Although not a product of Atlanta, W. E. B. Du Bois was an example of the sort of Black person that Blacks associated with the city. A professor at Atlanta University in 1906, Du Bois had been in Lowndes County doing research when the riot occurred. He rushed back to the city to see after his family. On the train home Du Bois composed a poem, "Litany of Atlanta," which includes this chilling line: "Surely, Thou too art not white, O Lord, a pale, bloodless, heartless thing?" Du Bois interpreted the riot as a political and economic phenomenon that disillusioned him thoroughly about the prospects of racial harmony in the United States.

Du Bois was thirty-eight at the time. A native of western Massachusetts, he had pursued graduate studies in Germany and had received his Ph.D. in history from Harvard in 1895. Because Blacks were not acceptable as instructors in the leading American universities that served Whites, Du Bois made his academic career in Black institutions. He had moved to Atlanta University in 1899 and was absorbed in the first sustained scholarly investigation of the status of Blacks in America, which became the multivolume Atlanta University Studies.

A collection of essays entitled *The Souls of Black Folk*, published in 1903, established Du Bois as the nation's premier Black intellectual and included an essay entitled "Of Mr. Booker T. Washington and Others," which was so temperate as to be condescending. Du Bois charged that Washington had hushed the "criticism of honest opponents" and accepted the "alleged inferiority of the Negro race."[9] Du Bois saw Blacks as victims of White supremacy, and he did not believe that southern Whites could be trusted to pursue the interests of southern Blacks.

Where Washington saw harmony, Du Bois saw conflict, and after 1903 the two men symbolized the two ends of the continuum of Black opinion. Most Blacks found it possible simultaneously to accept Washington's South-centered practicality and Du Bois's insistence on full civil rights. But after separate organizations came to embody the different approaches, combining the two became unwieldy. The National Negro Business League, which Washington had founded in Boston in 1900, deemphasized confrontational political questions and civil rights to concentrate on commercial successes, particularly in the South. In 1905 Du Bois and several other Black men and women organized the Niagara Movement to protest lynching, disfranchisement, Jim Crow, and the hegemony of the "Wizard of Tuskegee."

Shortly after the Atlanta riot Washington reported that conditions had returned to normal, that the best people, White and Black, were restoring racial tranquility.[10] But for large numbers of Blacks, Washington's reluctance to condemn Georgia's politicians and rioters disqualified him for race leadership. The 1906 meeting of the Afro-American Council passed resolutions calling for federal action against racial violence, providing one of several examples of the repudiation of Washington's style in the wake of the Atlanta riot.

The Afro-American Council was one of several Black organizations formed in the 1880s and 1890s to protest against extralegal executions of Blacks by White mobs. In 1892, 161 Blacks had been lynched, and the toll had continued to mount. Black journalist Ida B. Wells investigated the rape-lynch syndrome after three Black businessmen had been lynched in her hometown of Memphis. Her 1895 pamphlet, *A Red Record*, showed that the vast majority of Black lynch victims had not even been accused of rape, the most heinous of crimes said to excuse the actions of impassioned White lynch mobs.

A native of Mississippi, Wells had been educated at Rust University in Holly Springs but had had to find work as a schoolteacher before graduation, after both her parents died in a yellow fever epidemic. She taught in Memphis and continued her own education at Fisk University in Nashville. She sued a railroad company for demanding she sit in

a segregated coach but lost the case in an appeal in 1887. Wells began
writing for Black newspapers in the late 1880s and became half owner
of the *Memphis Free Speech* in 1892. While she was visiting in the East,
shortly after her investigation of the lynching of the Black grocers, a
mob destroyed her newspaper offices. Unable to return to Memphis,
Wells became a staff writer for the *New York Age*, the leading Black
newspaper of the time, and lectured against lynching throughout the
country, inspiring the organization of clubs among Black women. A
pioneer in the Black club movement, Wells organized in Chicago, where
she settled in the mid-1890s and where she wrote a pamphlet protesting the lack of recognition of American Blacks in the World's Columbian Exposition. Wells married Ferdinand Barnett, a Black lawyer and
newspaper publisher, in 1895 and became known as Ida Wells-Barnett.
She served as secretary of the Afro-American Council from 1898 to
1902 and was a member of the Niagara Movement and a signer of the
"Call" to the race conference out of which came the National Association for the Advancement of Colored People (NAACP), although she
thought that organization's approach to racial discrimination was too
moderate and did not continue to take an active part. Her concerns
encouraged Black clubwomen actively to oppose lynching.[11]

Black organizations spoke against racial discrimination tirelessly,
but at the turn of the century, Blacks mounted these protests very
nearly alone. As the mobs grew bolder and more sadistic, however, others became concerned. For the first time Whites like New York Socialist
and social worker Mary White Ovington attended meetings of Black
protest organizations. It took a race riot in the North to prompt several
Whites to take further action.

A LYNCH MOB had formed on August 14, 1908, in Abraham Lincoln's
hometown of Springfield, Illinois, after a White woman, Mrs. Earl
Hallam, had accused a well-known Black man, George Richardson, of
attempting to rape her. Although Richardson was the mob's main target,
any Black man on the streets of Springfield was considered fair game.
At one point the mob took off after a man who had sought refuge in

a crowd in front of the courthouse listening to a speech by the Prohibition party's presidential candidate, Eugene W. Chafin. When Chafin tried to shield the fugitive, someone in the mob smashed Chafin in the face with a brick, and a brawl broke out between the campaign crowd and the mob. The Black man escaped, but Chafin was injured seriously. The mayor tried to disperse the mob, but it handled him roughly for having appointed two Blacks to the police force. At least one Black had been killed and several Blacks and Whites had been injured by nightfall of the first day of rioting. After more than two nights of violence the state militia came to town to reimpose order. Several days later Mrs. Hallam admitted that George Richardson had not tried to assault her. A White, not a Black man had been involved in the affair, which evidently was not a rape at all.

ONE OF THE INVESTIGATORS of the Springfield riot was William English Walling, a member of a wealthy Kentucky family, resident of University Settlement on New York's Lower East Side, woman suffragist, and Socialist. He had devoted his life to the labor movement and had been one of the founders of the Women's Trade Union League in 1903. After his visit to Springfield he concluded that it was one thing for law and order to break down in the benighted South but that the spread of mob rule to the North threatened to undermine American society as a whole. He decided that a national organization of "fair-minded whites and intelligent blacks" was needed to combat racial oppression and stop the mobs.[12]

In New York Walling met with Mary White Ovington, who was completing *Half a Man: The Status of the Negro in New York* (1911), and Henry Moskowitz, a medical doctor who worked among immigrants. Both Ovington and Moskowitz were settlement workers. During early 1909 they laid plans for a conference on race and enlarged the group to include two Blacks, Bishop Alexander Walters of the African Methodist Episcopal Zion Church and the Reverend William Henry Brooks, a Methodist minister. Several more Whites joined the planners.

Bishop Walters, Oswald Garrison Villard, Lillian Wald, Florence

Kelley, and John Milholland were already well known in social reform circles. Walters had been a founder of the African American League in 1890 and was active in its successor organization, the Afro-American Council, serving as president twice. He was one of many Blacks who censured President Theodore Roosevelt for dishonorably discharging an entire battalion of Black soldiers at Brownsville, Texas, in 1906, after they had been goaded by White Texans and a few soldiers had fired back.

Lillian Wald was a nurse best known as the founder and head resident of New York's Henry Street Settlement. Like Walling, she was concerned with women workers and had organized a systematic investigation of women and children industrial workers in 1905 with the help of Florence Kelley, the general secretary of the National Consumers' League, who had been at Hull House in Chicago and now lived at Henry Street.

The grandchild of the abolitionist William Lloyd Garrison and son of Henry Villard, one of the most important railroad promoters of the mid-nineteenth century, newspaper publisher Oswald Garrison Villard had organized a Men's League for Woman Suffrage. In 1911 he became one of eighty-four men who were booed and hissed for marching in a New York suffrage parade led by his mother, Fanny Garrison Villard. A male supporter of woman suffrage like Villard, John Milholland was also a wealthy New Yorker. Active in many reform causes, he had founded the Constitutional League in 1903 to secure Black civil rights through litigation.

In 1909 Walling and his associates issued a "Call to Discuss Means for Securing Political and Civil Equality for the Negro," whose sixty signers included fourteen White and two Black women. The "Call" exhorted everyone who believed in democracy to renew the struggle for civil rights, beginning with a conference, which in 1911 became a permanent organization called the National Association for the Advancement of Colored People. At first the NAACP's only high-ranking Black member was Du Bois, editor of the association's organ, *The Crisis*. James Weldon Johnson, author, diplomat, and teacher, became the second in 1916. Thereafter Blacks gradually gained a larger leadership role until by the 1930s it was a predominantly Black organization. The

NAACP fought a long crusade against the disfranchisement of Blacks through poll taxes, the White primary, and grandfather clauses, all of which had been adopted by southern states in the late nineteenth and early twentieth centuries.

Poll taxes were head taxes of $1 to $2 per year whose payment was mandatory for voting, but for nothing else. Prospective voters had to pay poll taxes well in advance of elections, preserve their receipts, and pay any missed taxes cumulatively in order to vote. Because paying poll taxes was optional unless one wanted to vote, this burdensome fee proved an effective disfranchiser of the poor, who in the South were disproportionately Black. The White primary was a subterfuge by which the Democratic party, which monopolized political power in the one-party South, declared itself a private club that could determine its own standards for membership, the only salient criterion being Whiteness. And the grandfather clause provided a loophole for poor or illiterate Whites who could not qualify to vote under literacy or income restrictions by certifying men whose grandfathers had been able to vote before Reconstruction had extended suffrage to Blacks.

The NAACP's first successes in the campaign against racist laws came in 1915, when the U.S. Supreme Court struck down Oklahoma's grandfather clause, and in 1917, when it invalidated Louisville's residential segregation ordinance, which had designated certain blocks for Blacks and others for Whites, into which no one of the other race could move.

Although the NAACP contested racist laws, it did not undertake to reverse the late-nineteenth- and early-twentieth-century trends toward disfranchisement of the poor in general, which was occurring throughout the whole country and affected not only Blacks. Black disfranchisement in the South was the most blatant manifestation of a broader movement to reverse a century-long tendency toward widening the electorate.

DURING THE COLONIAL ERA suffrage had generally been restricted to male taxpayers (who were property owners), but states loosened these restrictions after the adoption of the Constitution, a process that accelerated in the 1820s. By the 1830s virtually all White men in the U.S., including immigrants who had merely expressed an intent—often quite casual—to become citizens, could vote. During the years when poor and ignorant White men gained the vote, however, states like North Carolina, New York, and Pennsylvania withdrew the vote from Black men who had previously qualified by virtue of education or property holding. By the Civil War Blacks could vote only in parts of New England. The Fifteenth Amendment to the U.S. Constitution extended suffrage in federal elections to Black men, but by 1900 southern states had disfranchised Blacks in practice and in law. To a far lesser degree but with a parallel intent, northern states followed suit regarding the working classes, many of whom were immigrants rather than Blacks.

In the North as well as the South many respectable people had concluded that too many men were voting and that political corruption could be corrected by reducing the size of the electorate. Educated northerners like the historian Francis Parkman of Boston and the Social Gospeler Washington Gladden saw suffrage as a privilege, not a right, that must be used to serve the ends of good government and public welfare, as they defined them. Gladden believed that immigrants should be made worthy of citizenship before voting, and he advocated not only literacy tests but certification of moral character. Professor John W. Burgess, who taught at Columbia University for thirty-six years, wanted men of his class and lineage, what he called the "Teutonic element," to control politics to the exclusion of all others. In circumstances such as those of New York, with its large immigrant population, Burgess argued that non-Teutons should not be permitted any participation in public life.

Northerners used registration months in advance of elections, the secret or "Australian" ballot, and literacy qualifications, which were also used in the South along with more stringent and effective measures. Between 1889 and 1913 nine states, not counting southern states, where literacy qualifications were aimed primarily at Blacks, required voters to be able to read English. Seven southern states imposed literacy tests, sometimes linked, as in North Carolina, with temporary grandfather clauses, to allow illiterate Whites to register within a stated period, or with temporary property exemptions, to allow wealthy but unschooled Whites to vote. Only in Mississippi was the property exemption for Whites permanent.

Between the late 1880s and the turn of the century eight southern and thirty nonsouthern states adopted secret ballots, replacing ballots printed and distributed by parties, which used symbols to guide voters who could not read. The Australian ballot, which the state or municipality distributed at the polls, effectively eliminated both controlled votes and illiterate voters by making it impossible for voters to receive help from a party worker in marking their ballots. By 1910 registration and secret ballots had disfranchised hundreds of thousands of voters, Black and White, inside and outside the South.[13]

IN THE EARLY twentieth century a new kind of municipal government, the city commission, also reduced the influence of working-class voters. The commission came to be associated with direct government: the initiative (voters could enact laws without going through the legislature); the referendum (voters could vote yes or no on issues that legislators wished to avoid); and the recall (voters could remove officeholders before the expiration of their terms). But in its purest form it included only three features: a small group of commissioners who combined both legislative and executive powers; nonpartisan elections and a merit system; and at-large instead of ward elections. Each of these features tended to weaken ward-based, party-dominated city government, which proponents of the commission system thought conducive to boss-run city rule and expensive government.

The commission system originated in Galveston, Texas, where, after a hurricane had destroyed the city in 1900, voters adopted this form of city government in 1901 amid a great deal of controversy. It was clear from the beginning that the commission form, reputedly managing a city like a business, favored businessmen and their interests over working people and minorities. At-large voting, especially, mitigated against the election of poor, obscure, or nonWhite candidates who were not likely to be known outside their wards. Although the commission vogue peaked around 1915, to be superseded by the city manager system, both forms of municipal government divorced city government from party organizations and radically reduced both the numbers of voters who participated in elections and the influence that poorer citizens were able to wield in city government. Unlike Tom Johnson's Cleveland, cities run like businesses offered few nonessential services like public baths, day care centers, public gardens, or recreational facilities. The point of running a city like a business was to reduce expenses, not to provide services.

THE ELECTORAL REFORMS of the turn of the century limited fraudulent voting by reducing the role of local party organizations and vote manipulations. But in limiting managed voting, the reforms drastically reduced voting as a whole. The higher voter turnouts of the nineteenth century, the product of robust party organizations, gave way to low turnouts and weak partisan affiliation in the twentieth.

Shrinking electorates were most pronounced in the South, where many poor Whites and all poor Blacks could no longer take part in the political process. Elsewhere, however, the narrowing of the franchise took part as another trend haltingly extended the vote toward White women. The former circumscribed democracy, but the latter redressed an injustice that had prevented half the population from exercising full citizens' rights.

9

WOMAN SUFFRAGE
AND WOMEN WORKERS

American thinking about gender was as multilayered and contradictory as that regarding race. But whereas Blacks of all income levels were stereotyped as a race in terms that had long been used in England and America against poor people (and that echoed mid-nineteenth-century nativists' stereotypes of the Irish), women were lumped together as a sex in generalities that applied only to the middle and upper classes. Women were said to be the weaker, gentler sex whose especial duty was the creation of an orderly and harmonious private sphere for husbands and children—as opposed to the public sphere, which men dominated. Respectable women, "true women," did not participate in debates on public issues and did not attract attention to themselves. In a society that denied the existence of a middle ground between purity and immorality, women who fell off the pedestal had to prove they were other than prostitutes. If a woman attracted public notoriety, she undermined her good reputation and courted infamy.

During the antebellum period, when a handful of Black and White women lectured on the abolition circuit and the issue of votes for women became a public issue for the first time, a young Ohio college teacher named James A. Garfield—who became President in 1880—summed up the prejudice against women in public life that sustained antisuffragists for three-quarters of a century:

... there is something about a woman's speaking in public that unsexes her in my mind, and how much soever I might admire the talent, yet I could never think of the female speaker as the gentle sister, the tender wife, or the loving mother. . . . The sacred place in my affections which Woman holds would be desecrated by the super addition of the business of public life and a contact with the coarser pursuits of Humanity.[1]

The notion that women should vote persisted throughout the nineteenth century in the face of deeply embedded prejudices like these.

The "woman question" first arose in the abolition movement, and after women were barred from abolitionist conventions, they formed the first National Female Anti-Slavery Society in 1837, but the movement for woman suffrage began at the Seneca Falls (New York) Convention in 1848, when pioneer suffragists drafted a Declaration of Sentiments demanding that the rights of citizens be extended to women. At that point the restriction of civil rights to men in the U.S. Constitution was unstated, for until the ratification of the Fourteenth Amendment (1868), the Constitution spoke of "persons," whom everyone understood to be male.[2]

The abolitionist movement had included strong elements of support for woman suffrage and temperance, both of which continued after emancipation. But several issues—the place of men in the woman suffrage movement, the use of funds, and Black male enfranchisement—split the woman suffrage movement. One faction, which opposed Black suffrage until White women could vote, became the National Woman Suffrage Association (NWSA), led by Elizabeth Cady Stanton and Susan B. Anthony and based in New York. The other faction saw Black male suffrage as a stepping-stone to woman suffrage and became the American Woman Suffrage Association (AWSA), based in New England and led by Lucy Stone and her husband, Henry Blackwell. During the latter part of the nineteenth century, however, the broadest support for woman suffrage was to be found not in the divided suffrage movement but in the Woman's Christian Temperance Union (WCTU).

Frances Willard, president of the Woman's Christian Temperance

Union, the largest organization supporting woman suffrage in the late nineteenth century, began persuading her organization of the need for woman suffrage in 1876. She spoke of the "home protection" ballot and argued that drunkenness ruined multitudes of homes and could be abolished only through temperance legislation, which men alone would not enact. Temperance, therefore, demanded woman suffrage. Although not everyone in the WCTU believed in woman suffrage, the organization adopted her position in 1881, and by the mid-1880s all the locals supported it at least formally. To Willard's satisfaction, the connection between woman suffrage and temperance was firmly established during the late nineteenth century. By the early 1880s she had the WCTU's support for woman suffrage and federal prohibition by constitutional amendment.[3]

Although middle-class White women constituted the great majority of WCTU members, the organization included departments dedicated to work among Blacks and among Native Americans. In the late 1880s the superintendent for colored work was the Black poet, novelist, and former abolitionist Frances Ellen Watkins Harper. Harper had been a suffragist since the 1870s, when she had attended meetings of the AWSA and had spoken on southern Black women's special need for the vote.[4]

Temperance was the WCTU's first concern, but pursuit of that goal in broad terms led the organization into many other arenas of social reform, including prisons and reformatories, workingwomen's centers, and public health. These sorts of public undertakings awakened middle-class women to the concerns of poor and working-class women and brought women together across class lines; this ultimately led to a demand for the vote. In the late nineteenth century the WCTU was active across a broader spectrum than most of the middle-class women's organizations that followed it, but it shared two characteristics with twentieth-century women's organizations. First, the religious convictions of WCTU members supported their belief that they were acting in the interests of the society as a whole. And second, the "Do everything" approach reached women across class lines.[5]

After Willard's death in 1898 the WCTU narrowed its purview to prohibition only, retreated into the racism and nativism that affected the entire country during the era of the Spanish-American War, and left the issue of votes for women to the labor movement—which had supported woman suffrage since the mid-nineteenth century, but not as a main priority—and to suffrage organizations. The two woman suffrage organizations merged in 1890 to form the National American Woman Suffrage Association (NAWSA), but the period between 1896 and 1908 was nonetheless the "doldrums," for the middle-class women's suffrage movement. During these years suffragists concentrated on 480 campaigns to get woman suffrage referenda on state ballots, producing a mere seventeen referenda, only two of which succeeded— one in Colorado in 1893, the other in Idaho in 1896. Two western states entered the Union with woman suffrage in their constitutions: Wyoming, in 1890, and Utah, in 1896. The 1896 California referendum, which gained the support of Mrs. Leland Stanford, wife of the railroad magnate and creator of Stanford University, and Mrs. William Randolph Hearst, seemed promising but was beaten badly by the liquor lobby, which believed—justifiably—that women would vote in prohibition. In New York in the late nineteenth century suffrage was the concern of upper-class women such as Josephine Shaw Lowell, a philanthropist active in charity work, and Mrs. Russell Sage, widow of the financier who had backed Jay Gould. Ignoring working-class women, they concentrated on securing the vote for women who owned property and paid taxes in New York State.

The lack of progress on woman suffrage did not indicate a lack of organization among women. The General Federation of Women's Clubs (1892) and the National Federation of African American Women (1895) were organizations of elite women, similar in their constituencies but not in their concerns. The National Federation of African American Women, whose first president was Mrs. Booker T. Washington, of Tuskegee, Alabama, supported woman suffrage from the beginning and took the condition of poor Black women as one of its prime concerns. The General Federation of Women's Clubs excluded Black

Breaker boys working in a coal mine separating coal from waste by hand. (Library of Congress / Underwood & Underwood)

(LEFT) *John Mitchell, head of the United Mine Workers, in 1902.* (Library of Congress) (RIGHT) *J. Pierpont Morgan, investment banker.* (Library of Congress)

William Randolph Hearst, publisher of the New York Journal *and New York gubernatorial candidate, in 1906.* (Library of Congress)

Tom Johnson, mayor of Cleveland, Ohio, in 1907. (Library of Congress)

Robert M. La Follette,
United States senator, in 1906.
(Library of Congress)

Booker T. Washington, founder and head of Tuskegee Institute, in 1915. (Library of Congress)

W. E. B. Du Bois, professor at Atlanta University and a founder of the National Association for the Advancement of Colored People. (Library of Congress)

Shirtwaist makers in the Uprising of the Twenty Thousand, 1909. (Library of Congress)

Ida B. Wells-Barnett, investigator of lynching and clubwoman. (The New York Public Library Digital Collections)

Woman suffrage parade, Washington, D.C., 1913. (Library of Congress)

*Elegantly dressed John D. Rockefeller walking with his son, John D.
Rockefeller, Jr.* (Everett Collection Historical / Alamy Stock Photo)

women's clubs, showed little interest in workingwomen, and did not endorse woman suffrage until 1914. But not all middle-class women limited their aims or circumscribed their constituency so closely. Educated women in the settlement movement, particularly, continued to take an interest in the welfare of women workers.

IN THE LATE nineteenth and early twentieth centuries the numbers of women who worked for wages outside the home challenged the assumption that women were naturally and exclusively homemakers. As technology made manufacturing jobs less arduous and less skilled, women increasingly found work in industry. In 1900, of the 5,319,400 women who worked for wages, some 932,000 were employed either in the clothing and garment trades or in textile mills, and nearly 2,000,000 women worked as domestic servants. Others were farm laborers, teachers, and salesclerks. Most workingwomen were young, poor, and unmarried, but in 1900, 21 percent of the female population over sixteen, many of whom were married, worked for wages in scattered vocations and regions. Throughout the country Black married women worked for wages as domestic servants and laundresses, and significant numbers of White married women worked in factories weaving cotton and woolen fabrics in New England and the Southeast. In the Northeast many married women did piecework at home.[6]

The question of respectability was an ambiguous one for working-class women. On the one hand, they had strong feelings about the relative respectability of various kinds of work. The professions, nursing and teaching, were most desirable, but they were open only to a trained few, fewer than half a million in 1900. Working-class women chose among domestic service, factory work, and salesclerking. These three kinds of workers occupied what amounted to three separate castes. Clerking in a store, even though the pay was low, the hours were long, and the expenses for good clothing high, was attractive, but open mainly to "American girls"—that is, White women born in this country who spoke unaccented English and looked Anglo-Saxon.

Factory work followed salesclerking in respectability. Although it did not bestow instant respectability, young women of working-class or farm background believed that a factory girl could enjoy social standing. According to one factory worker, "intelligent people set no stigma on factory workers who are well bred and ladylike. These girls are received in good circles anywhere. Many women of wealth and standing are interested in these girls and even invite them to their homes." But, she continued, women who worked as domestics forfeited their respectability, for "no one has ever invited someone's maid or cook to their home for afternoon tea or any other social affair."[7]

At the bottom of the job hierarchy were the domestic and service workers, foreign-born—especially Irish—and Black women who worked in the homes of others, twelve or more hours a day, often seven days a week. A young woman recalled her feelings on her first day at work as a servant: "Very slowly, I buttoned my apron, the badge of the servant. I knew Minnie and Sadie and all the other girls who worked in shops and factories would stop associating with me. I had dropped out of their class."[8] While wealthy women's organizations used their purchasing power to improve the working conditions of saleswomen, and the Women's Trade Union League and other union organizations for women worked to better conditions for female factory workers, almost no one was ameliorating the condition of domestic workers.

On the other hand, women who worked in fields or factories did not accept middle- and upper-class ideals of respectability unequivocally. For the 8,000,000 women employed outside the home in 1910, particularly for Black women, to whom the stereotype of the fallen woman (so easily applied to women of any race who worked) was attached, measuring up to the standards expected of the sequestered Victorian lady was neither desirable nor possible. Workingwomen dressed, talked, joked, and carried themselves differently from middle-class women. They frequented the dance halls and amusement parks and displayed an open sexuality that marked them off from genteel middle-class women.[9] The difference between the working-woman and the lady was first of all one of class, but Mother Jones warned that ladyhood was also a form of control: "God almighty made women and the Rockefeller gang of thieves made ladies."[10]

THE REFORMERS WHO worked with female factory workers were many of the same people who were concerned with the oppressed generally. Six years before William English Walling called his friends together to begin the process that led to the creation of the National Association for the Advancement of Colored People, he had encountered a long-established women's trade union league in Great Britain and brought the idea back to the United States. At the AFL convention of 1903 Walling, Mary Kenney O'Sullivan, Leonora O'Reilly, and women unionists, Socialists, and settlement leaders like Lillian Wald of Henry Street and Jane Addams of Hull House organized the Women's Trade Union League (WTUL) to advance the interest of women within the union movement. The WTUL brought together middle- and upper-class women, called allies, and working-class women like O'Sullivan and O'Reilly in a coalition that was sometimes uneasy.[11]

Mary Kenney—former AFL organizer, former Hull House resident, and former factory inspector under Florence Kelley—had married Jack O'Sullivan, a Boston trade unionist and labor editor for the *Boston Globe* in 1894, but by 1903 she was widowed. O'Sullivan was active with the WTUL local in Boston, but O'Reilly took a larger role. A member of the WTUL board from the beginning, O'Reilly became vice-president of the New York branch in 1909. Her parents both were working-class Irish immigrants whose poverty had sent her to work in a collar factory at age eleven. Among the family's friends were two veterans of the Paris Commune, Jean Baptiste Hubert and Victor Drury, who filled young Leonora with stories of "self-sacrifice, of renunciation of all those personal ties held dear by most of us, all their splendid, heroic deeds."[12] In 1886, when she was sixteen, O'Reilly joined a local assembly of the Knights of Labor and organized the Working Women's Club, which, by appealing to consumers, brought her to the attention of middle- and upper-class women. The Working Women's Society addressed society women as shoppers: "When a neatly made garment is offered to [you] as 'cheap,' do [you] stop to ask at whose expense is the cheapness?"[13]

Through the Working Women's Society O'Reilly met Florence Kelley, who lived at the Henry Street Settlement. O'Reilly and her mother moved to Henry Street in the 1890s, and O'Reilly continued to work ten to twelve hours a day in a shirtwaist factory, even while she worked with the WTUL, among other activities.

Although the WTUL was dedicated to ameliorating the condition of working-class women, its leaders, Mary Dreier, president in New York, and her sister, Margaret Dreier Robins, president in Chicago (and later nationally), as well as many of its leading members were allies, who, by virtue of their education and self-confidence, tended to overshadow the workingwomen, most of whom were quite young. In this respect the WTUL exhibited one of the main difficulties of organizing women across class lines. Although women were discriminated against as women, they still divided like men along lines of class, race, and political orientation. O'Reilly was one of the most sensitive to the irritation that elite women caused by patronizing workers. She told Walling that the allies "must drop the attitude of lady with something to give her sister, altogether—it never goes deeper than the skin." O'Reilly threatened to resign from the WTUL several times—actually leaving briefly in 1905—because of an "overdose of allies."[14]

The WTUL's first priority was organizing women industrial workers into AFL union locals. For the most part the league's successes were limited to a season or two and a handful of shops, because the work force varied yearly and women moved from one shop to another. The WTUL also faced a great deal of hostility from the AFL, whose union members preferred the idea of women at home rather than competing with them for jobs. The league fostered International Ladies' Garment Workers' Union (ILGWU) Locals 25 and 62, both in New York City.

The WTUL succeeded somewhat better in its other aims, especially lobbying for the passage of protective legislation, educating women of all classes to the value of the labor movement and of unions for women.

In New York, Chicago, and Boston the leagues worked primarily with women in the garment and textile industries.

AT THE SAME TIME that Leonora O'Reilly was organizing the Working Women's Society, a prominent New York charity worker was questioning her own usefulness. Josephine Shaw Lowell, a wealthy Civil War widow who had been the first woman appointed to the New York State Board of Charities in 1876, had begun to want to "leave the broken-down paupers to others," as she became more interested in the needs of working people. Not only were workers more numerous than paupers in New York City, but, Lowell observed, "if the working people had all they ought to have, we should not have the paupers and the criminals. It is better to save them before they go under, than to spend your life fishing them out when they're half-drowned and taking care of them afterwards!"[15] Lowell and O'Reilly both were instrumental in the founding of the New York Consumers' Society in 1890. By 1898 there were several local Consumers' Societies in the North and Midwest, and a National Consumer's League was formed; its executive secretary was Florence Kelley.

The principle behind the Consumers' League was straightforward. Women who shopped could boycott stores and exert pressure for the provision of decent wages and working conditions for women employees, primarily salespeople. The league publicized what it called a white list, which named stores that met its standards, including $6-per-week minimum wages for experienced workers, a six-day week, no more than twelve hours per day of work (eight to six, with three-quarters of an hour for lunch), paid half holidays in the summer, seats behind the sales counters, and an adequate place to eat lunch. Only eight stores in New York City met those standards when the first white list was published in 1891.

In the twentieth century Consumers' Leagues realized the limits of moral suasion and boycotts and began to lobby in state legislatures for laws protecting workingwomen, limiting hours of work, and stipulating safe working conditions. (Not all women workers favored preferential, protective legislation, however. Women who worked in traditionally male jobs, such as printing, consistently opposed different working standards for women, on the ground that such limitations justified discriminatory wages for women and put them at a disadvantage in competing with men for work.)

THE WTUL and the Consumers' Leagues were the largest and best-known organizations focusing on workingwomen, but they were not alone. Harriot Stanton Blatch, the daughter of pioneer suffragist Elizabeth Cady Stanton, returned from the United Kingdom, where she had lived with her British husband in the 1880s and early 1890s, after having graduated from college in the 1870s. During the 1894 suffrage campaign Blatch spoke in "parlor meetings" to wealthy suffragists (such as Mrs. Russell Sage and Mrs. John D. Rockefeller) of the centrality of working-women to the struggle for woman suffrage and the linkage of women's contributions as workers to the need for a voice in politics. Blatch joined the WTUL in 1905 as an ally and was a member of the executive council from 1906 to 1909.[16]

In 1907 Blatch formed the Equality League of Self-Supporting Women, two of whose most important figures were Leonora O'Reilly and Rose Schneiderman, a young, Jewish, Socialist capmaker. The Equality League's 19,000 members also included Florence Kelley and Charlotte Perkins Gilman, who had presented a telling argument for women's rights in an internationally influential book, *Women and Economics: A Study of the Economic Relation Between Men and Women as a Factor in Social Evolution* (1898). Ranging over human relationships of many sorts, Gilman dismissed theories that women's inferiority was biological. She showed how society, stressing the differences between the sexes, made women weak. "In our steady insistence on proclaiming sex-distinction," she wrote, "we have grown to consider most human attributes as masculine attributes, for the simple reason that they were allowed to men and forbidden to women." Women would become full-fledged members of society when people were no longer defined primarily by gender.[17] In 1916 Gilman serialized her novel *Herland* in her magazine *The Forerunner*. In this feminist utopian novel three young American men discover a country inhabited entirely by "highly civilized women" who have evolved a vigorous, advanced, vegetarian, androgynous culture. In their small country reasonableness is the rule, and women fill all roles, proving that women could fulfill their human potential when freed from the burdens of sex as decreed by society.

The Equality League brought together workers and clubwomen, but its great achievement was the full integration of workingwomen into suffrage activity, thanks to the prominence of the two working-class leaders, Schneiderman and O'Reilly. Blatch broke suffrage tradition by arranging for workingwomen to testify before the New York legislature in 1907. One of the witnesses, Clara Silver, told the legislators: "To be left out by the State just sets up a prejudice against us. . . . Bosses think and women come to think themselves that they don't count for so much as men."[18]

The Equality League of New York exemplified the broadening of the woman suffrage movement in several large cities in the East between 1905 and 1910. Reflecting the increased support for suffrage among women wage earners, the 1906 convention of the NAWSA considered reaching out to working-class women. The following year the WTUL established a Suffrage Department. Suffrage agitation began to awaken society women to the support as well as the needs of working-class women. Because so many Black women were poor, Black women's organizations were particularly sensitive to the interests of women who worked outside their own homes. Black women's organizations, such as the National Association of Colored Women, the National Federation of Afro-American Women, and the Northeastern Federation of Colored Women's Clubs, worked for suffrage along with White women, even though the White suffragists exhibited a good deal of racial prejudice.[19]

Repudiating the canons of middle-class respectability and the doctrine of separate spheres, Blatch built on workingwomen's own culture and borrowed tactics from the labor movement: demonstrations, street-corner speakers, and torchlight parades. These new methods succeeded in proving how central workers were to the suffrage movement and, by publicizing the suffrage cause, attracted elite women as well. By 1910 woman suffrage had become fashionable in drawing rooms and on college campuses in many parts of the country. One Nebraska college student wrote to her mother that women students were no longer "afraid of antagonising the men or losing invitations to parties by being suffragists."[20]

American suffragists also took note of the militant tactics of their British counterparts. Alice Paul and Lucy Burns of the Congressional Union had actually spent time in Britain studying the methods of British suffragists. Inspired by British examples and the labor-influenced Equality League, middle- and upper-class women became more assertive, thereby horrifying Americans who prized conventionality. Mainstream American magazines had already wondered about British suffragists "What Should Be Done with the Wild Women?"[21]

In 1909 Carrie Chapman Catt, who had been president of the NAWSA from 1900 to 1904, launched the Woman Suffrage party. In California a smoothly run campaign featuring fleets of automobiles won woman suffrage by a very narrow margin. The California victory brought to six the number of states, all in the West, in which women could vote. In 1912 in six suffrage referenda, three passed—in Arizona, Kansas, and Oregon—with Michigan narrowly lost. Illinois granted presidential suffrage in 1913, after a referendum had failed. Alice Paul led the most militant women out of the NAWSA in 1913 and founded the Congressional Union (later the National Woman's party), which pushed for the passage of a federal amendment. With 2,000,000 members in 1917, the NAWSA was the largest volunteer organization of American women, with the mass support necessary to sustain a campaign for the passage of suffrage amendments on both the state and federal levels.

WHILE MIDDLE- AND upper-class women were using labor tactics to secure woman suffrage, a strike of women workers became the first to receive national attention by attracting the support of elite women. The Uprising of the Twenty Thousand occurred in New York City's new shirtwaist-manufacturing industry, which produced the tailored blouses worn by legions of workingwomen. Unlike the piecework and homework done by the most oppressed garment workers, shirtwaists were factory goods. The industry was centered in New York, in hundreds of small factories and a handful of large ones, notably Leiserson's and the Triangle Shirtwaist Company. The young female work force, overwhelmingly Jewish, with some Italians and a scattering of Blacks, worked ten- to twelve-hour days, sometimes seven days a week, without overtime pay. Supplying their own thread and sometimes even sewing machines, they bargained for wages individually, were subject to layoffs during slack times, and worked around the clock in rush seasons. Their pay varied from $4 to $6 per week.

The vast majority of this work force was not unionized, and in the fall of 1909 a few women had tried to form a union in the Triangle Shirtwaist Company. After meeting with officials of the International Ladies' Garment Workers' Union (ILGWU), they were fired by the company in September 1909. The ILGWU could do little to protect them; the union was only nine years old, weak, small, and mostly male. The women responded with an independent strike against the Triangle company, which soon spread to Leiserson's. Both companies hired men and women to harass the strikers and beat them up as they walked the picket line. By October picket line violence had brought the New York Women's Trade Union League into the struggle.

When the society women of the WTUL joined the picket lines, the city's practice of arresting the strikers, hauling them to court, and slapping them with large fines backfired. The president of the New York WTUL, Mary Dreier, was a woman of considerable wealth and standing. The discovery that she was not a workingwoman dismayed the policeman who had arrested her along with several other strikers on the picket line. "Why didn't you tell me you was a rich lady? I'd never have arrested you in the world!"[22] Cooperation among women across class lines was new to most New Yorkers.

The strike received a boost on November 22, 1909, when a mass meeting at Cooper Union—New York's labor temple—attracted an overflow crowd that listened to Samuel Gompers, Dreier, other union supporters, and Socialists. After more than two hours of speeches urging moderation, a young striker named Clara Lemlich mounted the platform. She had been beaten on the picket line and was a heroine of the movement. She spoke in Yiddish: "I am a working girl, one of those who are on strike against intolerable conditions. I am tired of listening to speakers who talk in general terms. . . . What we are here for is to decide whether we shall or shall not strike. I offer a resolution that a general strike be declared—now."

The whole of Cooper Union took to its feet, shouting and waving hats and handkerchiefs. After a five-minute demonstration the crowd quieted enough for the chair to ask for a second to the motion for a general strike. Everyone in the hall shouted a second. The chair asked if the strikers really meant they would be faithful: "Will you take the old Jewish oath?" Two thousand right arms went up as the strikers repeated the oath: "If I turn traitor to the cause I now pledge, may this hand wither and drop off at the wrist from the arm I now raise."[23]

The strike of all the shirtwaist factories began the next day at 9:00 A.M. It took between 20,000 and 30,000 shirtwaist makers off the job and stunned observers with its unanimity and organization. As the strike continued through the end of the year and into 1910, strikers without winter coats strode the picket lines and marched to City Hall to demand proper protection against assailants.

By February 15, 1910, the strike had been won, and the shirtwaist makers returned to work. Women in all the factories had won improved wages, which still varied from shop to shop. Generally the strikers succeeded in limiting hours to fifty-two per week. Although the strike failed to get recognition for the union in the larger factories, it prepared the way for eventual union recognition in most factories of the ILGWU as the representative of the shirtwaist makers.

SHORTLY AFTER the shirtwaist makers and the WTUL's triumph in the Uprising of the Twenty Thousand, tragedy struck the New York garment workers. On March 25, 1911, a fire broke out in the Triangle Shirtwaist Company on the top three floors of the Asch building in Washington Square. Although the factory was new and reputedly fireproof, careless maintenance and the practice of locking doors and windows—supposedly to prevent employees from leaving the factory or stealing—transformed the burning building into an inferno. Either women remained trapped in the building to suffocate or burn to death or they jumped nine floors to death on the pavement. The Triangle fire took the lives of 146 women.

The New York WTUL and Local 25 of the ILGWU called protest meetings and collected relief funds, tapping a vein of anger that Rose Schneiderman articulated: "This is not the first time girls have been burned alive in the city. Every year thousands of us are maimed. The life of men and women is so cheap and property is so sacred. There are so many of us for one job it matters little if 14[6] of us are burned to death."[24]

The protests resulted in the appointment of a commission of investigation that included Frances Perkins (later Governor Franklin D. Roosevelt's New York State industrial commissioner and U.S. secretary of labor), who was then secretary of the New York Consumers' League. Familiar with the unsafe conditions in which large numbers of New Yorkers worked, she educated her co-commissioners: Robert Wagner (then a state senator, later a U.S. senator whose National Labor Relations Act [the "Wagner Act"] of 1935 secured workers the right to representation of their own choosing, which allowed spectacular growth in the labor movement), and Alfred E. Smith (then a member of the state legislature, later governor of New York for four terms, and Democratic presidential candidate in 1928). Perkins showed them exhausted workers, who after ten or more hours of work could no longer take needed precautions, and the machines they tended that could scalp a woman or take off a man's arm. The investigation resulted in several pieces of protective legislation, including a fifty-four-hour workweek in factories and stores and a broad new industrial code.

BY THE SECOND DECADE of the twentieth century women who had begun their social welfare work in women's organizations—such as the WTUL and the Consumers' League—and women-dominated institutions like the settlement houses, were exerting an important influence in the realm of public policy. In most instances, women acted on the state and local levels, to secure pure food, factory inspection, and health care for poor women and children. But increasingly they made their presence felt on the national level. Josephine Goldmark, lifelong friend of Florence Kelley and publications secretary and chair of the committee on the legal defense of labor laws of the National Consumers' League, prepared the "sociological" brief from which Louis D. Brandeis successfully supported protective legislation before the U.S. Supreme Court in *Muller v. Oregon* (1908).

Women had begun to leave the private sphere to obtain prohibition or the vote, and by the 1910s they were pursuing a wide range of issues, usually those concerned with women and children. Although women's rhetoric stressed gender, the aim was to heal the injuries of class, particularly as protective legislation for women and children was extended to workers in general.[25] To a very great degree, women's institutions laid down the agenda for the public health and social welfare reforms that in the twentieth century softened the impact of industrialization on working people.

10

THE PROGRESSIVE ERA

Women were not yet part of the congressional political response to the Panic of 1907, which had shown that a few hundred men in banks, trust companies, and the stock market could plunge the whole country into hard times. In the Republican-dominated Senate, insurgent Republicans and Democrats took on the Republican old guard. The latter group had the support of Roosevelt's handpicked successor, William Howard Taft, who epitomized a large group of officeholders who were more concerned with preserving stability than with embracing concepts of fairness. His presidency was a time of conflicting ideals.

To A FAR GREATER EXTENT than Roosevelt, William Howard Taft remained the captive of his social milieu. More conservative than enlightened, Taft came from a wealthy Cincinnati family and had been a federal judge (not known as a friend of labor) and the first governor-general of the Philippines before serving as Roosevelt's secretary of war. By 1908, however, he had seen a need for trustbusting and tax reform and seemed a safe custodian of Roosevelt's legacy of reform. Both Roosevelt and Taft thought that the high protective tariff needed lowering and that federal revenues should come from graduated taxes on incomes and estates.

The Panic of 1907 had renewed agitation for fairer tariffs, making tariff revision a key issue that was no longer strictly partisan. Early in 1908 Republican insurgent Senators Beveridge and La Follette had introduced bills to create a strong tariff commission, and the spring had witnessed growing resentment against protection among many sectors of public opinion. Editorials commonly repeated Ida Tarbell's contention that the poor could no longer afford warm clothing because the tariff made woolens too dear. Taft had spoken up for tariff reform, the main political issue of the presidential campaign, and most Republicans hoped the new President would usher in a tranquil period of moderate reform.

True to his campaign promises, President Taft called Congress into special session in the spring of 1909 to revise the tariff. But it was Taft's misfortune that the Congress, while nominally Republican, held enough insurgent midwestern Republicans to form an anticonservative block when they joined with Democrats. La Follette led the reforming Republicans in the Senate, including Jonathan Dolliver of Iowa, Joseph Bristow of Kansas, Albert Beveridge of Indiana, Albert Cummins of Iowa, and Moses Clapp of Minnesota, who attempted to serve the interests of consumers rather than manufacturers. Their endeavor to stymie conservative initiatives and to pass progressive legislation brought them into alliances with Bryan Democrats, led by Texas Democrat Joseph Bailey, and into conflict with conservative Republicans. Increasingly Taft found himself allied with the latter, notably Rhode Island Republican Nelson Aldrich.

Despite Taft's seeming agreement with Roosevelt on important matters of policy, the new President proved to be the ally of conservatives in Congress, virtually by default. Vacillating and lazy, he fell in with men whose political styles were more natural to him than was Roosevelt's after 1908. Conservatives in the Senate were pleased by Taft's reasonableness, but the President's ever-increasing numbers of opponents saw him otherwise. In William Allen White's words, "this genial, chuckling, courteous, kindly gentleman was in his heart a deep-dyed political and economic conservative, and bull-headed at that."[1]

THE SAGA OF the new tariff corroborated White's views completely. The new tariff, introduced in March by Representative Sereno Payne of New

York, chairman of the House Ways and Means Committee, revised rates downward and included an inheritance tax. But in April Senator Aldrich presented his amended version of the Payne bill that the House had passed. The Aldrich bill eliminated the inheritance tax and substituted a corporate income tax (which could easily be passed on to consumers). It also included 847 amendments that were exceedingly complicated and that the senator claimed to be in the spirit of downward revision. But insurgent Republican senators painstakingly analyzed the amendments and showed that most of them increased rates. Aldrich's cynical betrayal of public sentiment, which violated the President's campaign promises, provoked tremendous criticism of conservative Republicanism. This resentment surfaced as the Senate debated the various import duties.

During early May the Senate focused on Schedule K of the Aldrich bill, one of the most visible and least popular aspects of the tariff. Not only did the duties on wools and woolens raise the costs of consumer items, but Schedule K was also the oldest part of the tariff, which had protected the American woolens industry since the early nineteenth century. Schedule K had recently come under fire for other reasons as well. In December 1908 the House Ways and Means Committee had learned that the tariff on washed wool in the Dingley tariff of 1897 had been drawn to the specifications of the National Association of Wool Manufacturers.

Supporting high rates for Schedule K, Senator Aldrich called any assault on the wool schedule "an attack on the very citadel of protection." Democratic Senator Bailey of Texas, an opponent of protection, agreed with Aldrich on Schedule K's importance, but he argued that the woolen schedule symbolized the "fraud and injustice" of the whole protective system.[2] Meanwhile, Senator La Follette attacked Schedule K for having made woolen goods too expensive for the very workers who made them.

Despite the tremendous agitation in newspaper editorials and in Congress, which included a struggle in which the dictatorial powers of the archconservative speaker of the House were diminished, President Taft signed Aldrich's version of the Payne-Aldrich bill into law in August without having attempted seriously to reduce tariff rates. Now newspapers attacked the President and the conservatives for trying to fool the American people with the timeworn claim that tariffs protected American industries and wages. The Payne-Aldrich tariff was unpopular, and many saw it as a prime example of corporation pressure on conservatives in the Senate.[3] Even Senator Henry Cabot Lodge of Massachusetts, usually counted as a staunch conservative, blamed the tariff for high prices.

Amid this barrage of criticism an oblivious President Taft praised the tariff repeatedly, beginning in Winona, Minnesota, where he called it the "best bill that the Republican party ever passed." He continued to laud the tariff and the senators who had supported it, even as editorial opinion across the country excoriated him for siding with the bloated capitalists and reneging on his campaign promises. During 1910 and 1911 a coalition of Democrats and liberal Republicans attacked the Payne-Aldrich tariff piecemeal. They passed individual low tariff bills on cotton, wool, steel, and iron, every one of which Taft vetoed. The Payne-Aldrich tariff gave Democrats a perfect campaign issue, but a brouhaha over conservation in 1909 and 1910 did even more to bring Theodore Roosevelt back into electoral politics.

THEODORE ROOSEVELT had been the first President to identify himself with protection of the natural environment, and conservation had been one of his main concerns. Throughout his presidency his chief forester, Gifford Pinchot—who remained in office under Taft—had enthusiastically seconded Roosevelt's policies. Pinchot, like Roosevelt, advocated protecting public lands from abuse by extractive industries, but Taft's secretary of the interior, Richard A. Ballinger, reversed that policy.

A lawyer from Seattle, Ballinger shared the western enthusiasm for exploiting public lands. He wanted to open the public domain to business, a prospect which was anathema to conservationists. Not only did Ballinger attempt to lease public lands in Alaska to a combination of western businessmen and the notorious Morgan-Guggenheim mining syndicate (which combined the most powerful financial house in the country with the most powerful mining interests in the West), but his actions also suggested conflict of interest. The controversy that ensued grew complicated, setting Pinchot against Ballinger and President Taft. Fundamentally the split seemed to pit Roosevelt's policies of conservation against the corporations' heedless appropriation of public lands. Insurgent Republicans demanded a congressional investigation, which ultimately exonerated Ballinger. But the counsel for the Pinchot forces, Louis D. Brandeis, managed during the interrogation to paint Ballinger and Taft as the agents of rapacious capital and enemies of conservation.

DURING MOST OF 1909 and the first half of 1910, while the tariff and conservation controversies deepened the split in the Republican party, Theodore Roosevelt was out of the country. He returned vowing to eschew politics, but as insurgents trooped to his house, complaining about Taft, Roosevelt grew worried. By late summer he noted that "unless there is some progressive leadership, the great mass of progressives for lack of this legitimate leadership will follow every variety of demagogue and wild-eyed visionary."[4]

In fact, the Socialist party, which exemplified demagoguery and wild-eyed vision for Roosevelt, was attracting adherents in record numbers. In 1908 the Socialist party's presidential candidate, Eugene V. Debs, had polled 424,000 votes. Two years later Socialists fared better still at the polls across the country, notably in Wisconsin, where Milwaukee elected a Socialist mayor and congressman in 1910, and in the Southwest, especially Oklahoma, where men who would have been Populists twenty years before became Socialists. Still a small organization, the Socialist party collected dues from only 55,100 members, but it was growing by leaps and bounds.

In August and early September 1910 Roosevelt gave a series of speeches that delineated reform policies that came to be known as the New Nationalism. The reforms Roosevelt reeled off in his New Nationalism speeches had been circulating for years, but not among many Republicans: regulation of large corporations; tariff reform; graduated income and inheritance taxes; currency reform to forestall financial panics; the selling of public lands only in small parcels to bona fide set-tlers; a series of labor reforms; a strict accounting of campaign funds so as to limit the influence of money in elections; and the initiative, referendum, and recall.

Challenging the Hanna-Aldrich concept of politics, Roosevelt affirmed that "the object of the government is the welfare of the people. The material progress and prosperity of a nation are desirable chiefly so far as they lead to the moral and material welfare of all good citizens."[5] He had come 180 degrees from the standpat assumptions that had gov-erned his party when he had been elected Vice President in 1900. He no longer assumed that government's raison d'être was service to busi-ness in an understanding that what was good for business was good for the American people. He sought to bend the Republican party, the most powerful political organization in the land, the champion of big business, to suit what he saw as the needs of consumers, workers, and individuals of modest incomes. Having realized that identity of inter-est did not exist—although he would not have said that it had never existed—he aligned himself on what he saw as the proper side of a fundamental conflict of interests. Roosevelt's opposition to a Republi-can President split the party and marked the beginning of a new era in national politics in which standpatters were on the defensive.

TAFT WAS AGHAST at Roosevelt's attacks on the inviolables of the Repub-lican party. Spending money and manipulating patronage, the President and outraged Republican conservatives tried to defeat insurgents in the midterm-elections and failed. Conservative Republicans lost the pri-maries; then Democrats won the general elections by a landslide that surprised both parties. For the first time in the twentieth century the majority of the House of Representatives belonged to the Democratic party, whose leader was still William Jennings Bryan. In addition, in 1910 New Jersey elected a governor who looked like a President and who made Democrats think they had a chance to gain the presidency for the first time in years.

Woodrow Wilson, a Johns Hopkins Ph.D. who had taught at Bryn

Mawr in Pennsylvania and Princeton before becoming president of Princeton University in 1902, was a social conservative elected as a reform governor. Wilson distrusted democracy, suspecting that representative government worked best when restricted to the qualified few. He opposed labor unions and was wary of governmental regulation of utilities and big business. But as governor of New Jersey Wilson sloughed off his conservative skin. Despite meager support in the state legislature, he broke with the Democratic machine that had put him in office, prevented the election of the state's Democratic boss to the U.S. Senate, and pushed through a series of progressive reforms: workmen's compensation, prohibition of corrupt practices in government, direct primary elections, and meaningful regulation of railroads and utilities. By 1911 Wilson had emerged as a bona fide progressive, his party's best presidential hope for 1912.

The elections of 1910 also inspired reform Republicans. In January 1911 Robert La Follette and his associates formed the National Progressive Republican League to promote progressive causes and serve as a vehicle for La Follette's bid for the Republican presidential nomination in 1912. Although Theodore Roosevelt had accepted much of the insurgents' program, he drew back somewhat from his New Nationalism of 1910 and remained aloof from any group identified with La Follette, whom he thought extreme. Roosevelt's staunchest supporters, like Gifford Pinchot, began to lose hope that Roosevelt would run for President again, and toward the end of 1911 they joined La Follette's campaign with tempered enthusiasm. Then, in February 1912, La Follette delivered an angry, rambling, and—according to some—drunken speech at an important dinner for newspaper publishers, extinguishing whatever slender chances he had had for gaining the Republican nomination. At the same dinner the governor of New Jersey won acclaim. Meanwhile, an industrial crisis in Lawrence, Massachusetts, magnified the threat of social upheaval.

IN MID-FEBRUARY 1912 newspapers across the country carried shocking headlines about a police riot in Lawrence, Massachusetts. Strikers in the textile-manufacturing city were putting their children on trains to safer havens in New York, Pennsylvania, and New Jersey when police swooped down on the crowd at the Lawrence depot. Policemen beat several women and children before carrying them all off to head-quarters and several hours' detention. The violence focused attention on a strike that had started in January, when 500 Italian textile work-ers at the American Woolen Company mill had opened their envelopes to find their pay short. Spontaneously 10,000 men, women, and chil-dren had left the mills. The next evening, a Saturday, Joseph J. Ettor, an Italian American ironworker and union organizer from New York, had addressed the strikers and placed the Industrial Workers of the World squarely at the head of the leaderless strike.

On Monday several hundred strikers marched to the Pacific Mills, where they encountered the militia stationed to protect mill property. The police turned fire hoses on the thinly clad workers, the forceful stream of icy water knocking the strikers off their feet and rolling them across the Merrimack River bridge and down the street. On Thurs-day the strikers staged the first of several great parades. Four thousand strikers speaking several languages carried American flags and sang the "Marseillaise" and a lesser-known anthem, the "Internationale":

Arise, ye prisoners of starvation!
    Arise, ye wretched of the earth,
For Justice thunders condemnation,
    A better world's in birth.

No more tradition's chains shall bind us,
    Arise, ye slaves! No more in thrall!
The earth shall rise on new foundations,
    We have been naught, we shall be all.

'Tis the final conflict,
    Let each stand in his place,

The Industrial Union
Shall be the human race.

Singing came to characterize the strike. "The workers sang every-where," journalist Mary Heaton Vorse recalled, "at the picket line, at the soup kitchens, at the relief stations, at the strike meetings. Always there was singing."[6]

The causes of the strike lay in the confluence of the sort of protective legislation that social reformers had hoped would lighten the burdens of labor and the imperatives of factory production. Massachusetts had enacted a law limiting women and children to fifty-four hours per week after January 1, 1912, which had passed over the opposition of the textile industry. In the woolen and cotton mills of Lawrence, where women and children constituted about half the work force, employers had simply applied the law to all workers, regardless of sex or age, reducing the workweek by two hours and cutting wages correspondingly, by about 3.5 percent. This usually amounted to only a few cents, but, said one striker, that was a matter of four loaves of bread. Wages in Lawrence were so low that the cut spelled disaster. At the beginning the walkout was an act of simple desperation.

At no time did the United Textile Workers of America (UTWA), the AFL union in Lawrence, take any part in the strike, because mill managers had squarely defeated its attempts to organize even skilled workers. Until January 1912 the great majority of the workers, who were unskilled, were also unorganized, although about 300 men and women belonged to a local of the Industrial Workers of the World (IWW). Once the strike began, they had immediately called their organizer, Joseph Ettor. He quickly formed a multilingual coordinating committee and inspired the strikers with speeches in English and Italian.

THE IMMIGRANT TEXTILE WORKERS of Lawrence had come in three different waves. Lawrence's oldest immigrants, Irish and English, had begun to arrive as the weaving industry got started in the 1850s. In the 1870–

1895 period French-Canadians and Scottish immigrants had come to the mills. After 1895 Italian, Polish, Jewish, Syrian, German, Lithuanian, Portuguese, Belgian, and Armenian immigrants had come to Lawrence. Wages in Lawrence were too low for one wage earner to support a whole family; working thirty to forty weeks a year, including layoffs, the male head of a household made an average yearly wage of about $400. As a consequence, many women and children worked, and their wages increased the average yearly family income to about $660. Families also supplemented their incomes by taking in boarders or lodgers, which caused overcrowding.[7] After probing the conditions in which Lawrence workers lived, one of the many journalists covering the strike concluded that were he living in a miserable tenement, trying to feed a family on pitiable wages, "I should join any movement, however revolutionary, to put an end to such conditions."[8]

THE STRIKE'S LEADERS were avowed revolutionaries. Ettor (until his arrest on a pretext), then Elizabeth Gurley Flynn (who organized the European-style removal of the children) and William D. Haywood belonged to the Industrial Workers of the World ("Wobblies"), which set little store in political action. The IWW worked toward revolution through "direct action" leading to a general strike. A syndicalist organization ("syndicalist" from the French word for labor union), the IWW had as its aim the reorganization of society around industrial unions in the mines and mills where workers spent most of their lives. By IWW reasoning, workers and owners had no interests in common and class war was inevitable. Wobblies set out to organize American workers along industrial lines into one big union of the entire working class, an idea they shared with the Knights of Labor of the 1880s. Disdaining the AFL's acceptance of the wage system as a reactionary collusion with capitalists, the IWW preferred to abolish wages and capitalism completely.

Founded by Socialists in Chicago in 1905, the IWW had been active among unorganized workers on the fringes of industrial development: in the mines of Colorado and the lumber camps of Washington and Louisiana. Lawrence was its first major strike in the eastern industrial heartland, and it set easterners thinking. Because working conditions in Lawrence, appalling as they were, were no worse than those of industrial workers in other American cities, Lawrence came to symbolize the state of labor relations in general and the potential for profound unrest.

The acceptance the IWW seemed to enjoy in Lawrence alarmed many whom the poverty of the textile workers and the incendiary speeches of the IWW had already shocked. Haywood, especially, emerged from reports in newspapers as a violent revolutionary, an anarchist who would surely mislead the desperate. "It is a disquieting portent," one observer admitted, "that over 15,000 workers in a New England city of moderate size have accepted at a critical time the wild-eyed leadership of William Haywood."[9]

Lawrence threatened not only more strikes but strikes of a new sort. Some feared wage war on a national scale; others awaited a gigantic battle between the classes. One reporter referred skeptics to leading political figures: "Ask President Taft, if you are a Taft man, ask Colonel Roosevelt, if you follow him. Each will admit that the conflict is certainly coming if some radical step is not taken to check it."[10] Several observers saw the Lawrence strike as the beginning of a larger movement of workers to unite and take over the whole Western world, replicating the fictional underground in Ignatius Donnelly's dystopian novel *Caesar's Column*. The IWW leaders encouraged this impression by adopting many usages from the European left. Joseph Ettor told journalists that Lawrence might turn its fire hoses on the strikers, "but there is being kindled in the heart of the workers a flame of proletarian revolt which no fire hose in the world can ever extinguish."[11]

THE LAWRENCE STRIKE also reinvigorated debates about immigration. In 1912 much of the industrial working class outside the South (as opposed to farmers, clerks, and professionals) consisted of immigrants or the children of immigrants. Between 1901 and 1910 an immense wave of 6,300,000 immigrants arrived in the United States, many from southern and eastern Europe and the Middle East. By 1910 one-third of the American people had either been born outside the United States or had at least one foreign parent. The immigrants came to work, and they sought the centers of heavy industry, like Pittsburgh, with its iron and steel, New England, with its textiles, and Chicago, with its meat-packing. Along with their enormous labor power, immigrants brought unfamiliar languages and customs, and their working-class status and cultural distinctiveness fueled the middle-class nativism that had been growing since the late nineteenth century. By 1912 more Americans than ever feared that their free and democratic society was being subverted by the introduction of a proletariat that was actually European in origin and the rigid, Old World-style class distinctions that followed its appearance. Many Americans suspected that the masses of immigrants were so uncivilized as to be unassimilable, and others accused foreigners of carrying the germ of radicalism that would infect the American polity. Views like these, which gained currency after Lawrence, fueled rising demands for immigration restriction, which after the European War severely reduced immigration from southern and eastern Europe.

In sum, the Lawrence strike of 10,000 foreign workers, led by syndicalists who idealized class conflict, made many apprehensive. Americans expected the Industrial Workers of the World to gain a widespread following in the nation's great industrial centers, and they dreaded the class war that future strikes might provoke. The Lawrence strike ended victoriously in mid-March, but the IWW refused to sign contracts because it thought they would legitimize the capitalist wage system. Collapsing completely in Lawrence in 1913, the IWW left no lasting imprint in the textile industry there, but few anticipated that in 1912. As a social force the IWW seemed to be the wave of the future.

DURING THE EARLY SPRING, as the Lawrence strike reached public notice, the press was full of articles entitled "The Rising Tide of Socialism," which sought explanations for the apparently sudden appearance of socialism as a political force in the United States. In the elections of the fall of 1911 Socialists had won mayoral elections in eighteen cities and towns across the country, eight in Ohio alone. For the first time voters in New York and Rhode Island had elected Socialists to their state legislatures. In several cities (e.g., Buffalo) the Socialist vote had nearly doubled. And Schenectady, an industrial city in upstate New York, home of the General Electric Company, had elected a Socialist clergyman as mayor. With 1,150 Socialists holding office in 36 states and some 325 towns and cities, and with Socialists succeeding where none had ever been elected before, everyone wondered what it all meant.[12]

It did not mean a sudden American conversion to government ownership of the means of production. But it did indicate great dissatisfaction with the way things were. In Schenectady a union man said that "people got mighty sick of voting for Republicans and Democrats when it was a 'heads I win, tails you lose' proposition." In New York City a businessman explained that he was a Socialist "because it's the only way out of our miserable mess, and because the old parties are flim-flamming us all the time." Rising prices, uncertain employment, the defeat of the unions by employers' associations, and, above all, the conviction that something was radically wrong with the political system that the Republicans and Democrats could not fix moved people to vote Socialist.[13]

Socialists promised to provide uncorrupted, humane, and efficient government and to equalize tax burdens, so that ordinary citizens would no longer pay the bulk of property taxes while corporations paid little or none. They also promised municipal ownership of utilities, better housing, factory inspections, and recreation facilities for all. Their promises, in fact, recalled the non-Socialist reforming city administrations of the early 1900s like that of Tom Johnson of Cleveland.

While Socialist victories were most visible on the municipal level, they were discussed as a national phenomenon. To growing numbers of Americans, Socialists seemed to offer the last alternative to a bankrupt two-party political system before revolution, as had the People's party to the new constituencies after the Great Upheaval. Now an even broader spectrum of American opinion doubted that Republican insurgency and Bryan Democracy could envision reforms that were sufficiently far-reaching to save society from the revolutionaries preaching class war. Jacob Gould Schurman, president of Cornell University, spoke of a "spirit of discontent" that seemed more fundamental, permanent, and widespread than ever: "We are to-day like men moving about under a pall which stretches to the horizon and which cannot be broken through." After a thorough study of the 1911 elections a University of Chicago professor concluded that *the wonder is not that the Socialist party won so many victories in the last campaign but that it did not win more.*[14]

The Socialist upsurge was not merely a quirk of one election. By 1912 the Socialist party had grown to 118,000 ideologically diverse dues-paying members (from 55,000 in 1910). The largest state organization was in Oklahoma, which had a strong Populist tradition and where there were 12,000 party members and 53,000 Socialist voters. Many others across the nation were Christian Socialists, men and women like Mayor George Lunn of Schenectady, Walter Rauschenbusch, and Charlotte Perkins Gilman. One of the most prominent proponents of the Social Gospel, Rauschenbusch was a professor of church history at Rochester Theological Seminary who had published *Christianity and the Social Crisis* in 1907. Gilman called herself a Socialist, but she dismissed Marxism as "violent propaganda" and never accepted the Marxian notion of class struggle as desirable or necessary.[15] The Socialist party also included democratic socialists—called political socialists at the time. People like Victor Berger, whom Milwaukee sent to Congress in 1910, and Eugene Debs, the Socialist party's perennial presidential candidate, believed that when the majority of American voters favored socialism, the revolution would be achieved through the democratic process. Although Debs was skeptical of the value of conventional politics, he waged countless campaigns for their educative value.

On the party's left wing were the supporters of William D. Haywood, whose vision of the revolution was apocalyptic. Haywood turned out to be too radical for the Socialist party when, during the Lawrence strike, he gave speeches proclaiming, "I am not a law-abiding citizen," and suggesting sabotage.[16] Haywood's strongest backing came from IWW miners and loggers in the West.

Although the Socialist party looked forward to the 1912 elections as the "beginning of an epoch," serious controversies divided the movement: how to define industrial unionism, how the party should deal with the AFL and IWW, how to overcome American workers' resistance to socialism of any sort, whether to condone the use of sabotage, and whether to support unrestricted immigration. These controversies were fought out in the pages of the socialist press. Hundreds of weekly and a handful of daily periodicals that together circulated 2,000,000 copies a year served the various perspectives within the Socialist party. The most popular newspapers were the nationally read Girard, Kansas, *Appeal to Reason*, the St. Louis *National Rip Saw*, and the New York *Jewish Daily Forward*.

The *National Rip Saw*'s editors were Kate Richards O'Hare and her husband, Frank. O'Hare was one of several gifted women Socialists, whose ranks included Florence Kelley, birth control advocate Margaret Sanger, Ellen Gates Starr (Jane Addams's partner in Hull House), Mother Jones, and the late Frances Willard of the Woman's Christian Temperance Union.[17] Women came to the Socialist party from the same groups as men (the People's party, churches, Henry George's single tax movement, the labor movement) as well as from women's organizations such as the WCTU. About 10 percent of the Socialist party's membership was female, and women belonged and voted on the same basis as men. Unlike the two major parties, the Socialist party ran female candidates, and Socialist mayors appointed women to office.

WHILE SOCIALISTS SAVORED their victories and predicted a million votes in 1912, journalists broadcast their growth, the Lawrence strikers paraded and sang, William D. Haywood preached revolution, and the President praised the Payne-Aldrich tariff, Theodore Roosevelt wavered. Then, in mid-February, fearing that time was running out for nonsocialist reform, he decided to run for President. Roosevelt made a strong showing in states with primary elections, but the Taft forces controlled the Republican party and the credentials committee that would decide in the many contested cases whether to seat Taft or Roosevelt delegates in the nominating convention. Roosevelt realized that the fight would be tough. In an emotional speech before 6,000 of his followers in Chicago the day before the convention opened, he called Taft's people "the powers that prey, the representatives of special privilege in the world of business and their tools and instruments in the world of politics" and his own forces the plain people who represented the welfare of the nation, democratic government, and the future of American civilization.

The tone of Roosevelt's speech was apocalyptic, the summons to battle, sweeping. The country was in crisis, threatened on one side by the evils of plutocracy—the myopic reactionaries whom President Taft represented—and on the other side by the mob. Girding for war to save the country from impending disaster, Roosevelt rallied his forces: "We fight in honorable fashion for the good of mankind; fearless of the future, unheeding of our individual fates, with unflinching ears and undimmed eyes . . . we stand at Armageddon and we battle for the Lord."[18]

FOR ALL HIS ELOQUENCE, Roosevelt lost the nomination. With his reforming followers and his wealthy backers (including a Morgan partner), he bolted from the Republican party and formed the Progressive party, which scheduled its national convention in Chicago in August.

The National Progressive party's convention was singular. All its delegates were well educated and respectable—nothing of the professional politician or the party faithful here—and large numbers of them were women. Rather few were Black. Although Black delegates from northern states were seated and one made a speech, Roosevelt refused to recognize Black delegates from Florida and Mississippi, appealing instead to what he called the best White men of the South.

While the Socialist party had supported woman suffrage for years, the Progressive party was the only major party that supported votes for women in 1912. For the second time in history a woman, Jane Addams, seconded the presidential nomination. (Mary Elizabeth Lease had seconded the nomination of General James B. Weaver as the People's party nominee in 1892.) Introduced as "America's most eminent and most loved woman," Addams called the Progressive party "the exponent of that great American movement which is seeking the betterment of social conditions" and applauded the "splendid platform" as much as Theodore Roosevelt. As she left the rostrum, a group of women followed her down the aisle, carrying a banner that read VOTES FOR WOMEN.[19]

Well known as a proponent of woman suffrage, Addams symbolized the Progressive party's commitment to that reform. Another convention speaker, Judge Ben B. Lindsey of Denver, a pioneer of juvenile justice, symbolized the party's concern for the poor. The platform called for several labor reforms, the graduated income tax, lower tariffs, limits on campaign spending, regulation of the trusts, and currency reform.

Conservatives saw the goings-on at Chicago as outrageous, the Progressives as fanatics and dreamers. The *New York Times* called Roosevelt a socialist standing on a platform that contained "whole pages of socialist doctrine." There was, in fact, some area of agreement, on woman suffrage and the graduated income tax. The well-bred, sophisticated members of the Progressive party did not emphasize the kindredness of their aims with those of the rural southern and western masses of the People's party, but their fundamental goals were similar. The central idea of the Progressive party platform was the need to narrow economic inequities and to redistribute the nation's enormous wealth so that the blessings of American civilization would be enjoyed by everyone.

For all its concern for working people, the Progressive party was by no means a labor party. Very much a movement of cultured, middle-class people, the Progressives meant to help the workers, but from above and without their participation. This was a party of journalists, social workers, settlement house veterans, and young lawyers, not of members of the American Federation of Labor. Of socialists, syndicalists, or individual workers, there was never a question.

CONFIDENT OF their chances of success against a divided Republican party, Democrats met between the Republican and Progressive party conventions to choose the governor of New Jersey as their presidential candidate. In a year in which progressive reformers captured popular imagination, Woodrow Wilson was the only prospective Democratic candidate with progressive credentials. Although Bryan's long-running critique had shaped the ideas of people who after 1910 proclaimed themselves progressives, he was too old-fashioned, too popular among farmers—and too closely associated with defeat—to qualify as a progressive. Democratic progressives were urban, respectable, and more moderate than Bryan in his moral moments.

Wilson gained Bryan's support and the Democratic nomination. Speaking in elegant platitudes of progress and stability, he promised to bring in the era of the "New Freedom," a progressive credo similar to Roosevelt's New Nationalism. Wilson admitted at the time that "when I sit down and compare my views with those of a Progressive Republican I can't see what the difference is, except that he has a sort of pious feeling about the doctrine of protection, which I have never felt."[20]

Wilson's New Freedom and Roosevelt's New Nationalism were similar, but the two men approached reform from different angles. Most obviously, Roosevelt was a Republican and unopposed to vigorous federal action. Wilson was a Democrat who as a White southerner believed instinctively in states' rights. Since the Panic of 1907 Roosevelt had advocated the regulation of economic and political power that the wealthy—corporations and individuals—enjoyed and sometimes abused. He also favored protective legislation for workers and a federal woman's suffrage amendment.

Without being explicit on the point, Wilson wanted to keep the federal government small. He favored the little man against the trusts, wanted smaller businesses to be able to compete with the corporations, but he did not want the federal government to do a great deal to achieve those ends. As a states' rights Democrat Wilson distrusted federal action and thought federal legislation to protect various special groups, whether farmers, women, labor, or Blacks, was inappropriate.

Wilson won with only a plurality of the votes, 42 percent to Roosevelt's 27 percent. Taft won 23 percent of the votes, and Debs got 6 percent, nearly 1,000,000 votes, an astounding accomplishment for a

Socialist. Riding on the impressive increase in adherents to socialism, candidate Debs had announced during the campaign, "Comrades, this is our year."[21] In terms of the increase in the percentage of the vote garnered, 1912 was the year of socialism. But Socialists did not realize that the electoral victories were pleas for reform, not evidence of the spread of socialist class consciousness, and that the Socialist party was about to go downhill. Internal dissension between radicals and moderates over Haywood's positions and then over the European War lost the Socialist party thousands of members after 1912, and it never again enjoyed such popularity nationally.

THE DAY BEFORE Wilson's inaugural, Washington was the scene of a great parade down Pennsylvania Avenue for suffrage. Led by Inez Milholland, the sister of John Milholland, 5,000 marchers, nearly all women, carried banners that said WE DEMAND AN AMENDMENT TO THE UNITED STATES CONSTITUTION ENFRANCHISING THE WOMEN OF THE COUNTRY AND WOMEN OF THE WORLD, UNITE. Everyone wore something yellow, the color of woman suffrage. Several groups of women marched under professional banners: women in the clergy (six older women in long black dresses); businesswomen; writers; artists; women in education (including thirty-two Black women from Howard University); government workers; wives. Oswald Garrison Villard led a division of the National Men's League for Woman Suffrage.

The parade included floats depicting the status of women in 1840 and in 1913. But a rowdy crowd and ineffectual policing caused innumerable delays. A drunk, one of the 500,000 celebrants who had come to the capital for the first Democratic inaugural in twenty years, fell under the wheels of the 1840 float. The crowd jeered the marchers, pushing into the street and making walking difficult for the detachments of women.

Although the enormous parade proved that woman suffrage had attracted support from women in all walks of life, the lack of police protection outraged the marchers. Dr. Anna Howard Shaw, president of the National American Woman Suffrage Association and a veteran of many suffrage marches, said she had never seen a more disgraceful, uncontrolled crowd. Even the police insulted the marchers. A policeman told a congressman's wife that "if my wife were where you are I'd break her head."[22] For all the parade's enthusiasms and travails, however, President Wilson's speech the next day ignored woman suffrage entirely.

WILSON'S INAUGURAL ADDRESS laid out the three reforms of the New Freedom that the new President wanted to see enacted: a reduction of the tariff, restrictions on the trusts, and an overhaul of the nation's banking and currency system. Breaking long-standing tradition, the President appeared in person before a special session of Congress to ask for tariff reform. Congress cooperated, and in October Wilson signed the Underwood-Simmons bill, based largely on the tariff bills that Taft had vetoed in 1910 and 1911. This legislation also included a moderate but graduated income tax that was made possible by the ratification in February 1913 of the Sixteenth Amendment to the Constitution. (The *Pollock* decision of 1895 striking down the 1894 income tax had made the ratification of an amendment to the U.S. Constitution necessary for the enactment of an income tax.) From the beginning, income taxation was progressive, levying a 1 percent tax on annual individual and corporate incomes over $4,000 per year, rising to 7 percent of incomes over $100,000 per year.

ALTHOUGH THE MONEY question had provoked emotional dissension in the 1890s, between the depression of the 1890s and the Panic of 1907, banking and money had virtually disappeared as subjects of contention except among bankers, business leaders, and academic economists, who continued to discuss methods of making the money supply more flexible ("elastic") and centralizing decision making about currency. In the early twentieth century banking had grown more complicated than before the depression of the 1890s. Prosperity had created a need for more financial instruments, and banks and trust companies issued a plethora of paper that functioned as currency with more or less security, flexibility, and liquidity, including commercial paper (promissory notes and bills of exchange), bank credit, bank notes, certificates of deposit, and, to a certain degree, stocks and bonds. This jerry-built system worked fairly well until the financial Panic of 1907 closed down banks in New York, Chicago, and other cities, creating a nationwide currency crisis that forced people to find illegal substitutes for cash. This severe financial dislocation was brief, but it disturbed many—bankers, businessmen, Theodore Roosevelt, and ordinary people—who urged Congress to take action.

In 1908 Congress had appointed a monetary commission headed by Senator Nelson Aldrich to study currency and banking. Placing no confidence in the wisdom of the populace, Aldrich held no public hearings. "My idea," he said to a congressman, "is, of course, that everything shall be done in the most quiet manner possible, and without any public announcement."[23] Producing forty volumes of testimony and reports on every aspect of central banking, the Aldrich commission presented its recommendations in 1912. Framed by Paul M. Warburg, a partner in the Morgan-related investment house of Kuhn, Loeb & Company, the recommendations embodied the concerns of the biggest of New York bankers.

Reflecting a belief that private enterprise could best guarantee the health of the economy, the Aldrich plan called for a central bank (the National Reserve Association) and a flexible currency, reforms that bankers had supported for several years. The central bank would have branches, Aldrich's concession to a broad spectrum of public opinion that opposed further concentration of financial power in New York City. Owned and run by bankers, the central bank would issue its own currency.

These reforms were meant to rationalize banking and to end the financial panics that had periodically disturbed money markets and the nation's entire economic life. Although the idea of banking reform enjoyed support in many quarters, Senator Aldrich's plan answered only the needs of big bankers (smaller bankers, especially rural bankers, did not see issues in the same light at the big New York banks that were closely tied in with large corporations). In addition, Aldrich's reputation as a partisan of big business made it awkward politically for many

Republicans and nearly all Democrats to endorse his plan. Democrats were more concerned with policing the bankers and providing agricultural credit than with rationalizing financial institutions according to the dictates of New York financial houses.

Between Wilson's election and the inaugural Representative Arsène Pujo's special hearings on banking taught the country a great deal about how a few powerful New Yorkers controlled the nation's finances. A Democrat from Louisiana, Pujo set out to investigate the "money trust," and his committee summoned as witnesses J. P. Morgan and other important figures from the world of New York finance. (Morgan died later in the year, making 1913 a symbolic as well as a legislative watershed in banking.)

The testimony presented overwhelming evidence of the great concentration of banking power that had occurred during the "noteworthy prosperity" and the wave of mergers between 1897 and 1904 as well as the close relationship between banks and the Stock Exchange. The editor of the *Philadelphia North American* drew these conclusions: "The Money Trust is the Wall Street system. But it is clearer to say that the Stock Exchange is the machinery through which the Money Trust operates—in unloading upon the public its manufactured securities and in maintaining its control of prices, of cash, and of credit."[24] Speculation on the stock exchange, it appeared, was simply part of the process of accumulating money, and the Pujo committee hearings provoked an outcry for the regulation of the exchange.

The Pujo committee crystallized opinion against the great financiers of New York and the stock exchange (who were now routinely referred to as the money trust) and added a mandate for banking and currency reform to destroy the money trust and to regulate the stock exchange that conflicted with aims of the Aldrich report. To complicate matters further, William Jennings Bryan's midwestern and southern followers added two demands. Bryan men believed that money should be a governmental obligation because bankers were private citizens pursuing their own self-interest, which did not necessarily coincide with the interests of ordinary people. According to Bryan, only currency that was issued and controlled by the government—the representative of all the people in a democracy—could respond to the needs of all the people. Power so fundamental, he insisted, was too important to be lodged in private hands.

"All the people" included farmers, and Bryan supporters demanded some provision for agricultural credits. President Wilson opposed loans to farmers as special-interest legislation, but Bryanites insisted that agricultural credit was special only because agricultural credits needed to run longer than the usual sixty- or ninety-day limits of commercial paper that represented loans to businesses and industries. As they began to plant in the spring, farmers needed to borrow money they could not repay until they had sold their crops in the fall. (This was the problem that the Farmers' Alliances had tried to address with the subtreasury plan.) Under the best of conditions, cotton producers, who harvested well into the fall, routinely needed credit for longer than six months.

The debates over banking and currency reform embodied several conflicting demands: that the new system introduce a flexible currency to replace national bank notes and thereby end panics and depressions; that it create a central bank under unified, private management and with reserves that could prevent banks from closing in times of crisis; that it break the hold of the money trust; that it regulate the stock exchange; that it be publicly owned and operated in the interest of ordinary people; that the government issue currency; and that the bank operate equally in all sections of the country. No one system could possibly satisfy all these needs.

The act that President Wilson signed into law in December 1913 straddled many demands. The system consisted of twelve coequal banks owned by bankers, but the currency that the Federal Reserve Banks issued was declared an obligation of the government. In another compromise, the majority of the board of directors of each of the Federal Reserve Banks was to be elected by bankers, but the central board was to consist of presidential appointees. The Federal Reserve Act lacked provision for issuing long-term agricultural credits. Nor did it take steps toward curbing the money trust through regulation of banks or the stock exchange, which fell by the wayside until the mid-1930s. (The New Deal created the Federal Deposit Insurance Corporation [1933] and the Securities and Exchange Commission [1934] to insure bank deposits and regulate the stock exchange.) For the most part the framers of the Federal Reserve Act of 1913 agreed with the bankers.

The Federal Reserve Act aimed mainly to satisfy bankers' demand for what was called elastic currency through the issue of Federal Reserve notes, the dollars still in use today. (Until 1913 the basic currency, national bank notes, was secured in only one way, with government bonds, and therefore, the currency supply was relatively inflexible. Because the government issued bonds only when it needed money, the volume of currency in circulation depended on how much money the government needed to borrow. This was not the same as the amount of money consumers, businesses, farmers, and industries needed for their monetary exchanges. The government's demand for money fluctuated according to political as well as economic needs because taxes and tariffs were set for political as well as economic reasons. High protective tariffs were not meant to yield enormous payments of import duties. Quite the contrary, high protective tariffs were meant to shelter various American industries from overseas competition by reducing imports and so were not primarily intended as producers of revenue. Excise taxes on liquor and tobacco products were also meant in part to discourage use and therefore revenues. Because Congress prepared revenue bills and spending bills separately, there existed no coherent governmental budget mechanism that would indicate how much money the federal government spent and how much it collected.)

The Federal Reserve System was intended to replace this inflexible system based on government bonds with a bank that could issue currency based on its total assets (loans, deposits, and government bonds). Recalling the aims of nineteenth-century Greenbackers, the new system would be able to issue more currency in deflationary times and retire currency in inflationary times, thereby curing inflation and heading off panics. First and foremost, the Federal Reserve System was intended to abolish depressions and ensure that banks would never close for lack of money to cover deposits.

The Federal Reserve Act was the most important legislation of Wilson's administration, and the President hailed it as the dawning of a new day of permanent prosperity and happiness.[25] The system did provide flexible currency and efficient regional banking as well as more credit for loans to small businesses and later, with serious limitations, to farmers. But the Federal Reserve System failed in the task most people assigned to it at the time: the prevention of hard times.

WILSON'S ANTITRUST RECOMMENDATIONS were embodied in two bills, one of which, the Clayton bill, included a labor clause and the other of which created the Federal Trade Commission (FTC). As first proposed, the Clayton bill included stiff antitrust language but no exemption for labor, even though the American Federation of Labor had supported Democratic candidates in 1908 and 1912 with the understanding that any antitrust bill sponsored by Democrats would include an explicit exemption for labor. But President Wilson, caught between his sense of the conflicting claims of business and government, failed to put up a fight to secure the aims of Alabama Democrat Henry D. Clayton. Clayton's main reason for proposing the legislation that bears his name was to circumvent the Supreme Court's "rule of reason" in antitrust suits by listing practices that were unlawful. After strenuous lobbying by Samuel Gompers, the Wilson forces conceded the addition of a compromise amendment declaring that labor unions should not be enjoined when they were acting legally. This begged the question because for labor, the crux of the issue was the definition of strikes and boycotts as legal in the first place. After Wilson would go no farther, Gompers accepted the weak compromise, calling it "Labor's Magna Carta," a response, at last, to organized labor's preoccupation with the labor injunction.

Congress emasculated the antitrust provisions of the Clayton Act by prohibiting interlocking directorates and several other unfair trade practices in language so general as to be unenforceable. (Interlocking directorates are created when the same few people sit on the boards of directors

of numerous enterprises, so that several seemingly competing companies share the same leadership.) One western senator called the Clayton
Act "a sort of legislative apology to the trusts, delivered hat in hand, and
accompanied by assurances that no discourtesy is intended."[26] Congress
watered down the Clayton Act further by postponing enforcement of the
interlocking directorates provision before dropping it entirely.

The Federal Trade Commission completed Wilsonian antitrust
action. President Wilson's guide in the creation of the FTC was Louis
D. Brandeis, who had advised Wilson during the 1912 campaign and
whose muckraking treatment of the "money power," *Other People's
Money*, first published in installments in 1913 by *Harper's Weekly*, had
drawn heavily on the findings of the Pujo committee. Brandeis wanted
the FTC to exercise broad powers, and legislation did enable the commission to prevent business from employing "unfair methods of competition" by receiving complaints from the public, holding hearings, and
issuing cease-and-desist orders against businesses acting illegally. But
the FTC lacked enforcement power, and Wilson's appointees were not
distinguished. Judging the FTC's effectiveness during its first several
years, Brandeis called it "a stupid administration."[27]

BY LATE 1914 the three great reforms Wilson had outlined in his inaugural had become law, and the President declared the promises of the
New Freedom fulfilled and the reign of privilege undone. As far as
Wilson was concerned, all the reform that was necessary had been
enacted. He expected a new period of calm and readjustment to follow, as though the Underwood tariff, the Federal Reserve System,
the Clayton Act, and the Federal Trade Commission would cure the
many problems of twentieth-century American society. During this
time, however, Wilson had obstructed the passage of legislation that
he opposed. He blocked a bill to establish a system of long-term rural
credits that would have made low-interest mortgages available to
farmers, and he refused to support a child labor bill that he considered unconstitutional interference in the conduct of private business.
Believing that states had the right to define their electorate—a partic-

ularly prickly issue in the South—he withheld support from a federal amendment permitting women to vote.

WILSON'S EARLIEST SUPPORTERS had been White southerners who lived in the North, such as New York publisher Walter Hines Page, from North Carolina, and William G. McAdoo, a Georgian who built the Hudson River tubes. Wilson appointed several White southerners to his cabinet, including McAdoo as secretary of the treasury, Kentuckian James C. McReynolds as attorney general (whose successor in the Justice Department was a Texan, Thomas W. Gregory), North Carolinian newspaper publisher Josephus Daniels as secretary of the navy, and Texan Albert S. Burleson as postmaster general. Among the minority of nonsoutherners in the cabinet were Secretary of State William Jennings Bryan and the first ever secretary of labor, William B. Wilson.

The southernness of the administration became apparent immediately. Early in April 1913 Postmaster General Burleson suggested segregating Black government workers, and several departments implemented the new policy. Many Black officeholders lost their jobs to Whites, and Secretary of State Bryan appointed White ministers to Haiti and Liberia, breaking traditions that dated back to Reconstruction.

When leaders of the National Association for the Advancement of Colored People protested these policies, Wilson replied that he "honestly thought segregation to be in the interest of the colored people." When Oswald Garrison Villard, the head of the NAACP and one of Wilson's early supporters, met with the President to discuss the racial policies of the administration, Wilson told him that "there was really no discrimination along race lines but that there was a social line of cleavage which, unfortunately, corresponded with the racial line."[28] After the President and his cabinet had shown no inclination to reverse their racial policies in the governmental bureaucracy, Blacks across the country held mass meetings to protest. By December the most visible abuses were toned down, but Black bureaucrats still lost their jobs.

THE YEARS BETWEEN the election of 1910 and Wilson's announcement in 1914 that reform had been accomplished were unusual in the life of the nation. During this progressive era public opinion grew more tolerant of dissent and less bound by convention, and change to increase economic equity generally began to seem desirable. Shaken by the cynical manipulations of the Payne-Aldrich tariff and the revelations of the Pujo committee, the public began to lend reformers increasing support. Even larger numbers of Americans began to question standpattism and accepted, with Theodore Roosevelt, the idea that the nation's economic system operated unfairly or at least inefficiently. But the broadening consensus that change was necessary did not include agreement on the direction or extent of these changes. In the political arena the election of 1910 had tempered conservative Republican control of Congress, and the campaign of 1912 had brought advocates of change to the fore; three of the four presidential candidates promised reform. The hegemony of a united, business-oriented Republican party and the hierarchical identity-of-interest values that its influence entailed shattered.

Young people who came of age during these years shared a skewed set of assumptions about what was normal in public life that was based on unusually permissive times. They took for granted that the public wanted workers to be paid well and treated fairly, the powers of great corporations to be curbed, and wealth to be redistributed more equitably.

During the 1910–1914 years the country seemed to many to have changed once and for all for the better, to have shucked off the tyrannies of wealth and conventionality. Ray Stannard Baker remembered it as a new world, when "it seemed a genuine and sincere awakening to the social and economic and political ills that had so long afflicted the country."[29] A new era of fair play, democracy, and openness seemed to have begun.

Popular writing caught the excitement of the times. William Allen White, a barometer of public sentiment, published a book in 1910 entitled *The Old Order Changeth: A View of American Democracy*. Van Wyck Brooks, a Greenwich Village essayist, critic, and translator, was working on a book that he published in 1915, *America's Coming-of-Age*. Several other works celebrated the changing times, including Herbert Croly's *The Promise of American Life* (1909), which had convinced Theodore Roosevelt, whose thought was much like Croly's, to embark on the radical speaking tour that outlined the New Nationalism.

Walter Lippmann had served as secretary to George Lunn, the Socialist mayor of Schenectady. A promising young journalist from whom much would be heard after the European War, Lippmann published his first two books, *A Preface to Politics* (1913) and *Drift and Mastery* (1914), in these years, optimistic works that anticipated the rationalization of American life through liberal ideas. In 1914 Herbert Croly published *Progressive Democracy* and joined with Lippmann and Walter Weyl to launch *The New Republic*. Weyl had come from the settlement movement and had published *The New Democracy* in 1912. In the spirit of Rooseveltian reform, Croly promised that *The New Republic* would be "radical without being socialistic . . . pragmatic rather than doctrinaire."[30] This clarion of progressive reform published a range of liberal and a few radical voices. Its backers, Dorothy and Willard Straight, came out of the heart of the money trust. She, a Whitney, had inherited millions from Rockefeller enterprises; he was a Morgan banker.

Socialists represented only a minuscule percentage of Americans, but during the progressive years a society that talked about many sorts of reform tolerated their views and sometimes even made them fashionable. Greenwich Village in New York became the center of the colorful, cosmopolitan culture that brought together writers like Willa Cather and Edna St. Vincent Millay and various sorts of radicals—Wobblies, anarchists, birth control advocates, single taxers, and socialists—as well as older and younger liberals and moderates who called themselves progressives. They met at the Liberal Club and at what muckraking journalist Lincoln Steffens termed "the only successful salon I have ever seen in America," that of Mabel Dodge.[31] The daughter of a rich Buffalo, New York, banker, she had lived in a villa in Florence, Italy, for several years before returning to New York in 1912. Dodge wrote prolifically and was one of the creators of a new way of living that was called bohemian.

The Masses summed up bohemian New York. A radical periodical, it was founded in 1911 but blossomed in 1912 under the editorship of the Socialist critic and lecturer Max Eastman. According to John Reed, one of its best writers, "the broad purpose of *The Masses* is a social one—to everlastingly attack old systems, old morals, old prejudices— the whole weight of outworn thought that dead men have saddled upon us."[32] *The Masses'* backers were not as flush as the Straights, but they included some noteworthy names: Samuel Untermyer, the lawyer who had served as counsel for the Pujo committee; Amos Pinchot, brother of Gifford Pinchot; and E. W. Scripps, owner of the Scripps-Howard chain of "yellow" newspapers.

The Greenwich Village bohemian culture also spun off new pub- lishers for the new works, European and American. B. W. Heubsch published Van Wyck Brooks and, in the war years, the iconoclastic economist Thorstein Veblen, whose best-known work was *A Theory of the Leisure Class* (1899). In 1915, when he was twenty-three, Alfred A. Knopf launched his publishing house. At about the same time Albert and Charles Boni joined Horace Liveright to form Boni and Liveright, which published much of the new literature of the 1920s.

THE YEARS OF progressive ferment before the Great War were special but brief. Looking back, Walter Lippmann remembered them as "a happy time . . . it was easy for a young man to believe in the inevitability of progress, in the perfectibility of man and of society, and in the sublima- tion of evil." But in 1914 Lippmann was in Europe and writing home that "nothing can stop the awful disintegration now."[33] Not only had Woodrow Wilson called a halt to reform, but the time of wars soon dis- tracted attention from the halting but seemingly irresistible progress toward economic equity. Lippmann was witnessing the beginnings of the tragedy that finally engulfed the United States. But the war that cre- ated the first distraction occurred in the Western hemisphere.

WARS

The idea of the United States' going to war seemed distant when Woodrow Wilson took office early in 1913. But as the year wore on and Congress debated New Freedom legislation, the bloody and complicated Mexican Revolution, which had turned into a civil war, edged into the headlines. After the fall of the moderate government of Francisco I. Madero one government held Mexico City and a second controlled the northern region that bordered the United States. Occasional raids on American property exasperated southwesterners, but that was a local annoyance compared with the growing threat to what American investors termed a suitable climate for business. Americans were also beginning to worry about the activities of Britons, who had already invested heavily in Mexico, and Germans, who seemed poised to exploit both the disorder and the anti-Americanism that accompanied the revolution. By late 1913 President Wilson had come under great pressure to intervene militarily to protect "American interests" in Mexico. It quickly became apparent that what Americans saw as their interests in Mexico did not coincide with the various conflicting interests of Mexicans.

THE REVOLUTION AGAINST the oligarchy of President Porfirio Díaz had begun in 1910, while the president celebrated the centennial of the first battle in the Mexican struggle for independence from Spain. Díaz had ruled Mexico since 1876 but was now unable to contain reaction against a generation and a half of oppressive rule. His long dictatorship had combined internal repression, political stagnation, nepotism, and inefficiency with a rapid development of commercial agriculture and extractive industries. Díaz had allowed his favorites to acquire communal village lands for private exploitation because he thought entrepreneurs would develop agriculture more efficiently than peasants. This policy concentrated landownership in a few hands and divided the rural Mexican population on the best lands into rich owners of rural estates, hacendados, and landless workers, peons.

As in many other poor countries that welcomed private foreign investment, the Mexican economy was characterized by uneven development: a great many people were very poor, and a few were enormously wealthy. The Madero family of the northeastern state of Coahuila, for instance, owned mines, rolling mills, distilleries, flour mills, and textile factories as well as cotton plantations.[1] Taxes were low (but collected capriciously), and public services such as education were rudimentary in the towns and nonexistent in the countryside. Mexico exported cheap raw materials and imported expensive manufactured goods. Until Díaz's fall several repressive mechanisms kept order: federal rural police, state and municipal constabularies, and, often, the hacendados' personal police and Pinkertons.

THE DÍAZ GOVERNMENT had welcomed foreign investment, which had come from Germany, Great Britain, and, most of all, the United States. The United States was Mexico's most important trading partner, and Americans owned much of the visible wealth. American investments in Mexico had doubled between 1900 and 1910, so that by 1910 Americans owned about 43 percent of the property in Mexico, and other foreigners owned nearly a quarter.[2] Foreign companies, especially American companies, dominated important sectors of the Mexican economy— railroads, utilities, and extractive industries, such as coal mining and oil drilling.

Oil had been pumped in Mexico since 1900, and in 1910 Mexico was the world's seventh-largest producer of oil, by 1911, the third-largest. The exploitation of Mexican petroleum deposits by foreign interests was a particularly sensitive point, for many Mexicans believed that like other subsoil resources, they should belong to the nation as a whole and benefit all the Mexican people. Foreign oil companies did not share these views and, moreover, sent their oil and their profits out of Mexico as a matter of course.

Oil was not the only Mexican resource that foreigners controlled. In 1912 Americans owned well over three-quarters of the silver, lead, and copper mines (mostly in the hands of Hearsts and Guggenheims), nearly three-quarters of the smelters, almost 70 percent of the rubber, and 60 percent of the oil (Edward L. Doheny and Standard Oil). Under Díaz, Mexicans called their country "the mother of foreigners and the stepmother of Mexicans."[3]

As in China at the turn of the century, foreign economic domination had fostered nationalism, which became a political force to be reckoned with after 1900.[4] Mexicans wondered whether the government was giving the country away in the name of development, and the growing indignation against foreigners and foreign domination made anti-Americanism more obvious, especially in centers of American activity.

National control of extractive industries and land reform, the two central aims of the revolution, were closely intertwined. The revolution opposed the social and economic dislocations that rapid foreign-sponsored development entailed and demanded responsible development on behalf of the Mexican people, instead of exploitation that enriched foreigners and a few Mexicans. The revolutionary platform of 1910 demanded "Land for the landless and Mexico for the Mexicans."

The revolution against Díaz had soon turned into a civil war that mostly pitted Mexican armies against one another, although roving bands occasionally attacked, robbed, and murdered foreigners. Raids across the border into the United States occurred often enough to make President Taft put U.S. border troops on the alert in the winter of 1910–1911.

The Mexican Revolution had not been an issue in the 1912 presidential elections in the United States because Taft had avoided inflammatory action. But as the military phase of the revolution continued at the cost of American lives and property, pressure mounted for American intervention. Theodore Roosevelt volunteered to lead cavalry into Mexico, as he had done into Cuba. The Senate proposed the annexation of Lower California (Baja California) to settle American claims against Mexico.[5]

THE REVOLUTION HAD forced Díaz to resign in 1911, and the revolutionary haciendado from Coahuila Francisco I. Madero had taken office. But Madero backpedaled on land reform, and the revolution turned against him. In February 1913 Victoriano Huerta, one of Madero's generals, betrayed him and joined an anti-Maderist insurrection. Following the "tragic ten days" of slaughter in Mexico City, Huerta deposed, then murdered Madero and took over the government in a maneuver that strained legality. Huerta failed to gain the support of other important revolutionaries, who began to oppose him through force of arms.[6]

In Washington President Wilson broke the tradition of recognizing any foreign government that held power and refused to recognize Huerta, ostensibly because of the manner in which he had seized office, although the security of American investments in Mexico also carried weight. As 1913 progressed, Wilson not merely withheld recognition but did all he could to undermine Huerta by massing tens of thousands of American troops on the border and sending American warships to Mexican waters to hover around the oil fields near Tampico and the port of Veracruz. In November 1913 Wilson warned Huerta—who had imprisoned 100 deputies (legislators) and assumed dictatorial powers— that unless he stepped down, the United States would depose him.

While many Mexicans opposed Huerta and the general faced serious armed opposition, Mexicans resented the decision of the President of the United States to withhold recognition. What happened within Mexico, they thought, was not subject to approval from the United States, which seemed anxious to force its will upon Mexico.[7]

Although many Americans agreed that what happened in Mexico was the business of Mexicans, public pressure mounted for armed intervention to stop a seemingly interminable civil war. In the Senate Albert B. Fall of New Mexico, a leading proponent of intervention, who was also interested in oil, read a list of sixty-three murders and other crimes against Americans that had occurred in Mexico since the beginning of the revolution in 1910. He argued that the United States was responsible for maintaining order inside other countries in the hemisphere. According to this Rooseveltian interpretation of the Monroe Doctrine, Europeans were prohibited from undertaking military activities in the Western Hemisphere, and since European governments could not protect their nationals in the Americas, the United States must do it for them. "As soon as facts make it evident that civilized society in Mexico is in peril," *The Outlook* agreed editorially, "and life and property cannot be protected except by intervention, the United States is under moral obligation to intervene."[8]

Americans in Mexico—or in any other weaker country in the hemisphere—assumed that they held claims on the armed forces of the United States and believed that when they felt themselves or their interests to be endangered, the United States should not hesitate to violate Mexico's sovereignty to protect them. (Imperialist Europeans also construed the obligations of the state in this way.) Few Americans questioned the United States' right to police the hemisphere and to invade foreign countries at will, to protect Americans, American investments, or something vaguely called civilization.

Interventionists who argued that the United States should invade Mexico because Mexicans were not advanced enough to govern themselves resurrected racial assumptions about fitness for self-government from 1898. The Indian ancestry of most Mexicans supposedly explained why Mexicans were unable to establish what a Harvard professor called a modern civilized government. On the individual level, Indian descent was said to hold the key to General Huerta's character. "His ability, undoubtably remarkable, is closely allied to cunning," noted an American observer. "His intelligence has strange limitations."[9] As a White southerner Woodrow Wilson was particularly prickly about racial hierarchy, and he hounded General Huerta as though the latter were an "impudent" southern Black refusing a White man's orders.

MEXICO'S POVERTY—taken as proof that "in the hundred years of the Mexican Republic, the Mexican people have learned little or nothing about self-government or right living"—also seemed to weaken its people's claims to sovereignty and furnished a rationale for American annexation of regions adjacent to the United States that were lightly settled and undeveloped.[10] By this analysis, wealthy nations had the right to take over poor countries to develop natural resources. Citing lack of development, a Californian decided that "Mexico has no need of Lower California or northwestern Sonora. . . . We need them, could develop them, would develop them."[11]

Even Americans who shared the interventionists' basic assumptions might doubt that intervention was in the best interests of the United States, however. Three parallels warned them against invading a foreign country that would require pacification and occupation. Britain's bloody centuries-long occupation of Ireland and its desperate struggle to subdue the Boers in South Africa provided two examples. If the British experience lacked sufficient immediacy, Albert Bushnell Hart, a Harvard professor of government, reminded interventionists that for "sixteen years we have been civilizing the Filipinos up to the point where they are unanimous only on one thing, namely, that they want us to leave."[12]

WHILE WILSON'S IMPATIENCE with Huerta inclined him toward intervention, Governor O. B. Colquitt of Texas gave him a push in that direction. Ideology and economics exacerbated border troubles that had plagued U.S.-Mexican relations since the start of the Mexican Revolution. Not only was the revolution anti-American, but American wealth tempted Mexican raiders across the border. By early 1914 the governor of Texas had tired of Washington's policy of watchful waiting. When Hueristas kidnapped an American citizen, a Texan named Clemente Vargara, in February, Colquitt ordered an investigation of what turned out to be Vargara's murder and asked the State Department if Texas Rangers could go into Mexico to retrieve Vargara's body. Secretary of State Bryan reminded Colquitt that foreign relations were the responsibility of the federal government, but the governor still threatened to deal directly with the Mexican authorities to vindicate his state. To forestall future independent actions on the governor's part, the secretary of war sent United States troops to the Texas border, and the crisis passed. But just as the situation in Texas cooled down, Mexican raiders crossed over into Tecate, California, burned a customs office, and killed the postmaster. Border incidents and maverick actions at the state level increased tensions between the two nations.

As Wilson inched toward intervention, Huerta's Mexican opponents won several decisive battles. The "First Chief," Venustiano Carranza, a hacendado from the north, led the most serious opposition with the support of two effective generals from the other end of the social scale, Emiliano Zapata, whose base of operations lay in the southern agricultural state of Morelos, and Francisco ("Pancho") Villa, in the north.

FRANCISCO VILLA, Carranza's most successful general, captured American imaginations. In the early months of 1914 Villa led Carrancista forces and seemed to offer the best hope of defeating Huerta without direct American involvement. To the *New York World*, Villa was "the one strong, commanding military figure in Mexico . . . the man stands out as a strong, virile figure who commands the confidence of his followers in the highest degree."[13] Operating in the northern states and personally open, Villa was easily accessible to American journalists and movie companies such as the Mutual Film Corporation, with which he signed a contract in January 1914.

Villa looked like a Mexican Theodore Roosevelt. And like Roosevelt, he was often pictured on horseback. Roosevelt had made his reputation in the American war in Cuba, and Villa, too, had the panache of a military man. His impoverished childhood embellished the legend of "Pancho" Villa, who as a young man (named Doroteo Arango) was forced to flee the hacienda where he worked after avenging an insult to his sister by the landowner's son. In those days, it was said, the poor got no justice against the rich, and young Arango had had no choice but to join a gang of bandits in the mountains, where he took the name Francisco Villa. Villa's popularity transformed his bandit days into the picaresque adventures of a hero. In December 1913 the *New York Times* ran a photograph with the caption "Villa, the Robin Hood of Mexico." The story told of how the bandit Villa, angered by the misery of the peons of a large hacienda, looted the big house and distributed the spoils among the poor.

As a general Villa was engagingly unaffected. Unlike Zapata, whose manifestos bristled with words like *expropriation* and *exploitation*, Villa's dreams of Mexico after the revolution were pastoral and reassuringly vague. He envisioned a country without an army, because "armies are the greatest support of tyranny. There can be no dictator without any army."[14]

More comforting yet to his American admirers, Villa often spoke highly of his neighbors to the north. When he took over cities, he scrupulously protected Americans. He used American pilots in the airplanes that dropped bombs on the city of Torreón in the middle of 1913. And when other Mexican leaders unanimously opposed an American invasion in April 1914, Villa welcomed it.

VILLA'S PERSONAL POPULARITY in the United States in 1914 did not win the civil war or guarantee the safety of American investments in Mexico, and President Wilson continued to contemplate American intervention. Colonel Edward M. House, the President's close personal adviser, noted in his diary in late 1913 that Wilson had decided to go to war with Mexico, to establish a naval blockade, and to divide the country into two or three regions. If the governors would agree, U.S. forces would occupy the states of northern Mexico. Wilson needed only a pretext, which the events of April 9, 1914, in a region of great interest to Americans furnished.

Hueristas held Tampico, the major city in the oil fields, which Carrancistas were attacking. During the fighting American sailors from the USS *Dolphin*, one of several American warships stationed offshore, rowed a small boat to land to get gasoline. A Huerista colonel arrested the Americans for being in a war zone without a permit and held them for a couple of hours before releasing them with profuse apologies from his commanding officer. The officer also sent immediate apologies to the commander of the American fleet, Admiral Henry T. Mayo.

Admiral Mayo refused to accept apologies for what he saw as an insult to the United States, and he demanded a twenty-one-gun salute from the Mexican forces to the American flag within twenty-four hours. General Huerta's apology for the misunderstanding and his promise that the offending colonel would be punished satisfied Secretary of State Bryan and Secretary of the Navy Daniels. But President Wilson saw his chance and backed up Mayo's ultimatum, warning General Huerta that "the gravest consequences" would follow a refusal to salute the American flag. Huerta offered a "reciprocal salute" to be fired first by the Mexicans and then by the Americans, but Wilson insisted on an unconditional promise to salute the American flag. Huerta refused; Wilson suspended the negotiations.

On April 20, 1914, the President went before Congress to explain the Tampico affair, which he saw as one of a series of incidents proving that the Huerta regime intentionally imperiled American interests, and to ask for approval for the use of United States armed forces to obtain "the fullest recognition of the rights and dignity of the United States." Wilson wanted not only to destroy Huerta militarily but also to teach a public lesson in humility, another manifestation of the President's southern expectations.[15]

Wilson sent seven powerful new battleships, four troop transports full of marines, and a flotilla of destroyers to Mexico but was surprised when the Mexicans at Veracruz fought back. (The battle for occupation cost the Mexicans 126 casualties; the Americans, 19.) Wilson was also amazed that Huerta welcomed American intervention because it would unite Mexicans behind him against the Americans. Zapata and Carranza prepared to join Huerta in driving the Americans out of

Veracruz. Only Villa among the important Mexican leaders held back. Secretary of State Bryan appreciated Villa's response and called him a "high-minded and noble citizen" who showed a "comprehension of the whole situation that is greatly to his credit."[16]

The 6,000 American forces quickly settled into life in Veracruz. Applying lessons learned in the Philippines and Panama, the army employed large numbers of Mexicans to clean out the market, burn garbage, dig sewers, install screens and flytraps, spray mosquitoes, tear up hard-to-clean cobblestone sidewalks, and put down cement. Veracruz had never been cleaner than during the American occupation, but the American military ran the city completely and the City Council never met. Yet the occupation of Veracruz neither forced Huerta to salute the American flag nor ended the civil war. American forces withdrew after seven months. Cleaning up the city was their single accomplishment.

Huerta resigned in July 1914, during the American occupation of Veracruz, forced out of office by the Carrancistas, not by the American presence. Declaring it the provisional capital of Mexico, Carrancistas occupied Veracruz after the Americans had departed on November 23, 1914. But strains that had appeared earlier in the year deepened into a split between Carranza and his generals, Villa and Zapata, who now continued fighting against the "First Chief."

The President of the United States had tried to dictate policy and restore order in Mexico, but the revolution did not comply. The civil war continued, subject to a series of conflicting Mexican claims for power, true independence, and economic justice. The withdrawal from Veracruz marked the end of the first episode of direct United States involvement in the unruly Mexican Revolution. American policy was stymied in Mexico, but by then a new conflict had begun to obscure events south of the Rio Grande.

FROM THE VANTAGE POINT of the United States the assassination of the heir to the Austro-Hungarian throne at the end of June 1914 by a Serbian nationalist did not seem catastrophic. "The Hapsburgs were always being assassinated," an American woman journalist recalled.[17] The Serbian question was part of a larger political shifting in the Balkans in southeastern Europe, which had belonged to the Ottoman Empire— Turkey—since the sixteenth century. As the Ottoman Empire shrank, the Austro-Hungarian Empire expanded into recently independent Serbia. After the assassination—and with the assurance of German support—Austria declared war on Serbia. By early August Germany, Russia, France, Great Britain, and Turkey had entered the war, and Franz Ferdinand, Serbia, and Austria-Hungary faded from view, as the war allowed the settling of old scores and the pursuit of rivalries that were imperial, commercial, industrial, and colonial.

THE WAR CAUGHT Americans off guard, but having once realized that all Europe was embroiled, they, like Europeans, viewed it in apocalyptic terms. Whether or not they called it "white civilization," as did President Wilson, they agreed with the American ambassador in Paris that "civilization is threatened by demoralization."[18] A social reformer wrote that "suddenly, in the wink of an eye, three hundred years of progress is tossed into the melting-pot. Civilization is all gone, and barbarism come."[19] Samuel Gompers, president of the American Federation of Labor, remembered that he had been hearing speculation on the possibility of war between the major European powers for some time and that the last few years had witnessed an escalating arms race in Europe. Yet, he recalled, "I did not believe it was possible for civilized nations deliberately to undertake to settle differences through force of arms and to enter into the destructive horrors of war made possible by human inventions and our increased knowledge of science."[20] Others had viewed the arms race and a series of international crises with equal disquiet.

President Wilson had sent his personal envoy, Colonel House (not the secretary of state, William Jennings Bryan) to Europe in the spring of 1914 to seek means of soothing strained relations between the European governments. House found conditions in Europe appalling, what he called "jingoism run stark mad." Unless Wilson could find some way to pull Europeans back from the brink, House predicted the outbreak of "an awful cataclysm."[21] When the cataclysm broke within months, Americans employed the same imagery to express their incredulity: a horror; a horrid nightmare; a horrid dream.

Even though most Americans preferred the side of the Entente Cordiale (Britain, France, and Russia), which they called the Allies, they had little sympathy with what they saw as the forces that had caused the war—jingoism, militarism, and greed. Placing blame on one side or another mattered less than the existence throughout Europe of militarists competing for imperial possessions and investing in deadly arsenals. The European arms race had attained tremendous velocity after the last big European war in 1870. Between 1870 and 1914 Great Britain had spent more per capita for arms than any of its European rivals, but German arms procurement had increased most dramatically, especially in the years just before 1914. Not only were there far more arms and soldiers in 1914 than at any previous time (Germany and Austria-Hungary had universal male conscription), but the soldiers bore arms that seemed the ultimate in sophistication and deadliness. The new artillery and machine guns sprayed impenetrable curtains of fire, and gigantic mortars fired shells that devastated the landscape. Poison gases choked and permanently blinded their victims. The extraordinary destructiveness of the new weapons convinced Americans and Europeans that the war would prove too devastating to last.

By the winter of 1914, however, the two sides had reached a bloody stalemate that slaughtered millions without ending the war. Americans wanted nothing to do with this ugly, senseless fight, in which the idea of supremacy seemed to count for more than human life. But the war had repercussions in the United States anyway.

ALTHOUGH the war seemed far away to Americans who professed to want to let Europe stew in its own juice, the European crisis affected the U.S. economy immediately and disastrously.[22] As they went to war, the governments of Germany, Austria, France, and Great Britain all went off the gold standard. Frightened Europeans holding American securities—which could still be redeemed for gold—sold them in the United States or attempted to do so to get gold. The heavy volume of sales and the drain on U.S. gold threatened to ruin stock markets and banks in the U.S. as well as in Europe, because between $2.5 billion and $6 billion worth of American securities held abroad were being dumped simultaneously. European financial markets closed, the London Stock Exchange last of all, on July 31. Within hours the New York Stock Exchange had also closed, and the American economy plunged into a sharp recession. The New York Stock Exchange did not reopen until late November.

The banking and credit crisis squeezed American businesses, which laid off workers, thereby aggravating unemployment that had already been increasing since the fall of 1913. On the West Coast thousands of unemployed men formed armies reminiscent of the depression of the 1890s, one of which was led by "General" Charles T. Kelly, who had led an unemployed army from California to Washington in 1894. In the East the unemployed included many women, and in New York City the Women's Trade Union League organized a protest of women needing work. In the winter of 1913–1914 social workers had compared current unemployment and suffering with those of the winter of 1907–1908. By 1914–1915 their comparisons were to the catastrophic winter of 1893–1894. In many cities ministers and socialists improvised means of caring for the needy, whose numbers increased as the winter deepened. Late in the winter unemployment hovered around 11.5 percent nationally, with levels of 13 percent in Chicago, 20 percent in Duluth, and 14 percent in St. Louis.[23]

IWW leadership of the unemployed made the issue all the more volatile. Demanding food and shelter, Wobblies led the unemployed into churches during services. In February and March 1915 Frank Tannenbaum, a twenty-one-year-old busboy (later a Columbia history professor), led hundreds of men into churches in New York and inspired ministers to form committees to care for the unemployed and to locate temporary jobs.

Rising food prices made things worse. When the cost of bread increased 20 percent—from 5 to 6 cents—in New York City in February 1915, Mayor John Purroy Mitchel wrote President Wilson of the "immediate prospect [of] much hardship and suffering in New York and other cities caused by the recent increase in the price of bread . . . which is a very considerable burden on our poor people."[24] Former President Theodore Roosevelt added his voice to the rising chorus of concern at a meeting sponsored by the Church Federation on Unemployment in New York and contributed $10,000 of his Nobel Peace Prize money to the cause.

By the spring of 1915 European orders for war matériel from American factories had put American workers back to work, and manufacturers discovered that they could profit from Europe's misfortune in a variety of ways. The *Wall Street Journal* saw that not only could American exporters move into markets that Europeans had previously dominated, but the war would also provide a "chance to dissipate the prejudices against Wall Street created by dishonest politicians," like Arsène Pujo. It seemed that the war would accentuate a "tendency toward conservatism" that the *Journal* and other spokesmen for business applauded.[25]

THE EUROPEAN WAR cured an economic slump that it had previously aggravated, but prosperity was not its only bequest to the United States. With the war came conflict, as Americans began to divide into partisans of peace and partisans of preparedness. The first antiwar protest had occurred on August 29, 1914, in New York City, when 1,500 women dressed in mourning and accompanied by muffled drums marched silently down Fifth Avenue. At the head of the parade, a young woman carried a banner picturing a dove and olive branch and the word *PEACE*. The marchers included a division of nurses from the Henry Street Settlement, more than 100 Socialist women, a group of 20 Black women, and, in traditional dress, a Native American woman and a Chinese woman.

The Woman's Peace Parade marked a transformation of the peace movement from stuffy, male respectability to dramatic feminism unafraid of street demonstrations. This shift was influenced by the change in tactics in the woman suffrage movement, for many peace advocates were also suffragists. The Woman's Peace Parade committee was itself a coalition of suffragists, socialists, and social reformers, among whom were Lillian Wald of the Henry Street Settlement, author Charlotte Perkins Gilman, Leonora O'Reilly and Mary Dreier of the Women's Trade Union League, Anna Howard Shaw and Carrie Chapman Catt of the National American Woman Suffrage Association, historian Mary Beard, and Greenwich Village radical Crystal Eastman. They shared the long-standing conviction that women, whose morals were supposedly more elevated than men's, had a special interest in peace and therefore a particular antiwar mission. The Woman's Peace Parade Committee organized permanently as the Woman's Peace party, which ultimately became the Women's International League for Peace and Freedom.

In December 1914 men and women who had been associated with social reform during the progressive years, like Oswald Garrison Villard, Lillian Wald, and Carrie Chapman Catt, formed another influential antiwar organization, the League to Limit Armaments, predecessor of the American Union Against Militarism.

On the other side, the advocates of preparedness demanded universal military training for young men and the enlargement of the army and navy. The chief spokesmen for preparedness were Major General Leonard Wood, the hero of Cuba, and his friends United States Senator Elihu Root of New York, Theodore Roosevelt, and Wall Street investor Bernard Baruch.

The most articulate of the preparedness advocates, Roosevelt had always favored large armed forces. During the progressive years his followers had papered over his militarism with social reform. But now his renewed and unrestrained stress on the military distressed his progressive champions. William Allen White watched as Roosevelt turned away from the ideals of the Progressive party. "Social and industrial justice no longer interested Colonel Roosevelt," White noted ruefully. "He had a war, a war greater than ever he realized it would be, to engage his talents. He made a tremendous clamor for preparedness. He even won back many of his old enemies, the big businessmen who now saw eye to eye with him and applauded as the Colonel raged at Wilson."[26] Preparedness returned Roosevelt to the regular Republican fold.

Preparedness advocates wanted to remedy what they saw as the terrible weakness of the American armed forces, so as to reduce the nation's vulnerability to attack. Republican Senator Henry Cabot Lodge of Massachusetts supported preparedness, as he had supported military strength since the Spanish-American War, as a deterrent. Armies and navies served peaceful ends, he maintained, "because there is no such incentive to war as a rich, undefended, and helpless country, which by its condition invites aggression."[27] Because no aggressors threatened to cross the oceans, it remained true, as throughout most of the nineteenth century, that the American armed forces consisted of a small regular army of Indian fighters, national guards, and state militia and a navy that, despite a shipbuilding campaign early in the twentieth century, was still tiny when measured by European standards. As important as it was in the preparedness argument, defense provided only one postulate.

Theodore Roosevelt touted preparedness as a means of breaking down barriers in American life because, he said, "The military tent where they all sleep side by side will rank next to the public school among the great agents of democratization."[28] Universal (male) military training would strengthen Americans by lessening insidious social differences, thereby speeding "Americanization." The theme of Americanization quickly burgeoned into a nativist opposition to what were called hyphens, short for "hyphenated Americans"—that is, Americans whose identity was modified and supposedly conditional, as in Irish Americans and German Americans. Antihyphenism sprang from antipathy toward Americans of foreign parentage who had not enthusiastically assimilated American culture and values. Considering that 30 percent of Americans had been born overseas or had at least one foreign-born parent and that nearly all these people were farmers or workers who were not generally supporters of preparedness, antihyphenism's potential for mischief was enormous.

Antihyphenism began in fear of German intrigue in the United States and several unexplained attempts—some successful—to sabotage American shipyards and factories. By the middle of 1915, as the preparedness movement gathered momentum, anti-Germanism had merged into an undifferentiated antihyphenism and an ardent 100-percent-Americanism. Preparedness had become the issue not only of the military lobby but also of ultrapatriots.

Opponents of preparedness called it militarism and said it aped the worst aspects of Prussian authoritarianism. Antiwar spokesmen like William Jennings Bryan countered arguments for preparedness as a deterrent to war by pointing out that "if preparation prevents war, there would have been no war in Europe. They spent twenty years preparing for it."[29]

Bryan's argument did not convert the supporters of preparedness, who in December 1914 organized the National Security League, which numbered among its members prominent north-easterners such as the former ambassador to Britain Joseph H. Choate and former Secretary of War Henry L. Stimson. The league's financial backers included copper magnate Simon Guggenheim, railroad millionaire Cornelius Vanderbilt, and steel baron Henry Clay Frick.

In 1914 preparedness forces did not, however, advocate American entry into the European War. The National Security League promoted what it called patriotic education and financed congressional candidates who were probusiness and antilabor. Very early the preparedness lobby came to embody the views of well-off conservatives in the Northeast who were antagonistic to the economic and social liberalism of the preceding years. The peace/preparedness controversy was one of several dissensions brought by the war, for Americans lined up on both sides of the European conflict.

WHEN THE WAR STARTED, President Wilson asked Americans to be neutral in thought and deed, a politically expedient as well as high-minded request, considering the heterogeneous nature of the American people. Eight and one-quarter million Americans were of German parentage and, presumably, favored Germany and the Central Powers. Four and one-half million Americans were of Irish parentage and opposed Britain. Realizing that most other Americans saw Britain as the mother country and as a sister Anglo-Saxon democracy, Irish Americans joined German Americans in trying to keep the United States neutral. They formed organizations like the American Embargo Conference, the Friends of Peace, the American Neutrality League, and the American Truth Society. Although they did not represent the numerical and political strength of Irish and German Americans, the 3,000,000 American Jews also tended to oppose the Allies, which included anti-Semitic, autocratic czarist Russia, which many of them had fled.

With these important exceptions, Americans favored the Allies and took Allied victory for granted. For all the sympathy for Britain and France, however, virtually no one, not even Theodore Roosevelt, wanted to enter the conflict. Woodrow Wilson captured the mood in December 1914, when he opposed military training as counter to American tradition. The European conflict did not affect Americans, he said; it was "a war *with which we have nothing to do.*"[30] Like many Americans, journalist Ray Stannard Baker at first felt distant from the European conflict. But "suddenly, if imperceptibly, my world, the world of a majority of Americans, began to break up."[31] Bit by bit the following year made the war in Europe an American concern.

DIFFICULTIES AROSE first over the British blockade of Germany. Britain disregarded the traditional American value of freedom of the seas by mining the North Sea and seizing neutral American ships, which it took to British ports—where shippers lost time and, often, their cargoes—instead of searching them for contraband on the high seas. Declaring a long list of nonmilitary supplies, including cotton, contraband, Britain disrupted American trade, ruined cotton markets, and caused distress in the South. The British blockade and contraband policy kept the Wilson administration busy during late 1914.

In the spring of 1915 the war presented Americans with a new worry. The new German war boats, *Unterseebooten* (submarines), sank several British ships, killed several Americans traveling on British ships, and touched off a controversy in the State Department. The counselor of the State Department Robert Lansing wanted to hold Germany accountable for the loss of American lives, but Secretary of State Bryan wanted to reduce the risk of the United States' being drawn into the war by prohibiting Americans from traveling on the ships of the belligerent nations.

The sinking of the *Lusitania*, on May 7, 1915, precipitated a major crisis. This British Cunard liner, the largest luxury passenger ship in service on the North Atlantic, had disregarded torpedo scares and warnings and left New York bound for Liverpool carrying 1,257 passengers, a cargo of food, and a great deal of ammunition. Newspapers in New York City had carried some warnings about the presence of ammunition, but these seemed simply to be scare tactics to ruin British business and were not taken seriously. A German submarine torpedoed the *Lusitania* off the coast of Ireland, the liner sank quickly, and 1,200 passengers drowned: 124 Americans, 270 women, 94 children.

This attack on what was unmistakably a passenger ship introduced Americans to total warfare in a way that the German invasion of Belgium, the British food blockade against Germany, and the slaughter of soldiers by the hundreds of thousands did not. Newspapers called the Germans "miscreants" and "wild beasts," and Theodore Roosevelt branded the sinking "murder," demanding that Wilson declare war against Germany.[32]

Everyone else was angry, but a *New York Times* poll of representatives and senators revealed a great deal of wariness. President Wilson's first public statement on the *Lusitania* (before 4,000 newly naturalized American citizens in Philadelphia) expressed American abhorrence of the war. The United States, he said, was like "a man being too proud to fight" and had a special peace mission among the nations of the world. Roosevelt's reply to Wilson's pacifist sentiments and the audience to which he had spoken combined the preparedness camp's nativism and contempt for peace. Roosevelt branded Wilson a coward and his supporters "all the hyphenated Americans . . . the solid flubdub and pacifist vote."[33]

The debate within the administration mirrored this split in opinion, with Lansing demanding an immediate apology and reparations from

Germany for losses on the *Lusitania* and Bryan striving to maintain an evenhanded neutrality. Bryan wanted to address the German issue by submitting the *Lusitania* affair to arbitration and also to send a protest to Britain for interfering with American shipping. Bryan, the peacekeeper, met defeat on every score.

WITH MANY MISGIVINGS Bryan dutifully dispatched a formal American protest to Germany, holding the German government to strict accountability for American lives lost through submarine attacks. Fearing that the rigid response would bring the United States into the conflict, he resigned as secretary of state on June 8, 1915. Bryan's resignation provoked a storm of criticism. Although he was denounced as a contemptible coward who would not stand up for Americans' right to free travel, many shared his fear that the President was taking the country down the road to war. German Americans and Irish Americans repeated their calls for an arms embargo, and congressmen received avalanches of antiwar mail. American opinion was clearly divided, and Bryan, even out of office, spoke for millions.

William Jennings Bryan, representative of the rural and small-town Midwest of the 1890s, had been a peculiar secretary of state. Like many of his constituents, he treasured peace and hated liquor, but secretaries of state had not usually harbored Populist and temperance sympathies. Bryan had accepted the office with two goals in mind: omitting alcohol from official dinners and negotiating as many peace treaties as possible. He set about his business immediately. By August 1913 not only had he banned wine from his official table (he served grape juice instead), but he had also signed his first Treaty for the Advancement of Peace, with El Salvador. By the time he resigned, Bryan had negotiated twenty-nine more treaties.

Instead of erecting a system of alliances for war, Bryan's treaties arranged for the conciliation of disputes through cooling-off periods and investigating committees. After several of these bilateral treaties had been signed, Bryan held a ceremony to present all the ambassadors who had signed peace treaties paperweights in the shape of plows, which had been made from melted-down army swords. Each paperweight bore the legend "They shall beat their swords into plowshares."[34]

As secretary of state Bryan succeeded in limiting American incursions into Mexico and in avoiding a break with Japan over California legislation that prohibited Japanese immigrants from owning land and over Japanese encroachments on China while Europeans were threatening one another.

Yet this midwesterner, the "Great Commoner," was never at home with men familiar with foreign affairs, many of whom were upper-class eastern conservatives like Henry Cabot Lodge, who patronized Bryan for his kind heart and good intentions while deploring his ignorance of international relations. According to Lodge, the secretary of state had "the stump-speaking mind. . . . With him, words take the place of actions."[35] Lodge concluded that Bryan did not even know enough about foreign affairs to realize the depths of his ignorance. But when Wilson appointed him secretary of state in 1913, Bryan's strength in the Democratic party had outweighed his inexperience in diplomacy.

Bryan's departure deprived the cabinet of its most important moderating influence. Now the President's two closest advisers on foreign affairs were Secretary of State Lansing and personal adviser Colonel House, men without constituencies, Anglophiles who represented no one but themselves. After the sinking of the *Lusitania* they began to envision American entry into the war.

By mid-1915 discoveries of German and Austrian sabotage in the United States and the sinking of the *Lusitania* hardened American public opinion. The scope of permissible thought narrowed, so that anyone presenting a German interpretation of the war risked being branded a German agent, and German Americans, Irish Americans, and others who did not sympathize with the Allies were called disloyal, even though the United States was officially neutral. Disloyalty and hyphenism came to be seen as the opposites of 100-percent-Americanism, and 100-percent-Americanism came to mean preparedness. As preparedness grew more popular, nativism and other brands of bigotry, like anti-Semitism, increased. Once again Georgia provided a grisly example.

LEO FRANK WAS to be executed in June 1915 for the murder, two years previously, of Mary Phagan. Superintendent of an Atlanta pencil factory, Frank was a wealthy, prominent Jew. The victim was a pretty, popular fourteen-year-old Gentile pencil factory worker. During the trial Georgia newspapers had printed fabricated stories about Frank's reputed sexual perversions and treated the crime more like an interracial rape than a murder. In the drive to convict the "Jew pervert," the newspapers and the prosecution had disregarded overwhelming evidence against another suspect.

The Frank case attracted the attention of Tom Watson, who wrote up the case in his weekly *Jeffersonian* in hysterical, stereotyped, anti-Semitic terms. When the governor of Georgia commuted Frank's death sentence for lack of evidence, the *Jeffersonian* shrieked that Georgia had been "raped," "violated," and "betrayed." Watson demanded that Frank be lynched. On the night of August 16, 1915, twenty-five men from Mary Phagan's hometown who called themselves Knights of Mary Phagan took Frank out of the penitentiary, carried him back to Marietta, hanged him, and mutilated his body.[36]

Two weeks later, after the opening of the motion picture *Birth of a Nation* in Atlanta, a sometime Methodist minister, orator ("as full of sentiment as a plum is full of juice"), and honorary colonel from Alabama, William J. Simmons, appointed himself Imperial Wizard of the Invisible Empire of the Knights of the Ku Klux Klan.[37] Before a flag-draped altar, Simmons promised to further White supremacy, patriotism, and, when the United States entered the war, the sale of Liberty bonds. Meanwhile, in California, a state long familiar with anti-Oriental bigotry, leaflets warned: "Mr. White American if you have any race pride or patriotism" to organize against Jews and Blacks "for the protection of your race."[38]

IN 1915 THE United States was at peace, ostensibly, at least, but the revolution in Mexico and the European War had obstructed what in 1913 and 1914 had seemed to be an irresistible trend toward harmony, fairness, and increased democracy. The years that followed witnessed a speedy evolution, but in the opposition direction.

THE EUROPEAN WAR TAKES OVER

Peace and preparedness began to dominate American politics in 1915, and each spawned new organizations to promote its causes. The two issues were different from previous economic and social questions, but supporters on each side tended generally to divide along familiar lines. Women and men, like William Jennings Bryan, Jane Addams, and Oswald Garrison Villard, who had championed fairness, equity, and the existence of conflicting interests tended to belong to the peace camp. On the other side, preparedness forces, men like William Howard Taft and Henry Cabot Lodge, had supported hierarchical values that emphasized order and identity of interest. Theodore Roosevelt, having allied himself with both sides, represented a special but not unique case.

Jane Addams led the American delegation of the Woman's Peace party—including suffragists, Women's Trade Union League members, Socialists, and a single taxer—to a meeting at The Hague of the International Woman Suffrage Alliance.[1] After the conference two delegations of women visited European heads of state to promote permanent mediation by neutrals to end the war, according to the "Wisconsin plan," of Professor Julia Grace Wales of the University of Wisconsin. Hungarian peace activist Rosika Schwimmer led a delegation to neutral nations; Jane Addams led a delegation to belligerents. Addams returned from Europe enthusiastic about possibilities of ending the war through mediation, before Europe bled itself white on the battlefield.

About the time the Woman's Peace party delegation returned from Europe, several prominent men, many of whom had been active in the staid pre-1914 peace organizations—including former President William H. Taft and A. Lawrence Lowell, president of Harvard University—formed an organization that had far more influence than the Woman's Peace party. The League to Enforce Peace proposed the creation of a league of nations and borrowed heavily (with acknowledgment) from Bryan's peace treaties, the League's only debt to the former secretary of state.

According to the League to Enforce Peace, members of the projected league of nations would promise to submit to arbitration any disagreements that negotiation could not settle, the essence of Bryan's treaties. But the League to Enforce Peace went a step farther and committed its members to using economic and military force against any member that went to war. Bryan dismissed the idea of using force to prevent war as no more than fighting militarism with militarism, which seemed no improvement over 1914. Bryan's suspicions intensified when two leading preparedness advocates, Henry Cabot Lodge and Theodore Roosevelt, praised the League.

The League to Enforce Peace was strongly pro-Allies and propreparedness. Its members were mainly concerned with shaping the peace settlement after the war, announcing explicitly that the League did "not seek to end the present war." After the United States entered the war, the League to Enforce Peace printed the word *Enforce* on its letterhead in blood-red ink.[2]

While the League to Enforce Peace was successful in gaining widespread support in the Wilson administration and elsewhere, its league of nations idea stirred controversy, mainly in terms of the Monroe Doctrine. Democrats in particular suspected that by imposing the requirement to enforce peace worldwide, the league would take Americans outside the Western Hemisphere and forfeit the priceless advantage of isolation. It was one thing to secure the nation from outside attack but quite another to arrange a set of circumstances that would shed American blood to settle European quarrels, a danger inherent in preparedness.

An antiwar bloc of southern and western Bryan Democrats appeared in Congress late in 1915, led by North Carolinian Claude Kitchin. The antiwar congressmen saw preparedness as a cover for a multiplicity of evils, a pretext by which the wealthy lined their pockets. "It is a strange fact that only the rich people tolerate the thought of war," said Congressman Clyde H. Tavenner of Illinois, accusing "a very powerful group of men" of profiting from arms sales. Congressman Warren Worth Bailey of Pennsylvania called preparedness the "sheerest rot" because the United States was not liable to be invaded. In October 1915 Bryan made a speaking tour through Texas, Mississippi, Virginia, and New York, warning huge, enthusiastic crowds of the dangers of preparedness.

The President was moving in the opposite direction. In early November Wilson called for preparedness, "not for war, but only for defense," and sent plans to Congress to enlarge the army and navy and to create a continental army that would be a national force under federal control. These plans stirred still greater controversy. Congressman Kitchin accused Wilson of setting off an arms race that would make the whole world an armed camp. Outside Congress and the antiwar organizations, a well-known individual spoke up for peace.

"I don't believe in preparedness," said Henry Ford, who was famous for putting together the moving assembly line and interchangeable parts and for paying auto workers $5 a day (then a fabulous wage) to make the most popular automobile in the United States. "It's like a man carrying a gun. Men and nations who carry guns get into trouble. If I had my way, I'd throw every ounce of gunpowder into the sea and strip soldiers of their insignias."[3] Ford's words reached Rosika Schwimmer, one of the leaders of the international women's conference against the war, who came to Detroit to persuade him that mediation could bring peace. In the absence of any official peace efforts Ford decided to act.

In November 1915 Henry Ford traveled to New York, chartered a ship, and, a week before sailing, invited 115 well-known men and women to sail with him as peace commissioners and set up a permanent peace conference in Europe. At a press conference on November 24 he explained: "We're going to have the boys out of the trenches by Christmas. The main idea is to crush militarism and get the boys out of the trenches. Our object is to stop war for all times, and also preparedness."[4] William Jennings Bryan, Thomas Edison, and a host of other luminaries saw the peace ship off as a band played the most popular song of 1915, "I Didn't Raise My Boy to Be a Soldier":

> I didn't raise my boy to be a soldier
> I brought him up to be my pride and joy.
> Who dares to place a musket on his shoulder
> To shoot some other mother's darling boy?
> Let nations arbitrate their future troubles.
> It's time to lay the sword and gun away.
> There'd be no war today
> If mothers all would say:
> "I didn't raise my boy to be a soldier."[5]

In the absence of any clear indication of Henry Ford's intentions, the peace ship seemed a harebrained scheme. The *New York Times* drew Ford as David hurling a Model T at the gigantic god of war; the *New York Herald* showed him turning a crank in his own head. The ridicule, Ford's lack of a concrete plan for initiating and sustaining mediation, and division among the peace commissioners (some of whom never visited the permanent seat of the peace conference in Europe) doomed the Ford peace initiative to failure. But for all the jokes, the venture—financed entirely by Henry Ford—showed how far a private citizen would go to try to end the war. As 1915 ended and Henry Ford pursued peace, the President advocated preparedness and deplored the variety of opinions Americans held about the war.

DURING 1915 preparedness advocates had all too often combined their demands for military spending with attacks on immigrants and appeals for 100-percent-Americanism, initially perhaps because Irish Americans and German Americans endorsed neutrality. But bigotry had no roots in reason and acquired its own momentum. As though it were impossible to augment the armed services without indulging in nativism, President Wilson adopted the rhetoric of 100-percent-Americanism as he moved away from peace and toward preparedness. In December 1915 he called for bigger armed forces (a continental army) and criticized immigrants who expressed "alien sympathies" and who poured "the poison of disloyalty into the very arteries of our national life. . . . Such creatures of passion, disloyalty, and anarchy must be crushed out."[6] Although his antihyphenism was never as shrill as Theodore Roosevelt's, Wilson nonetheless tested the nativist waters. Less concerned with enforcing unanimity in American opinion, Bryan accused the President of "joyriding with the jingoes."[7]

Reflecting the lack of popular support for preparedness, Congress let the President's defense plans languish in early 1916. The continental army proposal came under criticism from advocates of states' rights who distrusted the idea of a large army entirely under federal control. While Congress pondered the continental army and its possible impact on southern race relations, events in Mexico spilled over into the United States and subjected preparedness to a real-life test.

ON JANUARY 10, 1916, the band of Francisco Villa—formerly the friend of the United States but now disgruntled by a lack of support in his struggle with Carranza—stopped a train near the tiny border settlement of Santa Isabel, New Mexico, and robbed and killed fifteen American engineers and miners. Interventionists, who were often preparedness advocates as well, called for retaliation, but most others hesitated. As American opinion divided over the appropriate response to the Santa Isabel massacre, Villa struck again.

On the night of March 9, 1916, Villa's army of 500 attacked the

United States Thirteenth Cavalry, stationed at Columbus, New Mexico, absconded with horses and guns, but lost nearly 100 men to army gunfire. In the six-hour battle 17 American soldiers died. Now the interventionists prevailed. Once again Wilson tried to teach Mexicans a lesson, this time by sending an American punitive expedition of 5,800 men into the northern state of Chihuahua in pursuit of Villa, without permission from the Mexican government.

Since the withdrawal of American forces from Veracruz in late 1914, conditions in Mexico had changed drastically. Huerta had resigned, and Carranza had declared himself head of the government; but he had failed to end the civil war. Zapata and Villa controlled much of the country and led massive armies. As in early 1914 Americans had looked to Villa to unify and pacify Mexico. But in the spring of 1915 Carrancistas had defeated the Villistas several times, and the Wilson administration began to have second thoughts about Villa. "If it should prove to be true that the Carranza forces have defeated Villa," mused then Secretary of State Bryan, "there is much to meditate upon."[8]

By late spring 1915 the Wilson administration had decided that Carranza was more likely to end the conflict and had withdrawn its support from Villa. It recognized Carranza's government on a de facto basis in October 1915 and allowed Carrancista forces to cross Arizona, circle Villa's army, and defeat it resoundingly at Agua Prieta on November 1. The erstwhile General Villa was now merely the head of a guerrilla band.

To supply his forces, compel the United States to invade Mexico, and embarrass Carranza (who Villa thought had made a deal with the American government), Villa robbed Americans and raided Columbus. His strategy bore fruit when Wilson ordered a punitive expedition under General John J. Pershing into Mexico. The American forces marched about Mexico after Villa, with Pershing feeling like a man looking for a needle in a haystack. George S. Patton, Pershing's lieutenant (and much later a hero of World War II), did not see much point in a futile search for Villa. Patton thought the United States should take over Mexico for good.

To many Americans and Mexicans, occupation to protect American investments seemed inevitable. From the moment the punitive expedition crossed the border, the Mexican government assumed that it would occupy the country, impose a settlement, and reduce Mexico to protectorate status. Their suspicions reinforced by one strand of American opinion that was demanding the imposition of a Cuban-style Platt Amendment, Mexican officials wondered aloud why an expedition supposedly hunting for a guerrilla would need infantry and artillery units rather than highly mobile cavalry.

The European War and Villa's raid had temporarily overshadowed a fundamental controversy between the Mexican and American governments about the aims of the revolution. The revolutionary state and federal governments of Mexico intended to bring foreign investments under Mexican control, to tax them, and to end appeals by foreign property owners for special protection from their governments. Between November 1916 and February 1917 Mexico's constitutional convention drafted a document that included several basic reforms that the American government opposed: land to the tiller, the government's right to nationalize foreign holdings, and the nation's right to subsoil resources. Aware of American opposition to these provisions, Mexicans saw the American punitive expedition as a counterrevolutionary force intended to protect American property. They demanded the withdrawal of the American expedition, which was now deep in Mexico.

The inevitable clash between Mexican and American soldiers occurred on April 12 at Parral, 350 miles south of the border. Still, the punitive expedition advanced. A second confrontation at Carrizal brought the two countries to the brink of war and to the realization that they did not wish to engage in an all-out conflict. But a negotiated settlement proved elusive.

THE UNITED STATES–MEXICAN COMMISSION formed to address the grievances of both sides could not agree on what was to be settled. For Mexicans, the withdrawal of the American punitive expedition was the first priority. But the first order of business for Americans was to force the

Mexican government to protect American lives and property or to allow the United States to reenter Mexico on its own initiative and provide protection itself. Since the Mexican government had not been able to end the fighting, to protect American property as Americans defined it would undermine the aims of the revolution. Mexicans concluded that the United States was demanding the right to invade Mexico at will.

Another stumbling block was the very definition of endangerment of property. Some businessmen thought taxing investments represented a peril, and American oil and mining companies were certain that their holdings were threatened by the exercise of controls over leases and operations envisioned by Mexican state and federal governments. The conflict between Americans and Mexicans proved intractable because limitations that Americans saw as endangerment of property appeared to Mexicans as legitimate exercises of sovereignty. In late 1916 the negotiations were at a stalemate and the punitive expedition was still deep inside Mexico.

Events in Europe dictated a hasty truce. As relations between the United States and Germany deteriorated sharply in early 1917, President Wilson decided to recall the punitive expedition. The withdrawal was completed on February 5, 1917, just as the Mexican constitutional convention promulgated its revolutionary document. Once again Wilson and the American expedition had not succeeded in imposing American concepts of order on Mexico. But rather than commit untold numbers of soldiers to the demands of protecting American property, the President decided to let the Mexican Revolution shift for itself while he concentrated on Europe.

During the time that Wilson was trying to manage Mexican problems short of a full-scale invasion, he took a different approach in the small, powerless nations of Nicaragua, Haiti, and the Dominican Republic whenever he thought disorder would threaten American investments or invite European involvement. None of these tiny countries presented the United States with foes as sobering as Venustiano Carranza, Francisco Villa, or Emiliano Zapata, and the United States disregarded their sovereignty freely. American forces occupied Haiti in 1915 and the Dominican Republic in 1916, imposing treaties of protection and taking control of national finances. American forces also intervened extensively in Nicaragua. Although the infringements of sovereignty in these countries were far more serious than in Mexico, they taught none of the lessons that Americans took from Villa's raid on Columbus and the punitive expedition.

The great discovery of the spring of 1916 was how ill prepared the American armed forces were for war. During the battle that repulsed Villa's raiders at Columbus, the Thirteenth Cavalry's machine guns had jammed badly. Before the punitive expedition could get under way, the quartermaster division had had to commandeer fifty-four trucks intended for the French Army. And the expedition's eight airplanes were old and tiny; within a month only two were still in working order. An army chief of staff called the American army the "most pathetic thing any nation every knew."[9] The Mexican crisis gave preparedness a boost, but contemporaneous events in Ireland pushed important segments of American opinion in another direction, deeper into neutrality.

IRISH AMERICAN SUPPORT of independence for Ireland from England was as old as Irish immigration, and most Irish Americans still supported Irish nationalists and damned British imperialism. In the early years of the war the American-Irish nationalist organization Clan na Gael (United Brotherhood) had financed the mission of Sir Roger Casement—formerly a British consular agent and now an Irish nationalist—to Germany to secure German aid for an Irish nationalist uprising. Although not all of Casement's plans materialized, the Irish revolt (with the token aid of a shipment of ineffectual old rifles from Germany) actually took place. On Easter Monday, April 24, 1916, the Irish Volunteer Army occupied the Dublin post office and proclaimed the existence of the Irish Republic.[10] Although the Irish nationalists surrendered to British forces on April 30, the Easter Rising marked a turning point in the struggle for Irish independence.

British reaction was swift and severe. Within a month of the Rising, leaders of the coup had been tried in secret courts-martial and fourteen of them executed before firing squads. The executions forced Irish Americans who had taken a moderate position on the war to denounce Britain and shocked many Americans who had been drifting into the Allied fold by calling into question Britain's liberalism and the strength of its commitment to the integrity of small nations.[11]

THE AFTERMATH of the Easter Rising and new British maritime policies strained relations between the United States and Great Britain in mid-1916. Toward the end of 1915 the British had begun arming merchant and passenger ships, endangering agreements between Germany and the United States on submarine warfare that assumed that passenger ships would not be armed. The British navy also extended its blockade of Germany, intercepting neutral ships serving neutral ports and seizing and opening United States mail. As a last straw, the British government in July 1916 published a blacklist of American firms said to be dealing with Britain's enemies and thereby prohibited from trading with British firms. President Wilson told Colonel House, "I am, I must admit, about at the end of my patience with Great Britain and the Allies."[12] At the same time the United States and Germany appeared to be resolving their differences on the limits of submarine warfare. On March 24, 1916, a submarine had torpedoed the unarmed Channel ferryboat *Sussex*, inflicting eighty casualties, four of whom were American. Wilson threatened to break diplomatic relations unless German submarines stopped sinking passenger boats without warning. Calling the *Sussex* sinking a mistake, the German government promised that submarine commanders would henceforth give warning. The *Sussex* pledge relaxed tensions between Germany and the United States without inclining Americans toward the Central Powers. President Wilson, annoyed with Britain and antipathetic toward Germany, began to prepare the United States to go it alone in a hostile world. That meant increased preparedness.

In Congress preparedness translated into previously unheard-of spending for men and war matériel. But how to raise the money? Who would pay? Bankers suggested that the defense spending be financed through loans; surely the wealthy would demonstrate their patriotism

by purchasing interest-bearing United States bonds. Social reformers wanted to finance the military buildup through steeply graduated
income, inheritance, and excess profits taxes that would not affect the
poor. The *Wall Street Journal* agreed that taxation was the best way to
pay, but its plan would not soak the rich. The *Journal* suggested that
the amount of income exempted from the income tax be lowered from
$4,000 (which meant only the upper-middle and wealthy classes paid
income taxes) to $1,000, to "bring home the war to all the people."[13]
The Wilson administration leaned more toward taxation than loans.

Antipreparedness forces in Congress saw the revenue issue as a
means of limiting the arms buildup. Representative Warren Worth Bailey wanted to raise the tax on very high incomes to 50 percent. "If the
forces of big business are to plunge this country into a saturnalia of
extravagance for war purposes in a time of peace," he announced, "it is
my notion that the forces of big business should put up the money."[14]
The issue of revenue continued to be controversial, but the Revenue
Act of 1916 set the pattern for war taxation.

In 1914 low- and middle-income Americans had borne a large
share of the burden of paying for the federal government. Of some
$734,675,000 total revenue, about $300,000,000 had been raised through
excise taxes on tobacco, liquor, wine, and beer—articles used by nearly
every family, regardless of wealth. Another $300,000,000 came from
customs duties (tariffs), which were also paid ultimately by all consumers. Indirect taxes of this sort were regressive—that is, they weighed
relatively more heavily on the poor than on the rich. Only $71,000,000
came from individual and corporate taxes on high incomes.[15]

The Revenue Act of 1916 increased tax rates on high incomes and
thereby shifted the cost of preparedness to those better able to pay—
and incidentally to those more likely to support preparedness. The Revenue Act of 1917 continued this trend, raising the rate on incomes of
more than $1,000,000 per year to 63 percent and instituting a series of
new taxes, including an excess profits tax that together with the income
taxes yielded two-thirds of government revenues. In the final analysis,
federal tax policies turned around during the war. Whereas nearly 75

percent of revenues had come from excise taxes and tariffs before the war, afterward 75 percent came from income, estate, and excess profits taxes.[16] In 1918 the revenue required for the war reached proportions that would have made financing half the cost of the war effort through taxation politically suicidal, and loans (especially Liberty bonds) supplied much of the financing.

Revenue was one of several issues that marked Wilson's swing back toward reform in 1916, when he faced a reunited Republican party. As a leader of preparedness Roosevelt turned his back on what was left of the Progressive party, which Wilson hoped to attract. By nominating Louis D. Brandeis, the "people's lawyer" and the most prominent reformer in Wilson's 1912 campaign, to the United States Supreme Court, the President took the first of several steps to renew his progressive credentials. In the spring the administration supported the Farm Loan Act, the Kern-McGillicuddy Act to give federal employees workmen's compensation, and the Keating-Owen Child Labor Act, legislation that Wilson had blocked in 1914 and 1915 as unconstitutional. He entered the presidential campaign restored as a progressive.

EVEN BEFORE the convention Wilson began to present his ideas about war and peace. Addressing the League to Enforce Peace in May, he called for a peace that guaranteed self-determination for all peoples and the respect of the sovereignty of weak as well as strong nations, committed the United States to an international peacekeeping organization, and offered American mediation to end the war. Given his willingness to invade neighbors in the Western Hemisphere, Wilson had in mind the small nations of Europe, not the Americas. This popular speech staked out the President's position as a peace candidate. The Democratic National Convention provided the slogan "He kept us out of war," but Wilson, realizing how fragile peace had become, never used it. "I can't keep the country out of war," he remarked to the secretary of the navy. "They talk of me as though I were a god. Any little German lieutenant can put us into the war at any time by some calculated outrage."[17]

Wilson's opponent was Supreme Court Justice Charles Evans

Hughes, former governor of New York and hero of the investigation of the New York insurance scandals. Both the Roosevelt (progressive) and Lodge (conservative) wings of the Republican party supported Hughes, and Roosevelt delivered several warlike, antialien speeches, in which he acted like a candidate and vented what had become a personal aversion to Wilson for not declaring war. Roosevelt was more interested in the war than in Hughes, whose campaign he did not help very much. Most of Hughes's campaigning was platitudinous and cold, making the campaign a contest between Roosevelt and Wilson. However, a piece of labor law provided Hughes an issue of his own, separate from Roosevelt's saber rattling.

A LABOR CRISIS beginning in June 1916 furnished an issue on which the presidential candidates, both of whom called themselves progressives, differed sharply. Negotiations between the railroad brotherhoods (the railroad unions) and twenty railroads had broken down over the brotherhoods' demands for an eight-hour day—with the same pay as for a ten-hour day—and time and half for overtime. After arbitration had failed, Wilson pressured each side to compromise to avert a nationwide strike. The brotherhoods insisted they had been working toward an eight-hour day for thirty years and would wait no longer. The managers maintained that the eight-hour day and time and a half for overtime would bankrupt them, and they steadfastly resisted the President's insistence on compromise. Wilson then backed passage of the Adamson eight-hour act, which prevented the railroad strike.

Hughes labeled this the "most shameful proceeding that has come to my attention since I have observed public life" and asked rhetorically "whether the Government shall yield to force. . . . This country must never know the rule of force. It must never know legislation under oppression."[18] The "force" that Hughes referred to was the threat of a strike. While Hughes attacked the Adamson Act, Wilson wrapped himself in it.

Backed by Samuel Gompers and the AFL, Wilson campaigned as the labor candidate. Hughes appeared increasingly antiunion, and hecklers would interrupt his speeches to ask about his vote in the Danbury Hatters' Case. (In 1915, as a Supreme Court justice, Hughes had sustained the 1908 conviction of the Danbury hatters.) Samuel Gompers pilloried Hughes's stand on labor, reminding workers that the Republican candidate endorsed the use of the hated labor injunction.

Certain of labor support, the Wilson campaign ignored Hughes and used Roosevelt's bellicosity against the Republican candidate. Just before the election, Democrats ran full-page advertisements in several leading newspapers that read:

You are Working—*Not Fighting!*
Alive and Happy;—*Not Cannon Fodder!*
Wilson and Peace with Honor?
or
Hughes and Roosevelt and War?
Roosevelt says we should hang our heads in shame because we are not at *war* with Germany in behalf of Belgium! Roosevelt says that following the sinking of the *Lusitania* he would have foregone [*sic*] diplomacy and seized every ship in our ports flying the German Flag. That would have meant *war!* Hughes says He and Roosevelt are in Complete Accord!

The Lesson is Plain:
If You Want WAR, vote for HUGHES!

If You Want Peace with Honor
VOTE FOR WILSON!
And Continued Prosperity.[19]

While Wilson enjoyed organized labor's support, woman suffragists campaigned against him, making woman suffrage a major national issue. The NAWSA and the Congressional Union were pushing for a federal amendment that would permit women to vote, which Hughes accepted and Wilson rejected. Without specifically endorsing Hughes, suffragists opposed Wilson's reelection in a whistle-stop railroad tour that was called the Golden Special.

A narrow victory in California won an uncomfortably close election for Wilson (9,100,000 votes to 8,500,000 for Hughes), making him the first Democratic President to succeed himself since Andrew Jackson. Although Wilson and Hughes had presented a liberal/conservative choice, the Socialist party's candidate, little-known journalist Allan L. Benson, polled more than half a million votes. (Eugene V. Debs had decided against running again to give a younger man a chance.) Benson got 580,000 votes, about 310,000 less than Debs in 1912. Thousands of Socialists (like John Reed) voted for Wilson on the basis of his record on peace and labor. On the local level, however, Socialist candidates attracted more support than they had in 1912, showing that significant numbers of voters were not satisfied with local Democratic and Republican candidates. In New York voters sent Socialist Meyer London to Congress. And in Washington the NAWSA and the Congressional Union prepared to implement their "Winning Plan" of lobbying Congress to pass the Nineteenth Amendment. Demonstrators from the Woman's party picketed the White House during the winter, carrying signs asking MR. PRESIDENT! HOW LONG MUST WOMEN WAIT FOR LIBERTY?[20]

FOR A MOMENT toward the end of 1916 it seemed that the war might come to a negotiated end. The German government announced a peace initiative at about the same time that Wilson invited the belligerents to state their war aims at a peace conference that would include the United States. But all prospects for a negotiated settlement disappeared in the face of German demands that vast territories in Europe and overseas (including the Belgian Congo) be ceded to Germany as the price of peace. German demands and Allied determination to defeat Germany and exact reparations made peace unlikely.

During Christmas week *The New Republic* ran an editorial by Walter Lippmann arguing that the President should reject the German peace proposal, which was nothing more than a grab for spoils. The German offer, if accepted, Lippmann warned, would mean "peace without victory," a bad thing. In late January 1917 President Wilson used Lippmann's phrase in a speech before the Senate in which he vowed to persevere in his attempt to end the war through a negotiated settlement based on the principles of equality, self-government and self-determination for all nations, freedom of the seas, and an end to great armies. Even though it was not a belligerent the United States had the right to help shape this enduring peace among equals, a peace without humiliation, a "peace without victory," a good thing.

In Europe the war was going badly for Germany. Its peace initiative having been refused, the German government prepared to wage all-out war in the hope of finally defeating the Allies. At the end of January Germany announced the resumption of unrestricted submarine warfare as of February 1. Wilson had stated clearly in the *Sussex* note that unrestricted submarine warfare would mean breaking diplomatic relations, and he recalled all United States diplomatic personnel from Germany.

DURING THIS uncertain twilight between peace and war, proponents of peace desperately pressed their point. A coalition of peace organizations formed the Emergency Peace Federation and called on the President with three demands: to defer all disputes with belligerents (e.g., losses caused by submarines) until the end of the war; to bar Americans from the war zone where submarines were active; and to go to war only after the declaration had been approved in a popular referendum instead of requiring merely a congressional declaration. Rather than take the country into the war, the Emergency Peace Federation argued that the government should keep Americans out of the war's way. The Socialist party advised workers to refuse to work if war was declared because "the six million men whose corpses are now rotting upon the battle-fields of Europe were mostly workingmen" and American workers would suffer a similar fate. William Jennings Bryan, who had been canvassing the country in the cause of peace, redoubled his efforts. At Madison Square Garden in New York, Bryan evoked America's mission to lift the morals of the world. "We will not get down with you," he thundered to the belligerents in Europe, "and wallow in the blood and mire to conform to your false standards of honor."[21]

After the resumption of unrestricted submarine warfare fewer Americans agreed with Bryan, and the exchanges grew heated. The *New York Tribune* accused antiwar activists of colluding with the German government. Food riots in Manhattan and Brooklyn in February were said to have been staged by the Central Powers. Charges and countercharges of war mongering and pacifist treason increased in stridency. German submarines sank several merchant vessels, shippers canceled Atlantic crossings, and goods piled up on the docks. Everyone feared that soon plants would close and workers would lose their jobs, and who could say what kinds of social unrest would follow widespread unemployment? To get shipping moving again, the President asked for authority to arm merchant ships (an act for which he had recently criticized the British) and to take any steps necessary to protect American lives and goods on the seas. Congress balked at handing him a blank check and began a filibuster. The President played his trump.

Wilson released a document he had held nearly a week, the text of a telegram that Arthur Zimmermann, the German foreign minister, had sent the German ambassador in Mexico, which the British had intercepted and decoded. Seeking to exploit the poor state of Mexican American relations, Zimmermann instructed the ambassador to suggest to Carranza a Mexican-German alliance that would regain for Mexico the "lost territories" of New Mexico, Arizona, and Texas should the United States declare war on Germany. The ambassador was also directed to prompt Carranza to approach Japan to form a three-way alliance against the United States. This news enraged Americans, who took the Zimmermann note as a signal for national unity against Germany and for war, against pacifists and for 100-percent-Americanism.

The Zimmermann telegram moved Congress to pass the armed ship bill, but before the United States could begin arming merchant ships,

German submarines sank three American vessels on March 18. Many Americans regarded the sinking and the consequent heavy loss of life and property the overt act that must take the United States into the war. Theodore Roosevelt called for war before 12,000 cheering supporters at Madison Square Garden. The ranks of the nation's most avowedly anti-war political party split, as several prominent Socialists repudiated the Socialist party national executive committee's antiwar resolution. The American Union Against Militarism fell apart, some members favoring war while others stood firm as pacifists.

In the midst of argument about the war, news arrived of the Russian Revolution against the czar, Europe's most despotic ruler, which seemed to bring some good out of the slaughter. Russian Jews, Poles, and Scandinavians in the United States now supported the Allied side enthusiastically. The Russian Revolution also seemed to presage a similar move toward democracy in Germany, perhaps elsewhere in Europe as well. Events in Russia held the promise that the European masses were ready at last to throw off the yoke of parasitic aristocrats. The war was now a war of the people against the autocrats, and Russian troops, fighting for a free Russia, would surely triumph over the Germans on the battlefield.

Otherwise, the news from the Allies was awful. The war on land had bogged down, and German submarines were taking a heavy toll on Allied shipping. In France the Aisne offensive failed, and the government of Aristide Briand fell in March 1917. Peace advocates distributed leaflets to troops bound for the trenches in which millions had died. On the front ten French divisions mutinied. Unable to raise sufficient volunteer manpower, the British government resorted to conscription to fill the ranks and was even considering the desperate strategy of conscripting Irishmen, which would have torn Ireland apart. Food was rationed in Britain. The Russian Revolution became a civil war in which Russians fought other Russians instead of the Germans. It seemed likely now that Germany would win the war, an outcome most Americans equated with the ruin of civilization.

William ("Big Bill") Haywood of the Industrial Workers of the World at Lowell, Massachusetts, 1912. (Library of Congress / George Grantham Bain Collection)

Presidents Woodrow Wilson (left) and William H. Taft at Wilson's inaugural, 1913. (Library of Congress)

Woman suffragists keep the watchfire before the White House during the European War.
(Library of Congress)

Francisco Villa (center) with General John ("Black Jack") Pershing (left), in 1914.
(DeGolyer Library, Southern Methodist University)

National Association of Manufacturers' poster advocating cooperation between employers and workers during the European War. (Wisconsin Historical Society, WHI-130380)

Whites pursue a Black man, Chicago, 1919. (The West Virginian)

Armed Pinkerton agents in Homestead, Pennsylvania, about to confront striking iron and steelworkers. (The Illustrated American)

ON APRIL 2, 1917, President Wilson asked Congress for a declaration of war to make the world safe for democracy, outlining the ideals that he would later amplify in the "Fourteen Points": democracy, self-government, rights for small nations, freedom of the seas, free trade, open diplomacy, and a league of nations that would provide collective security.

Despite the applause, the declaration of war did not pass unanimously. In the Senate the resolution passed with six dissents, including those of Robert M. La Follette, James K. Vardaman of Mississippi, and George Norris of Nebraska. In the House of Representatives the fifty votes cast against the declaration of war included those of Jeannette Rankin of Montana, the only woman in Congress, and Claude Kitchin of North Carolina.

Kitchin spoke for many dissenters inside and outside Congress when he said he was unwilling to take his country into a war that had made a slaughterhouse of half the civilized world. Calling the United States the last, best hope for peace, he predicted that American entry into the conflict would make the universe "one vast drama of horrors and blood, one boundless stage upon which will play all the evil spirits of earth and hell."[22] Woodrow Wilson himself confided to Ray Stannard Baker that he realized that the war would undo the New Freedom reforms. "War means autocracy," the President told Baker. "The people we have unhorsed will inevitably come into the control of the country, for we shall be dependent upon the steel, oil and financial magnates. They will run the nation."[23]

Wilson said he took the United States into the war for democracy, but the motives for American belligerency were largely material. If most Americans felt a sentimental attachment to Britain that made contemplation of a German conquest distressful, patterns of commerce that tied American manufacturers and workers to Allied markets and the protection of the British navy counted as much or more.

The strongest link between the American economy and the Allied cause was money. By April 1917 American bankers, led by J. P. Morgan and Company, had lent Allied countries more than $2 billion, all of which would be lost should Germany win the war. Losses of this magnitude would play havoc with American banks and, in turn, the entire economy. From Georgia Tom Watson railed against American belligerency in his own fashion: " 'The world must be made safe for democracy,' said our sweetly sincere President; what he meant was, that the huge investment, which our Blood-gorged Capitalists had made in French, Italian, Russian, and English *paper*, must be made safe. *Where Morgan's money went, your boy's blood must go*, ELSE MORGAN WILL LOSE HIS MONEY! That's all there is to it."[24]

Although many shared Watson's skepticism about the war, great numbers of Americans embraced a glorious cause and welcomed the end of uncertainty. Organizations that had opposed war split when faced with the actual fact of belligerency. The Socialist party held a special meeting that condemned American entry into the European War, but individual Socialists, many quite prominent (the writer Upton Sinclair and William English Walling, for instance) supported the war effort. The National Association for the Advancement of Colored People debated whether or not to support the war, then whether it was better to have no Black officers at all or to recognize the existence of racial segregation and approve a Jim Crow officers' training camp. The American Federation of Labor, with Samuel Gompers's enthusiastic leadership, supported the war, but with certain conditions. The government was to deal with workers through unions, workers were to be granted the right to organize, and labor, while promising restraint, did not surrender the right to strike. The head of the United Mine Workers remained antiwar, adding that he found "little sentiment among the working people in favor of this terrible war."[25]

College students responded with enthusiasm. Young women mobilized at Vassar as nurses and knitters of washcloths. At Princeton students honed their flying skills on two planes donated by an alumnus. Harvard's Hasty Pudding Club canceled its Easter performances and returned to Cambridge to drill. Half the undergraduates at the University of North Carolina were drilling, and the Carolina Medical School students organized an officers' medical corps.

William Alexander Percy, son of a Mississippi planter, hurried home to volunteer. He found Greenville "in the first throes of heroics": "Women were knitting and beginning to take one lump of sugar instead of two, men within draft age were discussing which branch of the service they had best enter, men above draft age were heading innumerable patriotic committees and making speeches. People found themselves all of a sudden with an objective in common, with a big aim they could share, and they liked it immensely. You could sense the pleasurable stir of nobility and the bustle of idealism."[26] In hometowns all over the country, people like Percy's friends and neighbors were gearing up for the war. Irish Americans and German Americans quickly declared their loyalty, the Irish after noting that the United States should also have declared war on England for violating neutral rights.

Much like the 100-percent-Americanism that had preceded it, this patriotic fervor was intolerant and increasingly paranoid. All too often being prowar was seen as the equivalent of patriotism, and patriotism came to require the sort of loyalty that could be jammed down the throat of anyone failing to demonstrate sufficient prowar enthusiasm. The mayor of New York divided the population into "Americans and traitors" and designated a Committee on National Defense that administered loyalty oaths to all city workers, including teachers. The oaths proved to be highly controversial but popular in several cities around the country. Being antiwar was now tantamount to being a coward or an anarchist or a traitor.

Wild enthusiasm was not the unanimous response to America's involvement in the war. An antiwar meeting at Madison Square Garden brought out thousands of working-class people who were more concerned about high food prices, which they blamed on the war, than the President's lofty rhetoric. They distrusted a cause whose leaders were men who had opposed unions and democratic reforms at home but who now championed America's fight for liberty and democracy overseas. Although *The New Republic* thought the United States had entered the war for the best of reasons, it feared that "the clean purpose and enthusiasm of the nation is poisoned by its own internal class struggle."[27] For many the war remained a distant conflict, easily lost sight of in the welter of everyday concerns, at least until the draft made large numbers of men liable for service in the armed forces.

WILSON HAD CALLED for universal (male) liability to service on the ground that only a manpower draft could avoid the favoritism, resentment, and draft riots that purchased substitutes had caused during the Civil War. He hoped also that a draft would avoid the atrocity stories and rabid hate campaigns against the enemy that European governments had used to persuade young men to sign up voluntarily. All in all, the draft seemed an equitable way to bring masses of men into the army. Yet universal military service did not meet universal approval. Southern congressman opposed an institution in which large numbers of Black men would learn how to handle weapons. Liberals feared that compulsory military service would destroy the individualism of American society and, in the words of Amos Pinchot, "mould the United States into an efficient, orderly nation, economically and politically controlled by those who know what is good for the people."[28]

Men were subject to considerable pressure, later heavy-handed coercion, to register for the draft. On registration day, June 5, 1917, 9,600,000 men registered. (Of the 337,000 who failed to register, the Justice Department prosecuted 10,000 before the armistice.) On July 20, the secretary of war pulled the first draft number out of a gigantic glass bowl, and the call-up began. Most men reported for physical examinations, but large numbers did not. They were called slackers, and generally their refusal was an individual, inarticulate opposition to going to war. In some places, however, opposition was collective, as in Tyler, Texas, and Chatham County, North Carolina.

The biggest protest, called the Green Corn Rebellion, took place in Oklahoma, where about 900 poor tenant farmers—Black, White, and Native American—planned to march on Washington, take over

the government, and end what they called a rich man's war. The rebels represented the vanguard of what had been planned as a massive
antiwar demonstration and uprising. They cut telegraph wires and ate
barbecued beef and green corn, waiting in vain for the convergence of
4,000,000 like-minded protestors in eastern Oklahoma. A local posse
took them to jail, and the rebellion ended.

The draft elicited divided responses, but it brought some 4,000,000
men into service in the armed forces before the armistice. Half of them
served overseas under General John J. Pershing, lately of Mexico. The
commander of the American Expeditionary Forces, Pershing was the
only American general with recent experience in the field. Several regiments had special personalities, including the "Fighting Sixty-ninth"
of New York, the pride of Irish America, whose recruits came from
Catholic athletic clubs and Irish societies and had Catholic priests
instead of Protestant chaplains. The only Black regiment allowed in
combat, the Ninety-second, a product of the War Department's policies of segregation, had been trained at seven separate cantonments
and was assembled only after leaving the United States. Its Black officers, who could not rise above the rank of captain, came from the Jim
Crow officers' training Camp Des Moines, created after the NAACP
had brought pressure on the War Department to make some provision
for Black officers. But for the NAACP's insistence on Black officers for
the Ninety-second, all its officers, not just field officers, would have
been White, probably southerners like William Percy, who served with
the Ninety-second in France. The War Department assumed that White
southerners knew best how to handle Blacks. The army prematurely
retired its only Black field officer, Lieutenant Charles Young, for the
duration of the war.[29]

The experience of Black troops in the war was unjust. The army
had always been segregated, and Black troops in the regular army had
been subject to harassment in southern encampments. Given the history of racial discrimination in American society, including the armed
forces, Blacks were initially divided on whether to support the war.
But W. E. B. Du Bois composed an influential editorial in *The Crisis,*

entitled "Close Ranks," advising Blacks to forget their grievances for the duration of the war and join their White fellow citizens. But in August 1917 the Twenty-fourth Infantry's Third Battalion, seasoned regulars, shot back at their White tormentors in Houston, Texas, where, after a hurried trial, thirteen Black soldiers were denied appeal and hanged. After the incident in Houston the Wilson administration halted Black recruitment until late September while pondering whether to keep all Black men out of combat. After Blacks across the country had protested, Black draftees were admitted to combat duty in principle, but in fact, most did labor duty. Black draftees received proportionately fewer deferrals than Whites, and they formed 13 percent of those serving, although Blacks constituted only 10 percent of the population.

LIKE THE DRAFT, the financial and administrative aspects of the war also called for extraordinary organization. In each case the Wilson administration's original means soon proved inadequate. Wilson and his secretary of the treasury, William G. McAdoo, had wanted to finance the war half through taxes, half through loans. McAdoo made Liberty loans (or Liberty bonds) available on credit, thereby reaching people who could not afford to save. He hoped not to disturb the routine operation of money markets and also to avoid the rancor that had followed the Civil War, when a few financiers had made killings by using inflated paper currency to purchase bonds whose interest and principal were paid in gold. The war's expense far outstripped McAdoo's estimates, however, because massive amounts of money were needed to tide over the Allies as well as to finance the American mobilization.

Five series of Liberty loans were issued, and each issue was oversubscribed. Of the $33.5 billion that the war cost outright, some $23 billion came from loans and $10.5 billion from taxes.[30] The Liberty loans succeeded wonderfully as revenue producers because the secretary of the treasury and a battery of famous salespeople continuously exhorted Americans to borrow money and buy bonds. But when people borrowed to buy bonds, they increased the money supply tremendously. Terrible inflation resulted, which contemporaries observed as rising prices for goods and services and called the high cost of living and abbreviated as the HCL. By increasing the money supply in this way, the government partially financed the European War through inflation, much as it had the Civil War through the use of fiat money (greenbacks).

Supplying American and Allied armed forces meant mobilizing the economy for war on a gigantic scale. The Wilson administration assembled a series of government agencies for this purpose, such as the Council of National Defense and the National Defense Advisory Commission (both created in 1916), which in turn spawned several more specialized boards. To the extent that the economy was successfully planned and organized during the war, the subsidiary organizations created in mid-1917 and 1918—such as the War Industries Board (run by Bernard Baruch after early 1918), the Fuel Administration, the Food Administration (run by Herbert Hoover), the Railroad Administration, and the War Labor Board—coordinated production.

In order to conserve grain, Congress passed laws limiting the production of alcoholic beverages. This legislation, along with the support that prohibition had attracted from men as influential as Supreme Court Justice Louis D. Brandeis and former President William Howard Taft, eased the passage in 1918 of the Eighteenth Amendment, which prohibited the manufacture, importation, exportation, transportation, or sale of alcoholic beverages. The certainty that prohibition would soon be the law of the land somewhat relaxed the influential liquor lobby's opposition to woman suffrage. The House of Representatives passed the Nineteenth Amendment, giving women the vote, in January 1918, the Senate in mid-1919. By August 1920 thirty-six states had ratified the Nineteenth Amendment, and women could vote in federal elections throughout the United States.

The wartime agencies brought private industry and government together cooperatively in a partnership that stressed maximum production and overlooked monopolies and soaring profits. With antitrust prosecutions suspended for the duration of the war, this government-industrial partnership set the tone for the 1920s and the New Deal agencies of the 1930s, notably the National Recovery Administration. Wartime cooperation extended to labor unions, which the National War Labor Board and the War Labor Policies Board tacitly recognized in order to extract no-strike contracts from workers. This recognition of workers' right to unionize revolutionized labor relations.[31]

THE COUNCIL OF National Defense and the various boards organized the production and distribution of goods, but this did not complete the mobilization. Eight days after the declaration of war the President created the Committee on Public Information (CPI), headed by George Creel, a Denver newspaperman, to mobilize public opinion and crush dissent. (Former muckraker Ida M. Tarbell was one of the journalists who served the CPI.) Seventy-five thousand "Four-Minute Men" and movie stars gave patriotic speeches to inspire draft registration, Liberty loan purchases, food conservation, and informing on neighbors who uttered disloyal remarks. The Committee on Public Information distributed millions of pamphlets on America and the war and the duties of Americans in wartime, placed posters in factories, ran newspaper ads calling for work and surveillance, and organized "Loyalty Leagues" among the foreign-born to encourage Americanization and ensure loyalty. The Committee aimed at unification of American thought through "expression, not repression" so that everyone would think and speak according to its definition of patriotism.

The barrage of exhortations to patriotism, sacrifice, and 100-percent-Americanism that came from the CPI, Herbert Hoover, and William G. McAdoo encouraged conformity and its companion, bigotry. School boards outlawed the teaching of the German language; German Americans were shunned by their neighbors, and in one instance near St. Louis in 1918 a German immigrant was lynched. The postmaster general subjected foreign-language newspapers to surveillance so strict that it forced them to wave the flag fanatically or go out of business. Two hundred and fifty thousand volunteers from the American Protective Association (a nativist organization founded in Iowa in 1887) helped the Justice Department keep an eye on immigrants from Germany and Austria-Hungary, with the aid of a subvention of $250,000 from the attorney general.

The Espionage Act of 1917 prohibited the publication of disloyal statements, as defined by the postmaster general, Albert S. Burleson. The act gave him authority to ban from the mail anything he thought advocated treason, insurrection, or resistance to law, including opposition to the draft. Burleson defined his powers broadly. If, in the words of Norman Thomas, a young Socialist, Burleson "didn't know socialism from rheumatism," he knew enough to bar Socialist newspapers from the mail.[32] Among two of the radical periodicals that the Espionage Act smothered were *The Masses* and *Appeal to Reason*. But mostly Burleson's targets were little foreign-language or western papers.

The attorney general asked Congress to strengthen the Espionage Act so he could prosecute disloyal speech as well as publications. Amendments to the Espionage Act of May 1918, known as the Sedition Act, prohibited "disloyal, profane, scurrilous, or abusive language" regarding the flag, the American government, or uniforms of the armed services. Under it Socialist orators like Kate Richards O'Hare and Eugene V. Debs went to prison.

LOCAL VIGILANTES enforcing 100-percent-Americanism saw themselves as good citizens protecting their country from secret agents and saboteurs. The Industrial Workers of the World provided a favorite target by refusing to support the war effort. In the West Wobblies went so far as to ridicule the war, singing antiwar parodies like this version of "Onward, Christian Soldiers":

CHRISTIANS AT WAR
Onward, Christian soldiers! Duty's way is plain;
Slay your Christian neighbors, or by them be slain.

Pulpiteers are spouting effervescent swill,

God above all is calling you to rob and rape and kill.

All your acts are sanctified by the Lamb on high;

If you love the Holy Ghost, go murder, pray and die.

———

Onward, Christian soldiers! Blighting all you meet,

Trampling human freedom under pious feet.

Praise the Lord whose dollar sign dupes his favored race!

Make the foreign trash respect your bullion brand of grace.

Trust in mock salvation, serve as pirates' tools;

History will say of you: "That pack of God damned fools."[33]

In July 1917 the sheriff of Bisbee, Arizona, and 2,000 deputies rounded up 1,200 strikers, half of whom were Wobblies, one-third of whom were Mexican Americans, and herded them onto a train where they spent two days imprisoned in the heat without food or water en route to New Mexico. A few weeks later in Butte, Montana, IWW organizer Frank Little encouraged striking copper miners in what he called their battle against an imperialist, capitalist war. Six masked men lynched Little for his transgression.[34]

Originally the American Federation of Labor had ignored the mounting toll of Wobblies beaten and killed in mob violence. The IWW's revolutionary internationalism and opposition to the war went against the grain of the AFL and seemed to have little to do with conventional unionism. But by mid-1917 the AFL had decided to take another look at anti-IWW violence. Emil Davidson, secretary-treasurer of the International Association of Machinists, noticed that some of its own members—not Wobblies at all—had been shut out after being branded IWW. Davidson suspected that "every big employer who is trying to prevent the workers in his employ from getting better conditions at this time is yelling that he is the victim of German plots."[35] Realizing that any worker could be called IWW, then victimized at will, the AFL began to object to violence against Wobblies.

THE FIRST SUMMER of the war produced an appalling outbreak of mob violence, not all of it directed against Wobblies, but most against workers. Much of the violence was aimed at southern Black migrants who had come to northern industrial cities to fill the jobs of European immigrants who were returning home to look after families or to serve in their countries' armed forces. White southerners migrated North in far greater numbers than Blacks, but their migration did not attract the same notice or violence. About 250,000 Black southerners moved North between 1915 and mid-1917.[36] They found conditions harsh, but an improvement on what they had left behind.

Black migrants sought higher wages and an escape from southern discrimination, segregation, and lynching. Despite the existence of considerable race prejudice in the North the color line was not drawn nearly so strictly as in the South, and racial humiliation was not so fundamental a part of society. In Philadelphia a forty-nine-year-old southern Black migrant said that for the first time in his life he had found peace and comfort.[37]

In Chicago, East St. Louis, Detroit, Pittsburgh, Philadelphia, New York, and Cleveland, Blacks found jobs in the meat-packing, auto, and steel industries, where they joined an industrial working class that already included immigrants and native Whites. Whites did not ordinarily welcome Blacks into the unions, and Blacks sometimes broke strikes, making it all the more likely that racial divisions in the workplace would spill over into the streets.

East St. Louis, Illinois, experienced a bloody antiBlack riot in July 1917 that a Russian Jew compared to a pogrom. With the connivance of the mayor, police, and local militia, Whites burned the houses of Blacks with the tenants still inside and massacred at least 200 men, women, and children. Ida Wells-Barnett went to East St. Louis immediately after the riot to secure legal aid for the victims.[38] Shortly afterward a similar riot occurred in Chester, Pennsylvania, an industrial city on the Delaware River. To protest the racist slaughter, 8,000 Black people wearing black armbands marched in silence in New York City carrying signs that read, WE ARE MALIGNED AS LAZY AND MURDERED WHEN WE WORK, and YOUR HANDS ARE FULL OF BLOOD, and MR. PRESIDENT, WHY NOT MAKE AMERICA SAFE FOR DEMOCRACY?

WORKERS STRUCK in record numbers in 1917, for two main reasons. One was a complex of issues that fell under the general rubric of "industrial democracy," and the other was soaring inflation that reduced the value of wages. *Industrial democracy* meant many things, depending on who used the phrase. Employers might create shop committees that advised on means of increasing productivity and allowed workers just enough say in the workplace to forestall the organization of unions. Government bureaus used the term as a way of pursuing the harmony that maximized production in factories supplying war matériel. For workers, however, industrial democracy meant assuring labor the right to influence or control working conditions. Posed as the antidote to the old, hierarchical ordering of industry—in which workers could choose only between unconditional obedience or quitting—industrial democracy would bring the ideals of political democracy into the workplace. Increasingly workers demanded what came to be called workers' control, the democratic management of factories by all the people who worked in them.[39]

Steadily rising gross wage figures meant little when the cost of living soared. The giant U.S. Steel Corporation raised its workers' pay by 10 percent five times between February 1916 and October 1917, increasing wages more than 60 percent in two years. But during the same period food prices doubled. While other costs, such as rent, did not increase as rapidly, workers nonetheless found themselves badly squeezed financially. Some companies, such as the Solvay Process Company in Detroit, the Franklin Automobile Company in Syracuse, New York, and the George Worthington Company in Cleveland, began experimenting with cost-of-living increases to help their workers keep up with inflation. Others gave wartime bonuses that helped temporarily.[40]

To bridge the gap between wages and the cost of running a household, more married women entered the paid work force. "I used to go to work when my man was sick or couldn't get a job," said one wife, after prices had been rising for four years. "But this is the first time I ever had to go to work to get enough money to feed the kids, when he was working regular."[41] War mobilization took women into new jobs. For the first time women worked in munitions plants, ran elevators, and delivered messages. Social workers worried about their long hours and night work, especially because many states had suspended protective labor legislation for the duration of the war. What bothered women workers most, however, was wages: women invariably earned less than men in exactly the same jobs. Even the Department of Labor advertised differently for male and female workers to run machines in munitions factories. If male, the workers would earn $2.24 to $2.64 per day; if female, $1.36 to $2.24.[42]

To protect their members against the competition of what they called cheap labor—women, Black, and, after late 1917, Mexican workers—union labor advocated (but did not pursue) equal pay for equal work. This demand, taken up by liberal reformers, died away after the armistice, as women were hustled out of the factories and what were seen as men's jobs. By 1920 fewer women worked for wages than in 1910. The whole point of the mobilization that affected millions of American workers was winning the war through money, matériel, and men sent to Europe. American troops went off as deliverers, who, after three years of inconclusive combat, would sort things out "over there" in the words of the popular song by the Irish American entertainer George M. Cohan.

ONLY 175,000 AMERICAN TROOPS reached Europe before the end of 1917, not enough to make a difference in a war that had claimed more than 6,000,000 lives or to reverse the Allies' disastrous losses. In the autumn of 1917 an Austrian victory nearly took Italy out of the war, and in November Bolsheviks took over the Russian government in a second revolution and negotiated a separate peace with Germany. The German Army then turned its full force on the western front. On March 21, 1918, 800,000 German troops staged an offensive along fifty miles of the front in France.

In the spring of 1918 American troops poured into Liverpool, Brest, and St.-Nazaire and headed straight to the front. In May, 245,000 American soldiers arrived in Europe; in June, 278,000; in July, 306,000. By sheer force of numbers, Americans stopped the German offensive, bringing Allied victory into sight. In November the Kaiser abdicated; a socialist government took over Germany and signed an armistice on November 11, 1918.

William Alexander Percy was in the midst of "the weary confusion of mid-battle" on the French front when at 2:10 A.M. he heard the soldier beside him gasp. " 'What's that?' and it was the Armistice! Signed, sealed, and delivered! Stop the artillery, no further advance is necessary; wake up the general; the hubbub outside is only the French returning from the line singing and calling to our men; 'La guerre est finie!' "[43]

At home, too, feelings ran high. "The war is won. All wars are at an end. This was a war to end wars and it is victoriously finished," a liberal editor exulted. "We are celebrating less a triumph over a fallen enemy than a veritable release of mankind from nightmare."[44] Europeans and Americans rejoiced over the end of the bloodletting. In Great Britain there was much talk of "reconstruction" to reshape the society and give workers, as represented in the Labour party and the trade unions, a larger say in national affairs. Although the leadership of the AFL was not anxious to pull away from the Wilson administration, urban labor federations and local leaders were poised to demand a more equitable postwar society. They were part of a worldwide insurgency of the rank and file that impressed the British prime minister, David Lloyd George, who commented on the "deep sense not only of discontent, but of anger and revolt among workmen against prewar conditions."[45] However strongly working people believed in the necessity for a fundamental postwar reconstruction of society, government and employers felt no such need.

THE 1918 ELECTIONS had dampened the Wilson administration's enthusiasm for fundamental economic and political reform. Before the elections Woodrow Wilson had asked voters for a mandate. If they approved of his leadership, he said, they should return a Democratic majority to Congress. The voters sent back Republicans. In the incoming Sixty-sixth Congress, both houses would have Republican majorities. In the Senate conservative Henry Cabot Lodge—who hated Wilson—would lead a reunited Republican party. Theodore Roosevelt announced to all that the American people had repudiated Wilson, who could no longer pretend to be their spokesman. After the disagreeable election Wilson abandoned all notions of any sort of reconstruction or even of planned demobilization. Once the armistice had been signed, the American wartime agencies simply closed their doors, and most were out of service within two weeks.

Thanks in large part to the guidelines of the War Labor Board, many employers had accepted changes during the war that unions had long fought for: the eight-hour workday; union recognition; collective bargaining; a living wage. Seeing that joining a union no longer meant risking the loss of one's job and that unions might well improve working conditions, more workers joined than ever before. The AFL unions gained 650,000 members in 1917 and 355,000 in 1918. In mid-1918 unionized workers numbered 2,725,000. The AFL's phenomenal growth repeated that of the Knights of Labor a generation earlier, when organization had also promised to pay off.

The War Labor Board had shown labor that industrial conditions were subject to political as well as economic pressures, a lesson not lost on many workers. Bolstered by the confidence of the British Labour party and following the reasoning of the workingmen's parties of the Knights of Labor in the 1880s, American workers sought to influence the political processes that affected them.

The British Labour party insisted on workers' having a say in reconstruction and encouraged meetings between representatives of labor from the Allies and the Central Powers. But Samuel Gompers, following President Wilson's lead, opposed the British approach to international class unity and political action. Nonetheless, several AFL unions, notably the United Mine Workers, began to discuss the Labour party's program of social reconstruction. Local labor federations met to formulate their plans to make postwar society more equitable materially. The California State Federation of Labor called for a minimum wage, government planning of demobilization, vocational rehabilitation for injured servicemen and workers, government ownership and operation of public utilities (including waterways and irrigation projects), more progressive income taxes, and the maintenance of the excess profit tax.

The Chicago Federation of Labor launched an Independent Labor party and adopted "Labor's Fourteen Points," which included the right to organize, a voice for labor in management, the eight-hour day and a minimum wage, equal rights for women, and the abolition of unemployment through public works on roads, housing, conservation, and the economic infrastructure. In conferences and national meetings around the country, organized labor discussed reconstruction.

The war had taught even conservatives that a minimum of concessions encouraged labor peace. As joint chairman of the War Labor Board William Howard Taft had learned that management must henceforth expect to deal with organized workers, not individuals. For some managers, this was a signal to form company unions. But no significant improvement in working conditions occurred until workers organized their own independent national unions. With this in mind, the 1918 AFL convention appointed a committee to begin a new undertaking (AFL unions had mainly organized skilled workers only, according to skill): the organization of unskilled and semiskilled industrial workers throughout the country, beginning with steel.

The end of the war brought American working people to what seemed the brink of success. Nearly 3,000,000 workers were unionized, and the possibility of exerting direct political influence made labor appear more potent still. It seemed to labor, ready to play a larger role in making postwar society more equitable, that the old bossism/strike nexus might give way to industrial democracy. But labor's initiative—

especially when coupled with a wave of strikes set off by the high cost of living—seemed to many in the middle and upper classes more like industrial warfare, a frightening upheaval they associated with a specter that they called bolshevism. Strictly speaking, the Bolsheviks had been the victorious party in the second, Soviet Russian Revolution. But when Americans spoke of bolshevism, they were thinking of bad things that they feared would happen in the United States. The term carried the negative connotations that in the 1870s and 1880s had attached to the Paris Commune—insurrectionary workers' seizing government, murdering, burning, and destroying civilization.

BEFORE APRIL 1917 Americans had differed profoundly about the war, dividing into preparedness and peace camps, but when the United States became a belligerent, the Wilson administration demanded unanimity and order. Without dissent, each person was to play his or her part in the war machine, but the enforcement of this hierarchical order entailed vigilante violence and repression. Americans had supposedly formed a united front to win the war, but now that the war was over, they disagreed on the price to be paid—and who should pay—for the fruits of victory.

13

THE GREAT UNREST

The armistice made everybody crazy. It was like Mardi Gras all over the country. Novelist James T. Farrell compared the Chicago Loop to "a nuthouse on fire. The sidewalks were swollen with people, the streets were clogged, and autoists honked their horns, and motor men donged bells in vain. Tons of paper and confetti blizzarded from the upper stories of buildings and sundry noise-makers echoed an insistent racket. People sang, shouted until it seemed that their lungs would burst from their mouths."[1] The war was over. President Wilson's concepts of freedom, self-determination, and collective security—the essence of his Fourteen Points—had shaped the truce. Now the President's idealism promised to make the peace treaty something loftier than a mere division of spoils.

Sensitive observers, however, realized that expectations for a more just world order did not reflect actual conditions. The ominous and unsettled domestic situation made William Allen White wish for a planned reconstruction of some sort. "I feel that if we drift," he wrote a friend, "we are in danger."[2] White feared the reaction of working people to the wartime preachments of sacrifice to make the world safe for democracy. Workers had made victory possible, and White expected them to insist on a payback. Trouble would result from any attempt to force them back into the kind of oppressive labor relations that had prevailed before the war. He worried that regression would generate "bolshevism."

While journalists like White discerned problems looming on the horizon in late 1918, many others did not. Woodrow Wilson's plans for attending the peace conference in person supplied a more absorbing topic of conversation, even though he was one of the few informed individuals who thought his Parisian venture a good idea. No American president had ever left the United States while in office, and no one knew how the Constitution intended the government to run in his absence.

It was all too possible, as well, that by actually taking part in the negotiations, the President would diminish his moral stature, that the inevitable compromises of the bargaining table would sully his reputation. Brushing such fears aside, Wilson insisted on going to Paris to defend his ideals and to protect the cornerstone of his vision of the new era, a league of nations. But former President William Howard Taft suspected that Wilson's real intention in Paris was "to hog the whole show."[3]

Criticism mounted as the President picked the delegation he would lead in Paris. Instead of selecting a bipartisan group that would represent several tendencies in American politics, Wilson chose only four men, none of whom answered to a constituency other than Woodrow Wilson. Only one could by any stretch of the imagination be considered a Republican. The humorist Will Rogers joked that Wilson was saying to the Republican party, "I tell you what, we will split 50–50. I will go and you fellows can stay."[4] Wilson did intend to run the American part of the show in his own way, to further his version of international order. This insensitivity to political realities was to haunt him once he had returned to the United States. Having lacked any share in the delegation, Republicans felt they had nothing to gain by supporting the treaty.

THE PRESIDENT and Mrs. Wilson left for France on the *George Washington* on December 2, 1918, and arrived at Brest on December 18 to a tumultuous welcome. The French greeted Wilson as a messiah, and they hung banners in the streets of Brest reading HAIL THE CHAMPION OF THE RIGHTS OF MAN and HONOR TO THE APOSTLE OF INTERNATIONAL JUSTICE. Paris embraced WILSON THE JUST. Everywhere it was "Vive Wilson" from the citizens lining the streets, throwing flowers and cheering the President and his lady. Workers and their representatives were especially enthusiastic because Wilson's ideals of democracy and self-determination seemed congruent with what unionists and Socialists had been demanding for years. Arriving in Europe well before the peace conference was ready to begin, the Wilsons toured Britain and Italy, where, again, the welcomes were warm from the masses of people who turned out to greet them. Reporters accompanying the presidential party dispatched detailed descriptions of the applause.

But once the actual peace conference had convened on January 12, 1919, news of the President slowed to a trickle. Jettisoning Wilson's ideal of open diplomacy at the outset, the conference conducted its business in small, secret meetings from which the press was barred. During January and February only vague rumors circulated in the United States about the conference. Without full press coverage the President's mission faded from public consciousness, as events in the United States provided ample diversion.

ON JANUARY 21, 1919, in the midst of a wave of strikes, 35,000 shipyard workers walked off the job in Seattle, Washington, after failing to gain wage hikes to offset soaring inflation through negotiation. Early in February the city was paralyzed when 60,000 additional workers of all sorts struck in support of shipyard workers, triggering the most famous general strike in American history.

The weeklong general strike was peaceful, but it raised nagging doubts nonetheless, because the underlying tensions between workers and employers were not confined to Seattle alone. Throughout the country employers were trying to reverse the higher wages, eight-hour workdays, and union recognition that had come with the drive for maximum wartime production. With equal determination, unionized

workers insisted that they would defend the improvements for which
they had struggled so long. The terms of the contest in Seattle were
the same as those in many other industrial communities, so that even
while the very idea of a general strike seemed foreign, the Seattle general strike, with its revolutionary rhetoric, conjured up the possibility
of a European-style labor takeover.[5]

Conservative newspapers like the *Los Angeles Times* saw in Seattle an indication that bolshevism was "a right-here now American
menace" that the American people must wake up to quickly. William
Howard Taft alerted his fellow citizens that Bolsheviks were "crusad-
ers, pushing their propaganda in every country, seeking to rouse the
lawless, the discontented, the poor, the lazy, and the shiftless to a mil-
lennium of plunder and class hatred."[6] In conservative circles Ole Hanson, the antilabor mayor of Seattle, became a hero overnight. After the
general strike had ended, he toured the country, telling how he had put
down a Bolshevik uprising.

At the same time as the Seattle general strike the textile workers
in Lawrence, Massachusetts—that reputed center of IWW agitation—
struck for a forty-eight-hour week without a reduction in pay. The
strike was strictly for hours, but a great deal of radical talk circulated
among the workers, feeding the presumption dating from 1912 that
strikes in Lawrence were inherently revolutionary. The discovery that
the largest of the Lawrence mills, the American Woolen Company, had
recently declared an extra dividend while protesting its inability to
increase wages gained support for the strikers. They won their cut in
hours with the pay they had earned for fifty-four hours' work. Despite
the dissimilarity of the two strikes, however, Lawrence joined Seattle as
another disturbing portent.

In response to these and other strikes, the United States Senate
ordered an investigation into the activities of Russian Bolsheviks in
the United States. One witness, the Reverend George A. Simons, head
of the Methodist Episcopal mission in Russia before 1918, based his
whole analysis of the Russian situation on the singular example of
Leon Trotsky, a Bolshevik leader who was Jewish and had spent time

in New York. Simons testified that bolshevism in Russia was largely a product of New York's Lower East Side, that he was not an anti-Semite, that many of his best friends were Jews. But it was a fact, he maintained, that the Bolshevik leaders were almost entirely Jewish.

In the early spring of 1919 such fantastical and bigoted testimony did not gain widespread credence. Most people believed that Americans were too free, too sophisticated, and too well off for bolshevism to make headway in the United States. Perhaps it might germinate in the United States and travel to Russia, as the Reverend Simons explained, but it could never take root here. American labor rejected communism, and the IWWs were in jail. Secure in the widespread assumption that revolutionary ideas and labor unrest could not be indigenous products, the *Louisville Courier-Journal* assured readers that there was "no need for alarm. . . . [T]here is no real Bolshevik menace in the United States."[7] Anomalous events soon threatened this equanimity.

Bolshevism was one of many phenomena that public opinion linked to labor. At the same time that Americans congratulated themselves on their immunity to bolshevism, Congress was discussing the fate of the railroads, which had been under governmental control during the war. The proposal that attracted the most attention was the plan drawn up by Glenn E. Plumb, counsel for the railroad brotherhoods. With the wholehearted support of the American Federation of Labor, liberals, and Socialists, the Plumb plan recommended the permanent ownership of the railroads by the federal government—as in virtually all other nations. A board of directors representing consumers, labor, and the government would set policy, but workers would manage the railroads on a daily basis. The public and the railroad workers would divide all profits. The Plumb plan was the epitome of "industrial democracy," a phrase still very much in vogue in labor circles in 1919.[8]

Besides the Plumb plan, other, less sweeping innovations fell under the rubric of industrial democracy in 1919. Grievance committees, boards of arbitration, employee representation on corporate boards, and profit sharing were the most common. Sometimes they would permit workers to exercise real influence; sometimes they served merely as conduits for employers' directives. One journalist dismissed industrial democracy as "easily the most ecumenically satisfying phrase now at large."[9] But one fundamental ideal that grew out of the wartime experience underlay the several interpretations of industrial democracy: the replacement of industrial conflict with cooperation, in which labor and management would share rights and responsibilities.

The Plumb plan reflected organized labor's new confidence, but few in the middle and upper classes besides labor reformers viewed society through workers' eyes. What organized labor saw as a plan for implementing industrial democracy, many Americans saw as a workers' grab for power—bolshevism, pure and simple. To conservatives, industrial democracy represented an attempt by workers to dictate railroad policy to the whole of the American people and, by extension, was "a blow at the foundations of representative government."[10] By the time the Plumb plan came up for a vote in August 1919, events had rendered it unpopular enough to be voted down handily.

To people who did not identify with labor, workers seemed to be intent on taking over not only the railroads and the factories but politics as well. In fact, the central labor committees of forty-five cities had endorsed plans for an American Labor party that had been drawn up in Chicago. The labor party movement allied itself with the Nonpartisan League, which had swept North Dakota and was spreading throughout the Middle West. As in 1886, farmers, labor, and the followers of Henry George seemed poised to parlay labor upheaval into political power.

IN THE MIDST OF the debate on labor's rightful place and the significance of the strikes that were sweeping the country, President Wilson returned from France to a massive, enthusiastic welcome in Boston on February 23. He had returned to present to the Senate and the American people a draft of the Covenant of the League of Nations, the constitution he had succeeded in drafting despite the coolness of the European participants in the peace conference.

Wilson, said William Allen White (who was covering the peace conference), "really had only one ship in the game, to secure justice for humanity in some kind of vital political organism that was in his own heart."[11] Wilson's heart was in the League of Nations, but the Allies were far more interested in making Germany, Austria, and Turkey pay for their sins by exacting reparations and dividing up their colonial possessions, which Britain and France had arranged to share in a series of secret treaties negotiated during the war.[12] Only Woodrow Wilson sought no territories, indemnities, or damages. Although he failed to halt the land grab, he did succeed in modifying the exchange of territories by substituting League of Nations mandates for outright colonial annexation.

Wilson intended the mandate system to reform imperialism by vesting control of former German and Turkish colonies, such as German Southwest Africa (now known also as Namibia) and Turkish Palestine (now divided between Israel and Jordan), in the League of Nations, which would entrust them to the Allies, notably Britain and France, under mandates that imposed limitations on the exploitation of subject peoples and resources. To the skeptical, the mandates were no improvement on ordinary colonies, the possessions of the powerful and victorious. But for Wilson, mandates would provide for the disinterested civilizing of backward peoples by those who were more advanced. Amending the transfer of colonies was only one part of Wilson's plan.

The President's greatest victory in Paris was the embedding of the League of Nations in the Treaty of Versailles. To a certain extent he achieved this by default. Other heads of state gave lip service to the idea of a league of nations in which all members would act as equals, but the Allies saw it as a hopelessly idealistic formulation. Faced with the Allies' indifference, Wilson made his League a reality by dint of extra work and sheer determination. After a full day's work with Vittorio Emanuele Orlando of Italy, Georges Clemenceau of France, and David Lloyd George of Britain, Wilson worked with a few others to draft the Covenant of the League of Nations. Serving both the Allies and the League, the President denied himself adequate rest.

Other Americans in Paris questioned Wilson's fixation on the League and his distraction from the rest of the treaty making, which had lapsed from the principles of his Fourteen Points into the sort of greedy distribution that he had denounced so eloquently. Convinced that eventual adjustments would rectify the temporary unfairness of the peace settlement—notably the refusal of independence to territories allotted to the Allies as mandates—and assure a lasting peace, Wilson disregarded these doubts. In his view, the necessity for the League overshadowed the peace treaty's injustices, which he now defended before a skeptical U.S. Senate.

The structure of the League of Nations resembled what later became the United Nations, with an executive council of the great powers and rotating delegates from the smaller nations, a general assembly of nations, and a world court. League members were obliged to take action—unspecified in the Covenant—to oppose aggression against the territorial integrity or independence of member nations. Wilson saw this provision of collective security as the heart of the League, but its possible application to American actions in Latin America provoked enormous controversy.

The President's senatorial critics presented several demands for modifications of the League Covenant to preserve American supremacy in Latin America, to incorporate provisions for withdrawal from the League, to protect purely domestic issues from League review, and to refuse undesired mandates (such as Armenia). They forced Wilson to incorporate their reservations into the Covenant when he returned to Paris. But he refused to bow to pressure to separate the League from the treaty. After less than two weeks in the United States he returned to Paris.

WILSON ARRIVED in France on March 13 to find that Allied leaders, taking advantage of his absence, had severed the League of Nations from the treaty, supposedly for consideration later. Negotiations entered what Ray Stannard Baker called the Dark Period, in which Wilson, subject to direct and insidious attacks in the peace conference and the European press, battled for the League alone. To make matters worse, Europe was disintegrating. American, Allied, and Japanese forces stationed temporarily in northern Russia and Siberia settled in for a protracted stay. But with revolutions erupting all over the Continent, the Allies could no longer seek simply to quarantine communism in Russia.

The revolutions had actually begun before the end of 1918. The Spartacist revolution had brought Communist rule to Germany briefly in January 1919. Hungary experienced a Communist revolution and a soviet government in March. Subsequent Communist uprisings occurred in the German cities of Berlin, Munich, and Düsseldorf. Vienna teetered on the brink of Communist revolution, and it seemed that the workers of Italy, perhaps even those of France, were prepared to seize their government. In March Communists from several countries met in Moscow to found the Third International (the Comintern), which quickly came to symbolize the aggressive self-confidence of Bolsheviks in Russia and throughout the world.

Nor was the rest of the world placid. Governments also trembled in the British colonies of Ireland, India, and Egypt, where nationalist revolts threatened imperial rule. With eighteen separate wars going on at once, the challenge in Paris seemed as much preventing anarchy in Europe and forestalling the loss of colonies as concluding the recent war.

Despite the spreading chaos, the British, French, and Italian delegations pursued their single-minded squabble over where to draw lines on maps. Against the background of a world in flames, the Allied leaders' contest for spoils seemed like an insane denial of reality. One American at the peace conference compared himself to a prisoner in a madhouse.

Whether liberal or conservative, Americans in Paris turned pessimistic. Although in theory they stood to profit handsomely from Wilson's insistence on global free trade, businessmen saw little promise of lucrative markets in an anarchic and Communist Europe. Both Bernard Baruch and Herbert Hoover, advisers to the American delegation, concluded that the treaty offered American business little hope in Germany. The Allies' demand for immense German reparations could be met only through heavy taxation, which would not leave German consumers enough purchasing power to buy goods from American facto-

ries and farms. Reparations also posed a political threat that especially
worried Hoover, who calculated the revolutionary potential of a tax
burden that invited revolt, which, in the current circumstances, would
be Communist.[13]

Oswald Garrison Villard, editor of *The Nation* and no longer an
admirer of the President, reported from Paris that everyone connected
with the American delegation but Wilson had lost interest in the League
of Nations "because they can really think seriously of nothing save the
terrible plight in which all Europe finds itself." Viewing the League
skeptically, Villard asked: "[O]f what use will a League of Nations be, if
Europe is to flare up in a revolution in which all the states east of the
Rhine will be joined in a veritable league to impose their extreme social
policies [i.e., communism] upon the rest of the world?" For Villard, as
for other Americans in Paris in the spring of 1919, it was "hard to take
interest in a League of Nations which is foredoomed to failure by the
insincerity of many of those who have accepted it, by the exclusion
from it of all the black races, and which holds out few attractions to the
small and the neutral nations." Like many other American liberals, Villard found the peace treaty imperialist and therefore undemocratic, and
he doubted it could last.[14]

Faced with the possibility that revolution would sweep aside Wilsonian moderation along with European vindictiveness, Americans
around Wilson argued all the harder for justice in the peace settlement,
which they saw as the last bastion against communism. The President's
secretary concluded: "If America fails now, socialism rules the world."[15]
Americans pressed for food aid to Germany and less punitive reparations but lost these arguments to the Europeans. The Treaty of Versailles emerged as a document of German humiliation. The settlement
with Germany lay at the core of the document, but treaty making also
affected the world beyond the borders of the defeated power. Millions
of Americans had stakes in what happened outside Germany.

IN THE UNITED STATES immigrants from southern and eastern Europe
and their children intently followed the peace conference's creation and

reconstitution of states like Yugoslavia and Poland. Many of these people saw themselves fundamentally as Europeans, but three large and
thoroughly American minority groups attempted to influence the terms
of the peace. Irish Americans, like Blacks and Jews, had applauded President Wilson's emphasis on self-determination. Like the President, they
initially overlooked the conflict between Wilsonian rhetoric of self-
government and the need to accommodate the world's greatest imperial
power, Great Britain. Secretary of State Lansing, however, recognized
the contradiction and worried about it. "The more I think about the
President's declaration as to the right of 'self-determination,'" he noted
confidentially, "the more convinced I am of the danger of putting such
ideas into the minds of certain races." "The phrase," he concluded, "is
simply loaded with dynamite." Among those "races" Lansing numbered
the Irish in the United States.[16]

The Irish case merited Lansing's apprehensions. Irish Americans
had petitioned the President, members of Congress, and state legislatures. They had organized mass meetings, culminating in December
1918 with "Self-Determination Week" in Boston, Chicago, Philadelphia, Denver, Baltimore, Louisville, New Haven, Omaha, New Orleans,
San Francisco, and several smaller cities. The British elections, held
at the same time, had also gratified Irish nationalists with several
parliamentary victories.

Early in 1919 Wilson himself began receiving resolutions from the
legislatures of several states, including California and Pennsylvania,
advocating Irish independence. (The Massachusetts legislature had
made this demand in March 1918.) The enormous political strength of
Irish Americans in the Democratic party explained both their success in
state legislatures and in Congress and their bitterness over the absence
of independence and self-determination for Ireland in the final draft of
the Versailles Treaty. The President's promises, it seemed, were meant
only for the subject peoples of enemies; the treaty set adjustments of
internal matters of the victorious nations outside the purview of the
League of Nations. The British Empire was an internal matter.

Irish Americans continued to press for Irish independence, but now

they assailed the treaty and the League as well. In the annual convention of the American Federation of Labor, for instance, Irish American
trade unionists amended a resolution supporting the League of Nations
(AFL leadership was closely allied with the Wilson administration) to
make clear that it must not preclude Irish independence. Scores of other
meetings passed Irish independence resolutions, and Irish American
delegations lobbied politicians at every level, including the President in
Paris. Wilson barely held his temper during the Irish onslaught, won-
dering in private how long he would be able to "resist telling them
what I think of their miserable mischief-making."[17] Irish independence
remained a lost cause in 1919.

AFRICAN AMERICANS also failed to influence the negotiations in Paris.
Even W. E. B. Du Bois, editor of the NAACP's The Crisis, encountered
State Department obstructions. Assigned to investigate the treatment
of Black troops in France, Du Bois reached Paris only by traveling with
Robert R. Moton, Booker T. Washington's successor at Tuskegee Institute, whom the government was sending to warn Black soldiers not to
expect any changes in race relations when they got home. In France
Du Bois discovered a series of official American documents that he said
proved that the armed forces had deliberately slandered Black troops
and had also demanded that the French adopt American patterns of
racial discrimination. He concluded that White American officers had
fought against Blacks as valiantly as against the Germans.[18]

Du Bois was one of many American Blacks who were disturbed that
the peace conference would decide, without African representation, the
fate of thousands of Africans living in German colonies. He organized
a Pan-African Congress in Paris, which was attended by some sixty
Blacks from the United States, Africa, and the West Indies. The meeting was smaller than intended because the British and American governments refused passports to their citizens who meant to attend. The
State Department also denied passports to businesswoman Madame C.
J. Walker and journalists Ida Wells-Barnett and William Monroe Trotter, editor of the Boston Guardian, who had been elected at a mass

meeting in Washington, D.C., to represent African Americans at the peace conference.

Undeterred, Trotter reached Paris by subterfuge, shipping out as a cook on a freighter. After a series of misadventures he arrived in Paris after the treaty had been submitted to the German government and too late to influence its wording. The treaty omitted any mention of equal rights for racial minorities and peoples victimized on account of race or color. It thus ignored the racial discrimination that burdened Black Americans and dark-skinned colonial peoples. Like Irish Americans, African Americans concluded that the lofty phrases about democracy did not apply to them.

At the end of the summer the great Allied triumphal parade in Paris delivered a parting demonstration of American racial politics in victory. The Black and Brown colonial troops who had fought in Europe marched along the boulevards beside the metropolitan soldiers of Britain and France, but the United States chose not to emulate that model. The American forces marching in the parade were lily White, as though the 400,000 Blacks who had served during the war had never existed and the 1,000 Black troops still stationed outside Paris were not there.

THE TREATY OF VERSAILLES disappointed Irish Americans and African Americans because the British and American delegates opposed their proposals on Ireland and racial discrimination. Jewish Americans, however, fared better. Both the British foreign secretary, Arthur Balfour (of the Balfour Declaration of November 1917, favoring the establishment of a national home for Jews in Palestine), and President Wilson supported the idea of Jewish settlement in Palestine, which had been a Turkish possession.[19] In both Britain and the United States many Jews were Zionists by the end of the war, but Zionism had not always been popular.

The late-nineteenth-century creation of a Viennese journalist, Theodor Herzl, author of *Der Judenstaat* (1896), Zionism made little headway among Jews in the United States and Great Britain in the early years of the twentieth century. In these two countries, assimilation promised to end anti-Jewish prejudice without recourse to expatriation, but in eastern Europe anti-Semitism grew more virulent in the twentieth century. Jews were subject to controls, humiliations, and terrorism. In the pogroms of 1903 and 1905, Russians massacred thousands of Jews. As Jewish refugees from Russia and other parts of eastern Europe immigrated to the United States in large numbers, they brought Zionism with them.

Before 1912 few successful American Jews were Zionists. Then Louis D. Brandeis joined the movement, bringing along Felix Frankfurter (a lawyer and Harvard professor, Brandeis's protégé). Brandeis adroitly combined American patriotism with Zionism and thereby attracted thousands of middle- and upper-class Jews who had hitherto assumed that Zionism would divide their loyalties. The persuasiveness and prestige of Zionists like Brandeis and Frankfurter, combined with the resurgence of anti-Semitism in Europe during and after the war, encouraged the growth of Zionism among American Jews.[20] The Leo Frank lynching was the salient American example, and European anti-Semites shed Jewish blood wholesale in the pogroms that started up again after the war. For many American Jews, concern for Jewish lives in Europe translated into support for a Palestinian homeland.

A meeting of the Jewish Congress in Philadelphia in December 1918 had elected a delegation to attend the Paris Peace Conference in pursuit of a Jewish homeland in Palestine. Initially the Jewish delegation encountered obstructions in the State Department, for Robert Lansing saw Zionists, like African Americans and Irish Americans, as troublesome people. Privately he wondered how Zionism, which Wilson supported, could be reconciled with self-determination, which the President also supported, in a territory most of whose inhabitants were not Jewish. President Wilson overrode his secretary of state, and the Jewish delegation received not only passports but also numerous small favors. In Paris Frankfurter shone as the Jewish delegation's most valuable member in the effort to protect British claims to the mandate for Palestine.

Secret wartime treaties between Britain and France had divided up the Turkish Middle East, both countries agreeing to share Palestine. But with only the British committed to the idea of a Jewish homeland, the American Jewish delegation endorsed British claims in Palestine. The British and Americans succeeded in limiting the French to Syria and Lebanon, thanks in part to the kind words of King Feisal of Arabia, who saw Zionists as "cousins in race" to whom he promised his support. Although the borders of the British protectorate over Palestine were not finally fixed until 1921, the American Jewish delegation came away from Paris victorious. In the United States Jews became the only large minority group that supported the Treaty of Versailles enthusiastically.

WHILE TREATY NEGOTIATIONS occupied President Wilson in Paris, some good news came out of Congress. In June the Senate passed the Nineteenth Amendment, permitting women to vote. (The House of Representatives had passed the woman suffrage amendment in January 1918.) Meanwhile the states were ratifying the Eighteenth (Prohibition) Amendment, which was to go into effect on January 1, 1920. But action on these popular issues belied the wider consequences of Wilson's absence, which had begun to cripple the federal government. Rudderless, the departments of the executive branch did nothing or drifted off in various directions, according to bureaucratic inertia or the proclivities of individual cabinet members. As early as January Congress also showed signs of aimlessness. *The Nation* called this "a period of hibernation" and warned of domestic problems that demanded the President's attention.[21] Twenty-six Democratic members of the Massachusetts legislature cabled Wilson to ask him to come back and deal with inflation, "which we consider *far more important than the League of Nations*."[22] Interest in foreign affairs had given way to other preoccupations: inflation, the epidemic of strikes, and bomb scares.

In March a Chicago newspaper revealed a plot to blow up the city. Nothing happened, but the revelation sent a shiver through the country. Before long actual bombs appeared. Mayor Ole Hanson, who had claimed the rout of the Seattle Bolsheviks, received a bomb in the mail on April 28. The next day a bomb arrived at the home of former Senator Thomas W. Hardwick of Georgia, who had chaired the Senate Committee on Immigration. On the thirtieth, sixteen similar bombs turned up in post offices around the country. A total of thirty-six prominent men had been sent bombs timed to explode on May Day (May 1), the international labor day. Nearly all the targets had some connection with immigration policy or the prosecution of radicals, but no political philosophy united them. They ranged from the liberal commissioner of immigration at Ellis Island, Frederic C. Howe, to the conservative Judge Kennesaw Mountain Landis, who had given Socialist Victor Berger and Wobbly William D. Haywood stiff sentences under the Sedition Act.

Bombs had also gone to Supreme Court Justice Oliver Wendell Holmes, Jr., Postmaster General Albert Burleson (by now the most hated member of the administration, whose resignation labor meetings regularly demanded), Secretary of Labor William B. Wilson (a former official of the United Mine Workers), John D. Rockefeller of Standard Oil, and banker J. P. Morgan, Jr. The identities of the bomb senders were never established. Despite the mystery, the blame quickly came to rest at the door of radicals or Bolsheviks or the IWW, which, in the minds of frightened conservatives, all were coming to mean the same thing: proof that some unAmerican entity was trying to overthrow the government by force.

May Day turned violent in several cities; it was worst in Cleveland, Boston, and New York. In Cleveland four different mobs circulated, attacking Socialists on parade and breaking into Socialist headquarters. One man was killed, and forty people were injured—all Socialists. The police arrested only Socialists. Wherever Socialist parades were broken up and marchers beaten, the assailants were servicemen. In New York City soldiers invaded an immigrant social center, the Russian People's House, confiscated literature, and forced everyone they found to sing "The Star-Spangled Banner." Other soldiers and sailors stormed the offices of the *New York Call*, a Socialist newspaper, beating up everyone there, male and female. A few days after the May Day riots, a man at a Victory Loan pageant in Washington, D.C., refused to rise for the playing of the national anthem. When the singing was over, a nearby sailor shot the unAmerican offender in the back three times. The crowd applauded as he fell.[23]

Throughout the United States newly returned veterans were prominent in attacking whomever they considered insufficiently patriotic or otherwise deviant, whether Socialists, Wobblies, or Blacks, but Blacks interpreted antiBlack attacks by servicemen as part of the long American tradition of racial violence. Many Black Americans reasoned that White supremacists, who resented the popularity of Black soldiers in France, were now trying to put Blacks back in their place. It remained true, however, that in 1919 servicemen in Europe were even more aggressive toward radicals and minorities than their counterparts in the United States. Assaults by soldiers were part of an international pattern of social and political upheaval that followed the war. In the United States the violent acts of veterans oddly aggravated fears that radicals were taking over the country. Another spate of bombings heightened tensions.

On June 2 mysterious bombs exploded in eight cities: two in Philadelphia, eight in Pittsburgh, and one, the most spectacular, in Washington, D.C., exploded on the doorstep of Attorney General A. Mitchell Palmer. Palmer's doorway was demolished, as was the unknown man (or men—two left legs were said to have been found among the bits of body strewn along the street) who planted the bombs. A fragment of anarchist literature survived the blast, and it seemed to prove that radicals were out to destroy America. The attorney general, remaining calm in the face of the destruction, dismissed the bombings as the work of "an anarchistic element." Judge Charles C. Nott of New York, another target, was not so sure that the terrorism was futile. He saw the bombs as a successful Bolshevik conspiracy to intimidate the upholders of law and order.

Along with many others, the secretary of the American Federation of Labor, Frank Morrison, assumed that the bombs had been planted by immigrants who had been imported to provide American industry a cheap labor force. Companies, he said, herded immigrants into large cities, where they continued to speak their native languages and experienced no more of America than "a petty boss and low wages." Morrison's remedy represented his own brand of 100-percent-Americanism: the assimilation of immigrants into American life.[24]

Public opinion differed on whether the unidentified bombers were foreign, but at midyear most agreed that education offered a means for restoring order. All strategies converged on teaching Americanism, whether they meant suppressing unAmerican speech and literature or fostering patriotism in schools and factories. Definitions of what constituted "American" narrowed as tolerance of dissent declined. Increasingly Americanism came to mean an unquestioning acceptance of conventional patriotism. Because education lay at the core of the task of fostering Americanism, teachers became targets in the campaign for conformity, and several cities forced teachers to sign loyalty oaths. In New York and Baltimore teachers lost their jobs for teaching about Soviet Russia. Fiddling with education, which was, after all, a long-term solution, did little to assuage anxieties over unAmericanism. To make matters worse, the short term produced new crises.

No sooner had the brouhaha over the June bombings subsided than a rumor of a Fourth of July nationwide general strike on behalf of Thomas Mooney began to spread. Mooney, a radical labor organizer, had been convicted of setting off a bomb that killed nine and injured forty at a Preparedness Day parade in San Francisco in 1916. The evidence against him was weak, and many liberals and labor supporters thought he had been framed. The governor of California, realizing that the case was not strong, had commuted the death sentences of Mooney and his associate, Warren K. Billings, to life imprisonment. But many in the labor fold demanded freedom for the man who had become a symbol of the workers' struggle for justice under capitalism. Radicals within and without the American Federation of Labor wanted to stage a nationwide general strike to demand Mooney's release. But radicals did not speak for organized labor as a whole. The annual meeting of the AFL defeated the Mooney resolution.

The AFL's rejection did not put an end to the rumors. Newspapers

all over the country discussed the Mooney general strike apprehen-
sively, embellishing predictions for the Fourth of July with images of
incendiarism and murder reminiscent of the Paris Commune. Recent
bombings and bomb scares, as well as a long general strike in Winnipeg,
Canada, fueled imaginations. New York City kept 11,000 police and
detectives on around-the-clock duty on the Fourth of July. In Chicago
two companies of the Fourteenth Infantry were ordered into the city.
In Philadelphia police patrolled the streets on a round-the-clock alert.

Independence Day passed uneventfully. But a peaceful Fourth of July
did not calm the apprehension or free organized labor of the stigmas of
radicalism and violence. The AFL was unswervingly anti-Communist,
anti-Socialist even. But for the frightened, labor's protestations of loyalty offered not reassurance but proof that the radicals were boring
from within—an old IWW tactic. How else to explain the mounting
toll of strikes? In March 175 strikes occurred; in April, 248; in May, 388;
in June, 303; in July, 360; in August, 373. More strikes had occurred
in 1917, but far more workers were involved in the strikes of 1919.[25]
The possibility that labor was controlled by Bolsheviks, dismissed early
in the year, now seemed increasingly plausible. As the hysteria over
strikes and bombs and radicalism mounted, the President came home.

AFTER THE SIGNING of the Treaty of Versailles, President Wilson returned
to the United States on July 8, weak and exhausted. During the dark
days of April he had contracted a case of influenza that affected his
brain and heart. (Wilson had had a long history of heart disease.) He
emerged from the illness mentally alert but altered temperamentally.
His opinions hardened, and he lost the flexibility that had previously
tempered the strength of his convictions. More than ever the League of
Nations was his all-consuming passion. Some of Wilson's fellow citizens assumed that he was only visiting—as before—but others were
delighted by the President's permanent return. "Just think," mused the
Macon, Georgia, *Telegraph*, "we will have a President all by ourselves
from now on!"[26]

Wilson returned to a country racked with fear of labor-radical-

Bolshevik-IWW-anarchist-Socialist revolution. However, racial strife cost far more lives in that season of blood that came to be known as the Red Summer (James Weldon Johnson, Black writer, diplomat, and NAACP official, coined the phrase). The antiBlack riots had begun in May, before the President's return. In Charleston, South Carolina, sailors attacked local Blacks in a riot that had begun as a Saturday night brawl and widened when White sailors charged into the Black district, beating the men and women they encountered. Two Blacks died and several White sailors were wounded before the violence ended.

As the President was returning to the White House in early July, Whites in Longview, Texas, acted out their resentments against Black neighbors whom they thought had grown too independent. A Black doctor had organized a cooperative store among Black cotton farmers that bypassed local White merchants. Longview Whites also suspected a Black schoolteacher of supplying dispatches to the *Chicago Defender* that violated the White southern code of racial etiquette. A Black newspaper, the *Defender* had been urging Blacks to leave the South, a line that had made its very existence a sore point with many southern Whites. Three Longview Whites beat up the teacher. Then a posse of Whites invaded the Black section of town and assaulted several Blacks. Blacks retaliated and killed four of the attackers. This confrontation in East Texas left five dead, a score wounded.

The first nationally prominent race riot occurred in Washington, D.C., between July 20 and 22. The *Washington Post*, then owned by the tabloid publisher Ned McLean, had run sensational crime stories all summer, playing up reports of alleged attacks by Black men on White women, including one on the wife of a naval officer. After this report White soldiers and marines ran amok, beating Black men and women at random. During the riot the *Post* published battle plans and meeting places.

The Washington riot became a free-for-all. Whites drove through Black districts, firing at everyone they saw; beleaguered Blacks responded by shooting at Whites. In one instance one car full of Blacks and one car full of Whites waged a running battle. The Washington police, at best, were unable to restrain the mobs. At worst they collaborated with violent White servicemen. Officials of the NAACP charged that the police would not intervene in the fighting until Whites had begun to lose the battles.

After the riot the *Post* admitted the assault that it had reported and that had triggered the violence had been verbal. The riot left 6 dead and more than 200 injured, but this was not the bloodiest outbreak in this murderous summer.

Late in June signs had gone up in Chicago's Black Belt, announcing "We will get you July 4."[27] Many Chicago Blacks heeded that warning and armed themselves against imminent assault. In the presence of thousands of soldiers in the city to prevent any uprising for Tom Mooney, the threat failed to materialize.

By late July the already jittery city of Chicago was in the midst of an unparalleled wave of strikes. Nearly 5,000 public employees—garbage collectors, street sweepers, city hall clerks, and fire department engineers—had walked out. On July 27, in the middle of extraordinary labor tensions, a Black boy swimming off a Lake Michigan beach drifted across an imaginary color line. Whites on the beach stoned him to death as a White policeman looked on impassively. Blacks mobbed the policeman, and the worst riot of a grim season began.

Crowds of armed Whites, led by Irish athletic clubs, roamed the Black section of Chicago on foot and in cars, firing upon Blacks indiscriminately. Blacks retaliated, killing all the Whites firing a machine gun from a truck that was driving through the Black Belt. Whites assaulted Blacks, and Blacks struck out at whatever White men were within reach. A Black soldier who had been wounded in Europe limped along the street, exclaiming that "this is a fine reception to give a man just home from the war." A crowd of Whites beat him to death.[28]

The riot in Chicago raged for five days. By the time it ended, more than 500 had been injured and 23 Blacks and 15 Whites were dead. Everyone noticed that Blacks had fought back.[29] Unlike the East St. Louis antiBlack pogrom two years earlier—nearly all of whose victims were Black—the violence in Chicago was less one-sided. It was the closest thing to race war that anyone could remember.

The *Chicago Defender* reported that "the youngest generation of black men are not content to move along the line of least resistance as did their sires."[30] George E. Haynes, a Black economist and director of Negro economics in the United States Department of Labor, traced the "shuffling off of the coil of servility" to the war and the migration of Blacks out of the South. For the first time, Haynes said, Blacks really understood what liberty meant, and the United States was face-to-face with a new Negro.[31]

Riots were one aspect of American racial violence; lynching was another that was on the increase: Thirty-six Blacks were lynched in 1917; sixty, in 1918; seventy-six, including ten veterans, some still in uniform, in 1919.[32] The ferocity and torture of the lynchings of 1919 were not new, but now several lynchings were advertised in advance, as though with official sanction. In June plans for the lynching of John Hartfield in Mississippi ran on the front pages of newspapers in Jackson and New Orleans.

Race riots and lynchings in the United States were part of a broader pattern of racial conflict that was also manifested in Johannesburg, South Africa, London and Liverpool, England, and Cardiff, Wales. Like labor unrest, racial violence was part of the postwar social dislocations.

During the war "force without stint," such as Wilson had demanded, had mobilized entire populations and, in the process, interrupted habits of oppression. As the war forced labor, management, and government into cooperative endeavor, organized labor had finally gained the recognition it had sought for years. A crucial component of wartime mobilization, labor had achieved reforms that it did not now intend to relinquish. The war gave workers (and other despised peoples) standing in their societies that they felt they had deserved all along. At the other end of the social and economic spectra, employers and others who thought they had something to lose saw themselves as having made unique, temporary concessions for the sake of productivity during the war. At war's end they intended to put their societies back to rights by reclaiming their former advantages. The convulsions of 1919 were conflicts between the forces of restoration and of resistance to the old ways, in relations between racial minorities and majorities, colonized peoples and imperialists, and workers and employers. The United States was one such battleground in July, when the President went before the United States Senate to present the Treaty of Versailles in its final form.

A GREAT DEAL OF opposition to the treaty already existed in the Senate. When Wilson appeared, two "irreconcilables" (senators opposed to the treaty in any form) refused to stand. Anticipating opposition to the League of Nations, the President told the Senate that it was an inseparable part of the treaty, its most important part, in fact. Praising the League, he asked the senators rhetorically, should "we or any other free people hesitate to accept this great duty? Dare we reject it and break the heart of the world?"[33] Conservative Republicans like Henry Cabot Lodge opposed the treaty as an infringement on American freedom of action in the Western Hemisphere; progressive Republicans like Hiram Johnson of California resented the President's imposition of "arbitrary will"; and liberal Republicans like Robert La Follette disliked the treaty's concessions to imperialists.[34] Democrats generally went along with the President, although White supremacists sniffed at a League of Nations in which nonWhites might be able to vote. Wilson insisted that the Senate ratify the treaty without any changes whatever.

Ratification of the treaty bogged down in the Senate Foreign Relations Committee, which was chaired by Wilson's nemesis, Henry Cabot Lodge. Lodge spent two weeks reading the contents of the treaty into the record, word by word. Then he called a parade of damaging witnesses, including Secretary of State Lansing, who revealed that he had played no part in the drafting of the Treaty, that Wilson alone had represented the United States.

The sensational testimony of William C. Bullitt, who, disgusted by the power plays and land grabbing in Paris, had resigned from a minor post with the American peace commission, further undermined the

President's position. Bullitt announced before the Senate Foreign Relations Committee that the Allies "had simply gone ahead and arranged the world to suit themselves." Reading from notes taken immediately after conversations with the secretary of state, Bullitt testified that Lansing had admitted that the League of Nations was a terrible idea. Such testimony from men who had been in Paris impressed undecided senators. Ratification began to appear doubtful.

Wilson believed correctly that public opinion was with him, but he did not realize that the public shared neither his passion for the treaty nor his conviction that it must be accepted without modification. Outside Washington, few knew of Wilson's rigidity or his fear that any senatorial modification of the Covenant of the League of Nations would invite other governments to demand changes of their own, which would amend the League out of existence.

Wilson counted on the people to pressure the Senate to ratify the treaty his way. But the American public was not concentrating on foreign affairs in August 1919. The influenza pandemic that had been raging since 1918 had killed 500,000 Americans and caused widespread private anguish, while other public issues continued to distract from Wilson's League. A midwestern congressman wished that he could tell the President "in all good faith that now where there is one man in a thousand who cares a rap about the League of Nations, there are nine hundred and ninety-nine who are vitally and distressingly concerned about the high cost of living."[35] Prices were still rising at a phenomenal rate, prompting fears of a terrible crash. Unless prices went down, said the president of the Brotherhood of Railway Trainmen, there would be "hell to pay in this country."[36] Yet the Wilson administration was slow to respond to the universal public preoccupation with inflation. The attorney general promised to prosecute the five big meat-packers for price-fixing, the President announced a plan to combat profiteering and hoarding and turned down the request of railroad workers for a raise, and as the railroad workers prepared for a nationwide strike, the President personally called a halt to strikes of all kinds before returning to the issue that interested him most.

BY THE END OF the summer it had become clear that if the treaty were to be ratified and the League of Nations accepted without reservations, the President would have to turn the Senate around or create a ground-swell of public support that would accomplish the same end. The Senate looked unpromising, so Wilson went directly to the people. Early in September he embarked on a speaking tour of nearly 10,000 miles, taking him to Ohio, North Dakota, Washington, California, Colorado, Arkansas, and Kentucky, to make forty formal speeches and countless informal appearances from the platform of his train. In view of the President's poor health, his physician and loyal Democrats advised against this undertaking, but Wilson persevered despite blinding headaches and double vision. Irish American orators preceded him, denouncing the treaty; irreconcilables trailed him, damning the League. The treaty's critics sneered at "the great international shell game by which [the President] seeks to preserve unbroken the heart of the world."[37]

On September 25 the strain proved too much for the weakened heart of this determined man. When a stroke paralyzed his left side temporarily, his physician canceled the trip, and Wilson returned to Washington. On October 3 he suffered a massive stroke that permanently paralyzed his left side, restricted his vision, and impaired his thinking. He never recovered and remained, at best, a part-time President until leaving office in March 1921.

ONCE AGAIN the President disappeared, and the country lurched from one crisis to another. In Boston on September 9, 1,117 of 1,544 Boston policemen went on strike, and mobs looted the city that Americans prized as their most civilized. As the police left their station houses, crowds booed and occasionally threw rotten fruit. In South Boston a young man in a tweed cap walked up to a striking policeman whose arms were full of gear. "I waited eleven years to get you!" the young man shouted. "You're not a cop now!" and he punched the policeman in the jaw. As the policeman went down, spilling his possessions, the crowd jeered and made no move to help.[38]

In the evening mobs formed in Scollay Square (now Government Center), Haymarket Square, and South Boston, robbing and beating up passersby and gang raping a woman. The bigger department stores like Filene's had stationed armed guards to protect their property, so the mob threw bricks and looted smaller stores, including the Irish groceries and saloons of South Boston.

The next day the police commissioner tried to reestablish order by using voluntary police (a tactic that dated back to 1877), consisting of Harvard students, officers of the Yankee Division of the American Expeditionary Force, and other representatives of the middle and upper classes. One woman volunteer directed traffic in a stylish suit and a fur boa. By Thursday the state guard reimposed order, but not before a total of eight people had died and seventy-one had been injured.

While the mayor and the police commissioner feuded, Governor Calvin Coolidge took over the city. Refusing Samuel Gompers's offer to settle the strike, Coolidge denied the right of the Boston police to form a union in the first place. "There is no right to strike against the public safety by anybody, anywhere, any time," the governor announced with a determination that earned him reelection in 1919 and the Republican vice presidential nomination in 1920.

The city dismissed all striking policemen and began to hire an entirely new force on September 13. A man from a small town offered the police commissioner some advice: "Would it not be a fine thing, when appointing new police officers to select a few old-fashioned Yankees—full blooded Americans on the force to instill a little Americanism into the situation? There [seem] to be altogether too many Irishmen in positions to impart the true Americanism which we so much need in these trying times."[39]

As the Boston police went on strike, the police of thirty-seven other cities, including Oklahoma City, Oklahoma; Peoria, Illinois; Meridian, Mississippi; Terre Haute, Indiana; Los Angeles and Richmond, California; Chattanooga, Tennessee; and Topeka, Kansas, were enrolled in unions affiliated with the AFL. The Boston police had formed their union as a last resort, after having requested a wage increase since 1917. The commissioner of police had put them off repeatedly, even though their most recent raise had come in 1913, with the implementation of a pay scale set in 1898. In 1919 the Boston police made less than common laborers, but unlike police, laborers did not work seventy-three to ninety-eight hours a week or perform unpaid parade duty.

In a period of rapidly rising prices the Boston police wanted better pay and improved working conditions. No one among them was a radical, but their strike was hailed as another victory for the Bolsheviks. A Philadelphia newspaper asked: "[W]herein do the police of the New England metropolis differ from the mad minority which overthrew Kerensky and ruined Russia . . . in their reckless defiance of the fundamentals of morality, in their bullying affront to the structure of civilization?" The paper's conclusion: "Bolshevism in the United States is no longer a specter. Boston in chaos reveals its sinister substance."[40] Another major strike reinforced such perceptions.

BEFORE THE BOSTON POLICE strike failed, 350,000 steelworkers went out on strike on September 22. The steelworkers struck after Judge Elbert Gary, chairman of United States Steel—which employed 268,000 of the 600,000 steelworkers in the United States in 145 different mills—had refused to meet with a union committee. President Wilson appealed to the steelworkers to postpone the strike until after the meeting of his Industrial Conference in early October, but the steelworkers went out anyway. Men in the mills complained that the company was discharging union members and that waiting would only decimate their union. Union leaders could not restrain the rank and file.

The Homestead strike of 1892 was the first of four big strikes that failed to secure recognition of unions in the steel industry. In 1901 and 1909 steelworkers had struck again for union recognition and lost. Since then they had remained unorganized. After the European War the American Federation of Labor had come finally to question the ability of the traditional craft unions to organize big, new industries like steel, few of whose workers were skilled craftsmen. The federation backed a new method of organizing its craft unions according to industry, which would produce one big union of skilled, semi-skilled, and unskilled workers, divided into several basic industrial sectors.

In 1918 twenty-four different unions had formed the National Committee for Organizing Iron and Steel Workers, of which Samuel Gompers was chairman, William Z. Foster, secretary. By early 1919 the committee had met in May with delegates from steel locals from Alabama, Colorado, Minnesota, and the major steel centers of Pennsylvania, Ohio, and Indiana. Although the delegates demanded a strike immediately, leaders of the national committee had held them in check, but by August this was no longer possible. The national committee took a strike vote. When Judge Gary refused to answer a letter from Gompers, the strike began.

The first basic demands of the strike called for an eight-hour day, a six-day week, and abolition of the long shift of twenty-four hours every two weeks when shifts changed. U.S. Steel had adopted the "basic eight-hour day" during the war, meaning that while the men continued to work twelve-hour shifts, they were paid time and a half overtime for the extra four hours. It was a raise, not an actual eight-hour day.

The other main demands were for union recognition and the right to bargain collectively through representatives of the workers' own choosing. In 1919 steelworkers lacked procedures for expressing grievances or concerns over working conditions. If, as in Clairton, Pennsylvania, a foreman ordered a gang of men scheduled to quit at six to remain on the job four more hours, the men had no right to object. If they went home anyway, as they did in this instance, the man who spoke up was fired. The steelworkers said, "[I]f you go to the foreman, he tells you 'if you don't like it you can quit.'" If they appealed to the superintendent, they would be fired. The very idea of appointing a committee to speak to the superintendent made a group of steelworkers from Homestead, Braddock, Clairton, and Donora laugh bitterly.[41]

Underlying the complaints and actions of the steelworkers was their determination to confront the autocratic management of U.S. Steel and the other smaller steel companies that followed the giant's lead. Steelworkers said that after the war had shown how critical their labor was to the economy as a whole, they deeply resented being treated like slaves. A Polish striker in Pittsburgh drew a different analogy with the same point: "Just like horse and wagon. Put horse in wagon, work all day. Take horse out of wagon—put in stable. Take horse out of stable, put in wagon. Same way like mills. Work all day. Come home—go sleep. Get up—go work in mills—come home. Wife say, 'John, children sick. You help with children.' You say, 'Oh, go to hell'—go sleep. No know what the hell you do. For why this war? For why we buy Liberty bonds? For mills? No, for freedom and America—for everybody. No more horse and wagon. For eight-hour day."[42]

In Ohio steel towns life went on in a fairly normal way during the strike. But the steel towns of western Pennsylvania turned into armed camps. Mayors and sheriffs, often the creatures of the steel companies, refused to let strikers hold meetings. Mounted state guards, whom the steelworkers called Cossacks, beat up organizers and strikers. From the moment it began, Pennsylvania newspapers regularly reported that the strike had failed.

In Gary, Indiana, 2,000 U.S. troops patrolled the streets under the command of Major General Leonard Wood, who believed that steelworkers were the dupes of alien, Bolshevik influences. The situation at Gary was grave, he reported, because of the presence of "a dangerous and extremely active group—the Red Anarchistic element—which is striving to bring about these extensive disturbances against law and order. These elements are working against everything which this country stands for."[43] Wood understood, at least, that the steel strike had implications for American industry in general.

The steel industry epitomized the changes that had occurred in American industry since the late nineteenth century. The U.S. Steel Corporation owned hundreds of steel mills in several states, and it used modern equipment that had drastically reduced the need for skilled workers. Most steelworkers were unskilled or semiskilled, and if one were fired or left his job, another could be trained quickly. By recruiting in Europe and the American South, steel companies had assembled a large, heterogeneous (heavily Slav) work force stratified according to language, nativity, and race.

Employers and their spokesmen played on the differences between English-speaking and European workers, maintaining that the strikers were all foreign and that the "American" workers stayed on the job. A poem published in a steel industry magazine made this point:

> Said Dan McGann to a foreign man who worked at the self-same bench.
> "Let me tell you this," and for emphasis, he flourished a monkey wrench,
> "Don't talk to me of this bourgoissee, don't open your mouth to speak
> "Of your socialists or your anarchists, don't mention the bolshevik,
> "For I've had enough of this foreign stuff, I'm sick as a man can be
> "Of the speech of hate, and I'm telling you straight, that this is the land
> for me."[44]

In fact, the degree to which foreign and English-speaking steelworkers clashed was not constant. In Johnstown, Pennsylvania; Cleveland, Youngstown, and Steubenville, Ohio; and Gary, Indiana, both groups supported the strike. In the Pittsburgh area, however, where social cleavages between "Americans" and "Hunkies" ran deep, "Americans" stayed on the job and Slavs struck, by and large. "Americans" spoke English as a first language and might be immigrants from Wales, Ireland, England, and Scotland. But a man born in the U.S. whose father or grandfather was Hungarian was labeled a "Hunky."

Judge Gary refused to meet with the strikers' representatives from the national organizing committee because, he said, they were not his employees and could not therefore speak for his workers. To meet with them would be tantamount to accepting what he called the "tyranny" of the closed shop (in which only union members could work). Judge Gary had insisted that he was waging a battle of principle, and conservative opinion upheld him. Agreeing with Gary, the *New York Tribune* saw the strike as an attempt by radicals and easily misled immigrants forcibly to nationalize basic industry. The *Wall Street Journal* thanked Gary for upholding the United States Constitution, and the *Chicago Tribune* announced that the American people must now choose between Gary and the American way, on the one hand, and the strikers and dictatorship of the proletariat, on the other.[45]

The issue of labor radicalism drew attention to the organizer of the steel strike, William Z. Foster. A former Wobbly who had founded the Syndicalist League of America, Foster had successfully organized Chicago's meat packers along industrial lines, as he was now undertaking to do in steel. Foster had come to see syndicalism as impractical, but his Wobbly past pursued him. He compounded fears that the IWW was taking over the AFL when he gave a Senate committee investigating the strike evasive answers about his political views. No matter how much AFL leaders, including Gompers, defended Foster as a convert to conservative unionism who was doing the work of the AFL, his past tainted the steel strike and the labor movement in general. The wave of industrial unrest, the steel strike in particular, looked to many like the beginning of an industrial revolution. The steel strike never gained public approval, and its failure marked a hardening of public opinion in labor matters. During the autumn conservative newspapers and politicians explicitly linked labor unrest with radicalism and radicalism with treason. The organ of the coal mining industry, the Chicago *Black Diamond*, said that "radicals are in the saddle within the ranks of organized labor, and strikes and threats of strikes are merely the prelude to a reign of lawlessness whose object is the overthrow of the American Government and the substitution of the Soviet form of government."[46]

Before the steelworkers had been out a full week, editors began to wonder "Where will Hades break loose next?"[47] It broke loose in Omaha, Nebraska. After weeks of racial tension fanned by sensational newspaper reporting, violence erupted on September 28. A White mob attacked the jail to get at a Black prisoner charged with the rape of a White woman. The young woman was not sure whether her assailant was Black or White, but William Brown was being held as the main suspect.

After beating up the mayor in order to get at Brown, those in the mob could not decide what to do with their captive. First they burned him; then they shot him hundreds of times; then they dragged his body through the streets at the end of a rope. They hung what was left of the torso from a trolley pole at one of the city's major intersections. By this time the governor had sent for General Leonard Wood, whose troops restored order. Brown's grisly death was hardly seen as serious in and of itself.

The Omaha riot was upsetting because it represented the invasion of chaos into an ordinary American town. Omaha could not be dismissed as either a wicked big city like Chicago or a savage southern place like Atlanta. If a gruesome lynching could take place in Omaha, it could happen anywhere. Omaha seemed to provide another example of the breakdown of civilization, which General Wood was quick to exploit. After pacifying the city, he toured the country, explaining the riots and strikes as the work of reds who traveled from place to place, breeding discontent. As the defender of order and the American way against the onslaughts of outside agitators, Wood attracted political support from frightened conservatives. By the fall of 1919 he was campaigning openly for the presidency in his uniform, becoming the leading Republican contender.

THE AUTUMN BROUGHT no respite. The bituminous (soft) coal miners had taken a strike vote in September and planned to walk out on November 1. As in other industries, union leadership could not restrain the United Mine Workers' restive rank and file. The steelworkers were still on strike, and hundreds of other strikes were in progress throughout the country; at the beginning of October more than 600,000 workers in twenty states were off the job. A quarter of a million railroad workers were staging wildcat strikes, and their brotherhoods were on the verge of calling a nationwide strike that would immobilize the entire country.

Even friends of labor who discounted the talk of Bolshevik conspiracy found the widespread discontent worrisome, because there seemed to be no end to the epidemic of strikes. As in the mid-1880s, when similar rank-and-file insurgency had overwhelmed the leadership of the Knights of Labor, workers' anger threatened to throw the labor movement into disarray in 1919. It was true that every strike that won union recognition and the right of collective bargaining secured a bit more industrial democracy. And each increment of collective power seemed to make the lives of workers less what the Polish steelworker had called "horse and wagon." But with the wartime agencies dismantled, that power could only be won piecemeal, strike by strike, with a cumulative effect that was devastating.

Compromise between labor and management that would serve the interests of both no longer seem possible. The President's National Industrial Conference had broken up over the steel strike and the refusal of the conference to accept the legitimacy of collective bargaining. (Members of the conference represented the public, employers, or labor. Elbert Gary and John D. Rockefeller, Jr., took part as representatives of the public.)

Meanwhile, talks in the coal industry broke down, and 425,000 miners prepared to strike, demanding increases in pay and a shorter workweek. On November 1, however, a judge on the federal court in Indianapolis issued a temporary restraining order, which he soon made permanent, against officials of the United Mine Workers. The Wilson administration resuscitated the Lever Fuel Act, part of the wartime legislation that had given the government power to prohibit obstructions in the production and distribution of fuel. Coal price controls under the Lever Act had been lifted in February, and coal prices had risen dramatically. But when the miners prepared to strike, the Wilson administration declared the Lever Act still in force and the strike, therefore, illegal. Wishing to avoid a conflict with the federal government, UMW leaders rescinded the strike order. But many miners, already defying the court order, did not return to the mines. The strike, now verging on political rebellion, continued without union leadership.

Conservatives warned that the United States would now have to choose between government by the people or government by labor unions. The miners having defied a federal court injunction, many editors characterized the strike as an attack by 425,000 miners on 110,000,000 citizens. This conviction deepened as a coal shortage forced schools and factories to close, limited rail transportation, and cut the generation of electricity for streetlights and household use. The strike ended in mid-November, before the lack of coal had reached crisis proportions. Even though a special commission studying the coal industry awarded the miners a raise, the justice of the miner's cause did not reassure millions who worried about their country. An organization of veterans acted out these fears.

THE WAR HAD BEEN over for a year on November 11, 1919, when the American Legion held its first annual convention, vowing to attack bolshevism and uphold Americanism. The president of the Grand Army of the Republic (the Civil War veterans' organization) passed the mantle of patriotism to the veterans of the European War, warning the legion to remain vigilant against the enemies within. While the convention was in full swing, word came of an encounter in Centralia, Washington, in which Wobblies killed four legionnaires on Armistice Day. Legionnaires and Wobblies had a long history of antagonism in Washington State, and Wobblies had fortified their hall in anticipation of trouble on Armistice Day, when legionnaires went on parade. After the marching legionnaires had halted in front of the IWW hall for a second time, the Wobblies opened fire.

In retaliation, legionnaires castrated and lynched Wesley Everest, an IWW organizer who was also a veteran. The lynching served to declare open season on radicals across the country. All along the West Coast mobs broke into IWW halls and beat up whomever they found. The United States Justice Department raided the Russian People's House in New York City. State justice departments throughout the country rounded up everyone called a radical.

By the end of November dragnets had yielded 249 deportable (noncitizen) radicals (citizens could not be deported), whom a "Red Special" took to Ellis Island in New York. On December 21 the 249 deportees, 3 of whom were women—including the famous anarchist Emma Goldman—took forced passage to the Soviet Union on the *Buford*, popularly labeled the "Soviet Ark." Stung into action by congressional impatience and public demand, Attorney General Palmer acted. Assuming that radicalism was a foreign product, Palmer promised to deport radicals by the thousands until, he said, the country was cleansed of the alien poison. He prepared a peacetime sedition law to facilitate the process and to lock away offending Americans. The red scare, like the Espionage and Sedition acts of wartime, ran roughshod over civil liberties. The Civil Liberties Bureau (later the American Civil Liberties Union), which had been formed during the suppression of dissent during the European War, continued its work against the ongoing attack on the freedoms of speech and assembly.

One British journalist visiting the United States in late 1919 found the public mind "hag-ridden by the spectre of Bolshevism. It was like a sleeper in a nightmare, enveloped by a thousand phantoms of destruction. Property was in an agony of fear, and the horrid name 'Radical' covered the most innocent departure from conventional thought with a suspicion of desperate purpose."[48] Another Briton who moved in wealthy circles heard a great deal about impending "social revolution in the United States along Bolshevik lines . . . Fifth Avenue swept by machine-gun fire. . . . Pittsburgh, Detroit, and Cleveland in the hands of revolutionary committees of workmen after wild scenes of pillage and mob passion . . . the rich daughters of millionaires stripped of their furs and their pearls."[49] The Paris Commune and *Caesar's Column* seemed right around the corner. But in Washington no one was in charge.

CLEARLY THINGS WERE AWRY. In the midst of social and political crises and with the President gravely ill, it was a mystery who was committing the government to enjoining strikers and rounding up foreigners wholesale. It turned out later that Mrs. Wilson and the President's secretary were doing the best they could. The executive and legislative branches barely functioned, as the breakdown of the national government became ever more distressing.

Despite the domestic crises, Congress had given sustained consideration to one issue only, the Treaty of Versailles. At the end of the year the Senate was deadlocked. Even Democratic senators who favored the treaty harbored misgivings about the League of Nations section, but the President would not let them make any alterations. Remaining inflexible, he insisted that the treaty be passed without reservations, yet without reservations the treaty could not pass. On November 21 the Senate defeated the treaty with and without the reservations to the Covenant drafted by Republican Henry Cabot Lodge. While Congress was occupied with the Treaty of Versailles, organized labor attempted to free itself of the taint of radicalism.

At the end of the year Samuel Gompers called a national labor conference that publicly repudiated bolshevism and Wobblyism as unAmerican and ordered all AFL unions to purge radical members. The conference's condemnation of revolutionaries met widespread approval, but its statement of Labor's Bill of Rights (the right to strike, the right of public employees to organize, the right of collective bargaining, and the continuation of governmental control of the railroads) was not so welcome. For many, Labor's Bill of Rights seemed to embody a defiant threat of more strikes and more talk of nationalization. The national labor conference did not free labor of the stigma of bolshevism because the very existence of labor demands fed the widespread fear of communism triumphant, furnishing the rationale for an antiradical red scare.

THE YEAR 1919 had at first promised an end to the regimentation of the war. It brought, instead, a mounting toll of disorder. Four million workers, one out of every five, struck in 1919, a proportion never since equaled. Nor has racial violence ever again reached 1919 levels. During the Red Summer antiBlack riots broke out in twenty-five cities and towns.

As in 1877 and 1886, the apparent enemies of 1919 seemed to spring from within and seemed ever so hard to ferret out and defeat. Socialists who had once stood for the visionary and impractical left end of the political spectrum now appeared to be bolshevism's entering wedge. People who spoke of economic equity seemed to want to take over the country and destroy it. In this panicky, anarchic universe of enemies, someone had to restore order, and many cared less about the means than the end.

In the absence of national leadership, states, localities, and voluntary associations entered the breach. State legislatures and local governments passed statutes against striking, speaking "disloyally," and displaying the red flag of socialism. The American Legion, Ku Klux Klan, and a diverse array of local societies began to enforce Americanism according to their own lights. Attorney General Palmer cracked down on the reds and began to look available as a Democratic presidential candidate. In the Republican ranks General Wood rode high. Supporters came from many sectors of the population, including businessmen like a Wood partisan who believed that only the general could "pull the ship of state off the shifting sands on which we are drifting."[50]

As the year of the Great Unrest closed, the seeming price of increased democracy—industrial and political anarchy—was deemed too high for most Americans to pay. The very fact of labor militancy led inexorably to the conviction that unAmerican radicals had fomented the trouble, as though only Bolsheviks caused strikes. The year ended with the rounding up of radicals in a brutal quest for law and order, a red scare that trampled civil liberties and civil rights. But large numbers of Americans had decided with Attorney General Palmer that in times like these the extremes of hierarchy were preferable to the extremes of democracy.

14

LOOKING FORWARD

O n January 2 and 3, 1920, the Justice Department arrested 5,000 people in surprise dragnet raids in thirty-three cities and twenty three states. Aimed at radical aliens, the "Palmer raids" on members of the tiny and divided Communist movement scooped up radicals and onlookers, citizens and noncitizens. During the month of January the New York legislature expelled its five Socialist members, heedless that as many as ten Socialists had served in the Assembly during the war. At the height of the red scare even five seemed to constitute a menace. Congress had taken action against its single Socialist and expelled Victor Berger of Milwaukee in late 1919. Berger had opposed the war, remarking afterward that all the American people got out of it was flu and inflation. Milwaukee voters had reelected Berger in a special election in December 1919, but Congress expelled him once again. This time there was no special election, and Milwaukee was not represented in the House of Representatives until after the regular election in November 1920, which Berger lost.

The red scare was at its most abusive in the winter of 1920, as the Palmer raids began to raise doubts about the justification for the wholesale rounding up of individuals, citizens or not. The expulsion of the New York Socialist legislators provoked widespread condemnation. Even Senator Warren G. Harding of Ohio, a very regular Republican, criticized the action. Each passing month called into question the credibility of the purveyors of the red scare.

Attorney General Palmer announced that the railroad strike of April 1920 was part of a worldwide Communist-IWW conspiracy whose leader in this country was William Z. Foster. Palmer planted agents among the strikers and arrested several for violating the Lever Act. But Palmer made the mistake of exposing his evidence. Before a congressional committee the attorney general presented his proof that the strike was IWW-inspired: Justice Department agents had overheard one striker say that "the IWW was not as bad as it was supposed to be," and another striker had said that "in his opinion Mr. Palmer . . . was the greatest Red in the United States."[1]

By the spring of 1920 the cry of "Bolshevik" no longer silenced questioners, and the charges received more careful scrutiny. Desperately trying to revive his popularity by reanimating the red scare, the attorney general fell farther out of step. He predicted a mass Communist uprising on May Day, and when nothing happened, newspapers began to ridicule Palmer's hallucinations.

On January 1 the country went dry, although Prohibition continued to be controversial throughout the 1920s. As Frances Willard had predicted in the 1870s, woman suffrage and prohibition had gone hand in hand, but not causally. She had expected enfranchised women to vote in prohibition, but Congress passed and the states ratified the prohibition amendment prior to granting women suffrage. Women voted for president for the first time in the 1920 election, which also marked another sort of watershed. For the first time the election returns were broadcast by radio.

In the middle of 1920 the American troops taking part in the Allied occupation of Siberia and Archangel came home from the Soviet Union, where they had been since 1918, initially to keep the Germans from seizing stocks of war matériel after the Communist revolution had taken Russia out of the war. When the Allied troops remained after the signing of the Treaty of Versailles, the Soviets accused the Allies of counterrevolution. Even anti-Communists in the United States began to question the wisdom of keeping American forces in Russia, agreeing with Senator William E. Borah of Idaho that it was not the business of the United States "to go there and engage in bloody riots with them."[2]

The internationalist in the White House, still terribly ill, cast a shadowy presence in Democratic politics, refusing to remove himself from the 1920 presidential race. Wilson's silence, which he expected to produce a movement to draft him in the nominating convention, paralyzed the strongest Democratic contender, his brother-in-law William McAdoo. Democrats and Republicans agreed upon the attractiveness of one man, Herbert Hoover, whom a perceptive Briton called the "only man who emerged from the ordeal of Paris with an enhanced reputation."[3] But Hoover's partisan identity was obscure. Moreover, he talked about wanting to correct what he saw as the basic problem of American society: the inequitable distribution of wealth. Republicans and Democrats looked elsewhere.

The Democratic National Convention settled on Governor James M. Cox of Ohio, a conservative who was not associated with the Wilson administration and who did not support prohibition. Vice presidential nominee Franklin D. Roosevelt of New York balanced the midwesterner and bore a famous last name. In a convention that was more wet than dry, William Jennings Bryan failed to get his plank endorsing Prohibition included in the platform. After nearly a quarter of a century Bryan could no longer rally masses of Democrats behind him. By the early 1920s only old-timers remembered him as the radical of the 1890s or the embodiment of forward-looking democracy. He moved to Florida, became a champion of fundamentalism against evolution, and died in 1925 shortly after the Scopes trial in Dayton, Tennessee. In his last years, as in Dayton, Bryan fixed himself in memory as an agent of ignorance, a seedy old man in a cheap white suit carrying a fan.

By the time the Republican Convention met, General Leonard Wood's 100-percent-Americanism had lost much of its appeal, and he proved to have few ideas beyond fighting bolshevism in the guise of labor unions. A deadlocked convention turned to Senator Warren G. Harding of Ohio, an inoffensive conservative. Harding's nomination symbolized the return of the Republican party to the standpattism that William McKinley and William Howard Taft (both fellow Ohioans) had represented.

Walter Lippmann of *The New Republic* wrote that Harding and Cox were "two provincial, ignorant politicians entirely surrounded by special interests, operating in a political vacuum. Nobody believes in anything."[4] The major candidates were clearly second-raters whose overarching achievement was not being Woodrow Wilson. Harding received 16,143,000 votes; Cox, 9,130,000. From the federal penitentiary, where he was serving out his Sedition Act conviction, Eugene V. Debs got 920,000 votes as the Socialist party candidate. The promise of labor politics in the heady atmosphere of 1918 had faded so badly by 1920 that labor party forces fused with the Nonpartisan League to create a Farmer-Labor party whose candidate, Parley P. Christensen, received only 265,000 votes.[5]

Lacking a candidate like Hoover, who wanted to tackle fundamental problems, the Republican victory represented a repudiation of many things—Wilson, political drift, labor unrest, the red scare, and the trampling of civil liberties—rather than a willingness to address the social and economic dislocations the war had caused. Lippmann wrote an old friend that he could "remember no time when the level of political discussion was so low." If there were such a thing as the "mind of the people," he concluded, "then it is fair to say that the American mind has temporarily lost all interest in public questions."[6]

THE ECONOMIC SITUATION changed at about the same time as politics shifted. The inflation that had caused so much desperation and so many strikes between 1917 and 1919 ended in the middle of 1920, and the country entered a recession that threw millions out of work. During the two years of deflation prices fell faster than wages. Many employers introduced new tactics, called the American plan of industrial relations, which improved the wages and fringe benefits of workers who promised not to join unions.

AFL unions lost a quarter of their membership as workers lost their jobs and chose jobs over unions when forced to give up one or the other. In addition, the United States Supreme Court invalidated several laws that labor had supported, striking down the exemption of unions from prosecution under the Clayton Act, declaring labor boycotts illegal, and seriously circumscribing the right of unions to picket. During the early 1920s workers collectively lost autonomy, but they gained purchasing power as individuals. By the time the recession let up in 1922, real wages were 19 percent higher than they had been in 1914, paving the way for the flourishing consumer society that has been the envy of the world ever since.

ANYONE WHO HAD known the United States in 1877 would readily acknowledge that fundamental changes had taken place by 1919. What had been a rural, agricultural nation had become an industrial society dominated by great cities that were far different from what they had been forty years earlier. Commercial cities had become manufacturing cities, and Asian, Irish, and German workers in industry had been joined by Slavs, Italians, Jews, and Blacks. More than ever before the workplace was a huge factory, powered by electricity, connected to suppliers and distributors by telephone, and producing goods that went out by truck as well as by rail. The trucks and other assorted motor vehicles were advertised in periodicals full of pictures, photos, and advertisements. Workers and employers alike saw themselves as consumers as well as producers, consuming leisure activities as well as material goods.

In the 1920s the makers of movies would reach out to middle- and upper-class audiences, but in 1919 moving pictures, like amusement parks and professional sports, appealed largely to working-class audiences, offering commercial mass entertainment that had not existed in the 1870s. Drinking in public places such as saloons had played a large part in working-class leisure, but movements advocating temperance and prohibition had steadily gained strength in the late nineteenth and early twentieth centuries, although their adherents were more likely to be Protestants than Catholics, middle- and upper-class rather than working-class, and female rather than male. By 1920 prohibition was the law of the land.

Railroads and great manufacturing enterprises still played an important part in the nation's economic life, but they no longer held the central spot as in the late nineteenth century. Finance capitalists now made most of the crucial economic decisions, so that the United States Steel Corporation, the great steel company that banker J. P. Morgan had assembled in 1901 and that had taken over the steel mills of Andrew Carnegie, was headed in 1919 by Judge Elbert Gary, who had come out of the financial world of J. P. Morgan and Company, not from the steel mills. After the European War, Wall Street was not only the financial capital of the country but the financial center of the world.

Social changes were easier to see. Cities had spread out, so that while workers might still live near the plants and mills in which they labored, the middle and upper classes of management and ownership now lived in clean and quiet suburbs, to which they commuted by automobile. Neighborhoods were more clearly demarcated by economic class, but the people in them looked ever more alike, at least at first glance. Increasing numbers of people purchased their clothes ready-made, so that class distinctions in clothing became a subtle matter of fabric and fit rather than simply of style.

During the 1870s virtually every one of the tiny minority of Americans who had attended college and practiced a profession was Anglo-Saxon, Protestant, and male. But by the end of the European War thousands of others had joined the professional ranks: women (mostly Anglo-Saxon and Protestant, but a few Blacks, Catholics, and Jews) and men from non-Anglo-Saxon backgrounds. The new professionals, often from families of modest means, faced considerable prejudice on account of their class, gender, race, and religion. Their numbers were so small that they never were more than tokens, but that was nonetheless an improvement over complete exclusion.

By the second decade of the twentieth century respectable political rhetoric had come to embrace views that had been relegated to the margins of politics in the 1870s. Whereas laissez-faire (leave alone) had supposedly characterized the political economy of the nineteenth century, in fact, governments on all levels had intervened in the marketplace to facilitate economic growth, by furthering the interests of business as opposed to those of consumers and workers. By 1919, however, officials at all levels of government had admitted that the welfare of citizens should also weigh in political decisions—or at least seem to count.

Meanwhile, the definition of citizen both narrowed and broadened during the period. In 1877 large numbers of Black men were voters, North and South. But during the late 1870s, 1880s, and 1890s political violence in the South limited their access to the ballot, and in the first decade of the twentieth century state laws disfranchised poor Black men as well as many poor Whites. During the very years that southern Blacks were losing the vote in the South, the idea of votes for women was growing more acceptable throughout the country. By 1920 most women could vote, but Black people of both sexes found it virtually impossible to exercise the franchise in the southern states, where 90 percent of them lived. Black and interracial organizations demanded equal access to the vote as they continued to protest against lynching and segregation.

In the twentieth century organized labor achieved a degree of political influence that would not have seemed possible in 1877. The AFL's alliance with the Democratic party discouraged the formation of an independent labor party but influenced the actions of President Wilson. Wilson acceded to one of labor's oldest demands in 1913, when he created a Department of Labor with cabinet rank and assigned a former union official the position of secretary of labor. In 1917 Wilson became the first President to address the annual convention of the AFL. As striking as it would have been to a member of the Knights of Labor, organized labor's proximity to political power did not prevent the recurrence of a pattern of red-baiting that dated back to the nineteenth century.

THE YEARS OF UNREST—1877, 1886, 1919—inspired ever more disturbing red scares, during which the reestablishment of order—that is, stopping the strikes—meant using as scapegoats whatever "reds" happened to be available, whether "communists/Communards" in 1877, anarchists in 1886, or "Bolsheviks" in 1919. Perhaps the jitteriness of 1877 should not be termed a red scare, for it amounted to little in comparison with 1886 and 1919, when governments rounded up everyone suspected of being a red. The railroad strike of 1877 produced a flurry of antiradical rhetoric and many warnings about the possibility of an American commune, but not the beatings, jailings, hangings, and deportations of 1886 and 1919. The great railroad strike of 1877 provides a clue to the relationship between events and red scares.

The railroad strike of 1877 was a spontaneous outbreak that inspired rather than stemmed from labor organization. The depression of the 1870s had begun in 1873 and had already dealt the two National Labor Unions a fatal blow when the great railroad strike occurred. This lack of organization explains the fairly tame red scare of 1877, as opposed to those of 1886 and 1919, when the Knights of Labor and the unions of the AFL represented hitherto unheard-of strength of numbers.

The trampling of civil liberties that characterized red scares was related to the organization of working people as well as to ideology, for red scares followed the combination of strikes and widespread labor organization, not the mere existence of "reds." Had red scares been directly related to the actual numerical strength of purported reds, the greatest red scare of all would have occurred in 1912, not 1919.

On another level, the question remains why socialists of various sorts inspired repression. Why not prohibitionists or single taxers? Why *red* scares? To answer these questions is to return to the contest between the ideals of identity of interest and of equity based on the acknowledgment of conflicting interests. Labor unions, Socialists, anarchists, and Communists all spoke on behalf of one part of society: workers, whom they saw as having interests that conflicted with those of capital. "Reds" insisted that all the people in society could not share an identity of interest, and when it came to choosing sides, they saw themselves as defenders of labor. They pointed to enduring class differences, which in an industrial society, they said, undermined fundamental tenets of American mythology—the possibility, the probability even, of upward mobility and the consequent impermanence of class differences. In tranquil moments people speaking for the workers could be tolerated on the sidelines, for they seldom entered the mainstream. But in 1886 and 1919 industrial conflict presented very real evidence of the class conflict that seemed to vindicate the reds. Then champions of identity of interest targeted reds and rooted them out as unAmerican. Red scares produced more than silence, however.

Red scares also encouraged the passage of antiunion legislation that made organizing, striking, and picketing difficult. The red scares of 1886 and 1919 were supposed assaults on distasteful ideologies, but the repression intentionally crippled the organizations that challenged the hierarchy; red scares were eerily effective at enforcing identity of interest as seen from the top.

RED SCARES assaulted workers' organizations and worker-centered ideologies. But the Spanish-American and European wars produced another sort of intolerance: the pressure for conformity of race. Racism has been an American ideology since the institutionalization of slavery in the late seventeenth century, and its manifestation at the turn of the century was not new.[7] But the Spanish-American War witnessed a frenzied pursuit of imperialism, White supremacy, and Anglo-Saxonism that redefined American society and characterized it by race. William Jennings Bryan had asked whether the United States would be a republic or an empire, and by the early years of the twentieth century the empire had triumphed. This was no multiracial, multicultural empire; it was stridently Anglo-Saxon. "This is a White man's country" was repeated in the South and in the Philippines, where disfranchised nonWhites were ordered to follow directions and take their places at the bottom of the society and the economy.

As Bryan had predicted, imperial ideals elevated the military. He had not been thinking of racial hierarchies, but racism was deeply embedded in the American military. The marines were proud of being lily White. The army was segregated by race, and with three exceptions Blacks had never even entered West Point, which trained the officer corps. The navy allowed Blacks only as servants. Whereas other groups (for instance, the United Mine Workers, educators, Socialists, woman suffragists, settlement workers) recognized Blacks at least as potential equals, the military was rigidly exclusionary. Proudly representing Anglo-Saxonism and 100-percent-American patriotism, the military epitomized White supremacy at the turn of the twentieth century.

During the European War 100-percent-Americanism, which was political, racial, and cultural, replaced Anglo-Saxonism. One-hundred-percent-Americanism demanded cultural conformity as well as strident patriotism. At the time some Americans confused culture with what they called race, assuming that culture was inherited as "racial traits." By this reasoning some immigrant groups—Italians, Jews, Slavs—were thought to be permanently unsuited to American life, having been prevented by "race" from acquiring American culture. At the same time others saw education as the means of turning foreigners into Americans. The clamor for 100-percent-Americanism produced both night schools in which immigrants learned English and the immigration restrictions of the 1920s that cut off immigration from southern and eastern Europe. There were further consequences of the intensified demand for conformity in the war years.

Wartime nationalism also reinforced the definition of 100-percent-Americans in Black and White. Blacks were seen as less than 100-percent-Americans on purely racial grounds, and they faced intense racial prejudice in the armed forces and violence in the streets of American cities. The summer of 1919, the Red Summer, saw the slaughter of Blacks by the score, the bloody culmination of the White supremacy in American militarism.

IN SUM, ideals of democracy and equity were as fundamentally American as ideals of hierarchy and order, but in two sorts of extraordinary times masses of Americans indicated that the quality of Americanness should be strictly defined. In years of labor upheaval Americanness was narrowed by class, and red scares suppressed working-class identities. In years of war militarism decreed that Americans with a claim to the name be White and Anglo-Saxon. Crisis produced demands that all Americans share an identity as well as an identity of interest, neither of which working people and racial/ethnic minorities could dictate. But peacetime allowed Americans to tolerate better the idea of a society consisting of several races and classes, and the years without wars or labor unrest permitted wide-ranging debates over economic and political issues.

ACKNOWLEDGMENTS

A book that has taken as long as this one piles up a lot of obligations that are a pleasure to acknowledge. The John Simon Guggenheim Foundation inadvertently supported some of the work on this book, a great help even so. Among scholars who have read parts of the manuscript and friends who have provided the moral support that is just as important are the late George Mowry, Arthur Link, William Harbaugh, Gil Joseph, Steve Channing, Armstead Robinson, Walter T. K. Nugent, Richard L. McCormick, Eric Foner, Leo Marx, Alan Trachtenberg, Marianne Debouzy, Nellie McKay, Thadious Davis, Nancy Clapp-Channing, Alden Whitman, Charles Phillips, Maura O'Donoghue, George Meyer, Randall Kenan, Wesley Brown, and, as ever, Frank and Dona Irvin. William Barney, Leon Litwack, and Sydney Nathans read entire drafts and made useful comments; Syd read even more and brought pumpkin bread as well. Derrick Bell, Ellen DuBois, Leonard Wallock, Kathryn Kish Sklar, David Montgomery, Nancy Schrom Dye, William Cooper, Michael Frisch, Nancy Cott, Leon Fink, Joyce Seltzer, John Semonche, Peter Filene, James Stewart, the Social History Project of the Graduate Center of the City University of New York, Thomas Browne, Michael Katz, and Andrew Gyory shared valuable information. I am especially grateful to Jerry Nowell and Tom Buske, two University of North Carolina at Chapel Hill students, who provided generous, voluntary research assistance during the summer of

1982. I leaned heavily on the staff of Wilson Library at the University of North Carolina, particularly on the microfilm staff headed by Robert France. In Chapel Hill, Rosalie Radcliffe, Julie Perry, and Patricia Reefe typed the manuscript. During the final revision I accumulated an enormous debt to the people at the unusually supportive Russell Sage Foundation in New York, led by Marshall Robinson and Peter de Janosi; I owe many thanks there, notably to librarian Pauline Rothstein; Madge Spitaleri, who changed my life by teaching me how to use a word processor; and my assistant, who wishes to remain unnamed. Very special thanks go to my real mensch of an editor, Robert Kehoe. This book is dedicated to my Harvard dissertation advisor and his wife, in appreciation for their essential support.

For the third edition, I thank Jacqueline Ko for smoothing the transition, Helen Thomaides for keeping everything in hand, and Rebecca Karamehmedovic for securing all those pesky permissions.

NOTES

1: LATE-NINETEENTH-CENTURY AMERICA BY THE NUMBERS

1. United States Department of Commerce, Bureau of the Census, *Historical Statistics of the United States* (1975), pp. 693–94, 684, 818.
2. In George E. Mowry, *The Era of Theodore Roosevelt and the Birth of Modern America, 1900–1912* (1959), p. 5.
3. *Historical Statistics of the United States*, p. 224.
4. Charles B. Spahr, *An Essay on the Present Distribution of Wealth in the United States* (1896), p. 69.
5. Ibid., pp. 128–29.
6. Steven Dubnoff, "A Method for Estimating the Economic Welfare of American Families of Any Composition: 1860–1901," *Historical Methods*, vol. 13, no. 3 (Summer 1980), p. 177.
7. Alexander Keyssar, *Out of Work: The First Century of Unemployment in Massachusetts* (1986), pp. 4–8, 300–07.
8. Richard M. Abrams, "Reform and Uncertainty: America Enters the Twentieth Century," in William E. Leuchtenburg, *The Unfinished Century: America Since 1900* (1973), p. 13, and C. Vann Woodward, *The Origins of the New South, 1877–1913* (1951), p. 407.
9. In David M. Katzman and William M. Tuttle, Jr., eds., *Plain Folk: the Life Stories of Undistinguished Americans* (1982), pp. 144–45.
10. In Meredith Tax, *The Rising of the Women: Feminist Solidarity and Class Conflict, 1880–1917* (1980), p. 39.
11. See Adam Przeworski, *Capitalism and Social Democracy* (1985), pp. 63–73.
12. See Roy Rosenzweig, *Eight Hours for What We Will: Workers and Leisure in an Industrial City, 1870–1920* (1983), pp. 27–32.
13. See John Bodnar, *The Transplanted: A History of Immigrants in Urban America* (1985), pp. 117–35.
14. In Katzman and Tuttle, op. cit., p. 190.

15. Laura Ellsworth Seiler, in Sherna Berger Gluck, *From Parlor to Prison: Five American Suffragists Talk About Their Lives* (1976, 1985 ed.), pp. 197–98.
16. Maury Klein, *The Life and Legend of Jay Gould* (1986), pp. 214–15, 219, 318.
17. Kerby A. Miller, *Emigrants and Exiles: Ireland and the Irish Exodus to North America* (1985), pp. 3–4; Hasia R. Diner, *Erin's Daughters: Irish Immigrant Women in the Nineteenth Century* (1983), p. 31: and Stephan Thernstrom, ed., *Harvard Encyclopedia of American Ethnic Groups* (1981), pp. 528–29.
18. See Eric Foner, *Politics and Ideology in the Age of the Civil War* (1980), p. 151.
19. In Daniel Rodgers, *The Work Ethic in Industrial America: 1850–1920* (1978), p. 35.
20. Morton Keller, *Affairs of State: Public Life in Late Nineteenth Century America* (1977), p. 239.
21. The ratio of departures to arrivals varied by decade and by ethnic group. The table below provides figures on arrivals and departures of all alien passengers to and from the United States, 1875–1919 (in thousands):

YEAR	ARRIVALS	DEPARTURES	DEPARTURES/ARRIVALS
1875–79	956	431	0.45
1880–84	3,201	327	0.10
1885–89	2,341	638	0.27
1890–94	2,590	838	0.32
1895–99	1,493	766	0.51
1900–04	3,575	1,454	0.41
1905–09	5,533	2,653	0.48
1910–14	6,075	2,759	0.45
1915–19	1,613	1,180	0.73

SOURCE: Simon Kuznets and Ernest Rubin, *Immigration and the Foreign Born* (1954), p. 95, and Gavin Wright, *Old South, New South: Revolutions in the Southern Economy Since the Civil War* (1986), p. 73.

One estimation of departures/arrivals by ethnic group yields the following figures for the period 1899–1924:

RACE OR PEOPLE	ARRIVALS	DEPARTURES	PERCENT DEPARTURES
Hebrew [Jewish]	1,837,875	93,344	5.2
Irish	808,762	100,108	12.4
Mexican	447,065	71,074	15.9
French	415,244	78,662	18.9
German	1,316,614	257,938	19.6
Czech	159,319	34,364	21.6
Scandinavian	956,308	227,620	23.8
English	1,067,659	261,295	24.5
Japanese	260,492	85,415	32.8
Polish	1,483,374	587,742	39.6
Greek	500,465	241,923	48.3
Italian, North	605,535	292,522	48.3
Croatian, Slovenian	485,379	246,098	50.7

RACE OR PEOPLE	ARRIVALS	DEPARTURES	PERCENT DEPARTURES
Slovak	536,911	298,689	55.6
Italian, South	3,215,451	1,812,943	56.4
Hungarian	492,031	177,484	63.9
Bulgarian, Serbian, Montenegrin	165,191	148,386	89.9
Chinese	59,079	76,332	129.2

SOURCE: Thernstrom, op. cit., p. 1036.

22. In Katzman and Tuttle, op. cit., pp. 168–69. Mott Street is located in New York City's Lower East Side.
23. Alan M. Kraut, *The Huddled Masses: The Immigrant in American Society, 1880–1921* (1982), p. 17, and Rodgers, op. cit., p. 170.
24. *Historical Statistics of the United States*, p. 177.
25. Ibid., pp. 164–65.
26. W. H. Orr, in *Report of the Committee of the Senate upon the Relations Between Labor and Capital* (1885), vol. 1, p. 219.
27. See Harry Braverman, *Labor and Monopoly Capital: The Degradation of Work in the Twentieth Century* (1974), pp. 85, 166–67, 271.
28. Robert Howard, in *Relations Between Labor and Capital*, vol. 1, p. 642.
29. Joseph T. Rinnerty, ibid., vol. 1, p. 741.
30. In Harry Emerson Fosdick, "After the Strike—In Lawrence," *The Outlook*, vol. 101, no. 15 (June 1912), p. 345.
31. In Katzman and Tuttle, op. cit., p. 7.
32. Orr, op. cit. vol. 1, p. 218. The United States Steel Corporation changed its name to USX in 1984.
33. See Robert L. Allen, *Reluctant Reformers: Racism and Social Reform in the United States* (1974), pp. 5–9, 263–80.
34. See Rodgers, op. cit., pp. 20–24 and Eric Foner, *Free Soil, Free Labor, Free Men: The Ideology of the Republican Party before the Civil War* (1970), pp. 19–20, 38.
35. John Caldwell Calhoun, in *Relations Between Labor and Capital*, vol. 2, p. 160.
36. Jay Gould, ibid., vol. 1, pp. 1085, 1088.
37. *John Swinton's Paper* (May 2, 1886).
38. R. Heber Newton, in *Relations Between Labor and Capital*, vol. 2, p. 595.
39. Walter A. Wykoff, *The Workers: An Experiment in Reality* (1899), vol. 2, p. 96.
40. Baptist Hubert, ibid., vol. 2, p. 945.
41. Jeremiah Murphy, ibid., vol. 2, p. 687.

2: THE TOCSIN SOUNDS

1. In William Gillette, *Retreat from Reconstruction: 1869–1879* (1979), p. 67.
2. Democratic candidate Samuel J. Tilden of New York seemed to have won the presidential election of 1876, but Republicans claimed that the results in the three southern states still under Republican control (Florida, South Carolina, and Louisiana) were fraudulent. After much negotiating, a special electoral commission

awarded all the contested votes to the Republican candidate, Rutherford B. Hayes. As part of the compromise Republicans assured Democrats control of all southern states by promising no longer to intervene in state politics in the South. See Vincent P. DeSantis, "Rutherford B. Hayes and the Removal of the Troops and the End of Reconstruction," in J. Morgan Kousser and James M. McPherson, eds., *Region, Race and Reconstruction: Essays in Honor of C. Vann Woodward* (1982), p. 417.

3. *The Nation*, vol. 13 (July 6, 1871), p. 4.

4. See Nell Irvin Painter, *Exodusters: Black Migration to Kansas After Reconstruction* (1976).

5. See Robert W. Rydell, *All the World's a Fair: Visions of Empire at American International Expositions, 1876–1916* (1984). George Henry Corliss, the most famous engine maker in the United States in the mid-nineteenth century, had in the 1840s attached a governor to reduce the motion of cutoff valves and introduced cylindrical rocking valves. He had shown the enormous steam engine that powered the machinery in Philadelphia in Paris nearly a decade earlier, so that the Corliss engine became famous in Europe as well as the United States. H. W. Dickinson, *A Short History of the Steam Engine* (1938, 1965 reprint ed.), pp. 137–39.

6. Alan Trachtenberg, *The Incorporation of America: Culture and Society in the Gilded Age* (1982), p. 39.

7. Alexander Keyssar, *Out of Work: The First Century of Unemployment in Massachusetts* (1986), pp. 1–5, 50–52.

8. See Eric Foner, *Politics and Ideology in the Age of the Civil War* (1980), pp. 114–17.

9. *Testimony Taken by the Joint Select Committee to Inquire into the Condition of Affairs in the late Insurrectionary States, South Carolina*, vol. II (1872), pp. 1219 and 1226.

10. In James M. McPherson, *Ordeal by Fire: The Civil War and Reconstruction* (1982), p. 594.

11. Despite their identifying with the "better classes" of the South who became redeemers, northern "best men" like Godkin, Adams, and Nordhoff were publicists rather than actual holders of political power. The northerners had far less power to implement their plans to limit mass suffrage than did southern redeemers.

12. Charles Nordhoff, "The Misgovernment of New York,—A Remedy Suggested," *North American Review*, vol. 113 (October 1871), pp. 321–22.

13. David Montgomery, *Beyond Equality: Labor and the Radical Republicans, 1862–1872* (1967), p. 455.

14. See Frank L. Norton, "Our Labor System and the Chinese," *Scribner's Monthly*, vol. II (May–October 1871), pp. 61–70, and Andrew Gyory, "Yan-kee vs. Yan-ki: American Workers React to Chinese Laborers in 1870," unpublished paper, 1986.

15. "A Striker"; "Fair Wages," *North American Review*, vol. 125 (September 1877), p. 323.

16. The National Colored Labor Union was split between members who were primarily working-class unionists and middle-class political figures like John Mercer Langston and Frederick Douglass. Although its original president was Isaac Myers, a Baltimore caulker, the politicians gained the upper hand in 1870 with the

election as president of Frederick Douglass, by then a spokesman for the Republican party. See Philip S. Foner, *History of the Labor Movement in the United States*, vol. 1, *From Colonial Times to the Founding of the American Federation of Labor* (1947), pp. 395–408.

17. In Montgomery, op. cit., p. 338.
18. "A Striker"; "Fair Wages," loc. cit., p. 324.
19. Editorial in *Scribner's Monthly*, vol. 14 (October 1877), pp. 852–53.
20. Quoted in Philip S. Foner, op. cit., vol. 1, p. 469.
21. In Gillette, op. cit., p. 348.
22. Leonard Wallock, "The B & O 'Monopoly' and the Baltimore Crowd: Patterns of Crowd Participation in the Riots of 1877," M.A. thesis, Columbia University, 1974, pp. 7–29.
23. James A. Dacus, *Annals of the Great Strikes* (1877), p. 70.
24. Robert V. Bruce, *1877: Year of Violence* (1959), p. 180.
25. In Philip S. Foner, op. cit., vol. 1, page 465.
26. David R. Roediger, "America's First General Strike: The St. Louis 'Commune' of 1877," *Midwest Quarterly*, vol. 21, no. 2 (Winter 1980), p. 205.
27. Dacus, op. cit., p. 122.
28. Stewart Edwards, *The Paris Commune: 1871* (1971), p. 301.
29. Ibid., p. 345.
30. Georges Bourgin, *La Commune* (1953), p. 98, and Edwards, op. cit., pp. 323–24, 346.
31. In Montgomery, op. cit., pp. 336–37.
32. Samuel Bernstein, "The Impact of the Paris Commune in the United States," in John Hicks and Robert Tucker, eds., *Revolution & Reaction: The Paris Commune 1871* (1973), p. 65. Oddly enough, the staid and Republican *Newburyport, Massachusetts, Herald* called the commune a "brave struggle" for human rights. Stephen Thernstrom, *Poverty and Progress: Social Mobility in a Nineteenth Century City* (1964, 1874 ed.), pp. 186–87.
33. *The Nation* (May 18, 1871), p. 333.
34. *New National Era* (May 11, 1871).
35. Thomas A. Scott, "The Recent Strikes," *North American Review*, vol. 5 (September 1877), pp. 360–61.
36. See Richard Slotkin, *The Fatal Environment: The Myth of the Frontier in the Age of Industrialization: 1800–1890* (1985), pp. 480–81.
37. In Martha Derthick, *The National Guard in Politics* (1965), p. 17.
38. Dacus, op. cit., p. 76, and W. M. Grosvenor, "The Communist and the Railway," *The International Review*, vol. IV (September 1877), p. 585.
39. Marx called the Paris Commune a "glorious harbinger of a new society" rather than the realization of socialism, in *The Civil War in France* (1871). See Edwards, op. cit., pp. 356–58, and Royden Harrison, "Marx, Engels, and the British Response to the Commune," in Hicks and Tucker, op. cit., p. 107.
40. A. C. Buell, *New Orleans Daily Democrat*, August 4, 1877.
41. Samuel Gompers, *Seventy Years of Life and Labor* (1925), p. 140. Gompers does not mention the Paris Commune at all in his discussion of the events of 1871, though he mentions having read Henry George's articles in the *Irish World*.

42. Henry George, *Progress and Poverty* (Modern Library ed., no date), p. 6.
43. Among the novels were Lee Harris, *The Man Who Tramps* (1878); *Nemo, King of the Tramps: or, the Romany Girl's Vengeance; A Story of the Great Railroad Riots,* an 1881 volume in Beadle's Dime Library; T. S. Denison, *An Iron Crown* (1885); Martin Foran, *The Other Side* (1886); George T. Dowling, *The Wreckers* (1886); and Paul Leicester Ford, *The Honorable Peter Stirling* (1894). Bruce, op. cit., p. 319.
44. John Hay, *The Bread-Winners: A Social Study* (1884), p. 215.
45. Bruce rightly terms Hay's novel "snobbish," op. cit., p. 319.
46. See Robert H. Walker, *Reform in America: The Continuing Frontier* (1985), pp. 30–40.
47. See Irwin Unger, *The Greenback Era: A Social and Political History of American Finance, 1865–1879* (1965), pp. 107–13.
48. Grand Master Workman Stephens lost his congressional election on the same ticket. Stephens relinquished leadership of the Knights of Labor to Terence Powderly in 1879 and died in 1882. Powderly was elected mayor of Scranton, Pennsylvania, on a Greenback-Labor ticket. Like many other Knights, Powderly was Irish American and became the first Irish American to be elected mayor of a city in the United States.
49. See Foster Rhea Dulles and Melvyn Dubfosky, *Labor in America: A History,* 4th ed. (1984), pp. 122–23.
50. In Philip S. Foner, op. cit., pp. 436–37.
51. In Joseph P. Goldberg and William T. Moye, *The First Hundred Years of the Bureau of Labor Statistics* (1985), p. 3.
52. In Maury Klein, *The Life and Legend of Jay Gould* (1986), pp. 335–36.
53. Paul Avrich, *The Haymarket Tragedy* (1984), p. 97, and Klein, op cit., pp. 484–97. Gould's reputation for sordidness and cupidity may have stemmed from the combination of his financial genius, poor press relations, and misplaced anti-semitism. Gould was not Jewish, but many assumed that he was. Cartoons showed him with the stereotyped features of a Jew.
54. In C. Joseph Pusateri, *A History of American Business* (1984), p. 156, and Klein, op. cit., pp. 88–145.
55. See Paul Sarnoff, *Russell Sage: The Money King* (1965), pp. 191–222, and Klein, op. cit., pp. 197–205, 310–14.

3: THE GREAT UPHEAVAL

1. Brooklyn did not become part of New York City until 1898.
2. In Alan Trachtenberg, *Brooklyn Bridge: Fact and Symbol* (1965), pp. 124–25.
3. Ibid., p. 93.
4. In John R. Stilgoe, *Metropolitan Corridor: Railroads and the American Scene* (1983), p. ix, and Leo Marx, *The Machine in the Garden: Technology and the Pastoral Ideal in America* (1964), p. 210. See also Leo Marx, "The Railroad-in-the-Landscape: An Iconological Reading of a Theme in American Art," *Prospects: An Annual of American Cultural Studies,* vol. 10 (1985), pp. 82–87.

5. In T. J. Jackson Lears, *No Place of Grace: Antimodernism and the Transformation of American Culture, 1880–1920* (1981), p. 8.

6. In 1865 there were 35,085 miles of railroads in operation; in 1877, 79,082 miles; in 1886, 136,338; in 1890, 166,654; and in 1900, 194,334. United States Treasury Department, Bureau of Statistics, *Statistical Abstract of the United States* (1902), p. 404.

7. In Trachtenberg, op. cit., p. 121.

8. *John Swinton's Paper,* April 18, 1886.

9. This meant that in the United States 1 out of 357 railroad workers was killed and 1 out of 35 was injured on the job. In England, by comparison, railroads killed 1 out of 875 and injured 1 out of 158 per year. Walter Licht, *Working for the Railroad: The Organization of Work in the Nineteenth Century* (1983), pp. 190–91.

10. *John Swinton's Paper,* March 21, 1886.

11. Scenes from the New York streetcar strike figure in the climax of William Dean Howells, *Hazard of New Fortunes* (1891).

12. See Terence Powderly, *The Path I Trod* (1940), p. 117.

13. Martin Irons, "Our Experience Meetings," *Lippincott's Monthly Magazine* (June 1886).

14. In Maury Klein, *The Life and Legend of Jay Gould* (1986), p. 359.

15. William Ross, "A Giant Is Rising," in *John Swinton's Paper,* April 18, 1886.

16. In John R. Commons et al., *History of Labour in the United States* (1918), vol. II, p. 379.

17. Philip S. Foner, *May Day: A Short History of the International Workers' Holiday, 1886–1986* (1986), p. 29. During the mid-1880s both May 1 and September 5 became popular as "Labor Day." By the early twentieth century socialists around the world recognized May 1 as Labor Day, but the AFL observed the first Monday in September.

18. See Paul Avrich, *The Haymarket Tragedy* (1984), pp. 79–98, 138–39.

19. Ibid., pp. 209–10. Evidence uncovered in 1985 indicates that George Meng, a German-born anarchist who disappeared before the Haymarket trials, was the actual bomb thrower.

20. Ibid., pp. 182, 185–86.

21. Brand Whitlock, ibid., p. 215.

22. Richard T. Ely, ibid., p. 222.

23. Avrich, op. cit., p. 272.

24. Ibid., pp. 283, 290.

25. William E. Farmer, in U.S. House of Representatives, 46th Congress, 2d Session, *Report 4174,* part II, pp. 243–49.

26. In Leon Fink, "The Uses of Political Power: Toward a Theory of the Labor Movement in the Era of the Knights of Labor," in Michael H. Frisch and Daniel J. Walkowitz, eds., *Working-Class America* (1983), p. 119.

27. Leon Fink, *Workingmen's Democracy: The Knights of Labor and American Politics* (1983), p. xiii.

28. Ibid., pp. xiii, 26–27.

29. See Eric Foner, *Politics and Ideology in the Age of the Civil War* (1980), pp. 183–99.

30. See John L. Thomas, *Alternative America: Henry George, Edward Bellamy, Henry Demarest Lloyd and the Adversary Tradition* (1983), pp. 223–24.

31. See L. Glen Seretan, *Daniel De Leon: The Odyssey of an American Marxist* (1979), pp. 16–25.

32. See Trachtenberg, op. cit, pp. 101–02.

33. Henry George, Jr., *The Life of Henry George* (1900), p. 273.

34. *Atlanta Constitution*, October 12, and October 10, 1886 respectively.

35. In Thomas, op. cit., p. 229.

36. See Lawrence Goodwyn, *Democratic Promise: The Populist Moment in America* (1976), pp. 42–43.

37. With locals in each state and territory, the WCTU in 1890 had 150,000 dues-paying members and a $30,000 annual budget. Ruth Bordin, *Woman and Temperance: The Quest for Power and Liberty, 1873–1900* (1981), p. 94, and *Frances Willard, A Biography* (1986), pp. 32–111.

38. In Bordin, *Woman and Temperance*, pp. 104, 107.

39. In Thomas, op. cit., p. 79.

40. See Martin Ridge, *Ignatius Donnelly, The Portrait of a Politician* (1962).

41. Alliance and Populist rhetoric often castigated bankers in anti-Semitic terms, leading historian Richard Hofstadter to identify paranoia as a central Populist trait in *The Age of Reform: From Bryan to FDR* (1955), especially pp. 61, 77–81.

42. In Thomas, op. cit., pp. 140, 298.

43. *John Swinton's Paper*, January 31, 1886.

4: REMEDIES

1. Ida M. Tarbell, *All in the Day's Work: An Autobiography* (1939), p. 82.

2. *New York Times*, December 7, 1886.

3. See Ida M. Tarbell, *The Tariff in Our Times* (1906, 1912 ed.), pp. 151–52. See also Kathleen Brady, *Ida Tarbell, Portrait of a Muckraker* (1984), pp. 37–38.

4. Rudyard Kipling, *American Notes* (1889), p. 47.

5. In *The Cross of Culture: A Social Analysis of Midwestern Politics, 1850–1900* (1970) and *The Third Electoral System, 1853–1892* (1979), Paul Kleppner argues that voting behavior varied according to dimensions of ethnoreligiosity that can be plotted along a pietistic-ritualistic continuum. This means that pietists who believed in free will—Yankee Congregationalists, Quakers, and Unitarians and German and Scandinavian Lutherans—tended to vote Republican, while ritualist Catholics who linked faith to knowledge and form—Irish, German, French-Canadian—tended to vote Democratic. This analysis does not hold up for the South, where most Whites and Blacks shared a Protestant religious culture but differed in partisan identity for reasons linked to slavery, the Civil War, and Reconstruction.

6. In Tarbell, *The Tariff in Our Times*, pp. 151–52.

7. R. W. Townshend of Illinois, *Congressional Record*, vol. 19, part 5, pp. 4054–55.

8. Ibid.

9. Ibid., pp. 3057–63.

10. Ibid.
11. Charles H. Allen, *Congressional Record*, vol. 19, part 5, p. 4054.
12. Ibid., pp. 4401–24.
13. *Relations Between Labor and Capital*, vol. 2, p. 14, and vol. 1, p. 643.
14. In Charles A. Beard, *Contemporary American History* (1914), pp. 103–04.
15. Frank W. Taussig, *The Tariff History of the United States* (1923 ed.), pp. 254–78, and Richard Franklin Bensel, *Sectionalism and American Political Development, 1880–1980* (1984), pp. 60–70.
16. See Milton Friedman and Anna Jacobson Schwartz, *A Monetary History of the United States, 1867–1960* (1963), p. 91.
17. John Kenneth Galbraith, *Money: Whence It Came, Where It Went* (1975), p. 85.
18. Walter T. K. Nugent, *Money and American Society, 1865–1880* (1968), p. 147.
19. Irwin Unger, *The Greenback Era: A Social and Political History of American Finance, 1865–1879* (1964), p. 363.
20. The 16 to 1 ratio embedded in the rhetoric of free silver was based on 371.25 grams of silver to the dollar and 23.22 grams of gold, which at mid-century adjusted the 15 to 1 ratio (established by Alexander Hamilton in the late eighteenth century) to take cognizance of increased silver supplies.
21. John Sherman, *Recollections of Forty Years in the House, Senate and Cabinet* (1895), pp. 829–32.
22. *Atlanta Constitution*, February 23, 1892.
23. In Morton Keller, *Affairs of State: Public Life in Late Nineteenth Century America* (1977), p. 428. See also Gabriel Kolko, *Railroads and Regulation, 1877–1915* (1965), and *The Triumph of Conservatism: A Reinterpretation of American History, 1900–1916* (1963), and Thomas K. McCraw, *Prophets of Regulation: Charles Francis Adams, Louis D. Brandeis, James M. Landis, Alfred E. Kahn* (1984).
24. In Beard, op. cit., p. 136. See also Hans B. Thorelli, *The Federal Antitrust Policy: Origination of an American Tradition* (1955), p. 153.
25. Sherman, op. cit. pp. 832–34.
26. This assumption held good in this country until the 1980s, when large corporations, notably oil producers, began to pare down their operations by selling off subsidiaries and contracting out services related to raw materials and distribution.
27. Andrew Carnegie, *Popular Illusions About Trusts* (1900), pp. 90–91.
28. Working people, particularly those who were Carnegie's employees, were skeptical of his philanthropy, which they regarded as appeasement or a distraction from what they saw as important concerns. Certainly men who worked twelve hours per day in steel plants and women who served their families and boarders had little time to take advantage of Carnegie libraries. Carnegie himself saw philanthropy as social engineering. At the dedication of a Carnegie library in Homestead, Pennsylvania, Carnegie said: "How a man spends his time at work may be taken for granted, but how he spends his hours of recreation is really the key to his progress in all the virtues" (in Francis G. Couvares, "The Triumph of Commerce: Class Culture and Mass Culture in Pittsburgh," in Michael H. Frisch and Daniel J. Walkowitz, eds. *Working-Class America* [1983], pp. 139–40).
29. Andrew Carnegie, *The Gospel of Wealth* (1889), pp. 14–16. Carnegie was also

known as the "horse-shit" capitalist for advocating feeding the sparrows by stuffing the horses.

30. Hamlin Garland, *A Spoil of Office* (new and rev., 1897), pp. 208–10. Garland initially published the novel serially in *The Arena*.

31. See David J. Rothman, *Politics and Power: The United States Senate, 1869–1901* (1966), pp. 4–7, 42, 62.

32. In 1895 Mary Lease published *The Problem of Civilization Solved*, which showed the Western world at the brink of catastrophe that might only be averted through mass migration and the establishment of global White supremacy. See Richard Hofstadter, *The Age of Reform: From Bryan to F.D.R.* (1955), pp. 83–84.

33. In Page Smith, *The Rise of Industrial America* (1984), pp. 445–46.

34. In James MacGregor Burns, *The Workshop of Democracy* (1985), p. 188. See also Sydney Nathans, *The Quest for Progress: The Way We Lived in North Carolina, 1870–1920* (1983), pp. 14–17.

35. See Indianapolis's *American Nonconformist*, July 5, 1890.

36. In *Atlanta Constitution*, May 20, 1891, and February 23, 1892.

37. In C. Vann Woodward, *Origins of the New South, 1877–1913* (1951), p. 257.

38. *Atlanta Constitution*, February 26, 1892.

39. See Robert L. Allen, *Reluctant Reformers: Racism and Social Reform Movements in the United States* (1974), pp. 49–79.

40. *Atlanta Constitution*, May 20, 1891.

41. Ibid., May 8, 1891.

42. Jacob Henry Dorn, *Washington Gladden: Prophet of the Social Gospel* (1967), p. 209.

43. Ibid., pp. 211–12.

44. Ruth Bordin, *Woman and Temperance: The Quest for Power and Liberty, 1873–1900* (1981), pp. 90, 94.

45. Ibid., pp. 97–98 and Ruth Bordin, *Frances Willard, A Biography* (1986), pp. 140–45.

46. Nancy Schrom Dye, "$acred Motherhood: Women and Progressive Reform" unpublished paper, 1986, pp. 6–10.

47. Coit's move to England in 1887 weakened the Neighborhood Guild, which several others (Edward King, Charles B. Stover) reorganized in 1891 as the University Settlement. See Allen F. Davis, *Spearheads for Reform: The Social Settlements and the Progressive Movement, 1890–1914* (1967), pp. 9–10, and *American Heroine: The Life and Legend of Jane Addams* (1973).

48. In Anne Firor Scott, "Jane Addams," in Edward T. James et al., eds., *Notable American Women* (1971), vol. I, p. 17.

49. Workingwomen and their middle-class allies had founded the Illinois Woman's Alliance in 1888, after a woman reporter had run a series of articles in the *Chicago Times* on workingwomen, entitled "City Slave Girls." See Meredith Tax, *The Rising of the Women: Feminist Solidarity and Class Conflict, 1880–1917* (1980), pp. 66–71.

50. See Kathryn Kish Sklar, "Hull House in the 1890s: A Community of Women Reformers," *Signs*, vol. 10, no. 4 (Summer 1985), pp. 670–71. Kelley improved

occupational safety for all workers by fighting for improved working conditions for women and children.

51. Ibid., p. 660.

5: THE DEPRESSION OF THE 1890s

1. Hamlin Garland, "Homestead and Its Perilous Trades," *McClure's Magazine*, vol. III, no. 1 (June 1894).
2. In Leon Wolff, *Lockout: the Story of the Homestead Strike of 1892* (1965), pp. 62–66.
3. In David Brody, *Steelworkers in America: The Nonunion Era* (1960), pp. 53–54.
4. *Senate Report No. 1280*, 53d Congress, 2d session, pp. 68–72, quoted in Richard Hofstadter and Michael Wallace, eds., *American Violence* (1970), p. 144.
5. See Arthur G. Burgoyne, *Homestead* (1893), p. 217.
6. *Atlanta Constitution*, February 23, 1892.
7. In Edmund Morris, *The Rise of Theodore Roosevelt* (1979), p. 399.
8. See Carlos A. Schwantes, *Coxey's Army: An American Odyssey* (1985), pp. 13–14.
9. Ray Stannard Baker, *American Chronicle* (1945), pp. 1–2.
10. In Donald L. McMurray, *Coxey's Army* (1929), page 31. Browne had been the private secretary of Denis Kearney in the San Francisco "Chinese Must Go" campaign of 1877 (Schwantes op. cit., p. 39).
11. Indianapolis *American Nonconformist*, April 26, 1894.
12. Robert Barltrop, *Jack London* (1976), p. 4, and Schwantes, op. cit., p. 130.
13. Indianapolis *American Nonconformist*, April 12 and May 3, 1894.
14. On the fiftieth anniversary of Coxey's Army in 1944 Coxey (at ninety) delivered the speech he had prepared for 1894 on the steps of the Capitol. Carl Browne married Coxey's daughter Mamie against Coxey's wishes and became a lecturer for the Socialist party and the Industrial Workers of the World in California. He died in 1914.
15. Baker, op. cit., p. 19.
16. See Stanley Buder, *Pullman, an Experiment in Industrial Order and Community Planning, 1880–1930* (1967), p. 103.
17. See Leon Stein, ed., *The Pullman Strike* (1969).
18. See Arnold M. Paul, *Conservative Crisis and the Rule of Law* (1960), p. 121.
19. Oswald Garrison Villard, *Fighting Years: Memoirs of a Liberal Editor* (1939), p. 100.
20. Indianapolis *American Nonconformist*, July 19, 1894.
21. Eugene V. Debs, "Liberty," at Battery D., Chicago, November 22, 1895, in Stein, op. cit., pp. 14–18.
22. Governor Lorenzo Lewelling, speech in Kansas City, July 1894, in George Brown Tindall, ed., *A Populist Reader* (1966), p. 157.
23. U. M. Fisk, in Indianapolis *American Nonconformist*, May 3, 1894.
24. This was not William B. Wilson, who became the first secretary of labor in 1912.
25. See Paul, op. cit., p. 191.
26. Ibid., pp. 204–05.

27. Richard Hofstadter, ed., *William H. Harvey, Coin's Financial School* (1963), p. 204.
28. In Allan Nevins, *Grover Cleveland: A Study in Courage* (1933), pp. 467–68.
29. In Harold U. Faulkner, *Politics, Reform and Expansion, 1890–1900* (1959), p. 156.
30. In Paolo E. Coletta, *William Jennings Bryan* (1964), vol. 1, pp. 140–41.
31. Ibid., p. 148.
32. In Faulkner, op. cit., p. 192.
33. William Allen White, *The Autobiography of William Allen White* (1946), p. 282.
34. In John A. Garraty, *Henry Cabot Lodge: A Biography* (1953), p. 176.
35. See Alexander Keyssar, *Out of Work: The First Century of Unemployment in Massachusetts* (1986), pp. 78, 159, 164.

6: THE WHITE MAN'S BURDEN

1. In Frank Freidel, *The Splendid Little War* (1958), p. 2.
2. The Platt Amendment gave the United States the right to intervene in Cuba to maintain order. In practice this meant that Cuban politics and the Cuban economy were dominated by Americans, as General Leonard Wood recognized in a letter to Theodore Roosevelt in 1901. "There is, of course, little or no independence left Cuba under the Platt Amendment." In Howard Zinn, *A People's History of the United States* (1980), p. 305. The United States occupied Cuba 1906–1909, 1912, and 1917–1922.
3. Whitelaw Reid, *Problems of Expansion* (1900), p. 189.
4. Alfred Thayer Mahan, *From Sail to Steam* (1907), p. xii.
5. See Walter LaFeber, *The New Empire: An Interpretation of American Expansion* (1963), p. 262.
6. Charles S. Olcott, *The Life of William McKinley* (1916), vol. 1, pp. 397–98.
7. See correspondence to Marion Butler, chairman of the People's party, Folders 50 and 90, Butler Papers, Southern Historical Collection, University of North Carolina at Chapel Hill.
8. In LaFeber, op. cit., p. 335.
9. Ibid., p. 334.
10. At the time Americans believed that a mine planted under the *Maine* had caused the explosion. Today it seems more likely that the explosion occurred within the ship.
11. Peter Finley Dunne, *Mr. Dooley in Peace and in War* (1898), p. 31.
12. James C. Thompson, Jr., Peter W. Stanley, and John Curtis Perry, *Sentimental Imperialists: The American Experience in East Asia* (1981), pp. 2–3, 122.
13. In John A. Garraty, *Henry Cabot Lodge: A Biography* (1953), p. 197.
14. Thompson et al., op. cit., p. 123.
15. Olcott, op. cit., vol. 2, p. 111. McKinley had also sought guidance through prayer as he agonized long and hard over declaring war in the first place. See Gerald F. Linderman, *The Mirror of War: American Society and the Spanish-American War* (1974), pp. 27–30, 33.
16. Thompson et al., op. cit., p. 96.

17. Josiah Strong, *Our Country* (1885), pp. 174–75.

18. In Linderman, op. cit., pp. 91–94, and T. J. Jackson Lears, *No Place of Grace: Antimodernism and the Transformation of American Culture, 1880–1920* (1981), p. 114.

19. In Albert K. Weinberg, *Manifest Destiny* (1935), p. 262.

20. Ibid., p. 263, and William Allen White, *The Autobiography of William Allen White* (1946), pp. 319–20.

21. In Thomas F. Gossett, *Race: The History of an Idea in America* (1963), p. 318.

22. Weinberg, op. cit., p. 308.

23. *Congressional Record*, 55th Congress, 2d Session, p. 6534.

24. Weinberg, op. cit., p. 307.

25. In Gossett, p. 329.

26. In Weinberg, op. cit., p. 301.

27. In Barbara W. Tuchman, *The Proud Tower* (1966, 1967 paperback ed.), p. 183.

28. In Richard E. Welch, Jr., *Response to Imperialism* (1979), pp. 41, 141.

29. William Jennings Bryan et al., *Republic or Empire* (1899), p. 83.

30. In Welch, op. cit., p. 126.

31. In Robert L. Beisner, *Twelve Against Empire* (1968), p. 113.

32. In George McMitchel, ed., *Anthology of American Literature*, 2d ed. (1980), vol. II, pp. 568–71.

33. Ibid., p. 588.

34. Henry Cabot Lodge, ed., *Selections from the Correspondence of Theodore Roosevelt and Henry Cabot Lodge* (1925), vol. 1, pp. 306, 322.

35. Charles Belmont Davis, *Adventures and Letters of Richard Harding Davis* (1917), p. 243.

36. Thomas J. Noer, *Briton, Boer, and Yankee* (1978), p. 71.

37. Ibid., p. 64.

38. Bryan et al., op. cit., p. 302.

39. Ibid., p. 258.

40. Ibid., p. 49.

41. Ibid., pp. 67, 85.

42. Ibid., p. 88.

43. Benjamin Tillman, *Congressional Record*, 55th Congress, 2d Session, p. 6532.

44. In Bernard C. Nalty, *Strength for the Fight: A History of Black Americans in the Military* (1986), p. 73.

45. In Bryan et al., op. cit., p. 577.

46. Ibid., pp. 579, 123.

47. Thompson et al., op. cit., p. 80.

48. I have used the term *non-Indian* instead of *Whites* because not only were Blacks to be found among the settlers, even in places like Montana and Nebraska, but the U.S. Army engaged in Indian wars depended heavily on Black units, notably the Ninth and Tenth Cavalries and the Twenty-fourth and Twenty-fifth Infantries.

49. In Willard B. Gatewood, Jr., *Black Americans and the White Man's Burden* (1975), pp. 135–36.

50. F. A. Coffin, *ibid.*, p. 115. One of the most prominent leaders of the White supremacist campaign that had preceded the Wilmington killings was journalist Josephus Daniels, later Woodrow Wilson's secretary of the navy.

51. In Gatewood, op. cit., p. 199.

52. Ibid., page 184. For more on Henry T. Johnson on the Boer War see Sylvia M. Jacobs, *The African Nexus: Black American Perspectives on the European Partitioning of Africa, 1880–1920* (1981), p. 145.

53. In George P. Marks III, *The Black Press Views American Imperialism* (1971), pp. 10–11.

54. Southern Society for the Promotion of the Study of Race Conditions . . ., *Race Problems of the South* (1900), p. 55.

55. Ibid., p. 43.

56. W. E. B. Du Bois, *The Souls of Black Folk* (1903), in John Hope Franklin, ed., *Three Negro Classics* (1965), p. 221.

57. During the war Congress passed the War Revenue Act of 1898, which, by widening the basis upon which national bank notes were issued, increased the money supply.

58. Ray Stannard Baker, *Our New Prosperity* (1900), p. 6, and *American Chronicle* (1945), p. 88.

7: PROSPERITY

1. See Louis Harlan, *Booker T. Washington: The Wizard of Tuskegee, 1901–1915* (1983), pp. 3–7.

2. See Robert Sklar, *Movie-Made America* (1975), pp. 5–13.

3. See John F. Kasson, *Amusing the Million: Coney Island at the Turn of the Century* (1978), pp. 3–9, 106–08. Francis G. Couvares calls the creators and purveyors of commercial mass culture the "merchants of leisure" in "The Triumph of Commerce: Class Culture and Mass Culture in Pittsburgh," in Michael H. Frisch and Daniel J. Walkowitz, eds., *Working-Class America* (1983), p. 124.

4. See Roy Rosenzweig, *Eight Hours for What We Will: Workers and Leisure in an Industrial City, 1870–1920* (1983), pp. 171–75, 180.

5. Walter LaFeber, *The Panama Canal: The Crisis in Historical Perspective* (1978), p. 42.

6. Ibid., p. 32.

7. Ibid., p. 41.

8. *The Commoner*, September 5, February 28, and August 29, 1902.

9. Richard M. Abrams, "Reform and Uncertainty: America Enters the Twentieth Century," in William E. Leuchtenburg, ed., *The Unfinished Century: America Since 1900* (1973), p. 29.

10. Morton Keller, *Affairs of State: Public Life in Late Nineteenth Century America* (1977), p. 373.

11. U.S. House of Representatives, 57th Congress, 1st Session, p. xvi.

12. James Livingston, *Origins of the Federal Reserve System: Money, Class, and Cor-*

porate Capitalism, 1890–1913 (1986), pp. 56–57, and James Oliver Robertson, *America's Business* (1985), p. 160. Because the federal government keeps figures on the consumer (not the financial) price index, it is difficult to translate early-twentieth-century financial statistics into late-1980s dollars. As best I can figure, $7,249,343,500 in 1904 equals about $8,076,500,000,000 in 1986 dollars.

13. Robertson, op. cit., pp. 163–64.

14. In *The Commoner*, June 17, 1902.

15. See Nick Salvatore, *Eugene V. Debs: Citizen and Socialist* (1982), pp. 204–05, and James Weinstein, *The Corporate Ideal in the Liberal State, 1900–1918* (1968), pp. 3–39.

16. In Harold U. Faulkner, *The Decline of Laissez-Faire, 1897–1917* (1951), p. 294, and in William Henry Harbaugh, *The Life and Times of Theodore Roosevelt* (1961, 1963 ed.), p. 768. See also Donald L. Miller and Richard E. Sharpless, *The Kingdom of Coal: Work, Enterprise, and Ethnic Communities in the Mine Fields* (1985), pp. 242–83.

17. In Elsie Gluck, *John Mitchell, Miner: Labor's Bargain with the Gilded Age* (1929), p. 114. The conservative *New York Times* said that Baer verged "very close to unconscious blasphemy" (in Foster Rhea Dulles and Melvyn Dubofsky, *Labor in America: A History*, 4th ed. [1984], p. 182).

18. In Robert J. Cornell, *The Anthracite Coal Strike of 1902* (1957), p. 174.

19. In Gluck, op. cit., p. 1126, and *The Commoner*, October 10, 1902.

20. Herbert Croly, *Marcus Alonzo Hanna, His Life and Work* (1912, 1923 ed.), p. 398.

21. *New York Times*, October 25, 1902.

22. Anthracite Coal Strike Commission, *Report to the President on the Anthracite Coal Strike of May–October, 1902* (1903), pp. 18, 29.

23. Mary Harris ("Mother") Jones, *Autobiography* (1925), pp. 30, 129.

24. *New York Times*, February 13, 1903.

25. Aldrich's daughter married John D. Rockefeller's son, and their son was Nelson Aldrich Rockefeller, governor of New York in the 1960s and briefly Gerald Ford's Vice President in the 1970s.

26. William Allen White, *The Autobiography of William Allen White* (1946), pp. 352–53.

27. In David P. Thelen, *Robert M. La Follette and the Insurgent Spirit* (1976), p. 52. See also Richard L. McCormick, *The Party Period and Public Policy: American Politics from the Age of Jackson to the Progressive Era* (1986), pp. 311–56.

28. Louis W. Koenig, *Bryan: A Political Biography of William Jennings Bryan* (1971), pp. 408, 412.

29. See Richard L. McCormick, *From Realignment to Reform: Political Change in New York State, 1893–1910* (1981), pp. 197–202.

30. In Louis Filler, *Voice of the Democracy, a Critical Biography of David Graham Phillips: Journalist, Novelist, Progressive* (1978), p. 101.

31. After President Roosevelt had delivered a speech condemning investigative journalists, which Phillips correctly understood to be aimed at himself and Hearst, Phillips moved away from journalism. He continued writing novels, one of which,

The Deluge (1905), predicted the Panic of 1907. *Susan Lenox* (1917), his best-known novel today, appeared six years after his assassination by a madman who thought that "Treason of the Senate" libeled members of his family.

32. In John K. Winkler, *William Randolph Hearst: A New Appraisal* (1955), p. 139.

33. Over the rest of his life Hearst's politics shifted dramatically. A Republican at his death in California in 1951, he had broken with the Democratic party during Franklin Roosevelt's first term.

34. Samuel Gompers, *Seventy Years of Life and Labor* (1925), vol. 2, p. 26.

35. In William H. Harbaugh, *Lawyer's Lawyer: The Life of John W. Davis* (1973), p. 58.

36. See Dulles and Dubofsky, op. cit., p. 189; Christopher L. Tompkins, *The State and the Unions: Labor Relations, Law, and the Organized Labor Movement in America, 1880–1960* (1985), p. 65; and Philip S. Foner, *The Policies and Practices of the American Federation of Labor, 1900–1909* (1964), p. 309.

37. In Gompers, op. cit., vol. 2, p. 212.

38. Foner, op. cit., pp. 308–09, 322.

39. Ibid., pp. 323, 325.

40. Dulles and Dubofsky, op. cit., pp. 174, 185–86, 196.

41. In Koenig, op. cit., p. 402.

42. White, op. cit., p. 392.

43. Elting E. Morison et al., eds., *The Letters of Theodore Roosevelt* (1951), vol. 5, p. 855.

44. Ibid., p. 859.

45. Ibid., vol. 6, p. 1842.

46. Charles Edward Russell, *Bare Hands and Stone Walls: Some Recollections of a Side-Line Reformer* (1933), p. 140.

8: RACE AND DISFRANCHISEMENT

1. One of Washington's supporters was John Merrick, who with six other Blacks had founded the North Carolina Mutual Life Insurance Company in Durham, North Carolina, in 1898. Merrick believed along with Washington that racial betterment would best be accomplished through the accumulation of property. After the Wilmington, North Carolina, riot of 1898, in which dozens of Blacks died, Merrick compared the wisdom of pursuing political office with that of going into business: "The Negroes have had lots of offices in this state and they have benefitted themselves but very little . . . Had the Negroes of Wilmington owned half of the city . . . there wouldn't anything happened to them [to] compare with what did." In Sydney Nathans, *The Quest for Progress: The Way We Lived in North Carolina, 1870–1920* (1983), p. 83.

2. Booker T. Washington, *Up from Slavery* (1901), in John Hope Franklin, ed., *Three Negro Classics* (1965), pp. 148–149.

3. In Louis Harlan, *Booker T. Washington: The Wizard of Tuskegee, 1901–1915* (1983), p. 298. The reporter for the *New York Evening Post*, owned by Oswald Garrison Villard, was Mary White Ovington.

4. *New York Times*, September 24, 1906.

5. Walter White, *A Man Called White* (1948, 1970 ed.), p. 9.

6. *Chicago Broadax*, October 6, 1906.

7. C. Vann Woodward, *The Origins of the New South, 1877–1913* (1951), pp. 330–33, 345.

8. In C. Vann Woodward, *Tom Watson, Agrarian Rebel* (1938, 1963 ed.), p. 379.

9. In Franklin, op. cit., pp. 243, 246, 251.

10. See Harlan, op. cit., pp. 295–309.

11. See Alfreda Duster, ed., *Crusade for Justice: The Autobiography of Ida B. Wells* (1970), pp. 35–66, 58–78, 322–28, 392–94, and Thomas C. Holt, "The Lonely Warrior: Ida B. Wells and the Struggle for Black Leadership," in John Hope Franklin and August Meier, eds., *Twentieth-Century Black Leaders* (1982), pp. 46–52.

12. Charles Edward Russell, *Bare Hands and Stone Walls: Some Recollections of a Side-Line Reformer* (1933), p. 224, and Allen Davis, *Spearheads for Reform: The Social Settlements and the Progressive Movement, 1890–1914* (1967), p. 99.

13. J. Morgan Kousser, *The Shaping of Southern Politics: Suffrage Restriction and the Establishment of the One-Party South* (1974), p. 47.

9: WOMAN SUFFRAGE AND WOMEN WORKERS

1. In Anne Firor Scott and Andrew MacKay Scott, *One Half the People: The Fight for Woman Suffrage* (1982), p. 6.

2. See Ellen DuBois, "The Radicalism of the Woman Suffrage Movement: Notes Toward the Reconstruction of Nineteenth-Century Feminism," *Feminist Studies*, Vol. 3, nos. 1 and 2 (Fall 1975), p. 65.

3. See Ruth Bordin, *Woman and Temperance: The Quest for Power and Liberty, 1873–1900* (1981).

4. See Rosalyn Terborg-Penn, "Nineteenth Century Black Women and Woman Suffrage," *Potamac Review*, Vol. 7, no. 3 (1977), pp. 17–18, and Gerda Lerner, *Black Women in White America* (1971), p. 321. In 1893 Harper published *Iola Leroy, or Shadows Uplifted*, the first novel by a Black author to deal with Reconstruction.

5. See Kathryn Kish Sklar, "Florence Kelley and the Integration of 'Women's Sphere' into American Politics, 1890–1921," paper, 1986, pp. 8–11.

6. Eleanor Flexner, *A Century of Struggle: The Woman's Rights Movement in the United States*, rev. ed. (1975), p. 236, and Robert Allen, *Reluctant Reformers: Racism and Social Reform Movements in the United States* (1974), p. 122. See also Jacqueline Jones, *Labor of Love, Labor of Sorrow: Black Women, Work, and the Family from Slavery to the Present* (1985).

7. In Alice Kessler-Harris, *Out to Work: A History of Wage-Earning Women in the United States* (1982), p. 136.

8. In ibid., p. 135.

9. See Sarah Eisenstein, *Give Us Bread but Give Us Roses: Working Women's Consciousness in the United States, 1890 to the First World War* (1983), pp. 39–46, 112, and Kathy Peiss, *Cheap Amusements: Working Women and Leisure in Turn-of-the-Century New York* (1986).

10. In Eisenstein, op. cit., p. 24.

11. See Nancy Schrom Dye, *As Equals and as Sisters: Feminism, Unionism and the Women's Trade Union League of New York* (1980), pp. 110–21.

12. In Meredith Tax, *The Rising of the Women: Feminist Solidarity and Class Conflict, 1880–1917* (1980), p. 97.

13. Ibid., p. 98.

14. Ibid., pp. 116–17.

15. In Flexner, op. cit., p. 212.

16. See Ellen DuBois, "Working Women, Class Relations, and Suffrage Militance: Harriot Stanton Blatch and the New York Woman Suffrage Movement, 1894–1909," *Journal of American History*, Vol. 74 (June 1987).

17. Charlotte Perkins Gilman, *Women and Economics* (1898), p. 51.

18. In DuBois, "Working Women . . ."

19. Nancy Cott, *The Grounding of Modern Feminism*, forthcoming, ch. 1.

20. Ibid.

21. Ibid.

22. In *The Outlook*, Vol. 93 (December 11, 1909), p. 800.

23. In *The Survey*, Vol. 23 (December 18, 1909), p. 385.

24. In Barbara Mayer Wertheimer, *We Were There: The Story of Working Women in America* (1977), p. 312.

25. See Kathryn Kish Sklar, "Hull House in the 1890s: A community of Women Reformers," *Signs*, Vol. 10, no. 4 (Summer 1985), p. 677.

10: THE PROGRESSIVE ERA

1. William Allen White, *The Autobiography of William Allen White* (1946), p. 426.

2. *Congressional Record*, Senate, 61st Congress, 1st Session, vol. 44, part 2, p. 1744.

3. The Payne-Aldrich tariff abolished tariffs on imported fine arts and allowed banker J. P. Morgan to bring his European art collection, valued at more than $20,000,000 to New York from London. Strict restrictions throughout the world on the exportation of national art treasures now prohibit the removal of artwork such as Morgan and many wealthy Americans acquired by the ton. See Doris Ackerman, "Pierpontifex Maximus: J. Pierpont Morgan as Renaissance Prince and Shaper of Arts Development in the United States," unpublished paper, 1986.

4. In William Harbaugh, *The Life and Times of Theodore Roosevelt*, rev. ed. (1963), p. 366.

5. Theodore Roosevelt, *The New Nationalism* (1910), p. 31.

6. Mary Heaton Vorse, *A Footnote to Folly* (1935), p. 12.

7. J. W. Lauck, "The Significance of the Situation at Lawrence," *The Survey*, vol. 27 (February 17, 1912), p. 1772.

8. Ray Stannard Baker, "The Revolutionary Strike," *American Magazine*, vol. 74 (May 1912), p. 22.

9. John Martin, "The Industrial Revolt at Lawrence," *The Independent*, vol. 72 (March 7, 1912), p. 492.

10. Lorin F. Deland, "The Lawrence Strike, a Study," *Atlantic Monthly*, vol. 109 (May 1912), p. 705.

11. In Harry Emerson Fosdick, "After the Strike—in Lawrence," *The Outlook*, vol. 101 (June 5, 1912), p. 341.

12. Robert F. Hoxie, "The Socialist Party in the November Elections," *Journal of Political Economy*, vol. 20 (March 1912), p. 205.

13. Henry Farrand Griffin, "The Rising Tide of Socialism," *The Outlook*, vol. 100 (February 24, 1912), p. 446, and Samuel P. Orth, "Is Socialism upon Us?," *World's Work*, vol. 24 (August 24, 1912), p. 453.

14. Schurman quoted in Griffin, op. cit., p. 448; also Hoxie, op. cit., p. 223, emphasis in original.

15. *The Living of Charlotte Perkins Gilman* (1935, 1974 ed.), pp. 131, 320.

16. James Weinstein, *The Decline of Socialism in America, 1912–1925* (1967), p. 14.

17. Willard had died in 1898, before the founding of the Socialist party, but she considered herself a socialist.

18. *New York Times*, June 18, 1912.

19. Allen F. Davis, *American Heroine: The Life and Legend of Jane Addams* (1973), p. 189, and *New York Times*, August 8, 1912.

20. In Gabriel Kolko, *The Triumph of Conservatism: A Reinterpretation of American History, 1900–1916* (1963, 1967 ed.), p. 207.

21. In Nick Salvatore, *Eugene V. Debs: Citizen and Socialist* (1982), p. 264.

22. *New York Times*, March 5, 1913.

23. In James Livingston, *Origins of the Federal Reserve System: Money, Class, and Corporate Capitalism, 1890–1913* (1986), p. 188.

24. *Literary Digest*, vol. 46 (January 4, 1913), p. 388.

25. See John Kenneth Galbraith, *Money: Whence it Came, Where it Went* (1975), p. 124.

26. In Arthur S. Link, *Woodrow Wilson and the Progressive Era, 1910–1917* (1954), p. 73.

27. In Thomas K. McCraw, *Prophets of Regulation: Charles Francis Adams, Louis D. Brandeis, James M. Landis, Alfred E. Kahn* (1984), p. 126.

28. Oswald Garrison Villard, *Fighting Years: Memoirs of a Liberal Journalist* (1939), p. 239.

29. Ray Stannard Baker, *American Chronicle* (1945), p. 295.

30. Randolph Bourne, a *New Republic* writer who was more radical than the progressive founders, soon found the magazine's posh liberalism timid and conventional. See Bruce Clayton, *Forgotten Prophet: The Life of Randolph Bourne* (1984), pp. 121–23.

31. In Christopher Lasch, *The New Radicalism in America, 1889–1963: The Intellectual as a Social Type* (1966), p. 107.

32. In Irving Howe's introduction to William L. O'Neill, ed., *Echoes of Revolt: The Masses 1911–1917* (1966), p. 6.

33. In Ronald Steel, *Walter Lippmann and the American Century* (1980), pp. 45, 72.

11: WARS

1. Alan Knight, *The Mexican Revolution*, vol. 1, *Porfirians, Liberals and Peasants* (1986), p. 55.

2. Paolo E. Colleta, *The Presidency of William Howard Taft* (1973), p. 175.

3. James M. Callahan, *American Foreign Policy in Mexican Relations* (1967), p. 519, and Robert Freeman Smith, *The United States and Revolutionary Nationalism in Mexico, 1916–1932* (1972), p. 8.

4. The Chinese Boxer Rebellion of 1899 was primarily an antiforeign uprising against the cultural and economic power of Westerners in China.

5. See Howard F. Cline, *The United States and Mexico* (1953), p. 129.

6. See Friedrich Katz, *The Secret War in Mexico: Europe, the United States and the Mexican Revolution* (1981), p. 123.

7. See Arthur S. Link, *Wilson: The New Freedom* (1956), p. 360.

8. *The Outlook*, vol. 103 (February 22, 1913), p. 379.

9. *Literary Digest*, vol. 48 (May 9, 1914), p. 1131.

10. *World's Work*, vol. 26 (September 1913), p. 513.

11. Arthur Richard Hinton, "Shall We Annex Northern Mexico?," *The Independent*, vol. 79 (July 27, 1914), p. 125.

12. Albert Bushnell Hart, "Postulates of the Mexico Situation," *American Academy of Political and Social Sciences*, vol. 24 (July 1914), p. 147.

13. *Literary Digest*, vol. 48 (May 16, 1914), p. 1167.

14. In John Reed, *Insurrection in Mexico* (1914, 1969 ed.), p. 145. See also *Review of Reviews*, vol. 50 (November 1914), p. 632.

15. See also Albert Bushnell Hart, "The Second Mexican War," *The Independent*, vol. 78 (May 4, 1914), p. 196.

16. Robert E. Quirk, *An Affair of Honor: Woodrow Wilson and the Occupation of Veracruz* (1962), p. 117.

17. Rheta Childe Dorr, *A Woman of Fifty* (1924), p. 306.

18. In Arthur S. Link, *Wilson* (1960), vol. 3, p. 5.

19. John Haynes Holmes, "War and the Social Movement," *The Survey*, vol. 32 (September 29, 1914), p. 629.

20. Samuel Gompers, *Seventy Years of Life and Labor* (1925), vol. 2, p. 322.

21. Link, op. cit., vol. 3, p. 2.

22. See Oswald Garrison Villard, *Fighting Years: Memoirs of a Liberal Journalist* (1939), p. 244.

23. *The Survey*, vol. 34 (June 5, 1915), pp. 210–211. See also Mary Heaton Vorse, *A Footnote to Folly* (1935), p. 56.

24. In Philip S. Foner, *History of the Labor Movement in the United States* (1965), vol. 4, p. 452.

25. In C. Roland Marchand, *The American Peace Movement and Social Reform, 1898–1918* (1972), p. 176.

26. William Allen White, *The Autobiography of William Allen White* (1946), p. 513.

27. In John A. Garraty, *Henry Cabot Lodge: A Biography* (1968), p. 315.

28. In David M. Kennedy, *Over Here: The First World War and American Society* (1980), p. 17.

29. In Lawrence W. Levine, *Defender of the Faith: William Jennings Bryan, the Last Decade, 1915–1925* (1965), p. 49.

30. In Link, op. cit., vol. 3, p. 139. Emphasis in original.

31. Ray Stannard Baker, *American Chronicle* (1945), p. 298.
32. Link, op. cit., vol. 3, p. 373, and William H. Harbaugh, *The Life and Times of Theodore Roosevelt* (1961, rev. ed., 1975), p. 448.
33. In Link, op. cit., vol. 3, p. 382.
34. Louis W. Koenig, *Bryan: A Political Biography of William Jennings Bryan* (1971), p. 511.
35. In John A. Garraty, *Henry Cabot Lodge: A Biography* (1953), p. 302.
36. See Joel Williamson, *The Crucible of Race: Black–White Relations in the American South Since Emancipation* (1984), pp. 468–72.
37. In George Brown Tindall, *The Emergence of the New South, 1913–1945* (1967), p. 187.
38. In John Higham, *Strangers in the Land: Patterns of American Nativism, 1860–1925* (1955, 1977 ed.), p. 186.

12: THE EUROPEAN WAR TAKES OVER

1. Leonora O'Reilly was the only American delegate from a working-class background.
2. C. Roland Marchand, *The American Peace Movement and Social Reform, 1898–1910* (1972), p. 157.
3. In Carol Gelderman, *Henry Ford, the Wayward Capitalist* (1981), p. 92.
4. Ibid., pp. 99–100.
5. In J. C. Furnas, *Great Times: An Informal Social History of the United States, 1914–1928* (1974), p. 213.
6. In John Higham, *Strangers in the Land: Patterns of American Nativism, 1850–1925* (1955, 1977 ed.), p. 200.
7. In Lawrence W. Levine, *Defender of the Faith: William Jennings Bryan, The Last Decade, 1915–1925* (1965), p. 58.
8. In Arthur S. Link, *Wilson* (1960) vol. 3, p. 467.
9. *Literary Digest*, vol. 52 (April 1, 1916), pp. 883–84.
10. See George Dangerfield, *The Damnable Question: A Study of Anglo-Irish Relations* (1976), pp. 179–80. The British government later hanged Casement for treason.
11. See Joseph E. Cuddy, *Irish-Americans and National Isolationism, 1914–1920* (1976), pp. 109–29.
12. In William E. Leuchtenburg, *The Perils of Prosperity, 1914–32* (1958), p. 22.
13. In David M. Kennedy, *Over Here: The First World War and American Society,* (1980), p. 17.
14. In Arthur S. Link, *Woodrow Wilson and the Progressive Era, 1910–1917* (1954), p. 194.
15. Ibid., pp. 192–93.
16. Kennedy, op. cit., p. 112.
17. In Leuchtenburg, op. cit., p. 24.
18. In Arthur S. Link, *Wilson,* (1965), vol. 5, p. 1032.
19. Ibid., p. 111.

20. In Anne Firor Scott and Andrew MacKay Scott, *One Half the People: The Fight for Woman Suffrage* (1982), p. 40.
21. *Literary Digest*, vol. 54 (February 10, 1917), p. 453.
22. Ibid., (April 14, 1917), p. 1044.
23. In Ray Stannard Baker, *American Chronicle* (1945), p. 301.
24. In C. Vann Woodward, *Tom Watson, Agrarian Rebel* (1938), p. 454, emphasis in original.
25. In Kennedy, op. cit., p. 28.
26. William Alexander Percy, *Lanterns on the Levee: Recollections of a Planter's Son* (1941, 1973 ed.), p. 169. In May Congress passed the Selective Service Act, under which men from twenty-one to thirty (later broadened to eighteen to forty-five) had to register for military service.
27. *The New Republic*, vol. 10 (April 7, 1917), p. 284.
28. In Kennedy, op. cit., p. 146.
29. See Bernard C. Nalty, *Strength for the Fight: A History of Black Americans in the Military* (1986), pp. 107–24.
30. Arthur S. Link and William B. Catton, *American Epoch: A History of the United States Since 1900* (5th ed., 1980), vol. 1, p. 201.
31. See Steve Fraser, "The 'New Unionism' and the 'New Economic Policy'" and Melvyn Dubofsky, "Abortive Reform: The Wilson Administration and Organized Labor, 1913–1920," in James E. Cronin and Carmen Sirianni, eds., *Work, Community, and Power: The Experience of Labor in Europe and America, 1900–1925* (1983), pp. 173, 175, 210.
32. In Kennedy, op. cit., p. 76.
33. In *The Survey*, vol. 39 (October 20, 1917), p. 75.
34. See Melvin Dubofsky, *We Shall Be All: A History of the Industrial Workers of the World* (1969), p. 392.
35. In *The Survey*, vol. 38 (August 11, 1917), pp. 428–29.
36. It is not possible to assign a number to the White southern migrants of the war years. But between 1910 and 1920, 663,000 White and 555,000 Black southerners left the South. Gavin Wright, *Old South, New South: Revolutions in the Southern Economy Since the Civil War* (1986), p. 201.
37. *The Survey*, vol. 38 (August 18, 1917), p. 448. See also Florette Henri, *Black Migration: Movement North, 1900–1920* (1975).
38. See also Elliott Rudwick, *Race Riot at East St. Louis, July 2, 1917* (1964).
39. See Bruce Nelson, *Workers on the Waterfront: Seamen, Longshoremen, and Unionism in the 1930s* (1990), pp. 18–22; Fraser, op. cit., pp. 173–74; David Montgomery, "New Tendencies in Union Struggles and Strategies in Europe and the United States, 1916–1922," in Cronin and Sirianni, op. cit., pp. 107–09; and David Montgomery, *Workers' Control in America* (1979), pp. 3–7, 113–14, 127–34.
40. *The Survey*, vol. 39 (October 20, 1917, pp. 59–60 and January 12, 1918, p. 412); vol. 40 (May 4, 1918), p. 122.
41. Ibid., vol. 40 (May 4, 1918), p. 122.
42. Ibid., vol. 37 (March 10, 1917), p. 655.
43. Percy, op. cit., pp. 212–13.

44. *The Survey,* vol. 41 (November 16, 1918), p. 179.
45. In James E. Cronin, "Rethinking the Legacy of Labor, 1890–1925," in Cronin and Sirianni, op. cit., p. 23, and Montgomery, "New Tendencies in Union Struggles," loc. cit., pp. 103–07, 132–34, and *Workers' Control in America,* loc. cit., pp. 132–33.

13: THE GREAT UNREST

1. James T. Farrell, *Young Lonigan* (1932, 1977 ed.), p. 185.
2. In John DeWitt McKee, *William Allen White: Maverick on Main Street* (1975), p. 149.
3. In Thomas A. Bailey, *Woodrow Wilson and the Lost Peace* (1944, 1947 ed.), p. 74.
4. Ibid., p. 93.
5. See Harvey O'Connor, *Revolution in Seattle: A Memoir* (1964), p. 133.
6. *Literary Digest,* Vol. 60 (February 22, 1919), p. 11.
7. Ibid., p. 13.
8. William L. Chenery, "The Railroad Crisis," *The Survey,* Vol. 42 (August 16, 1919), p. 722, and David Montgomery, *Workers' Control in America,* (1979), pp. 30–34.
9. In Daniel T. Rodgers, *The Work Ethic in Industrial America: 1850–1920* (1978), p. 60.
10. *Literary Digest,* Vol. 62 (August 16, 1919), p. 9.
11. In McKee, op. cit., p. 152.
12. Austria-Hungary yielded the new, independent states of Austria, Hungary, Yugoslavia (including Serbia), Czechoslovakia, and Poland (which included part of what had been Russia). Also out of Russia came the new nations of Finland, Estonia, Latvia, and Lithuania. France received Alsace-Lorraine, which had been part of Germany since 1871, and Japan received Germany's Asian colonies, notably the Chinese Shandong (Shantung) Peninsula. Britain and France took mandates for what had been the Turkish Empire in the Near East and North Africa and the German colonies in Africa.
13. Jordan A. Schwartz, *The Speculator: Bernard M. Baruch in Washington, 1917–1965* (1981), p. 150.
14. *The Nation,* Vol. 108 (April 26, 1919), pp. 646–47. See also *The Survey,* Vol. 41 (February 8, 1919), p. 660.
15. In N. Gordon Levin, Jr., *Woodrow Wilson and World Politics: America's Response to War and Revolution* (1968), p. 132.
16. Ibid., p. 247.
17. Baker, op. cit., pp. 407–35.
18. W. E. B. Du Bois, *Dusk of Dawn: An Essay Toward an Autobiography of a Race Concept* (1940, 1968 ed.), p. 262.
19. Morton Tenzer, "The Jews," in Joseph P. O'Grady, ed., *The Immigrants' Influence on Wilson's Peace Policies* (1967), p. 304.
20. Michael E. Parrish, *Felix Frankfurter and His Times: The Reform Years* (1982), pp. 134–36.
21. *The Nation* Vol. 108 (January 25, 1919), p. 111, and (March 29, 1919), p. 459.
22. In Thomas A. Bailey, *Woodrow Wilson and the Great Betrayal* (1945), p. 17. Emphasis in original.

23. Stanley Coben, *A. Mitchell Palmer: Politician* (1963), p. 196.
24. *Literary Digest*, Vol. 61 (June 14, 1919), p. 9.
25. Robert K. Murray, *Red Scare: A Study in National Hysteria, 1919–1920* (1955), p. 111.
26. In Bailey, *Woodrow Wilson and the Great Betrayal*, pp. 2–3.
27. Graham Taylor, "Chicago in the Nation's Race Strife," *The Survey*, Vol. 42 (August 9, 1919), p. 695.
28. Ibid., p. 698.
29. See William M. Tuttle, Jr., *Race Riot: Chicago in the Red Summer of 1919* (1970, 1972 ed.), p. 40.
30. *Literary Digest*, Vol. 62 (August 9, 1919), p. 11.
31. George E. Haynes, "Race Riots in Relation to Democracy," *The Survey*, Vol. 62 (August 9, 1919), p. 698.
32. Robert L. Zangrando, *The NAACP Crusade Against Lynching, 1919–1950* (1980), p. 6.
33. In Bailey, *Woodrow Wilson and the Great Betrayal*, p. 5.
34. Gene Smith, *When the Cheering Stopped: The Last Years of Woodrow Wilson* (1964), p. 55.
35. In Stanley Coben, op. cit., p. 162.
36. *Literary Digest*, Vol. 62 (August 16, 1919), p. 12.
37. *The Nation*, Vol. 109 (September 27, 1919), p. 326.
38. In Francis Russell, *A City in Terror, 1919, the Boston Police Strike* (1975), p. 124.
39. Ibid., p. 195.
40. *Philadelphia Evening Public Ledger*, in *Literary Digest*, Vol. 62 (September 27, 1919), p. 8.
41. In John A. Fitch, "The Closed Shop," *The Survey*, Vol. 43 (November 8, 1919), p. 56.
42. Ibid., p. 91.
43. In Jack C. Lane, *Armed Progressive: General Leonard Wood* (1978), p. 235. See also Herman Hagedorn, *Leonard Wood: A Biography* (1931), Vol. II, p. 334.
44. Edgar Guest in David Brody, *Labor in Crisis: The Steel Strike of 1919* (1965), pp. 132–33.
45. Fitch, op. cit., p. 56.
46. *Literary Digest*, Vol. 63 (October 25, 1919), p. 11.
47. Ibid., October 11, 1919, p. 16.
48. In Murray, p. 17.
49. In J. C. Furnas, *Great Times: An Informal History of the United States, 1914–1929* (1974), p. 256.
50. In Lane, op. cit., p. 239.

14: LOOKING FORWARD

1. In Stanley Coben, *A. Mitchell Palmer: Politician* (1963), p. 186.
2. In Burl Noggle, *Into the Twenties: The United States from Armistice to Normalcy* (1974), p. 141.
3. In David Burner, *Herbert Hoover: A Public Life* (1979), p. 138.

4. In Ronald Steel, *Walter Lippmann and the American Century* (1980), p. 169.
5. In the 1920 election the percentage of voter participation fell below 50 percent for the first time since 1824. Whereas 62 percent of eligible voters had voted in 1916, voter turnout did not rise above 50 percent until 1928.
6. In Steel, op. cit., p. 169.
7. See Barbara Fields, "Ideology and Race in American History," in J. Morgan Kousser and James M. McPherson, eds., *Region, Race, and Reconstruction: Essays in Honor of C. Vann Woodward* (1982), pp. 143–77; and Edmund S. Morgan, *American Slavery, American Freedom: The Ordeal of Colonial Virginia* (1975), pp. 316–37.

INDEX

Page numbers in *italics* refer to illustrations.